A Companion to Marx's *Capital*

A Companion to Marx's *Capital*

David Harvey

London • New York

First published by Verso 2010

1 3 5 7 9 10 8 6 4 2

Verso
UK: 6 Meard Street, London W1F 0EG
USA: 20 Jay Street, Suite 1010, Brooklyn, NY 11201
www.versobooks.com

Verso is the imprint of New Left Books

ISBN-13: 978-1-84467-359-9 (pbk)
ISBN-13: 978-1-84467-358-2 (hbk)

British Library Cataloguing in Publication Data
A catalogue record for this book is available from the British Library

Library of Congress Cataloging-in-Publication Data
A catalog record for this book is available from the Library of Congress

Typeset by Hewer Text UK Ltd, Edinburgh
Printed in the USA by Worldcolor / Fairfield

Contents

Preface

When it became known that the lectures I give annually on Marx's *Capital*, Volume I, were about to go online as a video series, I was approached by Verso and asked whether I would have any interest in preparing a written version. For a variety of reasons, I agreed to the idea.

To begin with, the failing economy and the onset of what threatens to be a serious global crisis, if not depression, have generated an upwelling of interest in Marx's analysis to see whether it can help us understand the origins of our current predicaments. The problem, however, is that the past thirty years, most particularly since the fall of the Berlin Wall and the end of the cold war, have not been a very favorable or fertile period for Marxian thought, and most certainly not for Marxian revolutionary politics. As a consequence, a whole younger generation has grown up bereft of familiarity with, let alone training in, Marxian political economy. It therefore appeared an opportune moment to produce a guide to *Capital* that would open the door for this generation to explore for itself what Marx might be about.

The timing for a constructive reevalution of Marx's work is opportune in another sense. The fierce oppositions and innumerable schisms within the Marxist movement that bedeviled the 1970s, affecting not only political practices but also theoretical orientations, have faded somewhat, as has the appetite for pure academicism which, on the one hand, helped keep interest in Marx alive in difficult times, but, on the other, did so at the price of arcane and often highly abstract arguments and reflections. My sense is that those who wish to read Marx now are far more interested in practical engagements, which does not mean they are fearful of abstractions but rather that they find academicism boring and irrelevant. There are many students and activists who desperately desire a strong theoretical base to better grasp how everything relates to everything else, so as to situate and contextualize their own particular interests and practical political work. I hope that this presentation of the basics of Marxian theory will help them do that.

In preparing this text, I worked from transcripts prepared by Katharina Bodirsky (to whom many thanks) of the audio recording of the lectures given in the spring of 2007. The video lectures (see davidharvey.org), organized by Chris Caruso (who also designed the website) and filmed by the Media College of the University of the Poor in New York and the Media Mobilizing Project in Philadelphia, were given in the fall of 2007. I want to thank Chris and everyone else for all their volunteer work on the project.

There were, however, significant differences between the audio and the video versions. These arose mainly because I always give the lectures in a somewhat *extempore* way, concentrating on different aspects of the text depending on political and economic events, as well as on my own interests (and even whims) of the moment. Class discussions also frequently redirect attention in unpredictable ways. Unfortunately, space would not allow for inclusion of the discussions, but I have several times incorporated elements from them into the main body of the text when that seemed appropriate. While I worked mainly from the audio version, I incorporated elements from the video materials as well. Of course, the editing of the transcripts had to be fairly draconian, in part for space reasons, but also because the translation from the spoken to the written word always requires significant and in some cases quite drastic modifications. I have also taken the opportunity to clear up some matters not covered in the lectures and to add a few further thoughts here and there. The text I use in the course is the translation by Ben Fowkes first published by Pelican Books and the *New Left Review* in 1976, republished by Vintage in 1977, and then in a Penguin Classics edition in 1992. The page numbers referred to are from these editions.

My hope is that this "companion"—and I really think of it as a companion on a journey rather than as an introduction or interpretation—will provide a helpful entry to Marx's political economy for anyone who wants to travel that road. I have tried to keep the presentation at an introductory level without, I hope, oversimplification. Furthermore, I have not considered in any detail the many controversies that swirl around diverse interpretations of the text. At the same time, the reader should understand that what is presented here is not a neutral interpretation, but a reading that I have arrived at over nearly forty years of teaching this text to all manner of people from all sorts of backgrounds (to whom I am indebted, since they have taught me a great deal), while also trying to use Marx's thought constructively in my own academic research in relation to political action. I do not seek to persuade people to adopt my own distinctive point of view. My ambition is to use my point of view as a gateway for others anxious to construct interpretations that are maximally meaningful and useful to them in the particular circumstances of their lives. If I have only partially succeeded in that, then I will be absolutely delighted.

Introduction

My aim is to get you to read a book by Karl Marx called *Capital*, Volume I, and to read it on Marx's own terms.[1] This may seem a bit ridiculous, since if you haven't yet read the book you can't possibly know what Marx's terms are; but one of his terms, I can assure you, is that you read, and read carefully. Real learning always entails a struggle to understand the unknown. My own readings of *Capital*, collected in the present volume, will prove far more enlightening if you have read the pertinent chapters beforehand. It is your own personal encounter with this text that I want to encourage, and by struggling directly with Marx's text, you can begin to shape your own understanding of his thought.

This poses an immediate difficulty. Everybody has heard of Karl Marx, of terms like "Marxism" and "Marxist," and there are all kinds of connotations that go with those words. So you are bound to begin with preconceptions and prejudices, favorable or otherwise; but I first have to ask you to try, as best you can, to set aside all those things you *think* you know about Marx so that you can engage with what he actually has to say.

There are still other obstacles to achieving this sort of direct engagement. We are bound, for example, to approach a text of this kind by way of our particular intellectual formations and experiential histories. For many students these intellectual formations are affected, if not governed, by academic considerations and concerns; there is a natural tendency to read Marx from a particular and exclusionary disciplinary standpoint. Marx himself would never have gotten tenure at a university in any discipline, and to this day most departmental apparatuses are disinclined to accept him as one of their own. So if you are a graduate student and want to read him right, then you'd better forget about what will get you tenure in your field—not in the long run, of course, but at least for the purpose of reading Marx. You have, in short, to struggle mightily to determine what he is saying beyond what you can easily understand by way of your

1. Karl Marx, *Capital: A Critique of Political Economy*, Volume I, trans. Ben Fowkes (London: Penguin Classics, 1990). Future references to this work are cited with page references only.

particular disciplinary apparatus, your own intellectual formation and, even more important, your own experiential history (whether as a labor or community organizer or a capitalist entrepreneur).

One important reason for taking such an open stance toward this reading is that *Capital* turns out to be an astonishingly rich book. Shakespeare, the Greeks, Faust, Balzac, Shelley, fairy tales, werewolves, vampires and poetry all turn up in its pages alongside innumerable political economists, philosophers, anthropologists, journalists and political theorists. Marx draws on an immense array of sources, and it can be instructive—and fun—to track these down. Some of the references can be elusive, as he often fails to acknowledge them directly; I uncover yet more connections as I continue to teach *Capital* over the years. When I first started I had not read much Balzac, for example. Later, when reading Balzac's novels, I found myself often saying, "Ah, that's where Marx got it from!" He apparently read Balzac comprehensively and had the ambition to write a full study of the *Comedie Humaine* when he got through with *Capital*. Reading *Capital* and Balzac together helps explain why.

So *Capital* is a rich and multidimensional text. It draws on a vast experiential world as conceptualized in a great diversity of literatures written in many languages at different places and times. I am not saying, I hasten to add, that you will not be able to make sense of Marx unless you get all the references. But what does inspire me, and I hope will inspire you, is the idea that there is an immense array of resources out there that can shed light on why we live life the way we do. In the same way that all of them are grist for Marx's mill of understanding, so we, too, can make them grist for our own.

You will also find that *Capital* is an astonishingly good book, just as a *book*. When read as a whole, it is an enormously gratifying literary construction. But we here find more potential barriers to understanding, because many of you will have encountered and read bits of Marx in the course of your education. Maybe you read the *Communist Manifesto* in high school. Maybe you went through one of those courses on social theory, spending two weeks on Marx, a couple on Weber, a few on Durkheim, Foucault and a host of other important characters. Maybe you have read excerpts from *Capital* or some theoretical exposition of, say, Marx's political beliefs. But reading excerpts or abstract accounts is entirely different from reading *Capital* as a complete text. You start to see the bits and pieces in a radically new light, in the context of a much grander narrative. It is vital to pay careful attention to the grand narrative and to be prepared to change your understanding of the bits and pieces or the abstract accounts you earlier encountered. Marx would almost certainly want his work to be read as a totality. He would object vociferously to the idea that he could be understood adequately by way of excerpts, no matter how strategically chosen. He would certainly not appreciate just two weeks of consideration in an introductory course on social theory, any more than he would himself have given over a mere two weeks to reading Adam Smith. You will almost certainly arrive at a quite different conception of Marx's thought from reading *Capital* as a whole. But that means you have to read the whole book as a book—and that is what I want to help you to do.

There *is* a way in which intellectual formations and disciplinary standpoints not only matter but also provide helpful perspectives on *Capital*. I am, of course, against the sort of exclusionary readings around which students almost invariably organize their understandings, but I have learned over the years that disciplinary perspectives can be instructive. I have taught *Capital* nearly every year since 1971, sometimes twice or even three times in a single year, to groups of all kinds. One year it was with the whole philosophy department—somewhat Hegelian—of what was then called Morgan State College in Baltimore; another year it was all the graduate students in the English program at Johns Hopkins; another year it was mainly economists who showed up. What came to fascinate me was that each group saw different things in *Capital*. I found myself learning more and more about the text from working through it with people from different disciplines.

But sometimes I found that learning experience irritating, even painful, because a particular group would not see it my way or would insist on going off onto topics I thought irrelevant. One year I tried to read *Capital* with a group from the Romance-languages program at Johns Hopkins. To my intense frustration, we spent almost the whole semester on chapter 1. I'd keep saying, "Look, we have to move on and get at least as far as the politics of the working day," and they'd say, "No, no, no, we've got to get this right. What is value? What does he mean by money as commodity? What is fetish about?" and so on. They even brought the German edition along just to check the translations. It turned out they were all working in the tradition of somebody I had never heard of, somebody who I thought must be a political if not intellectual idiot for sparking this kind of approach. That person was Jacques Derrida, who spent time at Hopkins during the late 1960s and early 1970s. Reflecting on this experience afterward, I realized this group had taught me the vital importance of paying careful attention to Marx's language—what he says, how he says it and what, also, he takes for granted—just from going through chapter 1 with a fine-toothed comb.

But don't worry: I don't intend to do that in these readings because not only do I want to cover Marx's discussion of the working day, I am determined to see you through to the end of the volume. My point is simply that different disciplinary perspectives can usefully open up the multiple dimensions of Marx's thought, precisely because he wrote this text out of such an incredibly diverse and rich tradition of critical thinking. I am indebted to the many individuals and groups with whom I have read this book over these many years, precisely because they have taught me so much about aspects of Marx's work that I would never have recognized on my own. For me, that education is never-ending.

Now, there are three major intellectual and political traditions that inspire the analysis laid out in *Capital*, and they are all propelled by Marx's deep commitment to critical theory, to a critical analysis. When he was relatively young, he wrote a little piece to one of his editorial colleagues, the title of which was "For a Ruthless Criticism of Everything That Exists." Clearly, he was being modest—and I do suggest that you actually go read it, because it is fascinating. He doesn't say, "Everybody is stupid and I, the great Marx, am going to criticize everybody out of existence." Instead, he argues that there have been a lot of serious people who have thought about the world hard, and they have seen certain things about the world that have to be respected, no matter how one-sided or warped. The critical method takes what others have said and seen and works on it so as to transform thought—and the world it describes—into something new. For Marx, new knowledge arises out of taking radically different conceptual blocs, rubbing them together and making revolutionary fire. This is in effect what he does in *Capital*: he brings together divergent intellectual traditions to create a completely new and revolutionary framework for knowledge.

The three grand conceptual frameworks that converge in *Capital* are these: first, classical political economy—seventeenth- to mid-nineteenth-century political economy. This is mainly British, though not solely so, and it runs from William Petty, Locke, Hobbes and Hume to the grand trio of Adam Smith, Malthus and Ricardo, as well as to a host of others, like James Steuart. There was also a French tradition of political economy (Physiocrats like Quesnay and Turgot and later on Sismondi and Say) as well as individual Italians and Americans (like Carey) who provide Marx with additional critical materials. Marx subjected all these people to a deep criticism in the three volumes of notes now called *Theories of Surplus Value*. He didn't have a photocopying machine and he didn't have the Web, so he laboriously copied out long passages from Smith and then wrote a commentary on them, long passages from Steuart and a commentary on them, and so on. In effect he was practicing what we now call deconstruction, and I learned from Marx how to deconstruct arguments in this way. When he takes on Adam Smith, for example, Marx accepts much of what Smith says but then searches for the gaps or contradictions which, when rectified, radically transform the argument. This kind of argumentation appears throughout *Capital* because, as its subtitle indicates, it is shaped around "a critique of political economy."

The second conceptual building block in Marx's theorizing is philosophical reflection and inquiry, which for Marx originates with the Greeks. Marx wrote his dissertation on Epicurus, and he was familiar with Greek thought. Aristotle, as you will see, provides a frequent anchor for his arguments. Marx was also thoroughly trained in the way in which Greek thought came into the mainly German philosophical critical tradition—Spinoza, Leibniz and, of course, Hegel, as well as Kant and many others. Marx puts this mainly German critical philosophical tradition into a relationship with the British and French political-economic tradition, though, again, it would be wrong simply to see this in terms of national traditions (Hume was, after all, as much a philosopher—albeit an empiricist—as he was a political economist, and Descartes' and Rousseau's influence on Marx was also substantial). But the mainly German critical philosophical tradition weighed heavily on Marx because that was his initial training. And the critical climate generated by what later came to be known as the "young Hegelians" in the 1830s and 1840s influenced him greatly.

The third tradition to which Marx appeals is that of utopian socialism. In Marx's time, this was primarily French, although it was an Englishman, Thomas More, who is generally credited with originating the modern tradition—though it, too, goes back to the Greeks—and another Englishman, Robert Owen, who not only wrote copious utopian tracts but actually sought to put many of his ideas into practice in Marx's lifetime. But in France there was a tremendous burst of utopian thinking in the 1830s and 1840s, inspired largely by the earlier writings of Saint-Simon, Fourier and Babeuf. There were, for example, people like Etienne Cabet, who created a group called the Icarians, which settled in the United States after 1848; Proudhon and the Proudhonists; August Blanqui (who coined the phrase "dictatorship of the proletariat") and many like him who adhered to a Jacobin tradition (such as that of Babeuf); the Saint-Simonian movement; Fourierists like Victor Considerant; and socialist feminists like Flora Tristan. And it was in the 1840s in France that many radicals, for the first time, cared to call themselves communists, even though they had no clear idea of what that might mean. Marx was very familiar with, if not immersed in, this tradition, particularly when in Paris before his expulsion in 1844, and I think that he draws from it more than he willingly acknowledges. Understandably, he wanted to distance himself from the utopianism of the 1830s and 1840s, which he felt accounted in many ways for the failures of the revolution of 1848 in Paris. He didn't like it when utopians configured some ideal society without any idea of how to get from here to there, an opposition made clear in the *Communist Manifesto*. He therefore often proceeds in relation to their ideas by means of negation, particularly with respect to the thought of Fourier and Proudhon.

These are the three main conceptual threads that come together in Marx's *Capital*. His aim is to convert the radical political project from what he considered a rather shallow utopian socialism to a scientific communism. But in order to do that, he can't just contrast the utopians with the political economists. He has to re-create and reconfigure what social-scientific method is all about. Crudely put, this new scientific method is predicated on the interrogation of the primarily British tradition of classical political economy, using the tools of the mainly German tradition of critical philosophy, all applied to illuminate the mainly French utopian impulse in order to answer the following questions: what is communism, and how should communists think? How can we both understand and critique capitalism *scientifically* in order to chart the path to communist revolution more effectively? As we will see, *Capital* has a great deal to say about the scientific understanding of capitalism but not much to say about how to build a communist revolution. Nor will we find much about what a communist society would look like.

* * *

I have already addressed some of the barriers to reading *Capital* on Marx's own terms. Marx himself was all too aware of the difficulties and, interestingly, commented on them in his various prefaces. In the preface to the French edition, for example, he reacts to the suggestion that the edition should be brought out in serial form. "I applaud [the] idea of publishing the translation of *Capital* as a serial," he wrote in 1872.

> In this form the book will be more accessible to the working class, a consideration which to me outweighs everything else . . . That is the good side of your suggestion, but here is the reverse of the medal: the method of analysis which I have employed, and which had not previously been applied to economic subjects, makes the reading of the first chapters rather arduous, and it is to be feared that the French public, always impatient to come to a conclusion, eager to know the connection between general principles and the immediate questions that have aroused their passions, may be disheartened because they will be unable to move on at once . . . That is a disadvantage I am powerless to overcome, unless it be by forewarning and forearming those readers who zealously seek the truth. There is no royal road to science, and only those who do not dread the fatiguing climb of its steep paths have a chance of gaining its luminous summits. (104)

So I, too, have to begin by warning all readers of Marx, however zealously concerned with the pursuit of truth, that yes, indeed, the first few chapters of *Capital* are particularly arduous. There are two reasons for this. One concerns Marx's method, which we'll consider further shortly. The other has to do with the particular way in which he sets up his project.

Marx's aim in *Capital* is to understand how capitalism works by way of a critique of political economy. He knows this is going to be an enormous undertaking. In order to get that project under way, he has to develop a conceptual apparatus that will help him understand all the complexity of capitalism, and in one of his introductions he explains how he plans to go about that. "The method of presentation," he writes in the postface to the second edition, "must differ in form from that of inquiry":

> The latter has to appropriate the material in detail, to analyse its different forms of development and to track down their inner connection. Only after this work has been done can the real movement be appropriately presented. If this is done successfully, if the life of the subject-matter [i.e.,

> the capitalist mode of production] is now reflected back in the ideas, then it may appear as if we have before us an a priori construction. (102)

Marx's method of inquiry starts with everything that exists—with reality as it's experienced, as well as with all available descriptions of that experience by political economists, philosophers, novelists and the like. He subjects that material to a rigorous criticism in order to discover some simple but powerful concepts that illuminate the way reality works. This is what he calls the method of descent—we proceed from the immediate reality around us, looking ever deeper for the concepts fundamental to that reality. Equipped with those fundamental concepts, we can begin working back to the surface—the method of ascent—and discover how deceiving the world of appearances can be. From this vantage, we are in a position to interpret that world in radically different terms.

In general, Marx starts with the surface appearance to find the deep concepts. In *Capital*, however, he begins by presenting the foundational concepts, conclusions he's already derived by employing his method of inquiry. He simply lays out his concepts in the opening chapters, directly and in rapid succession, in a way that indeed makes them look like *a priori*, even arbitrary, constructions. So, on first read, it is not unusual to wonder: where on earth are all these ideas and concepts coming from? Why is he using them in the way he does? Half the time you have no idea what he is talking about. But as you move on through the book, it becomes clear how these concepts indeed illuminate our world. After a while, concepts like value and fetishism become meaningful.

Yet we only fully understand how these concepts work by the end of the book! Now, that's an unfamiliar, even peculiar, strategy. We are far more familiar with an approach that builds the argument brick by brick. With Marx, the argument is more onion-like. Maybe this metaphor is an unfortunate one, because, as someone once pointed out to me, when you dissect an onion, it reduces you to tears. Marx starts from the outside of the onion, moving through layers of external reality to reach its center, the conceptual core. Then he grows the argument outward again, coming back to the surface through the various layers of theory. The true power of the argument only becomes clear when, having returned to the realm of experience, we find ourselves equipped with an entirely new framework of knowledge for understanding and interpreting that experience. By then, Marx has also revealed a great deal about what makes capitalism grow in the way it does. In this way, concepts that at first seem abstract and *a priori* become ever richer and more meaningful; Marx expands the range of his concepts as he goes on.

This is different from the brick-by-brick approach, and it is not easy to adapt to. What this means in practice is that you have to hang on like crazy, particularly through the first three chapters, without really knowing what is going on, until you can get a better sense of it all when you get further on in the text. Only then can you begin to see how these concepts are working.

Marx's starting point is the concept of the commodity. At first blush this seems a somewhat arbitrary if not strange place to start. When thinking of Marx, phrases like the *Manifesto*'s "all history is the history of class struggle" come to mind. So why doesn't *Capital* start with class struggle? In fact it takes about three hundred pages before there's more than a hint of that, which may frustrate those looking for an immediate guide to action. Why doesn't Marx start with money? Actually, in his preparatory investigations, he wanted to start there, but after further study he concluded that money needed to be explained rather than assumed. Why doesn't he start with labor, another concept with which he is deeply associated? Why does he start with the commodity? Interestingly, Marx's preparatory writings indicate that there was a long period, about twenty or thirty years, during which he struggled with the question of where to begin. The method of descent brought him to the concept of the commodity, but Marx makes no attempt to explain that choice, nor does he bother to argue for its legitimacy. He just starts with the commodity, and that is that.

It's crucial to understand that he is constructing an argument on the basis of an already determined conclusion. This makes for a cryptic beginning to his whole argument, and the temptation for the reader is to be either so bemused or irritated by the arbitrariness of it all as to give up by chapter 3. So Marx is quite correct to point out that the start of *Capital* is particularly arduous. My initial task is, therefore, to guide you through the first three chapters, at least; it does get plainer sailing after that.

I have suggested, however, that the conceptual apparatus Marx here constructs is meant to deal not just with the first volume of *Capital* but with his analysis as a whole. And there are, of course, three volumes of *Capital* that have come down to us, so if you really want to understand the capitalist mode of production, you have unfortunately to read all three volumes. Volume I is just one perspective. But, even worse, the three volumes of *Capital* are only about an eighth (if that) of what he had in mind. Here is what he wrote in a preparatory text called the *Grundrisse*, wherein he sets out various designs for *Capital*. I have the ambition, he says at one point, to deal with the following:

> (1) The general, abstract determinants which obtain in more or less all forms of society . . . (2) The categories which make up the inner structure of bourgeois society and on which the fundamental classes rest. Capital, wage labour, landed property. Their interrelation. Town and country. The three great social classes. Exchange between them. Circulation. Credit system (private). (3) Concentration of bourgeois society in the form of the state. Viewed in relation to itself. The 'unproductive' classes. Taxes. State debt. Public credit. The population. The colonies. Emigration. (4) The international relation of production. International division of labour. International exchange. Export and import. Rate of exchange. (5) The world market and crises. (104)

Marx never came near to finishing this project. In fact, he took up few of these topics in any systematic way or in any detail. And many of them—like the credit system and finance, colonial activities, the state, international relations and the world market and crises—are absolutely crucial for our understanding of capitalism. There are hints in his voluminous writings as to how to deal with many of these topics, how best to understand the state, civil society, immigration, currency exchanges and the like. And it is possible, as I tried to show in my own *Limits to Capital*,[2] to pin some of the fragments he left us with on these topics together in ways that make sense. But it's important to recognize that the conceptual apparatus presented at the beginning of *Capital* bears the burden of laying the foundation for this momentous but incomplete project.

Volume I, you will see, explores the capitalist mode of production from the standpoint of production, not of the market, not of global trade, but the standpoint of production alone. Volume II (never completed) takes the perspective of exchange relations, while Volume III (also incomplete) concentrates initially on crisis formation as a product of the fundamental contradictions of capitalism, then also takes up issues of distribution of

2. David Harvey, *The Limits to Capital* (London: Verso, 2006).

the surplus in the forms of interest, return on finance capital, rent on land, profit on merchant capital, taxes and the like. So there is a lot missing from the analysis of Volume I, but there is certainly enough there to furnish your understanding of how the capitalist mode of production actually works.

This brings us back to Marx's method. One of the most important things to glean from a careful study of Volume I is how Marx's method works. I personally think this is just as important as the propositions he derives about how capitalism works, because once you have learned the method and become both practiced in its execution and confident in its power, then you can use it to understand almost anything. This method derives, of course, from dialectics, which is, as he points out in the preface already cited, a method of inquiry "that had not previously been applied to economic subjects" (104). He further discusses this dialectical method in the postface to the second edition. While his ideas derive from Hegel, Marx's "dialectical method is, in its foundations, not only different from the Hegelian, but exactly opposite to it" (102). Hence derives the notorious claim that Marx inverted Hegel's dialectics and stood it right side up, on its feet.

There are ways in which, we'll find, this is not exactly true. Marx revolutionized the dialectical method; he didn't simply invert it. "I criticized the mystificatory side of the Hegelian dialectic nearly thirty years ago," he says, referring to his critique of Hegel's *Philosophy of Right*. Plainly, that critique was a foundational moment in which Marx redefined his relationship to the Hegelian dialectic. He objects to the way in which the mystified form of the dialectic as purveyed by Hegel became the fashion in Germany in the 1830s and 1840s, and he set out to reform it so that it could take account of "every historically developed form as being in a fluid state, in motion." Marx had, therefore, to reconfigure dialectics so that it could grasp the "transient aspect" of a society as well. Dialectics has to, in short, be able to understand and represent processes of motion, change and transformation. Such a dialectical method "does not let itself be impressed by anything, being in its very essence critical and revolutionary" (102–3), precisely because it goes to the heart of what social transformations, both actual and potential, are about.

What Marx is talking about here is his intention to reinvent the dialectical method to take account of the unfolding and dynamic relations between elements within a capitalist system. He intends to do so in such a way as to capture fluidity and motion because he is, as we will see, incredibly impressed with the mutability and dynamics of capitalism. This goes against the reputation that invariably precedes Marx, depicting him as some sort of fixed and immovable structuralist thinker. *Capital*, however, reveals a Marx who is always talking about movement and the motion—the processes—of, for example, the circulation of capital. So reading Marx on his own terms requires that you grapple with what it is he means by "dialectics."

The problem here is, however, that Marx never wrote a tract on dialectics, and he never explicated his dialectical method (although there are, as we shall see, plenty of hints here and there). So we have an apparent paradox. To understand Marx's dialectical method, you have to read *Capital*, because that is the source for its actual practice; but in order to understand *Capital* you have to understand Marx's dialectical method. A careful reading of *Capital* gradually yields a sense of how his method works, and the more you read, the better you'll understand *Capital* as a book.

One of the curious things about our educational system, I would note, is that the better trained you are in a discipline, the less used to dialectical method you're likely to be. In fact, young children are very dialectical; they see everything in motion, in contradictions and transformations. We have to put an immense effort into training kids out of being good dialecticians. Marx wants to recover the intuitive power of the dialectical method and put it to work in understanding how everything is in process, everything is in motion. He doesn't simply talk about labor; he talks about the labor *process*. Capital is not a thing, but rather a process that exists only in *motion*. When circulation stops, value disappears and the whole system comes tumbling down. Consider what happened in the aftermath of September 11, 2001, in New York City: everything came to a standstill. Planes stopped flying, bridges and roads closed. After about three days, everybody realized that capitalism would collapse if things didn't get moving again. So suddenly, Mayor Giuliani and President Bush are pleading the public to get out the credit cards and go shopping, go back to Broadway, patronize the restaurants. Bush even appeared in a TV ad for the airline industry encouraging Americans to start flying again.

Capitalism is nothing if it is not on the move. Marx is incredibly appreciative of that, and he sets out to evoke the transformative dynamism of capital. That's why it is so very strange that he's often depicted as a static thinker who reduces capitalism to a structural configuration. No, what Marx seeks out in *Capital* is a conceptual apparatus, a deep structure, that explains the way in which motion is actually instantiated within a capitalist mode of production. Consequently, many of his concepts are formulated around *relations* rather than stand-alone principles; they are about transformative activity.

So getting to know and appreciate the dialectical method of *Capital* is essential to understanding Marx on his own terms. Quite a lot of people, including some Marxists, would disagree. The so-called analytical Marxists—thinkers like G. A. Cohen, John Roemer and Robert Brenner—dismiss dialectics. They actually like to call themselves "no-bullshit Marxists." They prefer to convert Marx's argument into a series of analytical propositions. Others convert his argument into a causal model of the world. There is even a positivist way of representing Marx that allows his theory to be tested against empirical data. In each of these cases, dialectics gets stripped away. Now, I am not in principle arguing that the analytical Marxists are wrong, that those who turn Marx into a positivist model-builder are deluded. Maybe they are right; but I do insist that Marx's own terms are dialectical, and we are therefore obliged to grapple in the first instance with a dialectical reading of *Capital*.

One final point: our aim is to read Marx on Marx's own terms, but inasmuch as I am guiding that approach, those terms will inevitably be affected by my interests and experiences. I have spent much of my academic life bringing Marxian theory to bear on the study of urbanization under capitalism, of uneven geographical development and of imperialism, and that experience has obviously affected the way in which I now read *Capital*. To begin with, these are practical, rather than philosophical or abstractly theoretical, concerns; my approach has always been to ask what *Capital* can reveal to us about how daily life is lived in the grand cities that capitalism has produced. Over the thirty-odd years of engagement I have had with this text, all manner of geographical, historical and social shifts have occurred. Indeed, one of the reasons I like to teach *Capital* every year is that each time I must ask myself how it will read differently, what about it will strike me that I didn't notice before. I find myself coming back to Marx less for guidance than for potential theoretical insights as geography, history and people change. In the process, of course, I have in turn amended my understanding of the text. As the historical and intellectual climate confronts us with apparently unprecedented issues and perils, so the way we read *Capital* has also to shift and adapt.

Marx talks about this process of necessary reformulation and reinterpretation. Bourgeois theory understood the world in a certain way in the eighteenth century, he remarks, and then history moved on to make that theory and its theoretical formulations irrelevant (95–98). Ideas have to change or be reconfigured as circumstances change. Marx understood and represented the capitalist world luminously in the 1850s and 1860s, but the world has changed, and so the question must always be asked: in what ways is this text applicable to our own times? Unfortunately, in my view, the neoliberal counterrevolution that has dominated global capitalism over the past thirty years has done much to reconstitute globally those conditions that Marx so brilliantly deconstructed in the 1850s and 1860s in Britain. So in these readings I insert some of my own commentary on both the relevance of *Capital* to today's world and the reading of the text that seems best to fit the tenor of the times.

Mostly, though, I want you to come away with your own reading of *Capital*. That is, I hope you will engage with the text in terms of your own distinctive experience—intellectual, social, political—and learn from it in your own fashion. I hope you will have a good and enlightening time speaking to the text, as it were, and letting the text speak back to you. That kind of dialogue with the text is a wonderful exercise in seeking to understand what appears almost impossible to understand. It is the business of each reader to translate *Capital* into meaning for his or her own life. There is, and can be, no ultimate and definitive reading precisely because the world perpetually changes. As Marx would probably have said, *Hic Rhodus, hic salta!* Here is the ball, now run with it!

CHAPTER ONE

Commodities and Exchange

CHAPTER 1: THE COMMODITY

Section 1: Use-Value and Value

Let me begin by looking at the first section of chapter 1 in considerable detail. I do so in part because Marx here lays out fundamental categories in an *a priori* and somewhat cryptic, take-it-or-leave-it fashion that could do with elaboration. But I am also interested in getting you, as quickly as possible, familiar with the kind of close reading of *Capital* that is necessary if you are to understand it. Don't worry, I will not continue at this level of intensity!

The commodity is Marx's *a priori* beginning point. "The wealth of societies in which the capitalist mode of production prevails," he says, "appears as an 'immense collection of commodities'; the individual commodity appears as its elementary form. Our investigation therefore begins with the analysis of the commodity" (125). But notice something about the language. "Appears" occurs twice in the passage, and, plainly, "appears" is not the same as "is." The choice of this word—and watch out for it, because Marx makes frequent use of it throughout *Capital*—signals that something else is going on beneath the surface appearance. We are immediately invited to think about what this might be. Notice also that Marx is exclusively concerned with the capitalist mode of production. He is not concerned with ancient modes of production, socialist modes of production or even hybrid modes of production, but with a capitalist mode of production in a pretty pure form. It is always important to remember this in what follows.

Starting with commodities turns out to be very useful because everyone has daily contact with and experience of them. We are surrounded by them at every turn, we spend time shopping for them, looking at them, wanting them or spurning them. The commodity form is a universal presence within a capitalist mode of production. Marx has chosen *the* common denominator, something that is familiar and common to us all, irrespective of class, race, gender, religion, nationality, sexual preference or whatever. We know about commodities in an everyday way, and they are, furthermore, essential to our existence: we have to buy them in order to live.

Commodities are traded in the market, and this immediately poses the question: what kind of economic transaction is this? The commodity is something that meets a human want, need or desire. It is something external to us that we take possession of and make ours. But Marx immediately declares he is not interested in "the nature of these needs, whether they arise, for example, from the stomach, or the imagination." All he is interested in is the simple fact that people buy commodities and that this act is foundational to how people live. There are, of course, millions of commodities in the world, and all of them are different in terms of their material qualities and how they are described quantitatively (pounds of flour, pairs of socks, kilowatts of electricity, yards of cloth, etc.). But Marx pushes all this immense diversity to one side, saying that the discovery of "the manifold uses of things is the work of history," as is the "invention of socially recognized standards of measurement for the quantities of these useful objects" (125). But he needs to find some way to talk about the commodity in general. "The usefulness of a thing," can best be conceptualized as a "use-value" (126). This concept of use-value will be vital in everything that follows.

Notice how quickly he abstracts from the incredible diversity of human wants, needs and desires, as well as from the immense variety of commodities and their weights and measures, in order to focus on the unitary concept of a use-value. This is illustrative of an argument he makes in one of the prefaces, where he says that the problem for social science is that we cannot isolate and conduct controlled experiments in a laboratory, so we have to use the power of abstraction instead in order to arrive at similar scientific forms of understanding (90). In this opening passage you see this process of abstraction at work for the first, but certainly not the last, time.

But "in the form of society to be considered here" (i.e., capitalism), commodities "are also the material bearers . . . of . . . exchange-value." Be careful about the word "bearer," because bearing something is not the same as being something. Commodities are bearers of something else which has yet to be defined. So how do we discover what the commodity is a bearer of? When we look at actual exchange processes in the market, we witness an immense variety of exchange ratios between, for example, shirts and shoes and apples and oranges, and these exchange ratios vary a great deal even for the same products according to time and place. So at first sight it seems as if exchange ratios are "something accidental and purely relative" (but note the word "relative"). From this it would "appear" that the idea of "an intrinsic value, i.e. an exchange value that is inseparably connected with the commodity, inherent in it, seems a contradiction in terms" (126). On the other hand, everything is in principle exchangeable with everything else. Commodities can keep changing hands and keep moving in a system of exchanges. Something makes all commodities commensurable in exchange. From this it follows that "the valid exchange-values of a particular commodity express something equal, and secondly, exchange-value cannot be anything other than the mode of expression, the 'form of appearance', of a content distinguishable from it." I cannot dissect a commodity and find that element within it that makes it exchangeable. What makes it exchangeable must be something else, and that something else is discoverable only when the commodity is being exchanged (and here the idea of movement and process starts to emerge as crucial). As the commodity changes hands, so it expresses something about not only its own qualities but the qualities of all commodities, i.e., that they are commensurable with one another. So why are they commensurable, and whence does that commensurability derive? "Each of them" (the commodities), "so far as it is exchange-value, must therefore be reducible to this third thing" (127).

"This common element," Marx then argues, "cannot be a geometrical, physical, chemical or other natural property of commodities" (127). This leads to a significant turn in the argument. Marx is usually depicted as an unwavering if not fundamentalist materialist. Everything has to be material in order to be validly considered as real, but here he is denying that the materiality of the commodity can tell you anything you might want to know about what it is that makes them commensurable. "As use-values, commodities differ above all in quality, while as exchange-values they can only differ in quantity, and therefore do not contain an atom of use-value." The commensurability of commodities is not constituted out of their use-values. "If then we disregard the use-value of commodities, only one property remains"—and here we are going to make another of those *a priori* leaps by way of assertion—"that of being products of labour" (128). So commodities are all products of human labor. What commodities have in common is that they are all bearers of the human labor embodied in their production.

But, he then immediately asks, what kind of human labor is embodied in commodities? It can't be the actual time taken—what he calls the concrete labor—because then the longer taken to produce the commodity, the more valuable it would be. Why would I pay a lot for an item because somebody took a long time making it when I can get it at half the price from somebody else who produced it in half the time? So, he concludes, all commodities are "reduced to the same kind of labour, human labour in the abstract" (128).

But what does this human labor in the abstract look like? Commodities are residues

> of the products of labour. There is nothing left of them in each case but the same phantom-like objectivity; they are merely congealed quantities of homogeneous human labour ... As crystals of this social substance, which is common to them all, they are values—commodity values. (128)

What a crisp passage, yet with what incredibly condensed meanings! If human labor in the abstract is a "phantom-like objectivity," how can we possibly see it or measure it? What kind of materialism is this?

It has, you will notice, taken a mere four pages of rather cryptic assertions to lay out the fundamental concepts and move the argument from use-value to exchange-value to human labor in the abstract, and ultimately to value as congealed quantities of homogeneous human labor. It is their value that makes all commodities commensurable, and this value is both hidden as a "phantom-like objectivity" and passed on in the processes of commodity exchange. This poses the question: is value really a "phantom-like objectivity," or does it merely appear that way?

This allows us to reinterpret exchange-value as "the necessary mode of expression, or form of appearance, of value" (128). Notice the word "appearance" here once more, but now we can look at the relation the other way round because the mystery of what makes all commodities exchangeable is now understood as a world of appearances of this "phantom-like objectivity" called value. Exchange-value is a necessary representation of the human labor embodied in commodities. When you go into the supermarket you can find out the exchange-values, but you can't see or measure the human labor embodied in the commodities directly. It is that embodiment of human labor that has a phantom-like presence on the supermarket shelves. Think about that the next time you are in a supermarket surrounded with these phantoms!

Marx then returns to the question of what kind of labor is involved in the production of value. Value is "abstract human labour . . . objectified . . . or materialized" in the commodity. How can this value be measured? In the first instance, this plainly has something to do with labor-time. But as I already argued in setting up the difference between concrete and abstract labor, it cannot be the actual labor-time, because then the commodity would be "more valuable the more unskillful and lazy the worker who produced it." So "the labour that forms the substance of value is equal human labour, the expenditure of identical human labour-power." In order to get at what the "expenditure of identical human labour-power" might mean, he needs, he says, to look at "the total labour-power of society, which is manifested in the values of the world of commodities" (129).

This *a priori* assertion has huge implications. Marx does not, however, elaborate on them here. So let me do so, lest you misconstrue what the value theory is about. To speak of "the total labour-power of society" is tacitly to invoke a world market that has been brought into being under a capitalist mode of production. Where does this "society"—the world of capitalist commodity exchange—begin and end? Right now it's in China, it's in Mexico, it's in Japan, Russia, South Africa—it's a global set of relations. The measure of value is derived out of this whole world of human laboring. But this was true, though obviously on a lesser scale, of Marx's time, too. There is a brilliant description of what we now call globalization in the *Communist Manifesto*:

> The bourgeoisie has through its exploitation of the world-market given a cosmopolitan character to production and consumption in every country . . . it has drawn from under the feet of industry the national ground on which it stood. All old-established national industries have been destroyed or are daily being destroyed. They are dislodged by new industries, whose introduction becomes a life and death question for all civilised nations, by industries that no longer work up indigenous raw material, but raw material drawn from the remotest zones; industries whose products are consumed, not only at home, but in every quarter of the globe. In place of the old wants, satisfied by the productions of the country, we find new wants, requiring for their satisfaction the products of distant lands and climes. In place of the old local and national seclusion and self-sufficiency,

> we have intercourse in every direction, universal inter-dependence of nations.

It is on this dynamic global terrain of exchange relations that value is being determined and perpetually redetermined. Marx was writing in a historical context where the world was opening up very fast to global trade, through the steamship, the railways and the telegraph. And he understood very well that value was not determined in our backyard or even within a national economy, but arose out of the whole world of commodity exchange. But he here again uses the power of abstraction to arrive at the idea of units of homogeneous labor, each of which "is the same as any other, to the extent that it has the character of a socially average unit of labour-power and acts as such," as if this reduction to the value form is actually occurring through world trade.

This allows him to formulate the crucial definition of "value" as "socially necessary labour-time," which "is the labour-time required to produce any use-value under the conditions of production normal for a given society and with the average degree of skill and intensity of labour prevalent in that society." He concludes, "What exclusively determines the magnitude of the value of any article is therefore the amount of labour socially necessary, or the labour-time socially necessary for its production" (129). There is your definition. But it is plainly a contingent definition, because it is internal to the concept of "society"—but where does society begin or end? Is it closed or open? If that society is the world market, as it surely must be, then . . . ?

One reason Marx could get away with this cryptic presentation of use-value, exchange-value and value was because anybody who had read Ricardo would say, yes, this is Ricardo. And it is pure Ricardo with, however, one exceptional insertion. Ricardo appealed to the concept of labor-time as value. Marx uses the concept of *socially necessary* labor-time. What Marx has done here is to replicate the Ricardian conceptual apparatus and, seemingly innocently, insert a modification. But this insertion, as we shall see, makes a world of difference. We are immediately forced to ask: what is socially necessary? How is that established, and by whom? Marx gives no immediate answers, but this question is one theme that runs throughout *Capital*. What are the social necessities embedded within a capitalist mode of production?

This, I submit, continues to be the big issue for us. Is there, as Margaret

Thatcher famously remarked, "no alternative," which in a way is like saying that the social necessities that surround us are so implacably set that we have no choice but to conform to them? At its foundation, this goes back to a question of by whom and how "values" are established. We all like to think, of course, that we have our own "values," and every election season in the United States there is an interminable discussion about candidates' "values." But Marx is arguing that there is a certain kind and measure of value which is being determined by a process that we do not understand and which is not necessarily our conscious choice, and that the manner in which these values are being imposed on us has to be unpacked. If you want to understand who you are and where you stand in this maelstrom of churning values, you have first to understand how commodity values get created and produced and with what consequences—social, environmental, political and the like. If you think you can solve a serious environmental question like global warming without actually confronting the question of by whom and how the foundational value structure of our society is being determined, then you are kidding yourself. So Marx insists that we must understand what commodity values and the social necessities that determine them are all about.

Commodity values are not fixed magnitudes. They are sensitive, for instance, to changes in productivity:

> The introduction of power-looms into England, for example, probably reduced by one half the labour required to convert a given quantity of yarn into woven fabric. In order to do this, the English hand-loom weaver in fact needed the same amount of labour-time as before; but the product of his individual hour of labour now only represented half an hour of social labour, and consequently fell to one half its former value. (129)

This alerts us to the fact that value is sensitive to revolutions in technology and in productivity. Much of Volume I is going to be taken up with the discussion of the origins and impacts of revolutions in productivity and the consequent revolutions in value relations. But it is not only revolutions in technology that are important, because value is "determined by a wide range of circumstances; it is determined amongst other things by the workers' average degree of skill, the level of development of science and its technological application"—Marx is very taken with the significance of technology and science to capitalism—"the social organization of the process of production, the extent and effectiveness of the means of production, and the conditions found in the natural environment" (130). A vast array of forces can impinge on values. Transformations in the natural environment or migration to places with more favorable natural conditions (cheaper resources) revolutionize values. Commodity values, in short, are subject to a powerful array of forces. He does not here attempt a definitive categorization of all of them; he simply wants to alert us that what we are calling "value" is not a constant, but is subject to perpetual revolutionary transformations.

But then comes a peculiar twist in his argument. Right in the last paragraph of this section, he suddenly reintroduces the question of use-values. "A thing can be a use-value without being a value." We breathe air, and so far we haven't managed to bottle it and sell it as a commodity, although I am sure someone is already trying to figure out how to do that. Also, "a thing can be useful, and a product of human labour, without being a commodity." I grow tomatoes in my backyard, and I eat them. Lots of people within capitalism actually do a lot of things for themselves (particularly with a bit of help from do-it-yourself stores). A lot of laboring (particularly in the domestic economy) goes on outside commodity production. The production of commodities requires not only the production of use-values "but use-values for others." Not simply use-values for the lord of the manor, as the serf would do, but use-values that go to others through the market. But the implication of this is that "nothing can be a value without being an object of utility. If the thing is useless, so is the labour contained in it; the labour does not count as labour, and therefore creates no value" (131). Marx earlier seemed to dismiss and abstract from use-values in order to get to exchange-value, and it was this that got him to value. But now he says that if the commodity doesn't meet a human want, need or desire, then it has no value! You have, in short, to be able to sell it to someone somewhere.

Let us reflect a moment on the structure of this argument. We begin with the singular concept of the commodity and establish its dual character: it has a use-value and an exchange-value. Exchange-values are a representation of something. What is it a representation of? A representation of value, says Marx. And value is socially necessary labor-time. But value doesn't mean anything unless it connects back to use-value. Use-value is socially necessary to value. There is a pattern to this argument, and it looks like this:

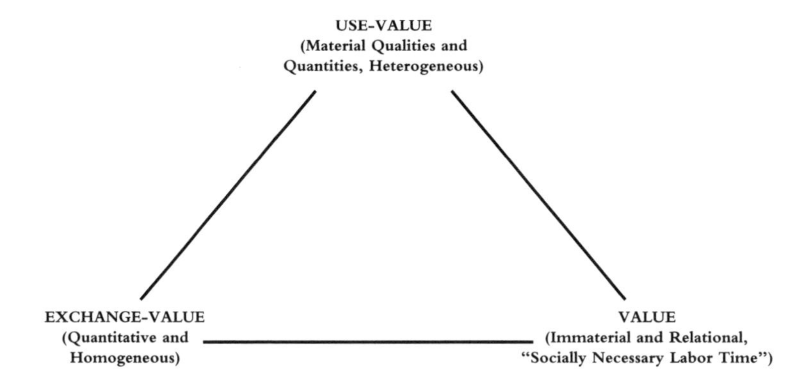

Consider, then, the implications of this argument. You own a commodity called a house. Are you more interested in its use-value or its exchange-value? You will likely be interested in both. But there is a potential opposition here. If you want to fully realize the exchange-value, you have to surrender its use-value to someone else. If you have the use-value of it, then it is difficult to get access to the exchange-value, unless you do a reverse mortgage or take out a home-equity loan. Does adding to the use-value of the house for oneself add to the potential exchange-value? (A new modern kitchen, probably yes; some special construction to facilitate a hobby, probably no.) And what happens to our social world when the house that was once conceptualized mainly in use-value terms as a home becomes reconceptualized as a way to build long-term savings (a capital asset) for a working-class family or even as a vehicle to be "flipped" by anyone who has access to credit for short-term speculative gain? This use-value/exchange-value dichotomy is, well, useful!

Consider the argument in greater detail. The commodity, a singular concept, has two aspects. But you can't cut the commodity in half and say, that's the exchange-value, and that's the use-value. No, the commodity is a unity. But within that unity, there is a dual aspect, and that dual aspect allows us to define something called value—another unitary concept—as socially necessary labor-time, and this is what the use-value of a commodity is a bearer of. But in order to be of value, the commodity has to be useful. On this link back between value and use-value, we will see all kinds of issues arising around supply and demand. If the supply is too great, the exchange-value will go down; if the supply is too little, the exchange-value will go up—so there is an element here of supply and demand involved in the "accidental and relative" aspects of exchange-value. But behind these fluctuations, the value can remain constant (provided all the other forces that determine value, such as productivity, do too). Marx is not terribly interested in the supply and demand relation. He wants to know how to interpret commodity-exchange ratios between, say, shirts and shoes, when supply and demand are in equilibrium. We then need a different kind of analysis which points to value as congealed elements of this social substance called socially necessary labor-time. We have, without noticing it, tacitly abstracted from supply and demand conditions in the market in order to talk about commodity-values (with supply and demand in equilibrium) as socially necessary labor-time.

How has Marx's dialectical method been working here? Would you say that exchange-values cause value? Would you say exchange-values cause use-value, or use-values cause . . . ? This analysis is not causal. It is about relations, dialectical relations. Can you talk about exchange-value without talking about use-value? No, you can't. Can you talk about value without talking about use-value? No. In other words, you can't talk about any of these concepts without talking about the others. The concepts are codependent on one another, relations within a totality of some sort.

I recognize that to use the word "totality" is to wave a huge red flag in certain intellectual circles. Marx had no idea what structuralism might be about and would have had even less idea about poststructuralism. We should be wary of cramming his thought into these categories (my own view is that he does not fit into them at all). But Marx certainly had the ambition to understand the capitalist mode of production as a totality, so the only question of interest is, exactly what concept of totality does he have in mind? What we know from this first section is that this totality can best be approached through the triumvirate of concepts of use-value, exchange-value and value built around the commodity. But he has acknowledged that use-values are incredibly diverse, that exchange-values are accidental and relative and that value has (or appears to have) a "phantom-like objectivity," which is in any case subjected to perpetual revolutions through technological changes and upheavals in social and natural relations. This totality is not static and closed but fluid and open and therefore in perpetual transformation. This is definitely not a Hegelian totality, but what else we can say about it will have to wait until we have gotten further along in the text.

* * *

The story so far is roughly this: Marx declares that his aim is to uncover the rules of operation of a capitalist mode of production. He starts with the concept of the commodity and immediately establishes its dual character: use-value and exchange-value. Since use-values have been around forever, they tell us little about the specificity of capitalism. So Marx puts them aside in order to study exchange-values. The exchange ratios between commodities at first appear accidental, but the very act of exchange presupposes that all commodities have something in common that makes them comparable and commensurable. This commonality, Marx cryptically asserts, is that they are all products of human labor. As such, they incorporate "value," initially defined as the socially necessary (average) labor time necessary to produce them under given conditions of labor productivity. But in order for the labor to be socially necessary, somebody somewhere must want, need or desire the commodity, which means that use-values have to be reintegrated into the argument.

In the analysis that follows, these three concepts of use-value, exchange-value and value are kept in a perpetual and sometimes tense relationship with one another. Marx rarely takes any one of these concepts in isolation, it is the *relations between them* that matter. He does, however, frequently examine the relationship between just two of them while holding the third tacitly to one side. In expanding on the dual character of labor embodied in a commodity in section 2, Marx focuses on the relationship between the use-value of laboring and the value that this useful labor embodies (holding exchange-value constant). In the following section, he brackets out use-value and examines the relationship between exchange-value and value in order to explain the origin and role of money. It's important to notice these changes of focus as the argument unfolds, because the statements in any one section are always contingent on which of the concepts is being set aside.

There is yet another mode of argumentation here that requires elucidation if we are to proceed. Having begun with use-value and exchange-value—a dichotomy—he then arrives at a unitary concept of value that has something to do with human labor understood as "socially necessary labour-time" (129). But what kind of human labor is socially necessary? The search for an answer reveals another duality, that between concrete (actual) and abstract (socially relevant) labor. These two forms of labor converge again in the unitary act of commodity exchange. Yet examination of this moment of exchange reveals another duality between relative and equivalent forms of value. These two modes of expression of value are reunited in the emergence of one commodity—the money commodity—which functions as a universal equivalent in relation to all other commodities. What we see here is a pattern in the mode of argumentation, a gradual unfolding of the argument that works through oppositions that are brought back into unities (like the money-form) that internalize a contradiction which in turn generates yet another duality (the relationship between processes and things, material relations between people and social relations between things). This is Marx's dialectical method of presentation at work, and it continues throughout the whole of *Capital*, as we will see.

Here is the pattern of argument unfolding in simple diagrammatic form:

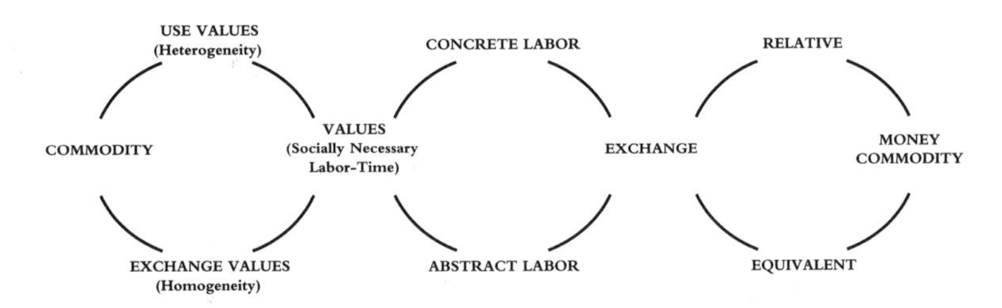

Mapping the argument in this way makes it much easier to see the woods for the trees. It is easier to situate the content of any one section within the overall line of argument. This is not Hegelian logic in the strict sense, because there is no final moment of synthesis, only a temporary moment of unity within which yet another contradiction—a duality—is internalized and then requires a further expansion of the argument if it is to be understood. This is how Marx's process of representation unfolds in *Capital*—and indeed, it is an unfolding and not a logical derivation. It produces a skeletal structure of argumentation around which all manner of conceptual matter can be arranged so that, as we proceed, there emerges a broader and broader understanding of the internal relations that keep capitalism in a perpetual state of contradictory unity and, therefore, in perpetual motion.

Section 2: The Dual Character of the Labour Embodied in Commodities

Marx begins this section with the modest claim that he "was the first to point out and examine critically this twofold nature of the labour contained in commodities. As this point is crucial to an understanding of political economy," he says, "it requires further elucidation" (132). He begins, as he did in section 1, with use-values. These are physical products, produced by useful, "concrete" labor. The immense heterogeneity of forms of concrete labor processes—tailoring, shoemaking, spinning, weaving, farming and so on—is important, because without it there would be no basis for any acts of exchange (nobody, obviously, would want to exchange similar products) or a social division of labor.

> Use-values cannot confront each other as commodities unless the useful labour contained in them is qualitatively different in each case. In a society whose products generally assume the form of commodities . . . this qualitative difference between the useful forms of labour which are carried on independently and privately by individual producers develops into a complex system, a social division of labour. (133)

Here Marx broaches a methodological theme that echoes throughout these chapters: the movement from simplicity to greater complexity, from the simple molecular aspects of an exchange economy toward a more systemic understanding. He then deviates from the rule of looking at relations in order to examine some of the universal properties of useful labor. He does so because "labour . . . as the creator of use-values, as useful labour, is a condition of human existence which is independent of all forms of society." Useful labor is "an eternal natural necessity which mediates the metabolism between man and nature, and therefore human life itself" (133).

This idea of "metabolism," with labor as the mediator between human existence and nature, is central to Marx's historical-materialist argument. He will come back to it at various points in *Capital* even as he leaves the idea rather undeveloped. This, too, is often typical of his approach. He says, in effect, "Look, there is something important here you should think about [in this case, the relation to nature]. I am not going to work with it in any detail, but I want to put it on the table as significant before going on to matters of more immediate concern." "Use-values," he writes, "are combinations of two elements, the material provided by nature, and labour." Hence, "when man engages in production, he can only proceed as nature does herself" (133). This again is an important foundational point: whatever we do has to be consistent with natural law.

> [We] can only change the form of the materials. Furthermore, even in this work of modification [we are] constantly helped by natural forces. Labour is therefore not the only source of material wealth, i.e. of the use-values it produces. As William Petty says, labour is the father of material wealth, the earth is its mother. (133–4)

With the help of this gendered metaphor (which dates back at least to Francis Bacon), Marx introduces a crucial distinction between wealth—the total use-values at one's command—and value—the socially necessary labor time these use-values represent.

Marx then returns to the question of values in order to contrast their homogeneity (all products of human labor) with the vast heterogeneity of use-values and of concrete forms of laboring. He writes,

> Tailoring and weaving, although they are qualitatively different productive activities, are both a productive expenditure of human brains, muscles, nerves, hands etc., and in this sense both human labour. They are merely two different forms of the expenditure of human labour-power. Of course, human labour-power must itself have attained a certain level of development before it can be expended in this or that form. But the value of a commodity represents human labour pure and simple, the expenditure of human labour in general. (134–5)

As such, it is what Marx calls "abstract" labor (135–7). This kind of generality of labor contrasts with the myriad concrete labors producing actual use-values. In creating this concept of abstract labor, Marx holds that he is merely mirroring an abstraction produced by extensive commodity exchanges.

So Marx conceptualizes value in terms of units of simple abstract labor; this standard of measurement "varies in character in different countries and at different cultural epochs, but in a particular society it is given." Here again we encounter a strategy frequently deployed in *Capital*. The standard of measurement is contingent on space and time, but for the purposes of analysis we assume it is known. Furthermore, in this instance, he then goes on to say, "complex labour," i.e., skilled labor, "counts only as *intensified*, or rather *multiplied* simple labour, so that a smaller quantity of complex labour is considered equal to a larger quantity of simple labour":

> Experience shows that this reduction is constantly being made. A commodity may be the outcome of the most complicated labor, but through its value it is posited as equal to the product of simple labor . . . In the interests of simplification, we shall henceforth view every form of labour-power directly as simple labour-power; by this we shall simply be saving ourselves the trouble of making the reduction. (135)

Notably, Marx never specifies what "experience" he has in mind, making this passage highly controversial. In the literature it is known as the "reduction problem," because it is not clear how skilled labor can be and is reduced to simple labor independently of the value of the commodity produced. Rather like the proposition about value as socially necessary labor time, Marx's formulation appears cryptic, if not cavalier; he doesn't explain how the reduction is made. He simply presumes for purposes of analysis that this is so and then proceeds on that basis. This means that the qualitative differences we experience in concrete labor, useful labor and the heterogeneity of it, is here reduced to something purely quantitative and homogeneous.

Marx's point, of course, is that abstract (homogeneous) and concrete (heterogeneous) aspects of labor are unified in the unitary act of laboring. It is not as if abstract labor occurs in one part of the factory and concrete labor occurs somewhere else. The duality resides within a singular labor process: making the shirt that embodies the value. This means there could be no embodiment of value without the concrete labor of making shirts and, furthermore, that we cannot know what value is unless shirts are being exchanged with shoes, apples, oranges and so on. There is, therefore, a relationship between concrete and abstract labor. It is through the multiplicities of concrete labors that the measuring rod of abstract labor emerges.

> On the one hand all labour is an expenditure of human labour-power, in the physiological sense, and it is in this quality of being equal, or abstract, human labour that it forms the value of commodities. On the other hand, all labour is an expenditure of human labour-power in a particular form

> and with a definite aim, and it is in this quality of being concrete useful labour that it produces use-values. (137)

Note that this argument mirrors that of the first section. The singular commodity internalizes use-values, exchange-values and values. A particular labor process embodies useful concrete labor and abstract labor or value (socially necessary labor-time) in a commodity that will be the bearer of exchange value in the market place. The answer to the problem of how skilled or "complex" labor can be reduced to simple labor partially lies, it turns out, in the next section, where Marx follows the commodity into the marketplace and takes up the relation between value and exchange-value. So let us move on to section 3.

Section 3: The Value Form, or Exchange-Value

This section incorporates, in my view, a lot of boring material that can all too easily mask the significance of the argument being made. Marx sometimes puts on, as I pointed out earlier, an accountant's hat, and the result is a form of exposition that can be tedious in the extreme: when this equals that and that equals this and this costs three pence and this fifteen, then the result is that something else is equivalent to . . . and so it goes, with the help of all manner of numerical illustrations to follow. The woods-for-the-trees problem, which often arises in Marx's writing, is at its worst here, so this is a good point to figure out how to approach it. I shall deal with this at two levels: I will skim over what is often a simple, technical argument, and then comment on its deeper significance.

Marx's objective is to explain the origin of the money-form. "We have to perform a task," he (again, so modestly!) claims, "never even attempted by bourgeois economics."

> That is, we have to show the origin of this money-form, we have to trace the development of the expression of value contained in the value-relation of commodities from its simplest, almost imperceptible outline to the dazzling money-form. When this has been done, the mystery of money will immediately disappear. (139)

He accomplishes this task in a series of heavy-handed steps, beginning with a simple barter situation. I have a commodity, you have a commodity.

The *relative value* of my commodity is going to be expressed in terms of the value (the labor input) of the commodity you hold. So your commodity is going to be a measure of the value of mine. Turn the relationship around, and my commodity can be viewed as the equivalent value of yours. In simple barter situations of this sort, everybody who has a commodity has something with a relative value and looks for its equivalent in another commodity. Since there are as many commodities as there are people and exchanges, there are as many equivalents as there are commodities and exchanges. All Marx really wants to show here is that the act of exchange always has a dual character—the poles of relative and equivalent forms—in which the equivalent commodity figures "as the embodiment of abstract human labour" (150). The opposition between use-value and value, hitherto internalized within the commodity, "gets represented on the surface by an external opposition" between one commodity that is a use-value and another that represents its value in exchange (153).

In a complex field of exchanges like the marketplace, my commodity will have multiple potential equivalents, and conversely, everybody out there has relative values in a potential relation with my singular equivalent. An increasing complexity of exchange relations produces an "expanded form" of value that morphs into a "general form" of value (§b, 154–7, and §c, 157–62). This ultimately crystallizes in a "universal equivalent": one commodity that plays the exclusive role of a "money commodity" (§d, 162–3). The money commodity arises out of a trading system and does not precede it, so it is the proliferation and generalization of exchange relations that is the crucial, necessary condition for the crystallization of the money-form.

In Marx's time, commodities like gold and silver had emerged to play this crucial role, but it could in principle be cowry shells, cans of tuna or—as has sometimes happened in disruptive conditions of war—cigarettes, chocolate or whatever. A market system requires a money commodity of some sort to function effectively, but a money commodity can only come into being through the rise of market exchange. Money was not imposed from outside, nor invented by somebody who thought it would be a good idea to have a money-form. Even symbolic forms, Marx argues, have to be understood in this context.

This gives rise to an interesting interpretive question, one that crops up a number of times in *Capital*: is Marx making a historical argument or a logical argument? The historical evidence supporting his explanation of how the money commodity arose would now, I think, be regarded as rather thin. Quasi-monetary systems and commodities, religious icons and symbolic tokens and the like, have long been in existence, and while expressive of some sort of social relation, these have had no necessary primitive relation to commodity exchanges even as they gradually became mixed up in such exchanges. If we were to consult the archaeological and historical records, many would now probably hold that the money-form didn't arise the way that Marx proposes at all. I am inclined to accept that argument, but then on top of it say the following—and this comes back to Marx's interest in understanding a capitalist mode of production. Under capitalism, the money-form has to be disciplined to and brought into line with the logical position that Marx describes, such that the money-form reflects the needs of a system of proliferating exchange relations. But by the same token (forgive the pun), it is the proliferation of commodity-exchange relations that disciplines any and all preceding symbolic forms to the money-form required to facilitate commodity-market exchange. The precursors of the money-form, which can indeed be found in the archaeological and historical record of coinage, have to conform to this logic to the degree that they get absorbed within capitalism and perform the function of money. At the same time, it should be clear that the market could not have evolved without that disciplining taking place. Though the historical argument is weak, the logical argument is powerful.

This section as a whole establishes, then, the necessary relation between commodity exchange and the money commodity and the mutually determinative role that each plays in the development of the other. But there is much more going on in this section to which we need to pay close attention. At the very beginning of the section, Marx describes the way in which

> the objectivity of commodities as values differs from Dame Quickly in the sense that 'a man knows not where to have it'. Not an atom of matter enters into the objectivity of commodities as values; in this it is the direct opposite of the coarsely sensuous objectivity of commodities as physical objects. We may twist and turn a single commodity as we wish; it remains impossible to grasp it as a thing possessing value. However, let us remember that commodities possess an objective character as values only in so far as they are all expressions of an identical social substance, human labour, that their objective character as values is therefore purely social. From this it follows self-evidently that it can only appear in the social relation between commodity and commodity. (138)

This is an absolutely vital point that cannot be overemphasized: value is immaterial but *objective*. Given Marx's supposed adherence to a rigorous materialism, this is, on the face of it, a surprising argument, and we have to wrestle a bit with what it means. Value is a social relation, and you cannot actually see, touch or feel social relations directly; yet they have an objective presence. We therefore have to carefully examine this social relation and its expression.

Marx proposes the following idea: values, being immaterial, cannot exist without a means of representation. It is, therefore, the rise of the monetary system, the rise of the money-form itself as a means of tangible expression, that makes value (as socially necessary labor-time) the regulator of exchange relations. But the money-form comes closer—step by step, given the logical argument—to expressing value only as commodity-exchange relations proliferate. There is, therefore, nothing universal out there called "value" that after many, many years of struggling finally gets to be expressed through monetary exchange. Rather, there is an internal and coevolving relation between the rise of the money- and the value-forms. The rise of monetary exchange leads to socially necessary labor-time becoming the guiding force within a capitalistic mode of production. Therefore, value as socially necessary labor-time is historically specific to the capitalist mode of production. It arises only in a situation where market exchange is doing the requisite job.

There are two conclusions and one major question that derive from Marx's analysis. The first conclusion is that exchange relations, far from being epiphenomena expressive of the deep value structure, exist in a dialectical relation with values such that the latter depend on the former as much as the former depend on the latter. The second conclusion confirms the immaterial (phantom-like), but objective, status of the value concept. All attempts to measure value directly will fail. The big question mark concerns how reliable and accurate the money representation is of value or, in other words, how the relation between immateriality (value) and objectivity (as captured by the monetary representation of value) actually unfolds.

Marx works through the problem in a number of steps. He comments,

> It is only the expression of equivalence between different sorts of commodities which brings to view the specific character of value-creating labour, by actually reducing the different kinds of labour embedded in the

> different kinds of commodity to their common quality of being human labour in general. (142)

Here we encounter a partial answer to the question of how the reduction from skilled and complex human labor to simple human labor occurs. But then he goes on to say: "human labour-power in its fluid state"—and it is striking how often Marx invokes the concept of fluidity in *Capital*—"or human labour, creates value, but is not itself value. It becomes value in its coagulated state, in objective form" (142). A distinction therefore needs to be made between the labor process and the thing that gets produced. This idea of a relationship between processes and things, along with the idea of fluidity, is important in Marx's analysis. The more he invokes it, the more he moves away from dialectics as a formal logic to dialectics as a philosophy of historical process. Human labor is a tangible process, but at the end of the process, you get this thing— a commodity—which "coagulates" or "congeals" value. While the actual process is what is significant, it is the *thing* that has value and the *thing* that has the objective qualities. Thus:

> The value of the linen as a congealed mass of human labour can be expressed only as an 'objectivity', a thing which is materially different from the linen itself and yet common to the linen and all other commodities. (142)

The problem is: how does value, this "thing which is materially different from the linen," get represented? The answer lies in the money-commodity form. But there are, he notes, some peculiarities in this relationship between value and its expression in the money-form. "The first peculiarity which strikes us," he writes, is that a particular use-value "becomes the form of appearance of its opposite, value," and this "conceals a social relation" (148–9).

> Hence the mysteriousness of the equivalent form, which only impinges on the crude bourgeois vision of the political economist when it confronts him in its fully developed shape, that of money. He then seeks to explain away the mystical character of gold and silver by substituting for them less dazzling commodities, and, with ever-renewed satisfaction, reeling off a catalogue of all the inferior

> commodities which have played the role of the equivalent at one time or another. (149–50)

"The body of the commodity," he goes on to say, "which serves as the equivalent, always figures as the embodiment of abstract human labour, and is always the product of some specific useful and concrete labour" (150). What does this say? Gold, for example, is a specific use-value, a specific commodity, produced under specific conditions of production, and yet we are using it as a means of expression of all human labor everywhere—we are taking a particular use-value and using it as a stand-in for all social labor. This raises complicated questions, as we will see when we get deeper into the theory of money in chapter 2.

The second peculiarity is that "concrete labour becomes the form of manifestation of its opposite, abstract human labour," and the third peculiarity is that "private labour takes the form of its opposite, namely labour in its directly social form" (150). This means not only that the universal equivalent, the money commodity, is subject to the qualitative and quantitative problems that beset the production of any use-value, but that the production and marketing of the money commodity as well as its accumulation (eventually as capital) lie in private hands even as it performs its universalizing social function. When gold was still a dominant commodity underpinning global money at the end of the 1960s, for example, the two primary gold producers were South Africa and Russia, neither of which was particularly friendly to international capitalism. The dematerialization of the whole financial system in the early 1970s and the system of floating exchange rates, free from any gold standard, that then came into being had the effect of disempowering the gold producers (even if this was not the primary reason it occurred).

These are the sorts of contradictions that Marx's analysis leads us to contemplate, and we later see—particularly in Volume III but also in chapter 3 of this volume—how these peculiarities and contradictions start to play out in the creation of possibilities for financial crises. In any case, the fundamental conclusion has to be that the relation between values and their representation in money-form is fraught with contradictions, and so we can never assume a perfect form of representation. This mismatch, as it were, between values and their representation turns out to have advantages even as it is deeply problematic, as we will see.

This brings us to an important passage on Aristotle. "There can be no exchange," says Aristotle, "without equality, and no equality without commensurability."[1] The relationship between the relative and equivalent forms of value presupposes an equality between those doing the exchanges. This attribute of equality within the market system is terribly important; Marx understands it as being fundamental to how capitalism theoretically works. Aristotle, too, understood the need for commensurability and equality in exchange relations, but he couldn't figure out what lay behind it. Why not? Marx's answer is that "Greek society was founded on the labour of slaves, hence had as its natural basis the inequality of men and of their labour-powers" (152). In a slave-holding society there can be no value theory of the sort that we are going to find under capitalism. Again, note the historical specificity of the value theory to capitalism.

This then brings Marx back to expand on the three peculiarities of the money-form in order to identify an emergent opposition:

> The internal opposition between use-value and value, hidden within the commodity, is therefore represented on the surface by an external opposition, i.e. by a relation between two commodities such that the one commodity, whose own value is supposed to be expressed, counts directly only as a use-value, whereas the other commodity, in which that value is to be expressed, counts directly only as exchange-value. (153)

This opposition between the expression of value and the world of commodities, an opposition that results in an "antinomy" between commodities and money, has to be interpreted as an externalization of something that is internalized within the commodity itself. Once externalized, the opposition becomes explicit. The relationship between commodities and money is a product of that dichotomy between use-value and exchange-value which we spotted as internal to the commodity at the very beginning.

So, what do we take from this? First, socially necessary labor-time cannot operate as a regulator of what is happening directly, because it is a social relation. Indirectly, it will do so through the medium of the money-form. Furthermore, the rise of the money-form is what permits value to start to crystallize out as the guiding principle of how a capitalist economy will

1. *Capital*, 151. The quotations from Aristotle, as cited by Marx, are from *Nicomachean Ethics*, Book V, chapter 5.

work. And, always remember, value is immaterial but objective. Now, this creates quite a lot of problems for commonsense logic that assumes value can actually be measured; even some Marxist economists spend a lot of time explaining how they can do so. My argument would be: you can't do it. If it is immaterial, you cannot measure it directly. To find value in a commodity by just looking at a commodity is like trying to find gravity in a stone. It only exists in relations between commodities and only gets expressed materially in the contradictory and problematic form of the money commodity.

Let me now take a moment to reflect further on the status of the three fundamental concepts of use-value, exchange-value and value that Marx sets out. In doing so, I will impose some of my own reflections that arise out of my specific interests, which you may accept or reject as you like. These three different concepts internalize fundamentally different spatiotemporal referents. Use-values exist in the physical material world of things that can be described in Newtonian and Cartesian terms of absolute space and time. Exchange-values lie in the relative space-time of motion and exchange of commodities, while values can be understood only in terms of the relational space-time of the world market. (The immaterial relational value of socially necessary labor times comes into being within the evolving space-time of capitalist global development.) But as Marx has already convincingly shown, values cannot exist without exchange-values, and exchange cannot exist without use-values. The three concepts are dialectically integrated with one another.

In the same way, the three forms of absolute, relative and relational space-time are dialectically related within the historical-geographical dynamics of capitalist development. This is my argument as a geographer. One of the major consequences is that the space-time of capitalism is not constant but variable (as happens with speed-up and what Marx elsewhere calls "the annihilation of space by time"[2] wrought through perpetual revolutions in transport and communications). I cannot refrain from injecting this into the discussion for your consideration! If you want to follow up on the question of spatiotemporal dynamics of capitalism, though, you will have to look elsewhere.[3]

2. Marx, *Grundrisse*, 524.

3. David Harvey, *Spaces of Global Capitalism: Towards a Theory of Uneven Geographical Development* (London: Verso, 2006).

Section 4: The Fetishism of the Commodity and Its Secret

This section is written in a completely different, rather literary, style—evocative and metaphoric, imaginative, playful and emotive, full of allusions and references to magic, mysteries and necromancies. There is a marked contrast with the dull accountancy style of the previous section. This is rather typical of Marx's tactics throughout *Capital*; he often shifts linguistic styles according to the subject under consideration. In this case, the switch can create some confusion as to the relevance of the fetishism concept in Marx's overall argument (a confusion exacerbated by the fact that this section was moved from an appendix in the first edition of *Capital* to its current position—along with section 3—only in the second, definitive edition). Those interested in developing a rigorous political-economic theory out of Marx, for example, sometimes seem to view the fetishism concept as extraneous, not to be taken too seriously. On the other hand, those of a more philosophical or literary persuasion often treat it as the golden nugget, the foundational moment to Marx's understanding of the world. So one of the questions we have to ask is: how does this section stand in relation to Marx's overall argument?

The fetishism concept was already signaled in his discussion of the ways in which important characteristics of the political economic system get "concealed" or confused through the "antinomies" and "contradictions" between, for example, the particularities of the money commodity on the one hand and the universality of phantom-like values on the other. Tensions, oppositions and contradictions that have already been opened up in the text now come in for detailed scrutiny under the heading "The Fetishism of the Commodity and Its Secret" (163). Throughout the rest of *Capital*, as we will see, the concept of fetishism emerges again and again (more often tacitly rather than explicitly) as a essential tool for unraveling the mysteries of capitalist political economy. I consider the concept of fetishism, therefore, as fundamental to the political economy as well as to Marx's wider argument. In effect, it conjoins the two at the hip.

The analysis proceeds in two steps. First, he identifies how fetishism arises and works as a fundamental and inevitable aspect of political-economic life under capitalism. Second, he examines how this fetishism is misleadingly represented in bourgeois thought in general and classical political economy in particular.

Commodities, he begins by observing, "abound in metaphysical subtleties and theological niceties":

> The mysterious character of the commodity-form consists . . . simply in the fact that the commodity reflects the social characteristics of men's own labour as objective characteristics of the products of labour themselves, as the socio-natural properties of these things. (164–5)

The problem is that "the commodity-form, and the value-relation of the products of labour within which it appears, have absolutely no connection with the physical nature of the commodity and the material . . . relations arising out of this." Our sensuous experience of the commodity as use-value has nothing to do with its value. Commodities are, therefore, "sensuous things which are at the same time supra-sensible or social." The result is that a "definite social relation between men themselves . . . assumes here, for them, the fantastic form of a relation between things." And it is this condition that defines "the fetishism which attaches itself to the products of labour as soon as they are produced as commodities." This fetishism is "inseparable from the production of commodities" (165).

This is so, he says, because "the producers do not come into social contact until they exchange the products of their labour," so that they only come to know "the specific social characteristics of their private labour" in the act of market exchange. In other words, they don't and can't know what the value of their commodity is until they take it to the market and successfully exchange it. "To the producers, therefore, the social relations between their private labours appear as what they are"—note please especially the important phrase, *appear as what they are*—"i.e. they do not appear as direct social relations between persons in their work, but rather as material . . . relations between persons and social relations between things" (165–6).

So what's going on here? You go into a supermarket and you want to buy a head of lettuce. In order to buy the lettuce, you have to put down a certain sum of money. The material relation between the money and the lettuce expresses a social relation because the price—the "how much"—is socially determined, and the price is a monetary representation of value. Hidden within this market exchange of things is a relation between you, the consumer, and the direct producers—those who labored to produce the lettuce. Not only do you not have to know anything about that labor or the laborers who congealed value in the lettuce in order to buy it; in highly complicated systems of exchange it is *impossible* to know anything about the labor or the laborers, which is why fetishism is inevitable in the world market. The end result is that our social relation to the laboring activities of others is disguised in the relationships between things. You cannot, for example, figure out in the supermarket whether the lettuce has been produced by happy laborers, miserable laborers, slave laborers, wage laborers or some self-employed peasant. The lettuces are mute, as it were, as to how they were produced and who produced them.

Why is this important? When I taught introductory geography classes at Johns Hopkins, I always started off by asking students where their breakfast came from. And they'd say, "Oh, I bought stuff at the deli." But when I asked them to think back further than that, they found themselves consider a whole incredible world of laboring in radically different geographical environments and under radically different social conditions that they knew nothing about and could know nothing about from staring at their breakfast ingredients or going into the deli. The bread, the sugar, the coffee, the milk; the cups, knives and forks, toasters and plastic plates—to say nothing of the machinery and equipment needed to produce all these things—linked them to millions of people laboring away all around the world. One of the tasks of geographical education is to impart something about the variety of socio-environmental conditions, spatial linkages and labor practices involved in every aspect of daily life, down to putting breakfast on the table every day.

The students did sometimes seem to think I was trying to guilt-trip them for not paying more mind to those poor sugar-cane cutters in the Dominican Republic who earned next to nothing. When it got to that stage they would sometimes declare "Sir, I didn't have breakfast this morning!" To that I would characteristically reply that they might want to do without lunch, dinner, and supper too for a week or so just to learn the truth of the basic Marxian maxim that we have to eat in order to live.

Issues of this kind do raise moral questions. There are those who, for various reasons, propose all manner of codes of moral conduct in interpersonal relations, but who then face the dilemma of whether or how to extend that moral code into the world of commodity exchanges in the world market. It is all very well to insist on "good" face-to-face relations and to be helpful to one's neighbor, but what is the point of that if we are totally indifferent to all those whom we do not know and can never know, but who play a vital role in providing us with our daily bread? These issues are sometime brought to our attention: by the "fair trade" movement, for example, which tries to articulate a moral standard for the world of commodity exchange, and the anti-poverty movement, which seeks to mobilize charitable contributions for distant others. But even these usually fail to challenge the social relations that produce and sustain the conditions of global inequality: wealth for the charitable donors and poverty for everyone else.

Marx's point is not, however, about the moral implications. His concern is to show how the market system and the money-forms disguise real social relations through the exchange of things. He is not saying that this disguise, which he calls "fetishism" (165) (and please note that Marx's use of this term is technical and quite different from other common usages), is a mere illusion, that it is a made-up construction that can be dismantled if only we care to try. No, in fact, what you see is the lettuce, what you see is your money, you see how much, and you make tangible decisions based on that information. This is the significance of the phrase "appear as what they are": it really is this way in the supermarket, and we can observe it so, even as it masks social relations.

This fetishism is an unavoidable condition of a capitalistic mode of production, and it has many implications. For example, people do not "bring the products of their labour into relation with each other as values because they see these objects merely as the material integuments of homogeneous human labour. The reverse is true: by equating their different products to each other in exchange as values, they equate their different kinds of labour as human labour" (166). Once again, we see that values arise out of exchange processes even as exchange relations increasingly converge to express value as socially necessary labor-time. But the producers

> do this without being aware of it. Value, therefore, does not have its description branded on its forehead; it rather transforms every product of labor into a social hieroglyphic. Later on, men try to decipher the hieroglyphic, to get behind the secret of their own social product: for the characteristic which objects of utility have of being values is as much men's social product as is their language. (166–7)

The dialectical relation between value formation and exchange and the immaterial, "phantom" qualities of value as a social relation could not be more starkly portrayed.

But how is this dialectic to be replicated in thought? Many of the political economists got it (and still get it) wrong, says Marx, because they look at prices in the supermarkets and think that's all there is, and that is the only material evidence they need to construct their theories. They simply examine the relationship between supply and demand and associated price movements. Others, more perceptive, came to "the belated scientific discovery that the products of labor, in so far as they are values, are merely the material expressions of the human labor expended to produce them." This "marks an epoch in the history of mankind's development" (167). Classical political economy did gradually converge on some idea of value that lay behind the fluctuations of the market (often referred to as "natural prices") and it recognized that human labor had something to do with it.

But classical political economy failed to understand the gap between the immateriality of values as "congealed" socially necessary labor-time and their representation as money and therefore also failed to understand the role that the proliferation of exchange played in consolidating the value form as something historically specific to capitalism. It assumed that values were a self-evident and universal truth, failing to see that

> the value character of the products of labour becomes firmly established only when they act as magnitudes of value. These magnitudes vary continually, independently of the will, foreknowledge and actions of the exchangers. Their own movement within society has for them the form of a movement made by things, and these things, far from being under their control, in fact control them. (167–8)

Thus Marx begins his attack on the liberal concept of freedom. The freedom of the market is not freedom at all. It is a fetishistic illusion. Under capitalism, individuals surrender to the discipline of abstract forces (such as the hidden hand of the market made much of by Adam Smith) that effectively govern their relations and choices. I can make something beautiful and take it to market, but if I don't manage to exchange it then it has no value. Furthermore, I won't have enough money to buy commodities to live. Market forces, which none of us individually control, regulate us. And part of what Marx wants to do in *Capital* is talk about this regulatory power that occurs even "in the midst of the accidental and ever-fluctuating exchange relations between the products." Supply and demand fluctuations generate price fluctuations around some norm but cannot explain why a pair of shoes on average trades for four shirts. Within all the confusions of the marketplace, "the labour-time socially necessary to produce [commodities] asserts itself as a regulative law of nature. In the same way, the law of gravity asserts itself when a person's house collapses on top of him" (168). This parallel between gravity and value is interesting: both are relations and not things, and both have to be conceptualized as immaterial but objective.

This then leads Marx directly into a critique of how bourgeois modes of thought have evolved in relationship to the proliferation of exchange relations and the rise of the money-form:

> Reflection on the forms of human life, hence also scientific analysis of those forms, takes a course directly opposite to their real development ... Consequently, it was solely the analysis of the prices of commodities which led to the determination of the magnitude of value, and solely the common expression of all commodities in money which led to the establishment of their character as values. It is however precisely this finished form of the world of commodities—the money form—which conceals the social character of private labour and the social relations between the individual workers, by making those relations appear as relations between material objects, instead of revealing them plainly. (168–9)

This failure of vision on the part of the classical political economists is epitomized in the way so many of them embraced Daniel Defoe's *Robinson Crusoe* as a model for a perfect market economy arising out of a state of nature: Robinson, all on his own, marooned on an island, logically constructs a way of life appropriate to dwelling in a state of nature and step by step reconstitutes the logic of a market economy. But as Marx amusedly points out, Robinson, besides supposedly learning from experience, had also conveniently "saved a watch, ledger, ink and pen from the shipwreck," and immediately began, "like a good Englishman, to keep a set of books" (169–70). In other words, Robinson carried with him to the island the mental conceptions of the world appropriate to a market economy and then went on to construct a relation to nature in that image. The political economists perversely used the story to naturalize the practices of an emergent bourgeoisie.

I have long thought that the political economists selected the wrong Defoe story. *Moll Flanders* is a far better model for how commodity production and circulation work. Moll behaves like the quintessential commodity for sale. She is constantly speculating on the desires of others, and others are constantly speculating on her desires (the great moment occurs when, effectively broke, she spends every last penny on hiring a grand outfit including coach and horses and appropriate jewelry to go to a ball where she enamors a young nobleman and elopes with him that night, only to find out the next morning that he is broke too, at which point they both see the humor of it all and amicably part ways). She travels the world (even goes to colonial Virginia), spends time in debtors' prison; her fortune fluctuates up and down. She circulates like a monetary object in a sea of commodity exchanges. *Moll Flanders* is a much better analogy for the way capitalism, particularly the speculative Wall Street variety, really works.

Plainly, the classical political economists preferred the Robinson Crusoe myth because it naturalized capitalism. But as Marx insists, capitalism is a historical construct, not a natural object. "The categories of bourgeois economics" are merely "forms of thought which are socially valid, and therefore objective, for the relations of production belonging to this historically determined mode of social production." A look at this history indicates the limitations of the supposed universal truths of bourgeois theory. "Let us now transport ourselves from Robinson's island, bathed in light, to medieval Europe, shrouded in darkness." While it may be "shrouded in darkness" the social relations are obvious. Under the *corvée* system, Marx points out, "every serf knows that what he expends in the service of his lord is a specific quantity of his own personal labour-power"; feudal subjects were very aware that "the social relations between individuals in the performance of their labour appear at all events as their own personal relations, and are not disguised as social relations between things, between the products of labour" (169–70). The same is true of a patriarchal rural industry of a peasant family: the social relations are transparent, you can see who is doing what and for whom.

Such historical comparisons, along with the analysis of fetishism, allow us to see the contingent, as opposed to the universal, nature of the truths laid out in bourgeois political economy. "The whole mystery of commodities, all the magic and necromancy that surrounds the products of labour on the basis of commodity production, vanishes therefore as soon as we come to other forms of production" (169). We can even finally imagine social relations organized as "an association of free men," i.e., a socialist world in which "the social relations of the individual producers, both towards their labour and the products of their labour, are . . . transparent in their simplicity, in production as well as in distribution" (171–2). By invoking the idea of association, Marx echoes much of French utopian socialist thought in the 1830s and 1840s (Proudhon, in particular, though Marx refrains from acknowledging so). His hope is that we might advance beyond the fetishism of commodities and try to establish, through associative forms, a different way of relating. Whether that is practical or not is a key question for any reader of Marx to consider; but here is one of the rare moments in *Capital* where we glimpse Marx's vision of a socialist future.

The fetishism of the market generates a good deal of ideological baggage around it. Marx comments, for example, on the way in which Protestantism is the most fitting form of religion for capitalism. He argues that our forms of thought—not just those of the political economists—reflect the fetish of their times; but this is a general tendency. His remarks on religion and its relation to political economic life are significant:

> Political economy has indeed analysed value and its magnitude, however incompletely, and has uncovered the content concealed within these forms. But it has never once asked the question why this content has assumed that particular form, that is to say, why labour is expressed in value, and why the measurement of labour by its duration is expressed in the magnitude of the value of the product. These formulas, which bear the unmistakable stamp of belonging to a social formation in which the process of production has mastery over man, instead of the opposite, appear to political economists' bourgeois consciousness to be as much a self-evident and nature-imposed necessity as productive labour itself. (173–5)

To this, Marx adds a lengthy and important footnote:

> The value-form of the product of labour is the most abstract, but also the most universal form of the bourgeois mode of production; by that fact it stamps the bourgeois mode of production as a particular kind of social production of a historical and transitory character. If then we make the mistake of treating it as the eternal natural form of social production, we necessarily overlook the specificity of the value-form, and consequently of the commodity-form together with its further developments, the money form, the capital form, etc. (174, n. 34)

You will err, he is suggesting, if you naturalize the value-form under capitalism, because it is then difficult, if not impossible, to conceive of alternatives.

This is what the bourgeois political economists have done: they have treated value as a fact of nature, not a social construction arising out of a particular mode of production. What Marx is interested in is a revolutionary transformation of society, and that means an overthrow of the capitalist value-form, the construction of an alternative value-structure, an alternative value-system that does not have the specific character of that achieved under capitalism. I cannot overemphasize this point, because the value theory in Marx is frequently interpreted as a universal norm with which we should comply. I have lost count of the number of times I have heard people complain that the problem with Marx is that he believes the only valid notion of value derives from labor inputs. It is not that at all; it is a historical social product. The problem, therefore, for socialist, communist, revolutionary, anarchist or whatever, is to find an alternative value-form that will work in terms of the social reproduction of society in a different image. By introducing the concept of fetishism, Marx shows how the naturalized value of classical political economy dictates a norm; we foreclose on revolutionary possibilities if we blindly follow that norm and replicate commodity fetishism. Our task is to question it.

Capitalism has no way of registering intrinsic, "natural" values in its calculus. "Since exchange-value is a definite social manner of expressing the labour bestowed on a thing, it can have no more natural content than has, for example, the rate of exchange"; it is illusory to believe, for example, that "ground rents grow out of the soil, not out of society" (176).

Bourgeois political economy looks at the surface appearance. Insofar as it had a labor theory of value, it never probed deeply into its meaning or the historical circumstances of its emergence. This leaves us with the task of getting beyond the fetishism, not by treating it as an illusion, but by addressing its objective reality (164–5, 176–7). One response is to take the "fair trade" path. Another is to devise a scientific path, a critical theory: a mode of investigation and inquiry that can uncover the deep structure of capitalism and suggest alternative value systems based on radically different kinds of social and material relations.

The two options are not mutually exclusive. A politics that deals with the conditions of labor on a global basis, developing into, say, an anti-sweatshop movement, can easily lead into the much deeper theoretical territory that Marx charts in *Capital* precisely because the surface appearance, while fetishistic, always indicates an objective reality. I recall, for example, when the students at Johns Hopkins put on a fashion show, featuring clothing from Liz Claiborne and the Gap, with a side commentary on both the items of clothing and the conditions of labor associated with their production. This was an effective way to talk about the fetishism and raise awareness with respect to global conditions, while suggesting the importance of doing something about it.

Marx's mission in *Capital*, though, is to define a science beyond the immediate fetishism without denying its reality. He has already laid a lot of the groundwork for this in the critique of bourgeois political economy. He has also already revealed the extent to which we are governed in what we do by the abstract forces of the market and how we are perpetually at risk of being ruled by fetishistic constructs that blind us to what is actually happening. To what degree can you say that this is a free society characterized by true individual liberty? The illusions of a liberal utopian order, in Marx's view, have to be debunked for what they are: a replication of that fetishism that displaces social relations between people into material relations between people and social relations between things.

CHAPTER 2: THE PROCESS OF EXCHANGE

Chapter 2 is not only shorter but easier to follow. Marx's purpose is to define the socially necessary conditions of capitalist commodity exchange and to create a firmer foundation for the consideration of the money-form that is to follow in chapter 3.

Since commodities do not themselves go to market, we need first to define the operative relationship between commodities and those who take them there. Marx imagines a society in which "the guardians" of commodities "recognize each other as owners of private property. This juridical relation, whose form is the contract, whether as part of a developed legal system or not, is a mirror between two wills which mirrors the economic relation . . . Here the persons exist for one another"—note the echo of the fetishism argument—not as people, but "as representatives and hence owners, of commodities." This leads him to make a broader point. Throughout *Capital*, "the characters who appear on the economic stage are merely personifications of economic relations," and it is "as the bearers"—please note the recurrence of this term—"of these economic relations that they come into contact with each other" (178–9). Marx is concerned with the economic roles that people play, rather than with the individuals who play them. So he will examine relations between buyers and sellers, debtors and creditors, capitalists and laborers. Throughout *Capital*, in fact, the focus will be on roles rather than persons, recognizing that individuals can and do often occupy several different roles, even deeply contradictory positions (as when, in our time, a worker has a pension fund invested in the stock market). This focus on roles rather than individuals is as perfectly legitimate as if we were analyzing the relations between drivers and pedestrians in the streets of Manhattan: most of us have taken on both roles and adapt our behaviors accordingly.

The roles in a capitalist mode of production are strictly defined. Individuals are juridical subjects who have private-property ownership of the commodity they wield, and they trade it under non-coercive, contractual conditions. There is reciprocal respect for the juridical rights of others; the principled equivalence of market exchanges that Aristotle noted is an honored virtue. What Marx describes here is the conventional political and legal framework for properly functioning markets as envisaged in liberal theory. In this world, a commodity is "a born leveller and cynic," because it "is always ready to exchange not only soul, but body, with each and every other commodity." The owner is willing to dispose of it, and the buyer wants to take it: "All commodities are non-use-values for their owners and use-values for their non-owners. Consequently, they must all change hands," but "only the act of exchange can prove whether that labour is useful for others, and its product consequently capable of satisfying the needs of others" (179–80).

This argument as to the socially necessary institutional and legal structure required for capitalism to work is historically specific. Failure to recognize the historical specificity of the bourgeois conception of rights and duties leads to serious errors. It is for this reason that Marx registers, in a lengthy footnote, a vigorous indictment of the anarchist Proudhon,

> who creates his idea of justice, of 'justice éternelle', from the juridical relations that correspond to the production of commodities: he thereby proves, to the consolation of all good petty bourgeois, that the production of commodities is a form as eternal as justice. Then he turns round and seeks to reform the actual production of commodities, and the corresponding legal system, in accordance with this ideal. (178, n. 2)

Proudhon in effect took the specifics of bourgeois legal and economic relations and treated them as universal and foundational for the development of an alternative, socially just economic system. From Marx's standpoint, this is no alternative at all since it merely re-inscribes bourgeois conceptions of value in a supposedly new form of society. This problem is still with us, not only because of the contemporary anarchist revival of interest in Proudhon's ideas but also because of the rise of a more broad-based liberal human rights politics as a supposed antidote to the social and political ills of contemporary capitalism. Marx's critique of Proudhon is directly applicable to this contemporary politics. The UN Universal Declaration of Human Rights of 1948 is a foundational document for a bourgeois, market-based individualism and as such cannot provide a basis for a thoroughgoing critique of liberal or neoliberal capitalism. Whether it is politically useful to insist that the capitalist political order live up to its own foundational principles is one thing, but to imagine that this politics can lead to a radical displacement of a capitalist mode of production is, in Marx's view, a serious error.

What follows is a recapitulation—and Marx frequently reiterates earlier arguments in somewhat different language—of the way in which money "crystallizes out of the process of exchange" in an institutional environment of this sort. He echoes this theme when he describes money as "the historical broadening and deepening of the phenomenon of exchange" that "develops the opposition between use-value and value which is latent in the nature of the commodity":

> The need to give an external expression to this opposition for the purposes of commercial intercourse produces the drive towards an independent form of value, which finds neither rest nor peace until an independent form has been achieved by the differentiation of commodities into commodities and money. At the same rate, then, as the transformation of the products of labour into commodities is accomplished, one particular commodity is transformed into money. (181)

There is nothing here that we have not already seen in earlier sections, but now Marx expounds on what this economic relation between things implies for relations between people. This economy of market exchange, he says, implies that we are dealing with "the private owners" of "alienable things," and this in turn implies that we have "persons who are independent of each other." "Alienable" refers to the fact that "things are in themselves external to man," i.e., freely exchangeable. This means that the exchangers are free of any personal attachment or other bond to the things they own. It also implies social relationships "of reciprocal isolation and foreignness" that are unique to capitalism and a concomitant of juridical ownership of commodities (182).

Such conditions did not prevail in the "patriarchal family, an ancient Indian commune or an Inca State"; exchange processes had to break down these preceding social structures. This happens gradually, he suggests, as occasional trade between communities evolves to the point where "the constant repetition of exchange makes it a normal social process" (182):

> In the same proportion as exchange bursts its local bonds [note the implication of geographical expansion], and the value of commodities accordingly expands more and more into the material embodiments of human labour as such, in that proportion does the money-form become transferred to commodities which are by nature fitted to perform the social function of a universal equivalent. These commodities are the precious metals. (183)

This is, as I have already pointed out, a somewhat dubious historical argument about the dissolution of preexisting social forms in the face of increasing exchange relations and the rise of money-forms. But its logical content is important for demonstrating that what is socially necessary is "an adequate form of appearance of value," and that requirement is best satisfied by precious metals such as gold and silver by virtue of their natural qualities. But, as he earlier pointed out, this means that the money commodity internalizes a duality, because it is both a commodity in the ordinary sense of being a product of labor *and* it also "acquires a formal use-value, arising out of its specific social function." In this formal social function, "the money-form is merely the reflection thrown upon a single commodity by the relations between all other commodities" (183).

Furthermore, in this role it is perfectly possible to replace the money commodity "by mere symbols of itself." This capacity for replacement is not surprising, however, given that "every commodity is a symbol, since, as value, it is only the material shell of the human labour expended on it" (185–6). Marx here opens up the possibility to incorporate many aspects of what is now often referred to as "the symbolic economy" directly into his analysis. He does not attempt to do so, and it would undoubtedly require modifications to the mode of presentation, but I think it important to note that the symbolic aspects of how capitalism works are not external to his argument. Those who argue that capitalism is different now because of the degree to which symbolic capital and the symbolic economy have come to the fore, and that capitalism has consequently changed its spots, should mark well that this is not necessarily so.

The danger lies in treating these symbolic qualities, which are very important, as purely imaginary or as "the arbitrary product of human reflection." What Marx is driving at here is that even the money commodity cannot realize its specific value without exchanging with all other commodities as equivalents, even as it postures as the universal equivalent for all other commodities. "The difficulty," he says, "lies not in comprehending that money is a commodity, but in discovering how, why and by what means a commodity becomes money" (186):

> What *appears* to happen is not that a particular commodity becomes money because all other commodities universally express their values in it, but, on the contrary, that all other commodities universally express their values in a particular commodity because it is money. (187, emphasis added)

In other words, once money exists, then commodities find a means of measuring their value easily to hand as if the gold drawn "from the bowels of the earth" is "the direct incarnation of human labour." This, he declares, is "the magic of money" that needs to be unpacked. "The riddle of the money fetish is therefore the riddle of the commodity fetish, now become visible and dazzling to our eyes" (187).

But there is one other vital point to this chapter. With the "magic" and "fetish" of money firmly in place,

> men are henceforth related to each other in their social process of production in a purely atomistic way. Their own relations of production therefore assume a material shape which is independent of their control and their conscious individual action. (187)

This sounds suspiciously like a tacit invocation of Adam Smith's vision of a perfectly functioning market whose hidden hand guides individual decisions. No individual is in command and everyone has to function according to what Marx later calls "the coercive laws of competition" (433).

In Smith's ideal world, the state would create the institutional framework for perfectly functioning markets and private property and then watch the wealth of the state and the welfare of the citizenry rapidly improve as individual initiative and entrepreneurialism coordinated through the hidden hand of the market would produce a result that was beneficial to all. In such a world, Smith thought, the intentions and motivations of individuals (varying from greed to social mission) did not matter, because the hidden hand of the market would do the work.

This chapter poses a conundrum. On the one hand, Marx devotes a footnote to condemning Proudhon's acceptance of bourgeois notions of rights and legality as providing absolutely no leverage in the construction of a revolutionary alternative. Yet in the main text of the chapter, Marx has seemingly accepted the liberal theory of property ownership, the reciprocity and equivalence of noncoercive market exchange between juridical individuals and even the hidden hand of the market as proposed by Adam Smith. How are we to reconcile this seeming contradiction? I think the answer is simple enough, but the answer does have important ramifications for how we read the rest of *Capital*.

Marx is engaged in a critique of classical liberal political economy. He therefore finds it necessary to accept the theses of liberalism (and, by extension to our own times, neoliberalism) in order to show that the classical political economists were profoundly wrong even in their own terms. So rather than saying that perfectly functioning markets and the hidden hand can never be constructed and that the marketplace is always distorted by political power, he accepts the liberal utopian vision of perfect markets and the hidden hand in order to show that these would not produce a result beneficial to all, but would instead make the capitalist class incredibly wealthy while relatively impoverishing the workers and everyone else.

This translates into a hypothesis about actually existing capitalism: that the more it is structured and organized according to this utopian liberal or neoliberal vision, the greater the class inequalities. And there is, it goes without saying, plenty of evidence to support the view that the rhetoric of free markets and free trade and their supposed universal benefits to which we have been subjected these past thirty years have produced exactly the result that Marx would expect: a massive concentration of wealth and power at one end of the social scale opposite the proliferating impoverishment of everyone else. But in order to prove that point, Marx has to accept the institutional foundations of liberal utopianism, and that is precisely what he does in this chapter.

This raises an important caveat into how we have to read *Capital.* We have to be careful to distinguish between when Marx is talking about and critiquing the liberal utopian vision in its perfected state, and when he is attempting to dissect actually existing capitalism with all of its market imperfections, power imbalances and institutional flaws. As we will see, these two missions sometimes confound each other. Some of the muddles of interpretation come from this confounding. So I will try in what follows to indicate when he is doing what and to pinpoint those moments of confusion that occasionally arise, including those in Marx's own analysis, when his desire to accomplish one objective—the critique of classical political economy—gets in the way of the additional task of understanding the actual dynamics of a capitalist mode of production.

For the most part, though, Marx has an ingenious way of using the theoretical critique of liberal utopianism in its various political-economic guises to shed devastating critical light on the actually existing capitalism of his own day. And this is fortunate for us, living in a world where the theses of neoliberalism echo and, in some respects, deepen those of liberalism, because Marx's critique of free markets and free trade can shed as much devastating light on our own actually existing capitalism as it did for the capitalism of Marx's own time and place.

CHAPTER TWO

Money

CHAPTER 3: MONEY, OR THE CIRCULATION OF COMMODITIES

By now it's clear that a particular notion of money has been crystallizing out of Marx's account of commodity exchange. It was implicit in the opposition between the relative and equivalent forms of value and this, with the proliferation of exchange into a general social act, led on to the emergence of a universal equivalent that took the form of a tangible money commodity that represented value even as it disguised the origins of value in socially necessary labor-time. We now inspect this money-form more closely.

Chapter 3 is long and quite intricate. It tells a simple story, though, in what by now should be a familiar fashion. Money is a unitary concept, but it internalizes dual functions that mirror the duality of use- and exchange-value within the commodity. On the one hand, money operates as a measure of value, as a golden representative, as it were, of socially necessary labor-time. In this role it must possess distinctive qualities so as to provide, as far as possible, an accurate and efficient standard measure of value. On the other hand, money also has to lubricate the proliferation of exchange and do so with the minimum of fuss and difficulty. In this way it functions as a mere medium and means for moving an increasingly vast array of commodities around.

There is a tension, a contradiction, between these two functions. As a measure of value, for example, gold looks very good. It is permanent and can be stored forever; one can assay its qualities; one can know and control its concrete conditions of production and circulation. So gold is great as a measure of value. But imagine if every time you went for coffee, you had to use a grain of gold to purchase it. This is a very inefficient form of money from the standpoint of the circulation of myriad small quantities of commodities. Imagine everyone with a little pouch with grains of gold in it—what if somebody sneezed while counting out the grains? Gold is an inefficient means of circulation, even as it is excellent as a measure of value.

So Marx contrasts money as a measure of value (section 1) and money as a means or medium of circulation (section 2). At the end of the day, though, there is only one kind of money (section 3). And the resolution of that tension between money as an effective measure of value and money as an efficient means of circulation is partially given by the possibility, or—and this is controversial—the *necessity*, of another form of circulation, which is the existence of credit moneys. The consequent relation between debtors and creditors opens up not only the possibility but also the necessity for another form of circulation, that of capital. In other words, what emerges in this chapter is the possibility for the concept, as well as the fact, of capital. In the same way that the possibility of money crystallized out of processes of exchange, so the possibility of capital crystallizes out of the contradiction between money as the measure of value and money as the means of circulation. This is the big story in this long chapter. If you keep it steadily in mind, a lot of the intricate and sometimes confusing details fall more easily into place.

Section 1: The Measure of Values

There is a distinction between "money" and "the money commodity." To consolidate his earlier argument—namely, that value is not in itself materially measurable but needs, rather, a representation to regulate exchanges—Marx begins by assuming gold to be the singular money commodity. This is "the necessary form of appearance of the measure of value which is immanent in commodities, namely labour-time" (188). Value gets expressed (or perhaps we should say "resides") in the relationship between the money commodity as "a form of appearance" of value and all the commodities that exchange with it. The value of commodities is unrecognizable and unknowable without its form of appearance.

This poses, however, some complications—and reveals some contradictions—that require close scrutiny. Marx focuses first on how prices get attached to commodities. Prices are, he says, imaginary, or ideal (meaning a product of thought or logical principle, as opposed to "real" or empirically derived conclusions) (189–90). He's referring to the fact that when I make a commodity, I have no idea what its value is before I take it to market. I go to the market with some imaginary, ideal notion of its value. So I hang a price tag on it. This tells the potential purchaser what I think the value of my commodity should be. I have no idea whether I'll get that price for it, though, because I can have no prior idea of what its value is "on the market":

> In its function as measure of value, money therefore serves only in an imaginary or ideal capacity. This circumstance has given rise to the wildest theories. But, although the money that performs the functions of a measure of value is only imaginary, the price depends entirely on the actual substance that is money. (190)

A relationship arises between the imaginary, ideal prices and the prices actually received in the marketplace. The received price should, "ideally," indicate true value, but it is only going to be the appearance, a representation—and an imperfect one, at that—of value.

We would obviously prefer the quantitative representation of value to be a stable standard of measurement. Gold is a specific commodity, though; its value is given by the socially necessary labor-time embodied in it, and this is not, as we have seen, constant. Fluctuations in the concrete conditions of production affect the value of gold (or any other money commodity). Since, however, such changes affect "all commodities simultaneously," then "other things being equal ... *the mutual relations* between their values [are] unaltered, although those values are now all expressed in higher or lower gold-prices than before" (191–3, emphasis added).

Marx also introduces silver as a potential alternative money commodity in order to make a simple point: although gold seems to be a solid standard of value for comparing the relative values of all other commodities, it is insecure when it comes to establishing the absolute value (192–3). If, as in the gold rush of 1848, an influx of gold floods the market, then suddenly the value of gold—the representative measure of socially necessary labor-time—declines, and all the commodity prices have to adjust upward (hence the grand inflation in the sixteenth century when the Spaniards brought in gold from Latin America). We are always dealing with the money commodity as something that has a concrete use-value, and the conditions of its own production have an impact on the way value is represented. In recent years, gold prices have been yo-yoing all over the place (for reasons we will come to shortly). What Marx wants to emphasize here is that even though any money commodity makes for a shifting measure of value, its inconstancy makes no difference to the *relative* values of the commodities being exchanged in the marketplace (192–3, see also 146).

Marx goes on to observe that, "as measure of value, and as standard of price, money performs two quite different functions." Here, a sub-duality within the theory of money emerges, not to be confused with the grand distinction between money as a measure of value and as a medium of circulation. The money commodity "is the measure of value as the social incarnation of human labour"—this is the "ideal" representation—but it is also "the standard of price as a quantity of metal with a fixed weight." It is the latter aspect that allows us to say that this commodity is really "worth" so many ounces of gold. This quantity, the weight of gold, is what we have in mind before, and hopefully in hand after, the exchange of the commodity. "For various reasons," though—and these turn out to be historical reasons—"the money-names of the metal weights are gradually separated from their original weight-names" (192–3).

Now, there is no explicit theory of the state in *Capital*, but if you trace its many appearances throughout the text, it becomes clear that the state performs essential functions within a capitalist system of production (we have already tacitly invoked this in imagining the institutions of private property and a properly functioning market in chapter 2). One of the state's most important functions, as we will see, has to do with organizing the monetary system, regulating the money-names and keeping the monetary system effective and stable.

> These historical processes have made the separation of the money-name from the weight-name into a fixed popular custom. Since the standard of money is on the one hand purely conventional, while on the other hand it must possess universal validity, it is in the end regulated by law. (194)

The money-name is, however, a fetish-construct. "The name of a thing is entirely external to its nature. I know nothing of a man if I merely know his name is Jacob. In the same way, every trace of the money-relation disappears in the money-names pound, thaler, franc, ducat, etc." That is, the relationship to socially necessary labor-time is further disguised by these money-names. "Price," Marx concludes, "is the money-name of the labour objectified in a commodity" (195). The money-name (pounds, ducats) is not the same as the money commodity (gold), and its relation to value as socially necessary labor-time becomes ever more opaque; but the definition of price as the money-name of the labor embodied in a commodity is important to remember.

Marx goes on to make two more important observations. The possibility exists, he writes, "of a quantitative incongruity between price and magnitude of value, i.e. the possibility that the price may diverge from the magnitude of value," and this possibility belongs inherently to the price-form itself. "This is not a defect, but, on the contrary, it makes this form the adequate one for a mode of production whose laws can only assert themselves as blindly operating averages between constant irregularities" (196). What he is saying here is this: if I take my commodity to market and hang a price (a money-name or proposed representation of value) on it, you bring a similar commodity to market and hang your price on it, somebody brings another and hangs a different price on it, we will have a marketplace full of different prices for the same commodity. The average price that will actually be achieved on a particular day will depend on how many people want the commodity and how many people come to market wanting to sell it. So, the average realized price will jump around depending on fluctuations in supply and demand conditions.

It is through this mechanism that an equilibrium price emerges. This equilibrium price, or what the classical political economists called the "natural" price, is the price achieved when supply and demand have come into equilibrium. At this equilibrium point, Marx will later claim, supply and demand cease to explain anything. Supply and demand do not explain why a shirt, on average, costs less than a pair of shoes and what the average differential price is between shirts and shoes. It is Marx's view that this average differential price is reflective of value, of the socially necessary labor-time congealed in the different commodities. On a given day, though, price fluctuations will tell you the state of demand and supply for shoes on that day and why it has gone up or down from yesterday. So the fact that we put money-names on commodities and convert the measure of value into this ideal form, the price-form, allows price fluctuations to equilibrate the market, and this brings us closer to identifying a proper representation of value as equilibrium or natural price. What the fluctuations in prices achieve is a *convergence on the average social labor necessary to produce a commodity*. Without this quantitative incongruity there would be no way of smoothing out demand and supply variations in the marketplace and converging on the social average price that represents value.

The second observation is even more difficult to absorb:

> The price-form . . . is not only compatible with the possibility of a quantitative incongruity between magnitude of value and price, i.e. between the magnitude of value and its own expression in money, but

> it may also harbour a qualitative contradiction, with the result that price ceases altogether to express value, despite the fact that money is nothing but the value-form of commodities. Things which in and for themselves are not commodities, such as conscience, honour, etc., can be offered for sale by their holders and thus acquire the form of commodities through their price. Hence a thing can, formally speaking, have a price without having a value. The expression of price is in this case imaginary, like certain quantities in mathematics. On the other hand, the imaginary price-form may also conceal a real value-relation or one derived from it, as for instance the price of uncultivated land, which is without value because no human labour is objectified in it. (197)

Once you can hang a price tag on something, you can in principle put a price tag on anything, including conscience and honor, to say nothing of body parts and children. You can hang it on a natural resource, on the view of a waterfall; you can certainly put a price tag on land and speculate on shifts in land prices. The price system can operate in these other dimensions to produce qualitative as well as quantitative incongruities. Which then raises the question: if prices can be put on anything independently of their value, and if they can in any case quantitatively fluctuate all over the place independently of value, then why is Marx so fixated on the labor theory of value? Aren't the conventional political economists—even to this day—correct to say that all we can observe and all that can have real meaning is contained in the concept of price, and that the labor theory of value is therefore irrelevant?

Marx does not defend his choice here; he didn't particularly have to, given that the labor theory of value was widely accepted by his Ricardian contemporaries. But today, with the labor theory widely questioned or abandoned, even by some Marxist economists, it behooves us to construct some sort of response. Marx would, I think, appeal to the concept of the material base: if everybody tried to live off the spectacle of waterfalls or through trading in conscience and honor, no one would survive. Real production, the real transformation of nature through labor processes, is crucial to our existence; and it is this material labor that forms the basis for the production and reproduction of all human life. We can't dress in conscience and honor (remember the fable of the emperor's new clothes), we can't dress in the spectacle of a waterfall; clothes do not come to us that way, they come to us through human labor processes and commodity exchange. Even in a city like Washington, D.C., where a vast amount of trading in conscience and honor seems to occur, there is always the question of where everybody's breakfast comes from, as well as the electronics, the paper, the automobiles, the houses and the highways that sustain daily life. To pretend this all arrives magically through the market, facilitated by the magic of the money that happens to be in our pocket, is to succumb totally to the fetishism of the commodity. We need the concept of value as socially necessary labor-time in order to break through the fetishism.

Whether or not you believe that Marx was right to take a position such as this is up to you to decide. To understand *Capital* on Marx's own terms, though, you have to be prepared to accept an argument somewhat along these lines, at least until you get to the end of the book. It is also important to recognize that Marx is, nevertheless, conceding something here that is terribly important. That is, the price system is indeed a surface appearance that has its own objective reality (it really is "as it appears") as well as a vital function—the regulation of demand and supply fluctuations so that they converge on an equilibrium price—and this system can easily get out of control on its own terms. As we will later see even in this chapter, the quantitative and qualitative incongruities have serious consequences for how market systems and money-forms work. (They can even yield not only the possibility, but also the *inevitability*, of financial and monetary crises!)

But Marx's presumption—and if you are to understand him, you must bear with him on this point—is that value as socially necessary labor-time lies at the center of things. If we assume that values are fixed (though perpetual shifts in technology and social and natural relations constantly remind us that in fact it's quite the contrary), then we'll see prices fluctuating over time around "natural" prices, the state of equilibrium between demand and supply. This equilibrium price is merely an appearance, a representation of socially necessary labor-time that generates the value crystallized in money. And *this* value is what the market prices are actually fluctuating around (196). Market prices perpetually and necessarily deviate from values; if they didn't, there would be no way of equilibrating the market. As for the qualitative incongruities, some of them (such as speculation in land values and land rents) have an important material role to play (not to be taken up until Volume III) in processes of urbanization and the production of space. But this is something that cannot be considered here.

Section 2: The Means of Circulation

It is useful to study Marx's introductory paragraphs carefully since they often signal a general argument or theme that needs to be borne in mind. Here he reminds us that "we saw in a former chapter that the exchange of commodities implies contradictory and mutually exclusive conditions" (198). What is he referring to? Look back at the section on relative and equivalent forms of value. There, he identified three peculiarities of the money commodity. First, that "use-value becomes the form of appearance of its opposite, value"; second, that "concrete labour becomes the form of manifestation of its opposite, abstract human labour"; and third, that "private labour takes the form of its opposite, namely labour in its directly social form" (148, 150, 151).

Gold is a particular commodity produced and appropriable by private persons, with a particular use-value, and yet all those particularities are somehow buried within the universal equivalent of the money commodity. "The further development of the commodity does not abolish these contradictions," Marx observes, "but rather provides the form within which they have room to move." There are some clues here—pay particular attention to that phrase, "the form within which [contradictions] have room to move"—as to the nature of Marx's dialectical method. There is, he says, a general "way in which real contradictions are resolved. For instance, it is a contradiction to depict one body as constantly falling towards another and at the same time constantly flying away from it. The ellipse is a form of motion within which this contradiction is *both realized and resolved*" (198, emphasis added).

Earlier, I described the dialectic as a form of expansionary logic. Some people like to think about the dialectic as being strictly about thesis, antithesis and synthesis, but what Marx is saying here is that there is no synthesis. There is only the internalization of and greater accommodation of the contradiction. Contradictions are never finally resolved; they can only be replicated either within a perpetual system of movement (like the ellipse) or on a grander scale. Yet there are apparent moments of resolution, as when the money-form crystallizes out of exchange to resolve the problem of how to circulate all those commodities efficiently. So we might breathe a sigh of relief and say, thank God, we have money, that's a nice synthesis, we don't have to think anymore. No, no, says Marx, we now have to analyze the contradictions that money-forms internalize—contradictions that become problematic on a much grander scale. There is, as it were, a perpetual expansion of the contradictions.

For this reason I get impatient with people who depict Marx's dialectic as a closed method of analysis. It is not finite; on the contrary, it is constantly expanding, and here he is explaining precisely how. We only have to review what we have already experienced in reading *Capital*; the movement of its argument is a perpetual reshaping, rephrasing and expansion of the field of contradictions. This explains why there is so much repetition. Each step forward requires Marx to return to an earlier contradiction in order to explain where the next one is coming from. Reflecting on introductory passages like this one helps to clarify Marx's meaning; it gives us a better idea of what he is trying to do in each section as his argument unfolds.

We see this process at work in the second section of the chapter on money, where Marx examines what he calls the "social metabolism" and "metamorphosis of commodities" through exchange. Exchange, as we have seen, "produces a differentiation of the commodity into two elements, commodity and money." When we put these into motion, we see that commodities and money move in opposite directions with each change of hands. While the movement of one (the exchange of money) is supposed to facilitate the other (the movement of commodities), there is an oppositional flow, which creates the possibility for the rise of "antagonistic forms" (198–9). This sets the stage for the analysis of the metamorphosis of commodities.

Exchange is a transaction in which value undergoes a change of form. Marx labels this chain of movements—commodity into money, money into commodity—the "C-M-C" relation. (This is different from the "C-C" or commodity-to-commodity movement of bartering; all exchanges are now mediated through money.) This process is a twofold metamorphosis of value from C into M and of M into C (199–200).

It would seem on the surface that these are mirror images and therefore in principle equivalent, but in fact they are asymmetrical. The C-M side of the exchange, the sale, involves the change in form of a particular commodity into the universal equivalent, the money commodity. It is a movement from the particular to the universal. In order to sell your particular commodity, you must find somebody in the market who wants it. What happens if you get to market and nobody wants your commodity? This provokes a whole series of questions about how need—and the production of needs through, for example, advertising—influences the exchange process:

> Perhaps the commodity is the product of a new kind of labour, and claims to satisfy a newly arisen need, or is even trying to bring forth a new need on its own account . . . Today the product satisfies a social need. Tomorrow it may perhaps be expelled partly or completely from its place by a similar product. (201)

So the transformation from C into M is complicated in large part by supply and demand conditions that exist in the market at a particular time:

> We see then that commodities are in love with money, but that 'the course of true love never did run smooth'. The quantitative articulation . . . of society's productive organism, by which its scattered elements are integrated into the system of the division of labour, is as haphazard and spontaneous as its qualitative articulation. (202)

That is, the hidden hand of the market—the chaos of market exchange, the chronic uncertainty of it all—places all kinds of barriers in the way of a direct conversion of the commodity into the universal equivalent.

C-M-C is a single process—an exchange—that can be viewed from either of its two "poles" (203). The M-C side of exchange, the purchase, is a transition from money to commodity; it entails a movement from the universal to the particular. This is not, however, simply C-M in reverse. Changing money into a commodity is in principle much easier: you enter the market with your money and buy anything you want. To be sure, potential buyers may on occasion be frustrated by not finding what they desire; but in that case, thanks to the universal equivalence of the money commodity, they can always buy something else.

So in the process of exchange, value in effect moves from one state (that of the commodity) into another (that of money) and back again. Viewed as a whole, this process

> appears in the first place [to be] made up of two opposite and complementary movements, C-M and M-C. These two antithetical transmutations of the commodity are accomplished through two antithetical social processes

> in which the commodity-owner takes part, and are reflected in the antithetical economic characteristics of the two processes . . . While the same commodity is successively passing through the two inverted transmutations . . . the owner of the commodity successively changes his role from seller to buyer. (206)

Marx's emphasis on antithesis signals a potential contradiction, but not one between buyers and sellers because these are "not fixed roles, but constantly attach themselves to different persons in the course of the circulation of commodities." The contradiction has to lie in the metamorphosis of commodities taken as a whole, i.e., within the circulation of commodities in general, since "the commodity itself is here subject to contradictory determinations," being at once a non-use-value from the standpoint of its owner and, as a purchase, a use-value to the buyer (206–7).

This process—the circulation of commodities—is increasingly mediated by money. Again, notice how important the proliferation of exchange relations is to Marx's argument:

> We see here, on the one hand, how the exchange of commodities breaks through all the individual and local limitations of the direct exchange of products, and develops the metabolic process of human labour. On the other hand, there develops a whole network of social connections of natural origin, entirely beyond the control of the human agents. (207)

So where in the process of the circulation of commodities is the contradiction? Whereas a purchased commodity, being a use-value to its consumer, might "fall out of circulation," the money does not drop out and disappear. It keeps on moving such that "circulation sweats money from every pore" (208). With this, Marx launches a definitive and violent attack upon something called Say's law, which was a powerful idea within classical political economy and continues to this day to be a strong tenet of belief among monetarist economists.[1] The French economist J. B. Say held that there can be no such thing as a general crisis of overproduction within capitalism, because every sale is a purchase and every purchase is a sale. By this logic, there is always some sort of aggregate equilibrium between purchases and sales in the market: while there may be an

1. See the sophisticated defense of the law in *Say's Law: An Historical Analysis* (Princeton, NJ: Princeton University Press, 1972) by the conservative economist Thomas Sowell.

overproduction of shoes relative to shirts, or oranges relative to apples, a generalized overproduction in society is impossible because of the overall equivalence of purchases and sales.

Marx objects as follows:

> Nothing could be more foolish than the dogma that because every sale is a purchase, and every purchase a sale, the circulation of commodities necessarily implies an equilibrium between sales and purchases. If this means that the number of actual sales accomplished is equal to the number of purchases, it is a flat tautology . . . No one can sell unless someone else purchases. But no one directly needs to purchase just because he has sold . . . To say that these mutually independent and antithetical processes [i.e., C-M and M-C] form an internal unity is to say also that their internal unity moves forward through external antitheses. These two processes lack internal independence because they complement each other. Hence, if the assertion of their external independence . . . proceeds to a certain critical point, their unity violently makes itself felt by producing—a crisis. There is an antithesis, immanent in the commodity, between use-value and value, between private labour which must simultaneously manifest itself as directly social labour, and a particular concrete kind of labour which simultaneously counts as merely abstract universal labour, between the conversion of things into persons and the conversion of persons into things; the antithetical phases of the metamorphosis of the commodity are the developed forms of motion of this immanent contradiction. These forms therefore imply the possibility of crises, though no more than the possibility. (208–9)

For the full development of this possibility of crises, I am sorry to say, you are going to have to read Volumes II and III, along with the three volumes of *Theories of Surplus Value*, because, as Marx points out, we need to know a lot more before we can explain in detail where crises might come from. For our purposes here, though, it's worth noticing how the "the conversion of things into persons and the conversion of persons into things" echoes the fetishism argument from the first chapter.

At the heart of Marx's objection to Say's law lies the following argument. I start with C, I go to M, but there is no force that compels me to spend the money immediately on another commodity. I can, if I want, simply hold on to the money. I might do that, for example, if I felt there was some insecurity in the economy, if I was worried about the future and wanted to save. (What would you rather have in your hand in difficult times: a particular commodity or the universal equivalent?) But what happens to the circulation of commodities in general if everybody suddenly decides to hold on to money? The buying of commodities would cease and circulation would stop, resulting in a generalized crisis. If everybody in the world suddenly decided not to use their credit cards for three days, the whole global economy would be in serious trouble. (Recall how we were all urged to get out our credit cards after 9/11 and get back to shopping.) Which is why so much effort is put toward getting money out of our pockets and keeping it circulating.

In Marx's time, most economists, including Ricardo, accepted Say's law (210, n. 42). And partly due to the influence of the Ricardians, the law dominated economic thinking throughout the nineteenth century and up until the 1930s, when there was a generalized crisis. Then followed the (typical, to this day) chorus of economists saying things like, "There would be no crisis if only the economy would perform according to my textbook!" The facts of the Great Depression made a dominant economic theory that denied the possibility of generalized crisis untenable.

Then, in 1936, John Maynard Keynes published his *General Theory of Employment, Interest and Money*, in which he totally abandons Say's law. In his *Essays in Biography* (1933), Keynes reexamines the history of Say's law and what he considered its lamentable consequences for economic theorizing. Keynes made much of something he called the liquidity trap, in which some ruction occurs in the market, and those with money get nervous and hold on to it rather than invest or spend it, driving the demand for commodities down. Suddenly people can't sell their commodities. Uncertainty increasingly troubles the market, and more people hang on to their money, the source of their security. Subsequently, the whole economy just goes spiraling downward. Keynes took the view that government had to step in and reverse the process by creating various fiscal stimuli. Then the privately hoarded money would be enticed back into the market.

As we've seen, Marx similarly dismisses Say's law as foolish nonsense in *Capital*, and since the 1930s there has been a dialogue about the relationship between Marxian and Keynesian theories of the economy. Marx clearly sides with those political economists who did argue for the possibility of general crises—in the literature of the time, these economists were referred to as "general glut" theorists—and there were relatively few of them. The Frenchman Sismondi was one; Thomas Malthus (of population-theory fame) was another, which is somewhat unfortunate, because Marx could not abide Malthus, as we will later see.

Keynes, on the other hand, praises Malthus inordinately in *Essays in Biography* but scarcely mentions Marx—presumably for political reasons. In fact, Keynes claimed he never read Marx. I suspect he did, but even if he didn't, he was surrounded by people like the economist Joan Robinson, who did read Marx and certainly told Keynes about Marx's rejection of Say's law. Keynesian theory dominated economic thinking in the postwar period; then came the anti-Keynesian revolution of the late 1970s. The monetarist and neoliberal theory that is predominant today is much closer to an acceptance of Say's law. So the question of the proper status of Say's law is an interesting one worthy of further inquiry. What matters for our purposes here, though, is Marx's emphatic rejection of it.

The next step in Marx's argument is to plunge into an analysis of the circulation of money. I won't spend much time on the details of this, because Marx is basically reviewing the monetarist literature of the time. The question he is posing here is: how much money does there need to be in order to circulate a given quantity of commodities? He accepts a version of what is called the "quantity theory of money," similar to that of Ricardo. After several pages of detailed discussion, he arrives at a supposed law: the quantity of the circulating medium is "determined by the sum of the prices of the commodities in circulation, and the average velocity of the circulation of money" (219). (The velocity of circulation of money is simply a measure of the rate at which money circulates—e.g., how many times in a day a dollar bill changes hands.) He had earlier noted, however, that "these three factors, the movement of prices, the quantity of commodities in circulation, and the velocity of the circulation of money, can all vary in various directions under different conditions" (218). The quantity of money needed therefore varies a great deal, depending on how these three variables shift. If you can find some way to speed up the circulation, then the velocity of money accelerates, as happens through credit-card use and electronic banking, for example: the greater the velocity of money, the less money you need, and conversely. Plainly, the concept of the velocity of money is important, and to this day the Federal Reserve goes to great pains to try to get accurate measures of it.

Considerations on the quantity theory of money bring him back to the argument I laid out at the beginning of this chapter—that when it comes to the circulation of commodities, little bits of gold are inefficient. It is much more efficient to use tokens, coins, paper or, as happens nowadays, numbers on a computer screen. But "the business of coining," Marx says, "like the establishing of a standard measure of price, is an attribute proper to the state" (221–2). So the state plays a vital role in replacing metallic money commodities with tokens, symbolic forms. Marx illustrates this with brilliant imagery:

> The different national uniforms worn at home by gold and silver as coins, but taken off again when they appear on the world market, demonstrate the separation between the internal or national spheres of commodity circulation and its universal sphere, the world market. (222)

The significance of the world market and world money comes back in at the end of this chapter.

Locally, the quest for efficient forms of money becomes paramount. "Small change appears alongside gold for the payment of fractional parts of the smallest gold coin" which then leads to "inconvertible paper money issued by the state and given forced currency" (224). As soon as symbols of money emerge, many other possibilities and problems arise:

> Paper money is a symbol of gold, a symbol of money. Its relation to the values of commodities consists only in this: they find imaginary expression in certain quantities of gold, and the same quantities are symbolically and physically represented by the paper. (225)

Marx also notes "that just as true paper money arises out of the function of money as the circulating medium, so does credit-money take root spontaneously in the function of money as the means of payment" (224). The money commodity, gold, is replaced by all manner of other means of payment such as coins, paper moneys and credit. This happens because a weight of gold is inefficient as a means of circulation. It becomes "socially necessary" to leave gold behind and work with these other symbolic forms of money.

Is this a logical argument, a historical argument or both? Certainly, the history of the different monetary forms and the history of state power are intricately intertwined. But is this necessarily so, and is there some inevitable pattern to those relations? Until the early 1970s, most paper moneys were supposedly convertible into gold. This was what gave the paper moneys their supposed stability or, as Marx would describe it, their relationality to value. Converting money into gold was, however, denied to private persons in many countries from the 1920s onward and mainly retained for exchanges between countries to balance currency accounts. The whole system broke down in the late 1960s and early 1970s, and we now have a purely symbolic system with no clear material base—a universal money commodity.

So what relationship exists today between the various paper moneys (e.g., dollars, euros, pesos, yen) and the value of commodities? Though gold still plays an interesting role, it no longer functions as the basis for representing value. The relationship of moneys to socially necessary labor-time, which was problematic even in the case of gold, has become even more remote and elusive. But to say it is hidden, remote and elusive is not to say it does not exist. Turmoil in international currency markets has something to do with differences in material productivity in different national economies. The problematic relationship between the existing money-forms and commodity-values that Marx outlines is still with us and very much open to the line of analysis that he pioneered, even though its contemporary form of appearance is quite different.

Section 3: Money

Marx has examined money as a measure of value and revealed some of its contradictions, particularly with respect to its "ideal" functions as price and the consequent "incongruities" in the relationship between prices and values. He has looked at money from the standpoint of circulation and revealed another set of contradictions (including the possibility of general crises). Now—typical Marx—he comes back to us and says, well, at the end of the day, there is only one money. This means that somehow the contradictions between money as a measure of value and money as a medium of circulation have to have "room to move" or perhaps even be resolved.

He thus begins by reiterating the foundational idea of money as "the commodity which functions as a measure of value and therefore also as the medium of circulation, either in its own body or through a representative" (227). So we are back to the unitary concept, but we must examine how the contradictions earlier identified can operate within it. The loosening of the connection between value and its expression provides room for maneuver, but it does so at the expense of contact with a real and solid monetary base. From this point, Marx probes deeper into the contradictions that characterize this evolved form of the money system. He begins by considering the phenomenon of hoarding:

> When the circulation of commodities first develops, there also develops the necessity and the passionate desire to hold fast to the product of the first metamorphosis. This product is the transformed shape of the commodity, or its gold chrysalis. Commodities are thus sold not in order to buy commodities, but in order to replace their commodity-form by their money-form. Instead of being merely a way of mediating the metabolic process, this change of form becomes an end in itself . . . The money is petrified into a hoard, and the seller of commodities becomes a hoarder of money. (227–8, emphasis added)

(This passage foreshadows another kind of circulation process, as we'll see, in which C-M-C is viewed as M-C-M with the procurement of money as an end in itself.)

But why would people do this? Marx offers an interesting twofold answer. On the one hand there is a passionate desire for money-power, but on the other there also exists a social necessity. Why is hoarding socially necessary for commodity exchange? Here he invokes the temporal problem of coordinating the sales and purchases of different commodities that take very different times to produce and bring to market. A farmer produces on an annual basis but also buys on a daily basis; he therefore needs to hoard reserves from one harvest to the next. Anyone wishing to purchase a big-ticket item (like a house or a car) needs to hoard money first—unless there is a credit system. "In this way hoards of gold and silver of the most various sizes are piled up at all the points of commercial intercourse" (229).

But the ability to hold the means of exchange (in defiance of Say's law) also awakens a passion, a "lust for gold." "The hoarding drive," he says, "is boundless in its nature." Witness Christopher Columbus: "Gold is a wonderful thing! Its owner is master of all he desires. Gold can even enable souls to enter Paradise" (229–30). Here Marx, quoting Columbus, returns to the idea that once you can hang a price tag on something, you can hang it on anything—even a person's soul, as his allusion to the

Catholic Church's infamous medieval practice of selling indulgences (i.e., papal pardons that promised entry into heaven) suggests:

> Circulation becomes the great social retort into which everything is thrown, to come out again as the money crystal. Nothing is immune from this alchemy, the bones of the saints cannot withstand it. (229)

The sale of indulgences is sometimes regarded as one of the first major waves of capitalist commodification. It certainly laid the basis for all that hoarded wealth in the Vatican. Talk about the commodification of conscience and honor!

So there is nothing that is not commensurable with money; in the circulation of commodities, it is "a radical leveller, it extinguishes all distinctions" (229). This idea of money as a radical leveler is very important. It indicates a certain democracy of money, an egalitarianism in it: a dollar in my pocket has the same value as one in yours. With enough money, you could buy your way into heaven no matter your sins!

But money is also "itself a commodity, an external object capable of becoming the private property of any individual. Thus the social power becomes the private power of private persons" (229–30). This is a vital step in Marx's argument. Notice how it echoes the third "peculiarity" of the money-form revealed in the section on relative and equivalent values—i.e., money's tendency to render private labor a means of expression for social labor. With this step, though, Marx reverses that initial formulation of the logical relation between money and labor. There, the problem was that private activities were involved in the production of the universal equivalent. Now, he is describing the way in which private persons can appropriate the universal equivalent for their own private purpose—and we begin to see the possibility for the concentration of private and, eventually, class power in monetary form.

This does not always go down well. "Ancient society . . . denounced it as tending to destroy the economic and moral order" (230). This is a theme that Marx explored at some length in the *Grundrisse*, where he writes on how money destroyed the ancient community by becoming the community itself, the community of money.[2] This is the kind of world in which we ourselves now live. We may have fantasies of belonging

2. Marx, *Grundrisse*, 224.

to this or that cultural community, but in practice, Marx argues, our primary community is given by the community of money—the universal circulatory system that puts breakfast on our tables—whether we like it or not:

> Modern society, which already in its infancy had pulled Pluto by the hair of his head from the bowels of the earth, greets gold as its Holy Grail, as the glittering incarnation of its innermost principle of life. (230)

The social power that attaches to money has no limit. But boundless though the hoarding drive may be, there is a quantitative limitation on the hoarder: the amount of money he has at any given time. "This contradiction between the *quantitative limitation* and the *qualitative lack of limitation* of money keeps driving the hoarder back to his Sisyphean task: accumulation" (231, emphasis added). This is the first mention of accumulation in *Capital*, and it is important to notice that Marx arrives at it by uncovering the contradiction inherent in the act of hoarding money.

The limitless potentialities for monetary accumulation are fascinating to reflect on. There is a physical limit to the accumulation of use-values. Imelda Marcos is reported to have had some two thousand pairs of shoes, but this enormous quantity is still a finite amount. How many Ferraris or McMansions can you own? With money-power, the sky seems to be the limit. No matter how much money they earn, all CEOs and billionaires want, and can get, more. In 2005 the leading hedge fund managers in the United States received around $250 million in personal remuneration, but by 2008 several of them, including George Soros, gained nearly $3 billion. The accumulation of money as unlimited social power is an essential feature of a capitalist mode of production. When people seek to accumulate that social power, they start to behave in a very different way. Once the universal equivalent becomes a representation of all socially necessary labor-time, the potentialities for further accumulation are limitless.

The consequences of this are legion. A capitalist mode of production is essentially based on infinite accumulation and limitless growth. Other social formations at some historical or geographical point reach a limit, and when they do, they collapse. But the experience of capitalism, with some obvious phases of interruption, has been characterized by constant and seemingly limitless growth. The mathematical growth curves illustrating the history of capitalism in terms of total output, total wealth and total money in circulation are astonishing to contemplate (along with the radical social, political and environmental consequences they imply). This growth syndrome would not be possible if not for the seemingly limitless way in which the representation of value can be accumulated in private hands. None of this is explicitly mentioned in *Capital*, but it helps us make an important connection. Marx is setting up his argument concerning the contradiction between the limitless potentiality of money-power accumulation and the limited possibilities for use-value accumulation. This, we'll see, is a precursor to his explanation of the growth dynamics and expansionary nature of what today we call "globalizing" capitalism.

At this point, however, he simply takes the standpoint of the hoarder, for whom the limitless accumulation of social power in the form of money is a significant incentive (leaving aside the added incentive of the aesthetic value attached to beautiful silver and gold objects). Marx notices that hoarding has a potentially useful function in relation to the contradiction between money as a measure of value and as a medium of circulation. The hoarded money constitutes a reserve that can be put into circulation if there is a surge in commodity production and can be retracted when the quantity of money needed for circulation shrinks (e.g., due to an increase in velocity). In this way, the formation of a hoard becomes crucial to moderating "the ebbs and flows" of the money in circulation (231).

The extent to which a hoard can perform this function depends, however, on whether it is used appropriately. How might hoarded money be enticed back into circulation when needed? Raising the relative price of gold and silver, for example, could tempt people to spend on commodities that have become relatively cheaper. The idea is that "the reserves created by hoarding serve as channels through which money may flow in and out of circulation, so that circulation itself never overflows its banks" (232).

Marx then considers the implications of money being used as a means of payment. Again, the basic problem addressed here arises out of the intersecting temporalities of different kinds of commodity production. A farmer produces a crop that can be put on the market in September. How do farmers live the rest of the year? They need money continuously but get their money all at one time, once a year. One solution, instead of hoarding, is to use money as a means of payment. This creates a time gap between the exchange of commodities and the money exchanges; a future date of settlement has to be set. (Michaelmas became a traditional date to settle up accounts in Britain, reflecting the agricultural cycle there.) The commodities circulate "on tick." Money becomes money of account, written down in a ledger. Since no money is actually moving until settlement date, less aggregate money is needed to circulate commodities, and this helps resolve tensions between money as a measure of value and as a medium of circulation (232–3).

The result is a new kind of social relation—that between debtors and creditors—which gives rise to a different kind of economic transaction and a different social dynamic:

> The seller becomes a creditor, the buyer becomes a debtor. Since the metamorphosis of commodities, or the development of their form of value, has undergone a change here, money receives a new function as well. It becomes the means of payment. (233)

But note well: "the role of creditor or of debtor results here from the simple circulation of commodities," but it is also possible for it to shift from transient, occasional forms to "a more rigid crystallization," by which he means a more definite class relation. (He compares this dynamic to the class struggle in the ancient world and the contest in the Middle Ages that "ended with the ruin of the feudal debtors, who lost their political power together with its economic basis" (233).) So there is a power relation within the debtor-creditor relation, though its nature has yet to be determined.

So what is the role of credit in the general circulation of commodities? Suppose I am a creditor. You are in need of money, and I lend it to you now with the idea I will get it back later. The form of circulation is M-C-M, which is very different from C-M-C. Why would I circulate money in order later to get back the same amount of money? There is no advantage to me in this form of circulation unless I get back more money at the end than I started with. (Perhaps it's already clear where this analysis is leading.)

There follows a crucial passage, the significance of which is all too easy to miss, partly because of the way Marx buries it in complicated language. I cite it nearly in full:

> Let us return to the sphere of circulation. The two equivalents, commodities and money, have ceased to appear simultaneously at the two poles of the process of sale. The money functions now, first as the measure of value in the determination of the price of the commodity

> sold . . . Secondly it serves as a nominal means of purchase. Although existing only in the promise of the buyer to pay, it causes the commodity to change hands. Not until payment falls due does the means of payment actually step into circulation, i.e. leave the hand of the buyer for that of the seller. The circulating medium was transformed into a hoard because the process stopped short after the first phase, because the converted shape of the commodity was withdrawn from circulation. The means of payment enters circulation, but only after the commodity has already left it. The money no longer mediates the process. It brings it to an end by emerging independently, as the absolute form of existence of exchange-value, in other words the universal commodity. The seller turned his commodity into money in order to satisfy some need; the hoarder in order to preserve the monetary form of his commodity, and the indebted purchaser in order to be able to pay. If he does not pay, his goods will be sold compulsorily. *The value-form of the commodity, money, has now become the self-sufficient purpose of the sale, owing to a social necessity springing from the conditions of the process of circulation itself.* (233–4, emphasis added)

Decoded, this means that there needs to be a form of circulation in which money is going to be exchanged in order to get money: M-C-M. This is a shift in perspective that makes a world of difference. If the objective is procuring other use-values through commodity production and commodity exchange, albeit mediated through money, we're dealing with C-M-C. In contrast, M-C-M is a form of circulation in which money is the objective, not commodities. In order for that to have a rationale, it requires that I get back more money than I started with. This is the moment in *Capital* when we first see the circulation of capital crystallizing out of the circulation of commodities mediated by the contradictions of money-forms. There is a big difference between the circulation of money as a mediator of commodity exchange and money used as capital. Not all money is capital. A monetized society is not necessarily a capitalist society. If everything revolved around the C-M-C circulation process, then money would be merely a mediator, nothing more. Capital emerges when money is put into circulation in order to get more money.

I want to pause now to reflect a bit on the nature of Marx's argument so far. At this point, we can say that the proliferation of commodity exchange necessarily leads to the rise of money-forms and that the internal contradiction within these money-forms necessarily leads, in turn, to the rise of the capitalist form of circulation, in which money is used to gain more money. This is, crudely summarized, the argument of *Capital* so far.

We first have to decide whether this is a historical or a logical argument. If it is the former, then there is a teleology to history in general, and capitalist history in particular; the rise of capitalism is an inevitable step in human history, emerging out of the gradual proliferations of commodity exchange. It is possible to find statements in Marx that would support such a teleological view, and his frequent deployment of the word "necessary" certainly supports such an interpretation. I myself am not convinced of it, and if Marx did indeed believe this then I think he was wrong.

This leaves us with the logical rationale, which I find much more persuasive. It focuses on the methodology at work as the argument unfolds: the dialectical and relational opposition between use-value and exchange-value as embodied in the commodity; the externalization of that opposition in the money-form as a way to represent value and facilitate commodity exchange; the internalization of this contradiction by the money-form as both a medium of circulation and a measure of value; and the resolution of that contradiction through the emergence of relations between debtors and creditors in the use of money as a means of payment. Now we are in a position to understand money as the beginning and end point of a distinctive circulation process, to be called capital. The logic of Marx's argument reveals the internalized dialectical relations that characterize a fully developed capitalist mode of production (understood as a totality) of the sort that evolved (for contingent historical reasons) from the sixteenth century onward in Britain in particular.

There may, of course, be some compromise to be made with the historical rationale, simply by converting the language from "necessity" to "possibility" or even "probability" or "likelihood." We would then say that the contradictions in the money-form created the possibility for the rise of a capitalist form of circulation, and perhaps even point to specific historical circumstances in which the pressures emanating from those contradictions might become so overwhelming as to directly cause capitalism to break through. Certainly much of what Marx attributes to "social necessity" would seem to indicate this. We could likewise point to the intense barriers that had to be developed in "traditional" societies to prevent the capitalist form of circulation from coming to dominate and the social instabilities those societies experienced as they were subjected to periodic feasts and famines of either commodity trading or gold or silver supply. Different social orders (such as China's) have, at various times, ridden out these contradictions in their own fashion without falling under the domination of capital. Whether contemporary China has already fallen into the capitalist camp or can manage to continue to ride the capitalist tiger is, however, a matter of great import and a subject of much debate. I must, however, conclude now with a series of questions to contemplate.

In *Capital*, Marx passes on to more particular matters. There is, he notes "a contradiction immanent in the function of money as the means of payment":

> When the payments balance each other, money functions only nominally, as money of account, as a measure of value. But when actual payments have to be made, money does not come onto the scene as a circulating medium, in its merely transient form of an intermediary in the social metabolism, but as the individual incarnation of social labour, the independent presence of exchange-value, the universal commodity. (235)

That is, when money comes into circulation to solve this disequilibrium, those who hold it don't do so out of the goodness of their hearts, responding to the needs of others or to the market's need for a greater supply of money. Rather, somebody who owns the universal equivalent puts it into the market purposefully, for some reason, and we have to understand what that reason might be. But the "independence" of the universal commodity and its separation from day-to-day commodity circulation have profound consequences.

From here Marx's argument takes a surprising turn:

> This contradiction bursts forth in that aspect of an industrial and commercial crisis which is known as a monetary crisis. Such a crisis occurs only where the ongoing chain of payments has been fully developed, along with an artificial system for settling them. Whenever there is a general disturbance of the mechanism, no matter what its cause, money suddenly and immediately changes over from its merely nominal shape, money of account, into hard cash. Profane commodities can no longer replace it. (236)

In other words, you can't settle your bills with more IOUs; you've got to find hard cash, the universal equivalent, to pay them off. This then poses the social question in general: where is the hard cash going to come from? Marx continues,

> The use-value of commodities becomes valueless, and their value vanishes in the face of their own form of value. The bourgeois, drunk with prosperity and arrogantly certain of himself, has just declared that money is a purely imaginary creation. 'Commodities alone are money,' he said. But now the opposite cry resounds over the markets of the world: only money is a commodity. As the hart pants after fresh water, so pants his soul after money, the only wealth. In a crisis, the antithesis between commodities and their value-form, money, is raised to the level of an absolute contradiction. Hence money's form of appearance is here also a matter of indifference. The monetary famine remains whether payments have to be made in gold or in credit-money, such as bank-notes. (236–7)

Back in 2005, there was a consensus that there was an immense surplus of liquidity sloshing around in the world's markets. The bankers had surplus funds and were lending to almost anyone, including, as we later found out, people who had no creditworthiness whatsoever. Buy a house with no income? Sure, why not? Money doesn't matter because commodities like housing are a safe bet. But then the prices of houses stopped rising, and when the debts fell due, more and more people could not pay. At that point the liquidity suddenly dries up. Where is the money? Suddenly the Federal Reserve has to inject massive funds into the banking system because now "money is the only commodity."

As Marx amusingly put it elsewhere, in boom economies everybody acts like a Protestant—they act on pure faith. When the crash comes, though, everyone dives for cover in the "Catholicism" of the monetary base, real gold. But it is in these times that the question of real values and reliable money-forms gets posed. What is the relation between what is going on in all those debt-bottling plants in New York City and real production? Are they dealing in purely fictitious values? These are the questions that Marx raises for us, questions that are forgotten during the halcyon years but regularly come back to haunt us at moments of crisis. Once the monetary system becomes even more detached from the value system than it does with a gold standard, then all sorts of wild possibilities open up with potentially devastating consequences for social and natural relations.

The sudden shortage of circulating medium, at a certain historical moment, can likewise generate a crisis. Withdrawing short-term credit from the market can crash commodity production. A good example of that took place in East and Southeast Asia between 1997 and 1998. Perfectly adequate companies, producing commodities, were heavily indebted but could easily have worked their way out of their indebtedness had it not been for a sudden withdrawal of short-term liquidity. The bankers withdrew the liquidity, the economy crashed and viable companies went bankrupt, selling out for lack of access to the means of payment. Western capital and the banks came in and bought them all up for almost nothing. Liquidity was then restored, the economy revived and suddenly the bankrupted companies are viable again. Except now they are owned by the banks and the Wall Street folk, who can sell them off at an immense profit. In the nineteenth century, there were several liquidity crises of this kind, and Marx had followed them closely. 1848 saw a profound element of a liquidity crisis. And the people who came out of that year exceedingly enriched and empowered were—guess who?—the people who controlled the gold, i.e., the Rothschilds. They brought down governments simply because they controlled the gold at that particular moment. In *Capital*, Marx shows how the possibility of this kind of crisis is immanent in the way contradictions within the monetary system move under capitalism (236).

This then leads Marx to modify the quantity theory of money, by insisting that less money is needed the more payments balance each other out and the more money becomes a mere means of payment. "Commodities circulate, but their equivalent in money does not appear until some future date." In this way, "credit-money springs directly out of the function of money as a means of payment, in that certificates of debt owing for already purchased commodities"—what on Wall Street is now institutionalized as collateralized debt obligations (CDOs)—"themselves circulate for the purpose of transferring those debts to others" (237–8).

> On the other hand, the function of money as a means of payment undergoes expansion in proportion as the system of credit itself expands . . . When the production of commodities has attained a certain level and extent, the function of money as a means of payment begins to spread out beyond the sphere of the circulation of commodities. It becomes the universal material of contracts. Rent, taxes and so on are transformed from payments in kind to payments in money. (238)

With this, Marx anticipates the monetization of everything, as well as the spread of credit and finance in ways that would radically transform both economic and social relations.

The bottom line is that "the development of money as a means of payment makes it necessary to accumulate it in preparation for the days when the sums which are owing fall due" (240). Again, accumulation and hoarding are paired, but they have different functions:

> While hoarding, considered as an independent form of self-enrichment, vanishes with the advance of bourgeois society, it grows at the same time in the form of the accumulation of a reserve fund of the means of payment. (240)

This leads Marx to modify the quantity theory of money earlier stated: the total quantity of money required in circulation is the sum of commodities, multiplied by their prices and modified by the velocity and the development of means of payment. To this must now be added a reserve fund (a hoard) that will permit flexibility in times of flux (240). (In contemporary conditions, of course, this reserve fund is not privately held but lies within the prerogative of a public institution, which in the US is appropriately designated the Federal Reserve.)

The final subsection of this chapter deals with world money. To work effectively, any monetary system, as we have seen, requires a deep participation on the part of the state as a regulator of coins and symbols and overseer of the qualities and quantities of money (and in our times as manager of the reserve fund). Individual states typically manage their own monetary system in a particular way and can exercise a great deal of discretion in so doing. There is still a world market, however, and national monetary policies cannot exempt states from the disciplinary effects that flow from commodity exchange across the world market. So while the state may play a critical role in the stabilization of the monetary system within its geopolitical borders, it is nevertheless connected to the world market and subject to its dynamics. Marx points to the role played by precious metals; gold and silver became, as it were, the *lingua franca* of the world financial system. This metallic base was vital both domestically and in external (international) relations (241–3).

So the security of this metallic base and the money-forms (coins, in particular) derived from it became critical to global capitalism. It is interesting to note that at the same time as John Locke was urging religious tolerance, condemning the practice of burning heretics at the stake, his close colleague Isaac Newton was being called on to defend to quality of moneys as master of the Royal Mint. He had to face the problem of the debasement of the currency through the practice of shaving some of the silver off silver coins to make more coins (an easy way to make money, when you think about it). Convicted coin-clippers were publicly hung at Tyburn—offences against God were to be forgiven, but offences against capital and mammon deserved capital punishment!

So this brings us to the problem of how relevant Marx's arguments are in a world where the financial system works without a money commodity, without a metallic base, as has been the case since 1971. You will notice that gold is still important and perhaps wonder, in these troubled times of roiled international currency markets, whether you want to hold gold, dollars, euros or yen. So gold has not entirely disappeared from the scene, and there are some who argue for a return to some version of a gold standard to counteract the instabilities and the chaotic speculation that often trouble international financial transactions. The gold, recall, is simply depicted by Marx as a representation of value, of socially necessary labor-time. All that has happened since 1973 is that the manner of representation has changed. But Marx himself also notes multiple shifts in representational forms with coins, paper moneys, credit and the like, so in a way there is nothing in the current situation that defies his mode of analysis. What has happened, in effect, is that the value of a particular currency vis-à-vis all other currencies is (or should be) determined in terms of the value of the total bundle of commodities produced within a national economy. Plainly, the overall productivity of a whole economy is an important variable in all this; hence the emphasis placed on productivity and efficiency in public policy.

Now, if we stick with Marx's logic, we should immediately observe the contradictions that derive from this situation. To begin with, there is the fiction of a national economy that matches the "national uniforms" of national moneys. Such an economy is an "ideal," a fiction made real by collecting vast amounts of statistics on production, consumption, exchange, welfare and the like. These statistics are crucial for evaluating the state of a nation and play an important role in affecting exchange rates between currencies. When the statistics on consumer confidence and jobs look good, the currency rises. These data actually construct the fiction of a national economy when really there is no such thing; in Marx's terms, it is a fetish construct. But then perhaps speculators may enter and challenge the data (much of which is organized on pretty shaky grounds) or suggest that some indicators are more important than others, and if they can prevail then they can make megabucks betting on currency moves. For example, George Soros made a billion dollars in a few days by betting against the British pound in relation to the European Exchange Rate Mechanism, by convincing the market that he had the better view on the national economy.

What Marx has built into his mode of analysis is a persuasive way to understand the fraught and problematic link between value (the socially necessary labor-time congealed in commodities) and the ways in which the monetary system represents that value. He unpacks what is fictitious and imaginary about those representations and their resulting contradictions, while showing how, nevertheless, the capitalist mode of production cannot function without these ideal elements. We cannot abolish the fetishism, as he earlier pointed out, and we are condemned to live in a topsy-turvy world of material relations between people and social relations between things. The way forward is to advance the analysis of the inherent contradictions, to understand the way they move and the ways they open up new possibilities for development (as with the credit system) as well as the potential for crises. Marx's method of inquiry, it seems to me, is exemplary even as we have to adapt it to understand our current perilous situation.

One final point. This chapter on money is rich, complicated and hard to absorb on first reading. For this reason, as I began by remarking, many people give up on *Capital* by chapter 3. I hope you have found enough that is intriguing to stay with it. But you will also be glad to know that you do not have to understand everything in the chapter in order to move on. Much of what is said here is more relevant to later volumes than to the rest of Volume I. Armed with some basic, but essential, propositions from this chapter, it is possible to grasp the rest of the material without too much difficulty. From here on in, the argument becomes much easier.

CHAPTER THREE

From Capital To Labor-Power

We now take on the three chapters dealing with the concepts of capital and of labor-power. These chapters, I think you'll find, are much more straightforward and clear than those we have been through. There are times when they seem almost obvious; one wonders sometimes why we are being treated to such elaborate discussions of fairly simple ideas, particularly when in earlier chapters such difficult ideas were presented almost without explanation. To some degree this is a product of the period when Marx was writing. Anyone interested in political economy at that time would have been familiar with the labor theory of value (albeit in Ricardian form), whereas we not only are unfamiliar with it but live in times when most economists, and even some Marxists, consider it indefensible. Were Marx writing *Capital* today, he would have to offer a strong defense of it rather than simply state it as obvious. By contrast, the materials covered in these following chapters were more radical departures from conventional thought in Marx's time, but appear far more familiar to us today.

We are, however, undertaking a macro-transition in the argument's location in these three chapters, and it is useful to note this at the outset. *Capital* starts out with a model of exchange based on the barter of commodities, in which it was (unrealistically) imagined that equivalent socially necessary labor-times were being exchanged. Marx then moves from this C-C relation to examine how exchanges get mediated and generalized through the rise of the money form. Careful analysis of this C-M-C exchange system brings us at the end of the money chapter to identify the M-C-M form of circulation, in which money became the aim and object of exchange. In the C-M-C circuit, an exchange of equivalent values makes sense because its aim is to acquire use-values. I want the shirts and the shoes but do not need or want the apples and pears I have produced. But when it comes to M-C-M, the exchange of equivalents seems absurd. Why go through all the trouble and risk of this process to end up with the same amount of money-value at the end? M-C-M only makes sense if it results in an increment of value, M-C-M + ΔM, to be defined as surplus-value.

This raises the question: where can this surplus-value come from when the laws of exchange, M-C and then C-M, as presupposed in classical political economy, mandate an exchange of equivalents? If the laws of exchange are to be observed as the theory states, then a commodity must be found that has the capacity to produce more value than it itself has. That commodity, Marx says in chapter 6, is labor-power. This is the broad transitional story told in these three chapters. The focus begins to shift from commodity exchange to capital circulation.

There is, however, one important feature in these chapters that deserves some preliminary scrutiny. Several times already I have asked whether Marx is making a logical argument (based on a critique of the utopian propositions of classical liberal political economy) or a historical argument about the evolution of actually existing capitalism. By and large I have preferred the logical reading to the historical one, even though there may be important historical insights to be gained in considering the circumstances necessary to facilitate the rise of a capitalist mode of production (such as the work of the state in relation to the different money-forms). This manner of approach would be consistent with the methodological argument he makes elsewhere, that we can only properly understand history by looking backward from where we are today. This was his key point in the *Grundrisse*:

> Bourgeois society is the most developed and the most complex historical organization of production. The categories which express its relations, the comprehension of its structure, thereby also allows insights into the structure and relations of production of all the vanished social formations out of whose ruins and elements it built itself up, whose partly still unconquered remnants are carried along within it, whose mere nuances have developed explicit significance within it, etc. Human anatomy contains a key to the anatomy of the ape.[1]

But while "the intimations of higher development . . . can be understood only after the higher development is already known," this should not delude us into seeing the prototypes of "bourgeois relations in all forms of society" or thinking "that the categories of bourgeois economics possess a truth for all other forms of society."[2] Marx does not accept a Whig

1. Marx, *Grundrisse*, 105.
2. Ibid.

interpretation of history or a simple teleology. The bourgeois revolution fundamentally reconfigured preexisting elements into fundamentally new forms, at the same time allowing us to see those preexisting elements in a new light.

CHAPTER 4: THE GENERAL FORMULA FOR CAPITAL

In these three chapters, the reading of history seems to have an important independent role to play in the theorizing. He starts off chapter 4, for example, with a historical statement: "World trade and the world market date from the sixteenth century, and from then on the modern history of capital starts to unfold." The logical starting point is given in the parallel statement that "commodity circulation is the first form of appearance of capital" (247). So the logical and historical arguments are immediately juxtaposed. We need, therefore, to pay careful attention to how these arguments work together in these chapters in order to understand how the methodological prescriptions set out in the *Grundrisse* are put into practice in *Capital*.

Marx begins by examining how capital historically confronted the power of landed property in the transition from feudalism to capitalism. In this transition, merchants' capital and usurers' capital—specific forms of capital—played an important historical role. But these forms of capital are different from the "modern" industrial form of capital that Marx considers central to a fully developed capitalist mode of production (247). The dissolution of the feudal order, the dissolution of the power of landed property and of feudal land control, was largely accomplished through the powers of merchant capital and usury. This is a theme you find strongly articulated also in the *Communist Manifesto*. Interestingly, it's a history that assumes a logical place in *Capital*, because what we see in usurers' capital in particular is the independent social power of money (and of the money holders), an independent power that he showed in the money chapter to be socially necessary within a capitalist mode of production. It is through the deployment of this independent power that usury and the usurers helped bring feudalism to its knees.

This brings him back to the starting point for understanding the role of money (as opposed to the commodity) in the circulation process. Money can be used to circulate commodities, it can be used to measure value, to store wealth and so on. Capital, however, is money used in a certain way. Not only is the M-C-M process an inversion of the C-M-C process, but, as Marx observed in the previous chapter, "money does not come onto the scene as a circulating medium, in its merely transient form of an intermediary in the social metabolism, but as the individual incarnation of social labour, the independent presence of exchange-value, the universal commodity" (235). The representation of value (money), in other words, becomes the aim and objective of circulation. This form of circulation, however, "would be absurd and empty if the intention were, by using this roundabout route, to exchange two equal sums of money, £100 for £100" (248). The exchange of equal values is perfectly fine with respect to use-values because it is the qualities that matter. But the only logical reason to engage in the M-C-M circulation, as we saw in chapter 3, is to have more value at the end than at the beginning. Marx laboriously arrives at the fairly obvious conclusion:

> The process M-C-M does not therefore owe its content to any qualitative difference between its extremes, for they are both money, but solely to quantitative changes. More money is finally withdrawn from circulation than was thrown into it at the beginning . . . The complete form of this process is therefore M-C-M', where M' = M + ΔM, i.e. the original sum advanced plus an increment. This increment or excess over the original value I call 'surplus-value'. (251)

With this we arrive for the first time at the concept of surplus-value, which is, of course, fundamental to all of Marx's analysis.

What happens is that "the value originally advanced . . . not only remains intact while in circulation, but increases its magnitude, adds to itself a surplus-value, or is valorized . . . And this movement converts it into capital" (252). Here, finally, is the definition of "capital." For Marx, capital is not a thing, but a *process*—a process, specifically, of the circulation of values. These values are congealed in different things at various points in the process: in the first instance, as money, and then as commodity before turning back into the money-form.

Now, this process definition of capital is terribly important. It marks a radical departure from the definition you'll find in classical political economics, where capital was traditionally understood as a stock of assets (machines, money, etc.), as well as from the predominant definition in conventional economics, where capital is viewed as a thing-like "factor of production." Conventional economics has in practice a hard time measuring (valuing) the factor of production that is capital. So they just label it K and put it into their equations. But actually, if you ask, "What is K and how do you get a measure of it?" the answer is far from simple. Economists come up with all kinds of measures, but they can't agree on what capital actually "is." It plainly exists in the form of money, but it also exists as machines, factories and means of production; and how do you put an independent monetary value on the means of production, independent of the value of the commodities they help to produce? As was shown in the so-called capital controversy of the early 1970s, the whole of contemporary economic theory is dangerously close to being founded on a tautology: the monetary value of K in physical asset-form is determined by what it is supposed to explain, viz. the value of the commodities produced[3] (208–9).

Again, Marx looks at capital as a process. I could make capital right now by taking money out of my pocket and putting it into circulation to make more money. Or I could take capital out of circulation simply by choosing to put the money back into my pocket. It then follows that not all money is capital. Capital is money used in a certain way. The definition of capital cannot be divorced from the human choice to launch money-power into this mode of circulation. But this poses a whole set of problems. To begin with, there is the question of how much of an increment capital can possibly yield. Recall that one of the findings in the chapter on money was that the accumulation of money-power is potentially limitless; Marx repeats that here (235, 256–7). Its full significance, however, will only be taken up much later (in chapters 23 and 24 in particular).

A capitalist, Marx says, is "the conscious bearer . . . of this movement, the possessor of money becomes a capitalist. His person, or rather his pocket, is the point from which the money starts, and to which it returns." From this it follows that "use-values must therefore never be treated as the immediate aim of the capitalist." That is, the capitalist produces use-values only in order to gain exchange-value. The capitalist doesn't actually care about which or what kind of use-value gets produced; it could be any kind of use-value, as long as it permits the capitalist to procure the surplus-value. The aim of the capitalist is, rather unsurprisingly, the

3. Marx cites the same tautological definition of capital in J. B. Say's theory of circulation.

"unceasing movement of profit-making" (254). This sounds like the plot of Balzac's *Eugenie Grandet*!

> This boundless drive for enrichment, this passionate chase after value, is common to the capitalist and the miser; but while the miser is merely a capitalist gone mad, the capitalist is a rational miser. The ceaseless augmentation of value, which the miser seeks to attain by saving his money from circulation, is achieved by the more acute capitalist by means of throwing his money again and again into circulation. (254)

Capital is, therefore, value in motion. But it is value-in-motion that appears in different forms. "If we pin down the specific forms of appearance"—notice this phrase again—"assumed in turn by self-valorizing value in the course of its life, we reach the following elucidation: capital is money, capital is commodities" (255). Marx now makes the process definition of capital explicit:

> In truth, however, value is here the subject of a process in which, while constantly assuming the form in turn of money and commodities, it changes its own magnitude, throws off surplus-value from itself considered as original value, and thus valorizes itself independently. For the movement in the course of which it adds surplus-value is its own movement, its valorization is therefore self-valorization . . . By virtue of being value, it has acquired the occult ability to add value to itself. It brings forth living offspring, or at least lays golden eggs. (255)

Of course, Marx is being heavily ironic here. I mention this because I once read a dissertation that took the magical qualities of self-expansion ascribed to capital seriously. In this dense text, it is often rather too easy to miss the irony. In this instance, the "occult" qualities of capital and its seemingly magical capacity to lay "golden eggs" exist only in the realm of appearance. But it is not hard to see how this fetish construct could be taken for real—a capitalist system of production depends on this very fiction, as we saw in chapter 1. You put money in a savings account, and at the end of the year it has grown. Do you ever ask yourself where the growth came from? The tendency is to assume that this expansion simply belongs to the nature of money. We have, of course, seen periods when the savings rate has been negative, i.e., when inflation has been so high and interest rates so low that the net return to the saver had been negative (as is the case now, in 2008). But it does really appear as if your money in the bank inherently grows at the rate of interest. Marx wants to know what is hidden behind the fetish. This is the mystery that has to be solved.

There is, he says, one moment in this circulation process that we always come back to and that therefore appears to be more important than the others, and that is the money moment: M-M. Why? Because money is the universal representation and ultimate measure of value. It is therefore only at the money moment—the moment of capitalist universality—that we can tell where we are in relation to value and surplus-value. It's hard to tell that just looking at the particularity of commodities. "Money therefore forms the starting-point and the conclusion of every valorization process" (255). In Marx's example, the conclusion should yield £110 from the £100 the capitalist started out with:

> The capitalist knows that all commodities, however tattered they may look, or however badly they may smell, are in faith and in truth money, are by nature circumcised Jews, and, what is more, a wonderful means for making still more money out of money. (256)

Remarks of this sort have been grist for a significant debate over Marx's supposed anti-Semitism. It is indeed perfectly true that these kinds of phrases crop up periodically. The context of the time was one of widespread anti-Semitism (e.g., the portrayal of Fagin in Dickens's *Oliver Twist*). So you can either conclude that Marx, coming from a Jewish family that converted for job-holding reasons, was subconsciously going against his past or unthinkingly echoing the prejudices of his time, or, at least in this case, you can conclude that his intent is to take all the opprobrium that was typically cast on Jews and to say that it really should be assigned to the capitalist as a capitalist. I will leave you to your own conclusions on that.

Back in the text we find Marx still chipping away at the fetishistic surface appearance:

> But now, in the circulation M-C-M, value suddenly presents itself as a self-moving substance which passes through a process of its own, and for which commodities and money are both mere forms. But there is more to come: instead of simply representing the relations of commodities, it now enters into a private relationship with itself, as it were. It differentiates

> itself as original value from itself as surplus-value, just as God the Father differentiates himself from himself as God the Son . . . Value therefore now becomes value in process, money in process, and, as such, capital. (256)

That's the next step in the fundamental definition of capital: value in process, money in process. And how different this is from capital as a fixed stock of assets or a factor of production. (Yet it is Marx, not the economists, who gets criticized for supposedly static "structural" formulations!) Capital "comes out of circulation, enters into it again, preserves and multiplies itself within circulation, emerges from it with an increased size, and starts the same cycle again and again" (256). The powerful sense of flow is palpable. Capital is process, and that is that.

Marx briefly returns to merchants' capital and usurers' capital (his historical, rather than logical, starting point). While industrial capital is what he is really concerned with, he has to recognize that there are these other forms of circulation—merchants' capital (buying cheap in order to sell dear) and interest-bearing capital, through which a seeming self-expansion of value can also be accomplished. So we see different possibilities: industrial, merchant and interest-bearing capital, all of which have the M-C-M + ΔM form of circulation. This form of circulation, he concludes, is "the general formula for capital, in the form in which it appears directly in the sphere of circulation" (257). It is this form of circulation that has to be put under the microscope and scrutinized in order to demystify its "occult" qualities. So: does capital lay its own golden eggs?

CHAPTER 5: CONTRADICTIONS IN THE GENERAL FORMULA

Marx begins the search for an answer by examining the contradictions within the M-C-M + ΔM form of circulation. The fundamental question is quite simply this: where does the increment, the surplus-value, come from? The rules and laws of exchange in their pure form (as presupposed in utopian liberalism) say there has to be a rule of equivalence in the transitions from M to C and in C to M. Surplus-value cannot, therefore, be derived from exchange in its pure form. "Where equality exists there is not gain." In practice, of course, "it is true that commodities may be sold at prices which diverge from their values, but this divergence appears as an infringement of the laws governing the exchange of commodities." These laws are those presupposed in the classical political-economic model of perfectly functioning markets. "In its pure form, the exchange of commodities is an exchange of equivalents, and thus it is not a method of increasing value" (260–1).

Faced with this conundrum, the capitalists and their economists, like Condillac, tried to attribute the increase to the field of use-values. But Marx rejects this. You can't suddenly appeal to use-values to cure a problem that derives from the equivalence of exchange-values.

> If commodities, or commodities and money, of equal exchange-value, and consequently equivalents, are exchanged, it is plain that no one abstracts more value from circulation than he throws into it. The formation of surplus-value does not take place. In its pure form, the circulation process necessitates the exchange of equivalents. (262)

But Marx knows full well that "in reality processes do not take place in their pure form" so he then goes on to "assume an exchange of non-equivalents." This gives rise to a number of possibilities. For one, the seller has "some inexplicable privilege . . . to sell his commodities above their value." But this doesn't work, when you start to think about the relationship between buyers and sellers in generalized markets, any more than it works to say that the buyer has a privilege to purchase commodities below their value. "The formation of surplus-value [cannot] be explained by assuming that commodities are sold above their value," or "are bought at less than their value" (262–3).

He then briefly considers the problem of what we now call effective demand, which was at the time mainly articulated by Malthus (although it is surprising that Marx doesn't reference Malthus's key text on the matter, *Principles of Political Economy*) (264–5). Malthus argued that there was a definite tendency toward a deficiency of aggregate demand in the market for the surplus commodities that capitalists produce in order to procure surplus-value. Who has the purchasing power to buy the commodities? The capitalists are reinvesting, so they are not consuming as much as they could. The workers cannot consume the totality of the product, because they are being exploited. So Malthus concluded that there was an important role for a class of landowners—or as Marx would call them, bourgeois parasites of all kinds—who did the benevolent thing of consuming as much as they could in order to keep the economy stable. Malthus thereby justified the perpetuation of a nonproductive consuming class (in the face of the Ricardian critique that also dismissed them as nonproductive parasites).

Malthus modified his argument somewhat by suggesting that this class of consumers could also be outside the nation—and that foreign trade and even foreign tribute (silver payments to an imperial power, for example) would also help solve the problem. This latter is one of Rosa Luxemburg's major arguments, that the necessary effective demand in a capitalist system (which she felt Marx hadn't sufficiently addressed in *Capital*) ultimately can only be guaranteed by establishing some relationship to the outside—in short, by imposing imperialist extractions of tribute. The British imperialist logic that led to the Opium Wars reflected this: there was a lot of silver in China, so the idea was to sell Indian opium to the Chinese, get all that silver out in that lucrative sale, and thereby pay for all the goods that were being produced in Manchester and sent to India. When the Chinese resisted opening their doors to the opium trade, the British response was to knock them down with military force.

Marx delivers a scathing dismissal of the idea that there is a class of consumers somewhere or other who get their value from God-knows-where, and who can somehow generate the surplus-value from within or from outside the system of capitalist social relations. Everyone (even members of the parasitic classes) within capitalism, he says, has to get their value from somewhere, and if they get their value from within the system then it is from appropriating values from others (like capitalists or workers) who are responsible for its production. The problem of surplus-value production cannot be solved by appeal to the market, and we most certainly cannot justify for this reason the perpetuation of a nonproductive class of consumers. Nor, in the long run, can foreign trade do the trick; at some point, the principle of equivalence has to prevail (265).

These passages on effective demand are problematic in certain respects, and Rosa Luxemburg provides a compelling challenge to Marx on this point, arguing that imperialism directed against noncapitalist social formations provided a partial answer to the effective demand problem.[4] There has been debate over these issues ever since. But in these passages Marx is simply concerned with how surplus-value is produced, not with how it might be paid for and realized through consumption.

4. Rosa Luxemburg, *The Accumulation of Capital* (New York: Routledge, 2003), 104–5.

The surplus-value has to be produced before it can be consumed, and we cannot appeal to processes of consumption in order to understand its production.

So these ideas on effective demand cannot explain how surplus-value is produced, particularly if we "keep within the limits of the exchange of commodities, where sellers are buyers, and buyers are sellers." Now, at first blush this seems an odd remark, given his earlier dismissal of Say's law. Nor does it seem to help when he adds that "our perplexity may perhaps have arisen from conceiving people merely as personified categories, instead of as individuals" (265), though we will see why he takes this path shortly. It is here, I think, that we encounter a real tension in Marx's text between his reliance on critique of the utopian tendencies of classical political economy and his desire to understand and illuminate for us the nature of actually existing capitalism. Marx is, in effect, saying that we have to seek an answer to the surplus-value origin problem in a geographically closed and perfected capitalist mode of production; in that ideal state, appeals to parasitic classes, consumerism or foreign trade have to be ruled out. He will later be explicit about these assumptions in *Capital*; here he tacitly invokes them by rejecting all external solutions. He dismisses effective-demand issues in general as irrelevant at this point in the analysis because here, in Volume I, he is concerned with production alone. Only in Volume II will he take up the problems of realization of values in the market and the world of consumption.

All this rules out any examination at this point in the analysis of geographical expansions, spatial fixes, imperialism and colonialism socially necessary to the survival of capitalism. He simply assumes a perfected and closed capitalist system, and it is on these terms alone that the origin of surplus-value is to be explained. While this assumption restricts the range of his theoretical capacity (particularly with respect to understanding the actual historical and geographical dynamics of capitalism), it deepens and sharpens his analysis. As I have shown elsewhere—particularly in *The Limits to Capital* and *Spaces of Capital*[5]—these broader questions were of deep concern to Marx when he sought to address the grander project of understanding the state, foreign trade, colonialism and the construction of the world market. But at this point

5. David Harvey, *Spaces of Capital: Towards a Critical Geography* (New York: Routledge, 2001).

in *Capital*, he is solely concerned to show that the production of surplus-value cannot arise out of market exchange regardless of what historical or geopolitical conditions may prevail. Some other way has to be found to solve the contradiction of how to produce a non-equivalence (i.e., the surplus-value) from the exchange of equivalents.

This adoption of such a narrow focus also explains why Marx momentarily switches to looking at individuals rather than social roles. Individuals can indeed best others by selling above value, and this indeed can and does happen all the time. But when looked at systemically and in aggregate social terms, the effect is simply to rob Peter to pay Paul. An individual capitalist may cheat another and get away with it, but then somebody's gain is somebody else's loss, and there is no aggregate surplus-value. A way must therefore be found for all capitalists to gain surplus-value. A healthy or properly functioning economy is one in which all capitalists earn a steady and remunerative rate of profit.

> However much we twist and turn, the final conclusion remains the same. If equivalents are exchanged, no surplus-value results, and if non-equivalents are exchanged, we still have no surplus-value . . . It can be understood, therefore, why, in our analysis of the primary form of capital, the form in which it determines the economic organization of modern society, we have entirely left out of consideration its well-known and so to speak antediluvian forms, merchants' capital and usurers' capital. (266)

It may have been historically true, as Benjamin Franklin observed, that "war is robbery, commerce is cheating" (267). Clearly, in the origins of capitalism, there was a lot of predation, fraud, robbery and stealing of surplus-values from around the world. And Marx does not deny the historical significance of that. The same applies to usurers' capital even in the face of long-standing and in some instances ultra-strict taboos against charging interest. Islamic law, for example, forbids charging interest. Probably not so well known, but up until the mid-nineteenth century, the Catholic Church had a prohibition on charging interest, and this had tremendous significance. For instance, at that time in France, conservative Catholics often compared investment houses to bordellos and viewed financial operations as a form of prostitution. There are some great political cartoons from that era that satirize this. One I used in *Paris: Capital of Modernity* depicts a young woman trying to entice this older and quite horrified man into this investment house, saying, "My rate of return is good for whatever amount you wish to invest. I'll treat you very gently."[6]

So merchant's capital and usurers' capital (or interest-bearing capital) both had important historical roles. But, Marx concludes,

> in the course of our investigation, we shall find that both merchants' capital and interest-bearing capital are derivative forms, and at the same time it will become clear why, historically, these two forms appear before the modern primary form of capital. (267)

These forms of capital circulation, he is saying, had a historical existence before industrial capital arrived on the scene. But, as we'll see, industrial capital is going to be *the* form of capital that defines a capitalist mode of production in its pure state. And once that industrial capital becomes dominant, it needs the merchant to sell the product, and it needs interest-bearing capital to be able to switch investments around to deal with the problems of long-term fixed capital investment and so on. In order for that to happen, the primary form of capital circulation has to subdue both finance capital and merchants' capital to its particular needs. In Volume III of *Capital*, Marx will take up the question of how this happened and with what consequences.

From our present perspective it is important to evaluate the positionality of merchants' and interest-bearing capital within capitalism in general. Certainly a plausible case can be made that they went from being hegemonic and dominant in the sixteenth and seventeenth centuries to becoming subservient to industrial capital during the nineteenth century. But many would now argue—myself included—that finance capital has become dominant again, particularly since the 1970s. If so, it is up to us to assess what this means and what it portends.

This is not a matter we can take up here, however. For our purposes, what is important to note is that Marx presumed (and this was probably correct at the time) that the circulation of capital in its industrial form had become hegemonic, and therefore it was within that framework that the question of surplus-value production had to be resolved. He therefore concludes:

6. David Harvey, *Paris: Capital of Modernity* (New York: Routledge, 2003), 119.

> Capital cannot therefore arise from circulation, and it is equally impossible for it to arise apart from circulation. It must have its origin both in circulation and not in circulation ... We therefore have a double result ... The transformation of money into capital has to be developed on the basis of the immanent laws of the exchange of commodities in such a way that the starting-point is the exchange of equivalents. The money-owner, who is as yet only a capitalist in larval form, must buy his commodities at their value, sell them at their value, and yet at the end of the process withdraw more value from circulation than he threw into it at the beginning. His emergence as a butterfly must, and yet must not, take place in the sphere of circulation. These are the conditions of the problem. Hic Rhodus, hic salta! (268–9)

Which in rough, colloquial translation means, "Here is the ball, now run with it."

CHAPTER 6: THE SALE AND PURCHASE OF LABOUR-POWER

The contradiction turns out to be easy to resolve. It is given away in the title of this chapter. Marx sets the argument up as follows:

> In order to extract value out of the consumption of a commodity, our friend the money-owner must be lucky enough to find within the sphere of circulation, on the market, a commodity whose use-value possesses the peculiar property of being a source of value, whose actual consumption is therefore itself an objectification . . . of labour, hence a creation of value. The possessor of money does find such a special commodity on the market: the capacity for labour . . . in other words labour-power. (270)

Labor-power consists of the physical, mental and human capacities to congeal value in commodities. But in order to be itself a commodity, labor-power has to have certain characteristics. First, "in order that its possessor may sell it as a commodity, he must have it at his disposal, he must be the free proprietor of his own labor-capacity, hence of his person." So the idea of the free laborer becomes crucial—slavery and serfdom will not do. The laborer cannot give up his or her person; all he or she can do is to trade the physical, mental and human capacities to create value. "In this way he manages both to alienate . . . his labour-power"—that is, to pass it over to somebody else—"and to avoid renouncing his rights of ownership over it" (271).

So the capitalist cannot own the laborer; all the capitalist owns is the *capacity* to labor and to produce value for a certain period of time.

> The second essential condition which allows the owner of money to find labour-power in the market as a commodity is this, that the possessor of labour-power, instead of being able to sell commodities in which his labour has been objectified, must rather be compelled to offer for sale as a commodity that very labour-power which exists only in his living body. (272)

Laborers, in other words, are not in a position to work for themselves.

> For the transformation of money into capital, therefore, the owner of money must find the free worker available on the commodity-market; and this worker must be free in the double sense that as a free individual he can dispose of his labour-power as his own commodity, and that, on the other hand, he has no other commodity for sale, i.e. he is rid of them, he is free of all the objects needed for the realization . . . of his labour-power. (272–3)

The laborer must, in short, already be dispossessed of access to the means of production.

Marx's commentary on freedom is really apposite to our own times. What did it mean, for example, when President George W. Bush went on and on about bringing freedom to the world? He used the words "freedom" and "liberty" in his Second Inaugural Address some fifty times. On Marx's critical interpretation, this would mean that Bush was mobilizing a campaign to free as many people in the world as possible of any direct control over, or access to, the means of production. Yes, indeed, individual laborers will have rights over their own body and individual legal rights in the labor market. In principle they have the right to sell their labor-power to whomsoever they choose and the right to buy whatever they want in the marketplace with the wages they receive. Creating such a world is what the capitalist form of imperial politics has been about for the past two hundred years. Indigenous and peasant populations were dispossessed of access to the means of production and proletarianized wholesale across the globe. In more recent neoliberal versions of this same process, more and more social strata in populations all around the world, including in the advanced capitalist countries, have been dispossessed of their assets, including independent access to means of production or other means of survival (e.g., pensions for older workers or state welfare payments).

The ideological and political ironies involved in the promotion of this "double-edged" form of bourgeois freedom are not lost on Marx. Today we are sold a bill of goods on the positive aspects of freedom and forced to accept as inevitable or even natural the negative aspects. Liberal theory is founded on doctrines of individual rights and freedoms. From Locke to Hayek and onward, all the ideologists of liberalism and neoliberalism have asserted that the best defense of such individual rights and liberties is a market system founded on private property and the bourgeois rules of independence, reciprocity and juridical individualism that Marx described (and, for purposes of inquiry, accepted) in chapter 2.

Since it is hard to protest against universal ideals of freedom, we are easily persuaded to go along with the fiction that the good freedoms (like those of market choice) far outweigh the bad freedoms (such as the freedom of capitalists to exploit the labor of others). And if it takes a little repression to dispossess people of their access to means of production and to ensure the sustenance of market freedoms, then that is justified as well. Pretty soon we find ourselves in the midst of McCarthyism or Guantánamo Bay without an oppositional leg to stand on. Woodrow Wilson, that great liberal president of the United States who sought to found the League of Nations, put it this way in a lecture he delivered at Columbia University in 1907:

> Since trade ignores national boundaries and the manufacturer insists on having the world as a market, the flag of his nation must follow him, and the doors of the nations which are closed against him must be battered down. Concessions obtained by financiers must be safeguarded by ministers of state, even if the sovereignty of unwilling nations be outraged in the process. Colonies must be obtained or planted, in order that no useful corner of the world may be overlooked or left unused.

Marx's essential ideological objective is to pinpoint the duplicity that lies at the heart of the bourgeois conception of freedom (much like he questioned Proudhon's appeal to bourgeois conceptions of justice). The contrast between George Bush's rhetoric of liberty and freedom and the reality of Guantánamo Bay is exactly what we should expect.

But how did the laborer come to be "free" in this double sense? *Why* the free worker approaches the capitalist with his labor in the market, Marx observes, "does not interest the owner of money . . . And for the present it interests us just as little" (273). Here Marx simply assumes that proletarianization has already occurred and that a functioning labor market already exists. But he does, however, want to make "one thing" clear:

> Nature does not produce on the one hand owners of money or commodities, and on the other hand men possessing nothing but their own labour-power. This relation has no basis in natural history, nor does it have a social basis common to all periods of human history. It is clearly the result of a past historical development, the product of many economic revolutions, of the extinction of a whole series of older formations of social production. (273)

That the wage-labor system had specific historical origins has to be acknowledged, if only to press home the point that the category of wage labor is no more "natural" than that of the capitalist or of value itself. The history of proletarianization will be taken up in greater detail later, in part 8. For now he simply wants to assume a full-fledged labor market already exists. He nevertheless acknowledges,

> The economic categories already discussed similarly bear a historical imprint. Definite historical conditions are involved in the existence of the product as a commodity . . . Had we gone further, and inquired under what circumstances all, or even the majority of products take the form of commodities, we should have found that this only happens on the basis of one particular mode of production, the capitalist one. (273)

The capitalist mode of production, not other modes of production, we are reminded, is Marx's exclusive focus.

The commodity production that has in the past existed in various forms, alongside the monetary circulation that historically has also existed in many forms, is clearly related in Marx's mind to the rise of wage-labor forms. None of these evolutions is independent of the other in the rise to domination of a capitalist mode of production. Again, the historical and logical arguments intertwine. The socially necessary relation that logically binds commodity production to monetization and both in turn to the commodification of wage labor has distinctive historical origins. The wage system and the labor market that to us appear obvious and logical almost certainly did not appear so even toward the end of European feudalism.

> The historical conditions of [capital's] existence are by no means given with the mere circulation of money and commodities. It arises only when the owner of the means of production and subsistence finds the free worker available, on the market, as the seller of his own labour-power. And this one historical pre-condition comprises a world's history. Capital, therefore, announces from the outset a new epoch in the process of social production. (274)

Labor-power is, however, a peculiar commodity, a special commodity unlike any other. First and foremost, it is the only commodity that has the capacity to *create value*. It is laborers whose socially necessary labor-time is congealed in commodities, and laborers who sell their labor-power to the capitalist. In turn, the capitalist uses this labor-power to organize the production of surplus-value. Note, however, that the form in which labor-power circulates is C-M-C (laborers take their labor-power into the market and sell it in return for money, which then permits them to buy the commodities they need to survive). So the laborer, remember, is always in the C-M-C circuit, while the capitalist works in the M-C-M' circuit. There will therefore be different rules for how they think about their respective situations. The laborer can be content with the exchange of equivalents because it is use-values that matter. The capitalist, on the other hand, has to solve the problem of gaining surplus-value out of the exchange of equivalents.

So what is it that fixes the value of labor-power as commodity? The answer is complicated because labor-power is not a commodity in the usual sense, not only because it alone can create value but also because the determinants of its value are different from those of shirts and shoes both in principle and in the details. Marx mentions the differences with scarcely any elaboration:

> The value of labour-power is determined, as in the case of every other commodity, by the labour-time necessary for the production, and consequently also the reproduction, of this specific article. In so far as it has value, it represents no more than a definite quantity of the average social labour objectified in it . . . For his maintenance he requires a certain quantity of the means of subsistence. Therefore the labour-time necessary for the production of labour-power is the same as that necessary for the

> production of those means of subsistence; in other words, the value of labour-power is the value of the means of subsistence necessary for the maintenance of its owner. (274)

The value of labor-power is fixed, therefore, by the value of all of those commodities that are needed to reproduce the laborer in a given state of life. We add up the value of the bread, the value of the shirts and the shoes and all the other things necessary to sustain and reproduce laborers, and the total is what fixes the value of labor-power.

It seems a simple enough calculation, seemingly no different in principle from any commodity. But how are "needs" determined? Needs distinguish labor from all other commodities. First off, in the course of laboring, "a definite quantity of human muscle, nerve, brain etc. is expended, and these things have to be replaced." If the laborers are required for a certain kind of laboring (e.g., down in a coal mine) they may need, say, more meat and potatoes to sustain their laboring. Furthermore, "his means of subsistence must therefore be sufficient to maintain him in his normal state as a working individual." Again, what is "normal"? There are "natural needs . . . such as food, clothing, fuel and housing" that "vary according to the climatic and other physical peculiarities of his country" (274–5). Workers' needs are different in the Arctic than in temperate zones. But then comes the really big shift:

> On the other hand, the number and extent of his so-called necessary requirements, as also the manner in which they are satisfied, are themselves products of history, and depend therefore to a great extent on the level of civilization attained by a country; in particular they depend on the conditions in which, and consequently on the habits and expectations with which, the class of free workers has been formed. In contrast, therefore, with the case of other commodities, the determination of the value of labour-power contains a historical and moral element. (275)

The implication is that the value of labor-power is not independent of the history of class struggles. Furthermore, "the level of civilization" in a country will vary according to, for example, the strength of bourgeois reform movements. The respectable and virtuous bourgeois are from time to time appalled to witness the poverty of the masses and, feeling guilty, conclude that it is unacceptable in a decent society that the mass of the people live in the way they do. They insist on the provision of decent housing, decent public health, decent education, decent this and decent that. Some of these measures can be seen as self-interested (because, for example, cholera epidemics do not stop at class borders), but there is no bourgeois society anywhere that does not have some sense of civilized values, and this sense plays a crucial role in determining what the value of labor-power should be.

Marx is appealing to the principle that there is a totality of commodities that sets the terms for what counts as a reasonable wage in a particular society at a particular time. He does not discuss any such particulars. Instead we can proceed with the theoretical inquiry as if the value of labor-power is fixed and known, even as the *datum* is perpetually moving and in any case has to be flexible, reflecting such other features as the reproduction costs of the laborer, from training and the reproduction of skills to raising a family and reproducing the working class (its qualities as well as its quantities) (275–6).

There is one other peculiarity of labor-power as a commodity that is worthy of note. The capitalist enters the marketplace and has to pay for all the commodities (raw materials, machinery, etc.) before putting them to work, but with labor-power the capitalist hires the labor-power and pays its providers only after they have done the work. In effect, the laborer advances the commodity of labor-power to the capitalist, hoping to get paid at the end of the day. This does not always happen, however; firms that declare bankruptcy can renege on wages (277–8). In contemporary China, for example, a large proportion of the labor force in certain industries (construction) and certain regions, particularly the North, have been denied their wages, prompting widespread protests.

Marx's point here is that the notion of an acceptable standard of living for the laborer varies according to natural, social, political and historical circumstances. Obviously, what is acceptable in one society (say, contemporary Sweden) is not the same as in another (contemporary China), and what was acceptable in 1850 in the United States is not acceptable today. So the value of labor-power is highly variable, depending not only on physical needs but also on conditions of class struggle, the degree of civilization in the country and the history of social movements (some of which go far beyond what the workers themselves might directly struggle for). There may be social democratic parties that insist on universal healthcare, access to education, adequate housing, public infrastructure—parks, water, public transportation, sanitation—as well as full employment opportunities at a minimum wage. All these things can be considered fundamental obligations of civilized countries, depending on the social and political situation.

The upshot is that labor-power is not a commodity like any other. It is the unique creator of value at the same time as a historical and moral element enters into the determination of its value. And this historical and moral element is subject to influence by a wide array of political, religious and other forces. Even the Vatican has produced powerful encyclicals on the conditions of labor, and the theology of liberation, when it was at its height in Latin America, played a key role in fomenting revolutionary movements in the 1960s and 1970s that focused on the standards of living of the poor. So the value of labor-power is not a constant. It fluctuates not only because the costs of subsistence commodities vary but also because the commodity bundle needed to reproduce the laborer is affected by all these wide-ranging forces. Plainly, the value of labor-power is sensitive to changes in the value of the commodities needed to support them. Cheap imports will reduce that value; the Wal-Mart phenomenon has thus had a significant impact on the value of labor-power in the United States. The hyperexploitation of labor-power in China keeps the value of labor-power down in the United States through cheap imports. This also explains the resistance, in many quarters of the capitalist class, to putting barriers to entry or tariffs on Chinese goods, because to do so would be to raise the cost of living in the US, leading to a demand from workers for higher wages.

Marx, having briefly mentioned issues of this sort, shunts them aside to conclude that, "nevertheless, in a given country at a given period, the average amount of the means of subsistence necessary for the worker is a known *datum*" (275). Marx fixes what he concedes is fluid and in perpetual flux as the "known *datum*" in a given country at a given time. How reasonable is this move? Theoretically, it permits him to move on to explain how surplus-value can be produced, but it does so at a price.

In most national economics, ways have indeed been found to determine what this *datum* might be. Legislation concerning a minimum wage, for example, recognizes the importance of a fixed *datum* in a given place and time, while the politics over whether to raise it or not is an excellent illustration of the role political struggle plays in determining the value of labor-power. Local struggles in recent years over a "living wage" also illustrate the idea of both a general *datum* and social struggle over what the *datum* should be.

An even more interesting parallel with Marx's formulation exists in the determination of the so-called poverty level. In the mid-1960s, Mollie Orshansky devised a method to define the poverty level by fixing it in terms of the money needed to buy that particular commodity bundle deemed necessary for the reproduction of, say, a family of four at some minimally acceptable level. This is the sort of known *datum* that Marx is referring to. Since the 1960s, however, there has been incessant debate regarding this definition, which became the basis of public policy (e.g., welfare and Social Security payments). Exactly what the market basket of commodities should be—how much for transportation, how much for clothing, how much for food, how much for rent (and do you really need a mobile phone nowadays?)—became a matter of controversy. The figure for a family of four now stands at more than $20,000 a year. The right wing says we have all along been looking at the wrong bundle and thereby overestimating poverty; in high-cost locations like New York City, however, studies suggest the level should be $26,000 or so. Obviously, historical, political and moral arguments are going to factor in here.

Let us return to the idea of the circulation of labor-power through the C-M-C circuit and the difference between that and the capitalists working in the C-M-C + ΔC circuit. Marx comments:

> The use-value which the [capitalist] gets in exchange manifests itself only in the actual utilization, in the process of the consumption of the labour-power ... The process of the consumption of labour-power is at the same time the production process of commodities and of surplus-value. The consumption of labour-power is completed, as in the case of every commodity, outside the market or the sphere of circulation. (279)

And now follows the large shift in perspective:

> Let us therefore, in company with the owner of money and the owner of labour-power, leave this noisy sphere, where everything takes place on the surface and in full view of everyone, and follow them into the hidden abode of production, on whose threshold there hangs the notice 'No admittance except on business'. Here we shall see, not only how capital produces, but how capital is itself produced. The secret of profit-making must at last be laid bare. (279–80)

Marx then concludes with a swinging indictment of bourgeois constitutionality and law. Leaving the sphere of circulation and exchange means leaving that sphere constitutionally set up as "a very Eden of the innate rights of man." The market is "the exclusive realm of Freedom, Equality, Property and Bentham."

> Freedom, because both buyer and seller of a commodity, let us say of labour-power, are determined only by their own free will. They contract as free persons, who are equal before the law . . . Equality, because each enters into relation with the other, as with a simple owner of commodities, and they exchange equivalent for equivalent. Property, because each disposes only of what is his own. And Bentham, because each looks only to his own advantage. The only force bringing them together, and putting them into relation with each other, is the selfishness, the gain and the private interest of each. Each pays heed to himself only, and no one worries about the others. And precisely for this reason, either in accordance with the pre-established harmony of things, or under the auspices of an omniscient providence, they all work together to their mutual advantage, for the common weal, and in the common interest. (280)

Marx's deeply ironic description of the standard form of liberal bourgeois constitutionality and market law brings us to the final phase of transition in his argument:

> When we leave this sphere of simple circulation or the exchange of commodities, which provides the 'free-trader vulgaris' with his views, his concepts and the standard by which he judges the society of capital and wage-labour, a certain change takes place, or so it appears, in the physiognomy of our dramatis personae. He who was previously the money-owner now strides out in front as a capitalist; the possessor of labour-power follows as his worker. The one smirks self-importantly and is intent on business; the other is timid and holds back, like someone who has brought his own hide to market and knows he has nothing else to expect but—a tanning. (280)

These further reflections on bourgeois rights, echoing the duality of the supposed freedom of the laborer, provide a segue in the argument into a consideration of the far less visible moment of production that occurs, typically, in the factory. And it is into this realm that we will follow Marx next.

CHAPTER FOUR

The Labor Process And The Production Of Surplus-Value

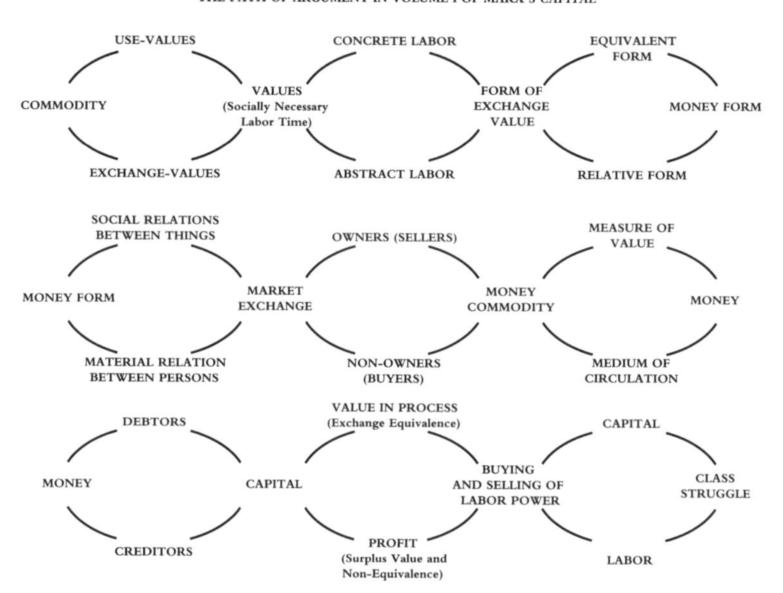

I want to cast a backward look at the direction Marx's argument has taken thus far. I do so with the help of a diagrammatic representation of his dialectical chain of argumentation (see figure above). Reducing Marx's argument to this format inevitably does an injustice to the richness of his thinking, but I think it useful to have some sort of cognitive map of his argument so that you can more easily navigate its swirling crosscurrents.

He begins with the unitary concept of the commodity, which embodies the duality of use- and exchange-values. What lies behind exchange-value is the unitary concept of value defined as socially necessary labor-time ("socially necessary" implies someone wants or needs the use-value).

Value internalizes a duality of concrete and abstract labor, which conjoin in an act of exchange through which value gets expressed in the duality of relative and equivalent forms of value. From this, a money commodity emerges as the representative of the universality of value, but this disguises the inner meaning of value as a social relation to produce the fetishism of commodities, understood as material relations between persons and social relations between things. In the marketplace, people relate to one another not as people but as buyers and sellers of things. Here Marx assumes, as in liberal theory, private property rights, juridical individuals and perfectly functioning markets. Within that world, money, the representation of value, takes on two distinctive and potentially antagonistic roles, as the measure of value and as the means of circulation. But finally there is only one money, and the tension between the two roles is seemingly resolved by a new money relation, that between debtors and creditors. This shifts the focus from a C-M-C form of circulation to M-C-M, which is, of course, the prototype of the concept of capital defined not as a thing but as a form of circulation of value that produces a surplus-value (profit), M-C-M + ΔM. This poses a contradiction between the equivalence supposed in perfect market exchange and the non-equivalence required in the production of surplus-value. This contradiction is resolved by the existence of labor-power as a commodity that can be bought and sold on the market and then used to produce value and therefore surplus-value. And so we arrive, finally, at the grand conception of a class relation between capital and labor.

This is not, please note, a causal chain of argument. It does entail the gradual unfolding, the layering of different levels of complexity, as the argument expands from a simple opposition within the commodity into more and more insights into different aspects of how a capitalist mode of production works. This dialectical expansion continues throughout the book, for example, in the emergence of a class relation and of class struggle and in the dual concepts of absolute and relative surplus-value. And the expansion jumps scale into the macro-dichotomy between the whole of Volume I, which concentrates on the world of production of surplus-value, and Volume II, where the primary focus is on the circulation and realization of surplus-value. The tensions (contradictions) between production and realization underpin the theory of crisis in Volume III. But I go way ahead in the story.

This cognitive map helps us envision how Marx has "grown" his argument organically and by what dialectical leaps. But please remember that the chart is a mere skeletal form around which Marx arranges an analysis of the real flesh and blood of a dynamic, evolving and contradictory capitalist mode of production.

CHAPTER 7: THE LABOUR PROCESS AND THE VALORIZATION PROCESS

We now leave the "noisy" sphere of the market, the sphere of freedom, equality, property and Bentham, and go inside the labor process, where the sign says: "No Admittance Except on Business." This chapter is, however, unusual in one respect. For the most part, Marx is emphatic that he is dealing only with the conceptual categories formulated within and appropriate to a capitalist mode of production. Value, for example, is not a universal category but something unique to capitalism arising out of the bourgeois era (Aristotle, as we have seen, could not have come up with it, given the conditions of slavery). But in this chapter, for the first ten pages or so, Marx launches into a discussion that is universal, applicable across all possible modes of production. We "have to consider the labour process," he says, "independently of any specific social formation" (283), thus confirming a position he took earlier, that labor is "a condition of human existence which is independent of all forms of society; it is an eternal natural necessity which mediates the metabolism between man and nature, and therefore human life itself" (133).

We should not interpret these statements, however, in familiar bourgeois terms that presuppose a clear separation between "man and nature," culture and nature, natural and artificial, mental and physical, and in which history is viewed as a titanic struggle between two independent forces, humanity and nature. There is, in Marx's view, no such clear separation in the labor process. That process is wholly natural and wholly human at the same time. It is construed dialectically as a moment of "metabolism" in which it is impossible to separate the natural from the human.

But within this unitary conception of the labor process, as happened in the case of the commodity, we immediately identify a duality. There is, says Marx, "a process between man and nature, a process by which man, through his own actions, mediates, regulates and controls the metabolism between himself and nature." Human beings are active agents in relation to the world around them. So man

> confronts the materials of nature as a force of nature. He sets in motion the natural forces which belong to his own body, his arms, legs, head and hands, in order to appropriate the materials of nature in a form adapted to his own needs. Through this movement he acts upon external nature and changes it, and in this way he simultaneously changes his own nature. (283)

This is where we most clearly encounter Marx's dialectical formulation of the relation to nature. We cannot transform what's going on around us without transforming ourselves. Conversely, we can't transform ourselves without transforming everything going on around us. The unitary character of this dialectical relation, even though it entails an "externalization" of nature and an "internalization" of the social, can never be displaced. This dialectic, of perpetually transforming oneself by transforming the world and vice versa, is fundamental to understanding the evolution of human societies as well as the evolution of nature itself. But this process is not unique to human beings—ants do it, beavers do it, all kinds of organisms do it. The whole history of life on earth is rife with dialectical interactions of this kind. James Lovelock argues in his Gaia hypothesis, for example, that the atmosphere which supports us right now wasn't always there but has been created by organisms that once lived off methane and produced oxygen. The dialectic of organic life and the evolution of the natural world has been central all along.

In his earlier works, Marx made much of the idea of a distinctively human "species being" (perhaps drawing on Kant's anthropology as well as the later anthropological formulations of Feuerbach). This idea takes a backseat in the formulations of *Capital*, but it does occasionally exercise a shadowy influence, as in this instance. So what makes our labor exclusively human? "A spider," he writes,

> conducts operations which resemble those of the weaver, and a bee would put many a human architect to shame by the construction of its honeycomb cells. But what distinguishes the worst architect from the best of bees is that the architect builds the cell in his mind before he constructs it in wax. At the end of every labour process, a result emerges which had already been conceived by the worker at the beginning, hence already existed ideally [i.e., mentally].

This is an important statement. We have an idea, Marx says, and then make it real. There is, therefore, always an "ideal" (mental) moment, a utopian moment, entailed in human productive activity. Furthermore, this moment is not haphazard: "man not only effects a change of form in the materials of nature; he also realizes . . . his own purpose in those materials." The activity is purposive. "And this is a purpose he is conscious of, it determines the mode of his activity with the rigidity of a law, and he must subordinate his will to it. This subordination is no mere momentary act." He needs—we need—to pay close attention, and

> the less he is attracted by the nature of the work . . . and the less, therefore, he enjoys it as the free play of his own physical and mental powers, the closer his attention is forced to be. (284)

There are a number of points to be made about these crucial passages—and they really are crucial. To begin with, there is no question that Marx is here contesting Fourier's ideas about the labor process. Fourier thought laboring should be about joy, passionate and erotic engagement, if not pure play. Marx is saying it's never like that. A lot of hard work and self-discipline are required if the imagined is to be made real on the ground, if a conscious purpose is to be realized. Second, Marx here accords a vital role to mental conceptions, to conscious and purposive action, and this contradicts one of those arguments so often attributed to him, namely that material circumstances determine consciousness, that how we think is dictated by the material circumstances in our life. Here he clearly says, no, there is a moment when the ideal (the mental) actually mediates what we do. The architect—and I think it is important to treat the architect here as a metaphor rather than as a profession—has the capacity to think the world and to remake the world in that image. Some analysts argue either that Marx simply forgot his own maxims in this passage or that he is in effect schizophrenic, that there are two Marxisms: one the Marx of this passage, allowing for the free play of ideas and mental activities, and one the deterministic Marx, who indeed holds that our consciousness, as well as what we think and do, is determined by our material circumstances. I think neither view is plausible. It is unlikely that in *Capital*, of all places, in a central chapter of a work that was revised carefully for publication (and later modified in response to criticism), Marx would take a position that was not deeply consistent with the way in which he understood the world. If these passages were in one of his notebooks, or even in the *Grundrisse*, that would be one thing. But this is a central transitional moment in

Capital's argument. It deserves, therefore, a serious reading and a careful interpretation.

Marx's dialectical understanding of the labor process as a metabolic moment immediately implies that ideas cannot possibly come out of nowhere. Ideas are in some sense wholly natural (this is a position fundamentally at odds with Hegelian idealism). So there is nothing strange about saying ideas arise from within the metabolic relation to material nature and always bear the mark of that origin. Our mental conceptions of the world are not divorced from our material experiences, our central engagements with the world, and therefore, they are not independent of those engagements. But there is (and the parallel with the case of money and the commodity is here instructive), an inevitable externalization of an internal relation, and in the same way that the world of money (particularly when it assumes symbolic forms) can both appear to be and "really is" (see the fetishism argument) in opposition to the world of commodities and their use-values, so our mental conceptions move into an external relation to the material world we seek to reshape. There is, therefore, a dialectical movement, when the imagination soars free, when it can and does say I am going to build this rather than that, reshaping material elements using natural forces (including human muscle) in such a way as to produce something new and different (e.g., the potter at the wheel). There is a certain openness to ideas and mental conceptions that is captured here in Marx's formulation. And in exactly the same way that the monetary system can get out of hand and generate financial crises, so our mental conceptions (our ideological fixations) can get out of hand and generate crises. Indeed, this is exactly the position that Marx takes with respect to the whole bourgeois vision of the world, with its Robinson Crusoe fantasies and its celebration of a fictional possessive individualism and perfectly functioning markets. In the same way that the monetary system is forced at some point to return to its senses in relation to the material world of socially necessary labor, so the bourgeois conception of the world, which is still so very much with us, has to give way to a more appropriate configuration of mental conceptions if we are to address the spiraling social and environmental problems of contemporary capitalism. In this, the struggle over appropriate mental conceptions (usually cast as "merely" superstructural, though note that Marx did specify that this is the realm in which we "become conscious" of issues and "fight them out") has a significant role to play. Why else would Marx struggle so mightily to write *Capital*? This moment, when Marx positions mental conceptions, consciousness, purposiveness and commitment, is therefore in no way aberrant in relation to the dynamics of social evolution and the transformation of nature, and human nature, through laboring. It is, instead, fundamental.

Marx is also saying that projects (like building a house) take hard work to complete and that once we have embarked on a project we all too often become imprisoned within its confines. We have to submit to its demands, subject ourselves and our passions to its purposive intensity, if we are to complete it. Every time I write a book, for instance, I start with an idea that sounds brilliant and exciting, but by the time I'm done, it feels like getting out of prison! But there is a far broader meaning here. At the heart of Marx's critical sensibility lies the idea that human beings can all too easily fall prisoner to their own products and projects, to say nothing of their false mental conceptions of the world. This critical sensibility can be applied just as ruthlessly to communism, socialism and ancient Rome as to capitalism, where Marx will most powerfully and persuasively deploy it.

There is something else about these passages that makes them interesting. Marx, it seems to me, attaches a sense not only of creativity but also of nobility to the labor process. I find the argument deeply Romantic. Marx was undoubtedly influenced by early-nineteenth-century Romanticism. His early writings are infused with Romantic sentiments and meanings. And while this sensibility is subdued in his later writings, it is not hard to detect its presence (even as concepts of alienation move from deeply agonistic in the *Economic and Philosophical Manuscripts* to more technical meanings in *Capital*). But here he says directly that human beings can transform the world in radical ways, according to their imagination and with an idea of a purpose, and be conscious about what they are doing. And in so doing, they have the power to transform themselves. We must therefore think about our purposes, become conscious of how and when we intervene in the world, transforming ourselves. We can and must seize hold of that dialectical possibility creatively. There is, therefore, no neutral transformation of an externalized nature in relationship to us. What we do "out there" is very much about us "in here." Marx makes us think about exactly what this dialectic means for us, as well as for nature, of which we are but one part: hence the universalistic approach to understanding the labor process. This implies that human nature is not a given but perpetually evolving.

Marx's positioning here is controversial (as is, perhaps, my own reading of it). There are abundant opportunities to dispute it. You can take Fourier's position, for example, or some version of the Marxist autonomistic positions of Tony Negri, John Holloway and Harry Cleaver, whose *Reading* Capital *Politically*[1] offers an intensive inquiry into the matters now before us. But you have to come to terms here with some understanding of what Marx is saying, see that this is how he is positioning himself, that this is his vision of what the potentiality for creative labor and changing the world is really all about.

So how then can the labor process, as a universal condition of possibility of human existence, be characterized? Marx distinguishes three distinctive elements: "purposeful activity, that is work itself . . . the object on which that work is performed, and . . . the instruments of that work" (284). Initially, the object on which work is performed is given in the concept of land, raw nature. But he quickly moves away from this to distinguish raw nature from raw materials, which are aspects of the world that have already been partially transformed, created or extracted by human labor. A similar distinction arises in the case of the instruments of labor. These can be given directly—sticks, stones, etc., that we can use. But then there are the consciously made instruments of labor such as knives and axes. So while the earth may be our "original larder" and "our original tool house," human beings have long succeeded in transforming both the land and the instruments of labor according to conscious design. "Man," Marx says, quoting Ben Franklin with some modicum of approval, can be defined "as a tool-making animal." "The use and construction of instruments of labour, although present in germ among certain species of animals, is characteristic of the specifically human labour process" (285–6). Marx then offers a side observation on which he will elaborate in detail later:

> It is not what is made but how [it is made], and by what instruments of labour, that distinguishes different economic epochs. Instruments of labour not only supply a standard of the degree of development which human labour has attained, but they also indicate the social relations within which men work. (286)

---

1. Harry Cleaver, *Reading* Capital *Politically* (Leeds: AK/Anti-Thesis, 2000).

The implication is that transformation in our instruments of labor has consequences for our social relations and vice versa; that as our social relations change, so our technology must change, and as our technology changes, so our social relations change. So he here sets up the idea of a dialectic between technologies and social relations which will be significant later on. This is, as we have seen, a typical Marx strategy—to insert a comment of this sort as a precursor to what comes later.

But we are not only concerned with tools in the conventional sense. Physical infrastructural conditions, also produced by human labor, are not directly involved in the immediate labor process but are necessary to its performance. "Instruments of this kind, which have already been mediated through past labour, include workshops, canals, roads, etc." (287). The labor process depends not only on the extraction of materials from raw nature but also on a built environment of fields, roads and urban infrastructure (sometimes referred to as "second nature").

So what about the actual labor process itself? Here Marx reverts to a consideration of process-thing relationships. Labor is a process; it's transforming something into something else. This transformation extinguishes an existing use-value and creates an alternative. Furthermore, "what on the side of the worker appeared in the form of unrest"—that is, motion—"now appears, on the side of the product, in the form of being . . . as a fixed, immobile characteristic. The worker has spun, and the product is a spinning" (287). This difference between process and thing is always there.

This is something I always appreciate about Marx's formulation. As an educator, I am constantly confronted with the process-thing relation. The process of a student's learning gets judged in the end by performative things, like written papers. But it is sometimes hard, if not impossible, to evaluate the process through the things produced. Students may find the process astonishingly enlightening and learn a lot, but if they produce a lousy paper, they get an F. Then they say, "But I learned so much taking this course!" And I say, "How can you possibly write a paper like that and say you've learned anything?" But this is a problem that frequently confronts us all. We can totally screw up in producing the thing, but we learn a fantastic amount in the process.

For Marx, the heart of laboring is the process. In exactly the same way that capital is construed as a process of circulation, so labor is construed as a process of making. But it is a process of making use-values, and under capitalism this means making use-value for someone else in commodity form. Does this use-value have to be of immediate use? Not necessarily, because past labor can be stored up for use in the future (even primitive societies usually maintain a surplus product to tide them over). In our world, a massive amount of past labor is stored up in our fields, cities and physical infrastructure, and some of that came from long ago. The daily activity of laboring is one thing, but the way that laboring gets stored up in products and things also plays a critical role. Furthermore, the labor process often produces different things simultaneously. This is what is known as a "joint products" issue. The raising of cattle produces milk, meat and hides, while sheep raised for their meat produce wool whether you like it or not. This will pose problems under capitalism: how, for example, are these multiple joint products to be separately valued? Then there is the problem of how the products of past labor relate to present activities of laboring. This becomes particularly important in the case of the value of machines: "a machine which is not active in the labour process is useless." The implication is that

> living labour must seize on these things, awaken them from the dead, change them from merely possible into real and effective use-values. Bathed in the fire of labour [and this is again Marx coming back to the centrality of labor as process] appropriated as part of its organism, and infused with vital energy for the performance of the functions appropriate to their concept and to their vocation in the process, [the machines] are indeed consumed, but to some purpose, as elements in the formation of new use-values, new products, which are capable of entering into individual consumption as means of subsistence or into a new labour process as means of production. (289–90)

It is, therefore, contact with living labor which resuscitates the value of the dead labor congealed in past products. This points to a vital distinction between productive and individual consumption. Productive consumption is past labor that gets consumed in a current labor process to make an entirely new use-value; individual consumption is what gets consumed by people as they reproduce themselves.

"The labour process," Marx argues in a concluding passage, "is purposeful activity aimed at the production of use-values. It is an appropriation of what exists in nature for the requirements of man. It is the universal condition for the metabolic interaction ... between man and nature" (note again how important this idea of metabolic interaction is in Marx's analysis), "the everlasting nature-imposed condition of human existence" (which is what he said back on page 133),

> or rather it is common to all forms of society in which human beings live. We did not, therefore, have to present the worker in his relationship with other workers; it was enough to present man and his labour on one side, nature and its materials on the other. The taste of porridge does not tell us who grew the oats, and the process we have presented does not reveal the conditions under which it takes place. (290)

What Marx has done in these few pages is to offer universal physical dissections and descriptions of the labor process independent of any social formation, stripped bare of any particular social meaning. I can describe somebody digging a ditch in all its physical detail, including its relation to past labor embodied in the shovel, but I can't tell from this description whether this is some nutty aristocrat who does it just for exercise, whether it's a peasant, whether it's a slave, whether it's a wage laborer or a convict. So there is a way to look at the labor process as a purely physical process without actually knowing anything whatsoever about the social relations in which it is embedded and without reference to the ideological and mental conceptions that arise within, say, a capitalist mode of production. What remains is to consider how capitalism makes distinctive use of these universal capacities and powers.

The Capitalist Form of the Labor Process

"Let us now return to our would-be capitalist. We left him just after he had purchased, in the open market, all the necessary factors of the labour process; its objective factors"—that is, the means of production—"as well as its personal factor, labour-power." Two conditions attach, however, to the contract between capital and labor in the buying and selling of labor-power as a commodity. The first is that "the worker works under the control of the capitalist to whom his labour belongs" (291). That is, when I enter into contract with a capitalist, the capitalist has the right to direct my work and assign my tasks. Now, there will likely be contestation over this if that work is dangerous to life and limb, but nevertheless, the general principle is that the laborer will get the money to survive and in return the capitalist can direct the laborer to do this or that. Labor-power is a commodity that belongs to the capitalist for the period of the contract. The second condition is that whatever the laborer produces during the period of the contract belongs to the capitalist, not to the laborer. Even though I am the one who makes the commodity and who embeds concrete labor and value in it, it does not belong to me. This is an interesting violation of the Lockean view that those who create value by mixing their labor with the land are entitled to private property in that value. In general, I think you can see that these two conditions amount to the total alienation (though Marx does not use that word here) of the laborer from the creative potential that attaches both to laboring and to the product. "From the instant he steps into the workshop, the use-value of his labour-power and therefore also its use, which is labour, belongs to the capitalist. By the purchase of the labour-power, the capitalist incorporates labour, as a living agent of fermentation"—again we encounter the *Grundrisse*'s "form-giving fire" of laboring as an activity—"into the lifeless constituents of the product, which also belong to him" (292).

These two conditions, however, permit the capitalist to so organize production as

> to produce a commodity greater in value than the sum of the values of the commodities used to produce it; namely the means of production and the labour-power he purchased with his good money on the open market. His aim is to produce not only a use-value, but a commodity; not only use-value, but value; and not just value, but also surplus-value.

So the capitalist brings together the "labour process and the process of creating value" to create a new kind of unity (293). This is what the capitalist has to do, this is the capitalist's conscious aim, because the origin of profit lies in surplus-value, and the role of the capitalist is to seek profit.

"Every condition of the problem is satisfied," says Marx,

> while the laws governing the exchange of commodities have not been violated in any way. Equivalent has been exchanged for equivalent. For the capitalist as buyer paid the full value for each commodity, for the cotton, for the spindle and for the labour-power. He then did what is done by every purchaser of commodities: he consumed their use-value.

In so doing, he is enabled to produce commodities with more value than those purchased at the outset, hence the production of surplus-value. "This whole course of events," Marx concludes, involves "the transformation of money into capital," in such a way that it "both takes place and does not take place in the sphere of circulation" (301–2). The materials and labor-power are bought in the marketplace at their value but put to work to congeal more value in the commodities produced in the process of production, out of sight of the marketplace. The conditions that are "satisfied" are those set out at the end of chapter 5: that the money owner "must buy his commodities at their value, sell them at their value, and yet at the end of the process withdraw more value from circulation than he threw into it at the beginning" (269). The result appears magical, because not only does capital appear able to lay golden eggs but

> by incorporating living labour into . . . lifeless objectivity, the capitalist simultaneously transforms value, i.e. past labour in its objectified and lifeless form, into capital, value which can perform its own valorization process, an animated monster which begins to 'work', 'as if its body were by love possessed' [here Marx quotes Faust]. (302)

The form of circulation looks like this:

$$M\text{—}C \begin{matrix} LP \\ \\ MP \end{matrix} \;\ldots\ldots\; P \;\ldots\ldots\ldots\; C\text{—}M + \Delta M$$

Let us look more closely at the different steps in this process. The capitalist has to buy means of production (MP): raw materials, machinery, semi-manufactured items, all products of past labor (congealed values). The capitalist has to pay for those commodities at their value according to the rules of exchange. If a spindle is needed, then the socially necessary labor-time embodied in spindles fixes value. If somebody uses a gold spindle, then that is not socially necessary. For the labor process to work, the capitalist requires adequate access to means of production in the marketplace. What the purchase of labor-power (LP) enables is the reanimation of these "dead" means of production through the process of laboring (P).

> During the labour process, the worker's labour constantly undergoes a transformation, from the form of unrest . . . into that of being . . . , from the form of motion . . . into that of objectivity . . . At the end of one hour,

> the spinning motion is represented in a certain quantity of yarn; in other words, a definite quantity of labour, namely that of one hour, has been objectified in the cotton. We say labour, i.e. the expenditure of his vital force by the spinner, and not spinning labour, because the special work of spinning counts here only in so far as it is the expenditure of labour-power in general, and not the specific labour of the spinner. (296)

In other words, it is abstract labor which is being incorporated into this act of spinning, it is value being added in the form of socially necessary labor-time congealed in the yarn. The result is that

> definite quantities of product, quantities which are determined by experience, now represent nothing but definite quantities of labour, definite masses of crystallized labour-time. They are now simply the material shape taken by a given number of hours or days of social labour. (297)

Furthermore, "in the process we are now considering it is of extreme importance that no more time be consumed in the work of transforming the cotton into yarn than is necessary under the given social conditions" (296).

But at the end of the workday, if all goes well, the capitalists find themselves, magically, in possession of surplus-value. The "capitalist stares in astonishment," writes Marx with heavy irony. Should not the value of the product be "equal to the value of the capital advanced," a simple adding up of all the values of the inputs (297)? Where does the surplus-value come from, given the law of equivalence in exchanges? "The road to hell," writes Marx with equal irony, "is paved with good intentions" (298).

So the capitalists look for virtuous reasons to explain the surplus-value. First off, consider abstinence. Capitalists abstain from present consumption and invest the money they save. Do they not deserve some reward for their abstinence? This is a theme that echoes loudly in the long debate over the role of the Protestant ethic in the rise of capitalism. Second, capitalists provide employment to people. If capitalists didn't invest their money, there would be no employment. Poor workers! Capitalists are doing them a favor by investing their money. Don't the capitalists deserve some rate of return for that? This is a pretty general and on the surface rather convincing argument—does not investment create jobs? I used to have this argument with my mother all the time. She'd say, "But of course we need capitalists!" I'd say, "Why, why?" And she'd say, "Who would employ workers if we didn't have capitalists?" She could not imagine that there might be other ways in which you could employ people. "Capitalists are vital," she would say, "and it is very important we keep them around and treat them nicely, because if they didn't employ laborers, the world would become a terrible place—look what happened in the 1930s!" The third argument is that capitalists say they work hard. They set up the production process, manage things, put in their own labor-time and take all this risk. Yes, indeed, many capitalists work, and some of them work hard, but when they work they usually pay themselves twice over, i.e., they pay themselves the rate of return on the capital they invest and they pay themselves as managers. They pay themselves as CEOs and then take stock options.

Marx regards all these explanations as subterfuges and conjuring tricks:

> The whole litany [the capitalist] has just recited was simply meant to pull the wool over our eyes. He himself does not care twopence for it. He leaves this and all similar subterfuges and conjuring tricks to the professors of political economy, who are paid for it. He himself is a practical man, and although he does not always consider what he says outside his business, within his business he knows what he is doing. (300)

Capitalists may indeed be frugal and abstain, and they may also sometimes exhibit a benevolent attitude toward their workers (desperately trying to maintain their workforce in employment when times are bad, for example). Marx's point is that capitalists could not possibly sustain the whole system by appeals to virtue, morality or benevolence, that the individual behavior of capitalists, varying from benevolence to vicious greed, is irrelevant to what capitalists must do in order to be capitalists, which is, quite simply, to procure surplus-value. Furthermore, their role is defined, as Marx will later point out, by "coercive laws of competition," which push all capitalists to behave in similar fashion no matter whether they are good people or proverbial capitalist pigs.

The full answer to the problem of explaining surplus-value follows. You pay the value of labor-power, which is set, recall, by the value of the commodities needed to reproduce the laborer at a given standard of living. The laborer sells the commodity labor-power, gets money, then goes and gets that bundle of commodities needed to live. But it will only take a certain number of hours each day for the laborer to reproduce the equivalent of the value of labor-power. Therefore, "the daily cost of maintaining labour-power" and its daily creation of value are two totally different things. "The former determines the exchange-value of the labour-power, the latter is its use-value." Labor, recall, is in the C-M-C circuit, while capital is in the M-C-M + ΔM circuit.

> The fact that half a day's labour is necessary to keep the worker alive during 24 hours does not in any way prevent him from working a whole day. Therefore the value of labour-power, and the value which that labour-power valorizes . . . in the labour-process, are two entirely different magnitudes; and this difference was what the capitalist had in mind when he was purchasing the labour-power . . . What was really decisive for him was the specific use-value which this commodity possesses of being a source not only of value, but of more value than it has itself. This is the specific service the capitalist expects from labour-power, and in this transaction he acts in accordance with the eternal laws of commodity-exchange. In fact, the seller of labour-power [the laborer], like the seller of any other commodity, realizes . . . its exchange-value, and alienates . . . its use-value. (300–1)

There is a key distinction between what labor gets and what labor creates. Surplus-value results from the difference between the value labor congeals in commodities in a working day and the value the laborer gets for surrendering labor-power as a commodity to the capitalist. Laborers, in short, are paid the value of labor-power, and that is that. The capitalist then puts them to work in such a way that not only do they reproduce the value of their own labor-power, they also produce surplus-value. The use-value of labor-power to the capitalist is that it is the one commodity that can produce value and hence surplus-value.

There are, of course, lots of subtleties to be considered. We know from the previous chapter, for example, that the value of labor-power is not a fixed magnitude but varies according to physical needs, the degree of civilization in a country, the state of class struggle and all the rest of it. So the value of labor-power in Sweden is radically different from that in Thailand or China. But Marx, in order to simplify the analysis, here assumes the value of labor-power is a fixed *datum*. And in a given society at a given time, we can say roughly what the value of labor-power is. This allows Marx to presume that capitalists will pay the full value of that labor-power (even though they may struggle mightily in practice to pay their workers less) and still use it, whatever that full value is, to create surplus-value by milking the gap between what labor gets and the value that labor makes. This gap can be procured because the capitalist has control over (a) what the laborer does in the factory and (b) the product. But hidden within this argument is another variable that Marx has yet to analyze explicitly: how long is the laborer contracted to work during the day? If laborers produce the equivalent value of their labor-power in six hours, then plainly the capitalist can procure surplus-value only by contracting them to work more hours than that. If the workday is ten hours, then the capitalist gains four hours' worth of surplus-value. This is what permits the extraction of surplus-value in a way that does not in any way violate the rules of exchange.

It is at this point that we need to remind ourselves of the duality of Marx's project. What he wishes to show here is that even in a perfected liberal society where all the rules of exchange are perfectly obeyed, capitalists have a way of extracting surplus-value from laborers. The liberal utopia turns out to be not so utopian after all, but potentially dystopian for the laborers. Marx is not saying that wage determination actually works this way, but that the theses of classical liberal political economy (and this carries over to our neoliberal times) are seriously warped in favor of capital. The world of freedom, equality, property and Bentham is a mask, a ruse, to permit the extraction of surplus-value from laborers without violating the laws of exchange.

Marx, having set out his fundamental theorem—that surplus-value originates from the difference between what labor gets for its labor-power as a commodity and what the laborer produces in a labor process under the command of capital—immediately states a host of caveats. He observes, for example, that "the time spent in production counts only in so far as it is socially necessary for the production of a use-value," and this depends on labor-power functioning under "normal conditions." This raises the question: what is normal? The labor-power should, moreover, be of "normal effectiveness," again leaving open the question of what normal is, except to say that this will vary from one trade to another and that it means possessing "the average skill, dexterity and speed prevalent in that trade." The labor must also

> be expended with the average amount of exertion and the usual degree of intensity; and the capitalist is as careful to see this is done, as he is to ensure that his workmen are not idle for a single moment. (303)

The casual introduction of the question of "usual intensity" here is significant, for it erupts later as a crucial aspect of labor control because "moments" are "the elements of profit" (352). In all this, the capitalist "insists on his rights" under the law of exchanges, to full use of the commodity that has been purchased and the right to penalize those who do not cooperate fully with his desires. These rights include that labor not be wasted, that

> all wasteful consumption of raw material or instruments of labour is strictly forbidden, because what is wasted in this way represents a superfluous expenditure of quantities of objectified labour, labour that does not count in the product or enter into its value. (303)

What we here see outlined is a charter covering the capitalist control over the labor process, and it is through the implementation of these controls that the question of what is socially necessary in the labor process becomes more clearly defined. The outcome is, surprise, a duality!

> The production process, considered as the unity of the labour process and the process of creating value, is the process of production of commodities; considered as the unity of the labour process and the process of valorization, it is the capitalist process of production, or the capitalist form of the production of commodities. (304)

Again, Marx distinguishes between the production of commodities in general and the specific capitalist form which uses commodity production to gain surplus-value, thus establishing a different kind of unity.

Finally, he returns to the fraught question of how to account for the impact of skill differentiations within the labor process. Skilled labor is considered as simple labor "with a higher specific gravity as it were." This is labor of "a more costly kind, labour-power whose production has cost more time and labour than unskilled or simple labour-power, and which therefore has a higher value," and in turn "becomes objectified, during an equal amount of time, in proportionally higher values" (304–5). In the footnote (305), however, he points out that many of these skill distinctions are illusory or arbitrary and themselves determined socially and historically. There is a long history of this, which Marx briefly alludes to but which could do with some elaboration. I found in my own work on Second Empire Paris, for example, that the definition of "skill" was highly gendered. Any work that women could do was viewed as unskilled, so when women began to enter a trade, the effect was to deskill the labor. This partly accounts for the hostility of some artisanal groups to women's employment and for Proudhon's insistence that women did not belong in the workshop but should stay at home. The issue of women's employment then became a major source of tension within the First International in the 1860s. This does not help, however, with the issue of how to account for labor which is highly trained and therefore costly to produce and maintain. Marx again bypasses this thorny issue by assuming that "in every process of creating value," the "higher type of labour" can be reduced to "average simple labour" and that we can thereby assume "that the labour of the worker employed by the capitalist is average simple labour" (306). There are in fact some serious difficulties with this argument, which is known as the reduction-from-skilled-to-simple-labor problem. But I, too, will bypass it here, leaving you with a question mark to be examined later.

The lengthy footnote on the relationship between slavery and wage labor (303–4) deserves some comment. When the two labor systems collide and become competititve with each other, the effects are particularly pernicious. Slavery becomes more brutal under the competitive lash of market integrations into capitalism, while, conversely, slavery exerts strong negative pressures on both wages and conditions of work. Any kind of human relationship that might have previously existed between master and slave will likely be destroyed. Of course, slavery varies a great deal in what it is about, but it is not about the production of value in the sense that Marx means it. It entails a different kind of labor process. There is no abstract labor in a pure slave system. This was why Aristotle could not formulate a labor theory of value—because this theory only works in the case of free labor. Remember, value for Marx is not universal but specific to wage labor within a capitalist mode of production.

CHAPTERS 8 & 9: CONSTANT CAPITAL, VARIABLE CAPITAL AND THE RATE OF SURPLUS-VALUE

In the next two chapters, Marx seeks to both clarify and consolidate his theory of surplus-value, a theory that, as Engels notes in his introduction to Volume II of *Capital*, "struck home like a thunderbolt out of a clear sky." These chapters are not complicated, so I will go over them fairly lightly.

Marx first establishes a distinction between what he calls constant and variable capital. Constant capital is past labor already congealed in commodities that are used as means of production in a current labor process. The value of the means of production is already given, and so the question is what happens to that value when it is incorporated into the new labor process. Marx argues that the value simply gets transferred into the new commodity. This value varies according to the productivity of those industries producing raw materials, machinery, etc., so to call this capital "constant" is not to regard it as fixed. All Marx wants to signal here is that the value of the means of production flows through the labor process to be congealed in the new commodity. The value remains constant as it flows.

The actual process of transfer of value is complicated by a variety of special circumstances. Cotton goes into a shirt, and in this instance the cotton physically ends up being the substance of the shirt, so it is reasonable to say that the value of the cotton is incorporated into the shirt. But the energy used in producing the shirt doesn't end up in the shirt. And you certainly wouldn't like it if bits of a machine ended up in the shirt. A distinction exists, therefore, between the physical transfers and the circulation of values. The two circulation processes are different because cotton is a physical, material use-value but value is immaterial and social (but nevertheless, as was earlier argued, objective). The raw materials also contain a certain amount of past value, as do the machines and other instruments of labor. All these accumulated past values are brought into a new production process in the form of dead labor that living labor reanimates. So the laborer in effect preserves the values already congealed in raw materials, partially manufactured products, machines and the like and does so by using them up (in productive consumption). Marx is going to make a great deal of the fact that the laborer does this favor for the capitalist gratis.

These past use-values and their congealed values don't and can't create anything new. They are simply used and preserved. Machines, for example, cannot create value. This is an important point, since it is often held, fetishistically, that machines are a source of value. But in Marx's accounting schema, they absolutely are not. All that happens is that the value of the machine is transferred into the commodity during the labor process. But with machines there is a problem, because a machine may last for twenty years, and you are producing lots of shirts with it, so the question is how much of the value of the machine ends up in each shirt? The simplest way to account for the flow of value from the machine into the shirt is to say that, for example, one-twentieth of the value of a machine that lasts twenty years will flow each year into the shirts produced in that year. The labor process preserves all these values by passing them through into the commodity to be sold on the market. This can happen, notice, only because value is immaterial but objective, so it is open to being socially accounted for in this way.

Then there is the variable capital, the value given over to hiring the laborers. How does this circulate, and with what consequences? Dead labor is resuscitated and passed on into the value of the new commodity by living labor. This is a very important idea for Marx, and you can see immediately its political significance. Laborers have the power to destroy constant capital (e.g., machines) simply by refusing to work with it. If labor is withdrawn (and "productive consumption" ceases), then the transfer of capital from the machine to the final product stops, and the value of the constant capital is decreased or totally lost. Clearly, the laborer is potentially empowered by this, and to the degree that laborers perform this function they should surely claim some sort of remuneration for so doing. After all, if capitalists can argue for the right to surplus-value on the grounds that they bring employment to laborers, why cannot laborers argue that they deserve surplus-value because without their efforts all the constant capital held by capitalists would be valueless?

The laborers also add value by congealing socially necessary labor-time in products. But the value they create has two components. First, the laborers have to produce enough value to cover the costs of their own hiring. This, when rendered into money-form, permits the reproduction of labor-power at a given standard of living in a given place and time. The laborers spend their money to buy the commodities they want, need or desire in order to live. In this way, variable capital literally circulates through the body of the laborer in the C-M-C circulation process that reproduces the living laborer through individual consumption and social reproduction. The second aspect of variable capital concerns the production of surplus-value, the production of value over and above that which would be required to reproduce the laborers at a given standard of living. This surplus-value produces and reproduces the capitalist. Marx is, in effect, proposing a value-added theory of surplus-value production.

The total value of the commodity is made up of the value of constant and variable capitals plus the surplus-value (c + v + s). If the capitalist is to gain surplus-value, then it is the variable part that needs to be controlled. After all, machines don't go on strike, and machines don't behave in cantankerous ways (though they can sometimes appear to be temperamental). The active element in the labor process is variable capital. This is the "form-giving fire" of living labor applied to production. Again, there is a political point to this argument. "Look, dear workers," Marx is saying, "*you* are the ones who are really doing all the work here. You are the ones who preserve values from the past. You are the ones who reproduce yourselves by way of your laboring. And you are the ones who produce the surplus-value that capital appropriates so that capitalists can live, all too often in luxury. Obviously, it is very much in the interest of the capitalists to make sure that you don't recognize your central role and your massive powers. They prefer that you imagine yourself just going out and getting a job with a decent wage so that you can go home and reproduce yourself and your family, preferably fit enough to come back to work the next day. You are in a C-M-C circulation process, and they think you should confine your ambitions to that station in life." Marx wants to counter this deliberate fetishization by alerting the working class to its true position in relation to surplus-value production and capital accumulation.

So the full circulation process of capital has been defined, and the definitions of constant and variable capital are laid out. "That part of capital," he writes in summary form,

> which is turned into means of production, i.e. the raw material, the auxiliary material and the instruments of labour, does not undergo any quantitative alteration of value in the process of production. For this reason, I call it the constant part of capital, or more briefly, constant capital . . . On the other hand, that part of capital which is turned into labour-power does undergo an alteration of value in the process of production. It both reproduces the equivalent of its own value and produces an excess, a surplus-value . . . I therefore call it the variable part of capital, or more briefly, variable capital. (317)

This leads into chapter 9, where Marx uses the categories he has just defined and examines the relationships between them in a more structured way. He here puts his accounting hat back on. Ostensibly, he is looking "for an exact expression" of the degree of exploitation of labor-power. But there are several ratio measures he comes up with that are of interest. Consider, for example, the ratio of constant to variable capital, c/v. This ratio is a measure of the productivity of labor, the value of means of production that a single value unit of labor-power can transform. The higher the ratio, the more productive the labor. Then consider the ratio of surplus-value to variable capital, s/v. This measures the rate of exploitation of labor-power. It is the amount of surplus-value that a single value unit of labor-power can produce. The higher the ratio, the greater the exploitation of labor-power. Finally, there is the rate of profit, which is the ratio of the surplus-value to the total value used (constant plus variable capital) or s/(c + v). The rate of profit is different from the rate of exploitation. The latter captures how much extra labor the laborers give up to the capitalist in return for the value they receive to reproduce themselves at a given standard of living. Of course, you can see straight away that the rate of profit is always lower than the rate of exploitation. If you complain about a high rate of exploitation, then the capitalists may show you their books to prove that their rate of profit is low. So you then are supposed to feel sorry for the capitalist and forget the high rate of exploitation! The more constant capital employed, the lower the rate of profit (with everything else held equal). A low rate of profit can accompany a high rate of exploitation. This is going to be a crucial argument for Volume III of *Capital*. Capitalists themselves work on the basis of the rate of profit, and they tend to allocate their capital according to wherever the rate of profit is highest. The result is a tendency (driven by competition) toward the equalization of the rate of profit. If I look at a situation and I think I can get a higher rate of profit over there, I take my capital over there. But that doesn't necessarily lead me to make good decisions from the standpoint of maximizing the rate of exploitation, which is the key element the capitalist should be interested in. In fact, this is where the fetishism of the system captures the capitalist. Even if capitalists recognized all this, there wouldn't be anything they could do about it. Competition drives them to make decisions on the basis of the rate of profit rather than the rate of exploitation. If they go to a bank to borrow money, then the bank will make its decisions based on the rate of profit, not on the rate of exploitation.

> Of course, the ratio of surplus-value not only to that portion of the capital from which it directly arises, and whose change in value it represents, but also to the sum total of the capital advanced, is economically of very great importance. We shall therefore deal exhaustively with this ratio in our third book. (323)

In Volume III, Marx seeks to show that this is one of the mechanisms that drives capitalism into periodic crises of falling rates of profit. I cannot elaborate on this here any more than Marx can, so all I want to emphasize at this point is that you should carefully note the distinction between the rate of profit, $s/(c + v)$, and the rate of exploitation, s/v.

For Marx, and for the workers, it is the rate of exploitation that really matters. Furthermore, an understanding of the dynamics of capitalism requires an analysis of the rate of exploitation rather than the rate of profit. So this is what Marx concentrates on in this chapter. The rate of exploitation can, he says, be looked at in a number of different ways. You can think of it as the relationship between surplus-labor (appropriated by the capitalist) and necessary labor (the labor required to reproduce the value of labor-power), as necessary labor-time in relation to surplus labor-time or, more formally, as the ratio of the value laid out to purchase labor-power versus the total value produced minus that paid for labor-power. The problem, however, is that while all these ratios make sense, there is no way we can observe them in practice. It is not as if a bell rings the moment in the working day when laborers have reproduced the value of v (or spent the time necessary to produce v), so they know that thereafter they are producing surplus-value for (or giving over their time free to) the capitalist. The labor process is a continuous process which ends with a commodity whose value is composed of $c + v + s$.

While the different elements of value congealed in the commodity are invisible to the naked eye, Marx is going to make the claim, which you may not like, that this mode of analysis actually produces a far better science of political economy precisely because it gets beyond the fetishism of the market. The bourgeoisie had produced good enough science from the standpoint of the market, but they don't understand how the system works from the standpoint of the labor process, and to the degree that they do, they plainly want to disguise it. They have a vested interest in saying to the workers that labor is just one factor of production that you bring to market, and that is your contribution, for which you will receive a fair remuneration at the going wage rate. They cannot possibly concede that labor is the form-giving, fluid, creative fire in the transformation of nature that lies at the heart of any mode of production, including capitalism. Nor can one imagine the capitalist praising workers for all the value they produce, including, of course, the surplus-value that underpins capitalist profit.

Marx ends this chapter with a fantastic piece critiquing a typical bourgeois representation of the world of laboring. This arose when

> one fine morning in the year 1836, Nassau W. Senior . . . a man famed both for his economic science and his beautiful style, was summoned from Oxford to Manchester, to learn in the latter place the political economy he taught in the former. (333)

The Manchester industrialists were upset at the political agitation to limit the length of the working day to a "civilized" ten hours, after the shallow and not very effective Factory Act of 1833 had shown that the state apparatus was at least in principle prepared to legislate the legal hours of laboring. Senior argued in a detailed pamphlet that what the worker had to do during the first eight hours of the day was to produce the equivalent value of all the means of production used up (constant capital, in Marx's terms). So Senior had no concept that the worker might be transferring the values already congealed in commodities and took the ludicrous view that the worker had to actively reproduce those values. The next three hours were taken up reproducing the value of the labor-power employed (the variable capital), and only in the final hour was the profit of the capitalist (the surplus-value) produced. Therefore, a twelve-hour day was absolutely essential to gaining a profit. If the length of the working day were reduced from twelve to eleven hours then all the profit would disappear, and industry would cease to function. Marx's response is scathing: "and the professor calls this an 'analysis'!" he exclaims (334). "Senior's last hour" is a vulgar economic argument, solely designed to promote the interests of the manufacturers.

In a funny kind of way, however, Senior confirms Marx's own theorization. It is the workers' time that is of crucial value to the capitalists, and that is why they so desperately need that twelfth hour. The struggle to command the worker's time lies at the origin of profit, which is exactly what Marx's theory of surplus-value posits. This reaffirms the relevance of Marx's definition of value as socially necessary labor-*time*.

What, then, is socially necessary about the temporalities of laboring? Not only must capitalists command the labor process, the product and the time of the laborer, but they must also strive to command the social nature of temporality itself. Senior recognizes this fundamental truth, and Marx, using his critical tools and his situatedness on the side of the workers, turns the dross of Senior's argument into a revelatory moment. The critique of Senior's last hour therefore acquires a double significance. On the one hand, it allows Marx to depict the depths to which the economists can sink in trying to create apologetic arguments for the capitalist class, while on the other it neatly positions Marx to take on the fundamental truth revealed by Senior's polemic: that command over time is a central vector of struggle within a capitalist mode of production. The examination of Senior's last hour therefore makes for a crafty transition to the next chapter, which is all about capitalist time.

CHAPTER FIVE

The Working Day

CHAPTER 10: THE WORKING DAY

Chapter 10 is constructed in a different way and written in a different style than are the preceding chapters. It is light on theory and laden with historical detail. Yet it also invokes abstract categories not yet encountered. This is so because Marx here focuses on the history of class struggle over the length of the working day. I have commented before on the complex interweaving of logical and historical argumentation in *Capital* and for the most part argued that we are on safer ground with the logical argument. But here it is the historical narrative that counts—though it is not bereft of theoretical significance. We here encounter a deep theorization of the nature of time and temporality under capitalism at the same time as we more clearly see why a capitalist mode of production is necessarily constituted through and by class struggle.

Marx begins by reminding us that there is a world of difference between the labor theory of value and the value of labor-power. The labor theory of value deals with how socially necessary labor-time is congealed in commodities by the laborer. This is the standard of value represented by the money commodity and by money in general. The value of labor-power, on the other hand, is simply the value of that commodity sold in the market as labor-power. While this commodity is like other commodities in certain respects, it also has some special qualities because there here enters in a historical and moral element. A failure to distinguish between the value of labor-power and the labor theory of value can generate fundamental misunderstandings.

"We began with the assumption," writes Marx, "that labour-power is bought and sold at its value" and that "its value, like that of all other commodities, is determined by the labour time necessary to produce it" (340). This is equivalent to the labor-time taken to produce those commodities needed to reproduce the laborer at a given standard of living. Marx assumes that this value is fixed, even though we know (as does he) that it is perpetually changing, depending on the costs of commodities, the state of civilization and the state of class struggle.

As workers add value to commodities in the labor process, there arrives a point in the day when workers will have created the exact equivalent of the value of their own labor-power. Let us suppose, says Marx, that this occurs after six hours of laboring. Surplus-value arises because workers labor beyond the number of hours it takes to reproduce the value equivalent of their labor-power. How many extra hours do they work? That depends on the length of the working day. This length is not something that can be negotiated in the market as a form of commodity exchange in which equivalent exchanges for equivalent (as is the case with wages). It is not a fixed but a fluid quantity. It can vary from six hours to ten hours to twelve hours to fourteen hours, with an outer limit of twenty-four hours—which is impossible because of "the physical limits to labour-power," and because "the worker needs time in which to satisfy his intellectual and social requirements . . . The length of the working day therefore fluctuates within boundaries both physical and social" (341).

Marx then sets up a fictitious discussion between a capitalist and a laborer. The capitalist, as purchaser of the labor-power, says he has the right to use it as long as he can. He is, after all, "only capital personified" (recall that Marx deals with roles, not persons). "His soul is the soul of capital," and "capital has one sole driving force, the drive to valorize itself, to create surplus-value." Capital, Marx says, "is dead labour which, vampire-like"—and this is a chapter where we'll get a lot of vampires and werewolves running around, a major departure from usual modes of political-economic theorizing—"lives only by sucking living labour, and lives the more, the more labour it sucks." If the laborer calls time-out or takes time off, "he robs the capitalist . . . The capitalist therefore takes his stand on the law of commodity-exchange. Like all other buyers, he seeks to extract the maximum possible benefit from the use-value of his commodity" (342).

Workers, unlike machines and other forms of constant capital, answer back. They note that they own this property called labor-power and that their interest is to conserve its value for future use. The capitalist has no right to squeeze so much out of them in each day as to shorten their working life. This is, says the worker,

> against our contract and the law of commodity exchange. I therefore demand a working day of normal length, and I demand it without any appeal to your heart, for in money matters sentiment is out of place . . . I

> demand a normal working day because, like every other seller, I demand the value of my commodity. (343)

Notice, both workers and capitalists take their positions according to the laws of exchange. Marx is not, as you might expect from a revolutionary thinker, advocating abolition of the wages system, but has both the workers and the capitalists agree to abide by the laws of market exchange, equivalent for equivalent. The only issue concerns how much use-value (the capacity for congealing values in commodities) the laborer is going to give up to the capitalist. Marx makes this move because, as I have emphasized, a key objective in *Capital* is to deconstruct the utopian propositions of classical liberal political economy on their own terms. "The capitalist maintains his right as a purchaser when he tries to make the working day as long as possible," and

> the worker maintains his right as a seller when he wishes to reduce the working day to a particular normal length. There is here therefore an antinomy, of right against right, both equally bearing the seal of the law of exchange. Between equal rights, force decides. Hence, in the history of capitalist production, the establishment of a norm for the working day presents itself as a struggle over the limits of that day, a struggle between collective capital, i.e. the class of capitalists, and collective labour, i.e. the working class. (344)

So finally, after 344 pages, we get to the idea of class struggle. Finally!

There are a number of issues that call for clarification here. The acceptance by both sides of a notion of "rights" is a statement of fact concerning the hegemony of bourgeois notions of rights. But Marx immediately indicates that the problem of the length of the working day cannot be solved by appeal to rights and the laws and legalities of exchange (this parallels his earlier attack on Proudhon's concept of eternal justice). Issues of this kind can be resolved only through class struggle, in which "force" decides between "equal rights." This finding has ramifications for understanding the politics of contemporary capitalism. In recent times, there has been a remarkable upsurge in "rights talk," and a lot of political energy has been invested in the idea that the pursuit of individual human rights is a way (if not *the* way) to shape a more humane capitalist system. What Marx is signaling here is that there is no way that many of the important questions posed in rights terms can be resolved without being reformulated in class-struggle terms. Amnesty International, for example, deals well enough with political and civil rights but has a hard time extending its concerns to economic rights because there is no way that these can be resolved without taking a side, either that of capital or that of labor. So you can see Marx's point. There is no way to adjudicate "fairly" between equal rights (both bearing the seal of the law of exchange). All you can do is to fight for your side of the argument. This chapter therefore ends on a very skeptical note about some "pompous catalogue of 'the inalienable rights of man,'" as opposed to what can be achieved through class struggle (416).

"Force," in this context, doesn't necessarily mean physical force (though there have clearly been instances when this has been crucial). The main thrust of this chapter concerns political force, the capacity to mobilize and to build political alliances and institutions (such as trade unions) to influence a state apparatus that has the power to legislate a "normal" working day. In Marx's account, there are moments of possibility that can be grasped or lost, depending on the contingencies of the political situation and the relations of force in play. The technique here is similar to that so superbly represented in Marx's study in *The Eighteenth Brumaire* of how Louis Bonaparte came to power in France in the wake of the failed 1848 revolution in Paris. The materials in this chapter shed a special light on Marx's way of jointly pursuing a theory of a capitalist mode of production on the one hand and a deep understanding of processes of historical transformation of actually existing capitalist social formations on the other. Class-struggle outcomes are not determined in advance.

The introduction of class struggle marks a radical departure from the tenets of both classical and contemporary economic theory. It radically changes the language in which the economy is depicted and shifts the focus of concern. Introductory courses in economics are unlikely ever to focus on the length of the working day as a serious issue. It was not discussed in classical political economy, either. Yet historically there has been a monumental and ongoing struggle over the length of the working day, the working week, the working year (paid vacations) and the working life (the retirement age), and this struggle is still with us. This is clearly a fundamental aspect of capitalist history and a central issue in a capitalist mode of production. What are we to make of economic theories that ignore it?

Marx's value theory, in contrast, leads directly into this central question. This is so because value is socially necessary labor-*time*, which means that time is of the essence within capitalism. As the old saying has it, "Time is money!" Control over time, other people's time in particular, has to be collectively fought over. It cannot be traded. Class struggle therefore has to move center stage in political-economic theory as well as into all attempts to understand the historical and geographical evolution of capitalism. It is at this point in *Capital* that we can start to appreciate the "use-value" of Marx's labor theory of value and of surplus-value. And while it would be wrong to treat this as some kind of empirical proof of the theoretical apparatus, it certainly illustrates its utility when it comes to the practice of theoretically informed empirical inquiry.

So how, then, does Marx lead us through this history of struggle over the length of the working day? He begins by noting that capitalism is not the only kind of society in which surplus labor and a surplus product is extracted for the benefit of some ruling class:

> Wherever a part of society possesses the monopoly of the means of production, the worker, free or unfree, must add to the labour-time necessary for his own maintenance an extra quantity of labour-time in order to produce the means of subsistence for the owner of the means of production. (344)

But under capitalism, surplus labor is converted into surplus-value. So the production of a surplus product is a means for the capitalist to gain surplus-value. This imposes particular qualities on capitalist exploitation because value accumulation in money-form, as we earlier saw, is without limit.

> In any economic formation of society where the use-value rather than the exchange-value of the product predominates, surplus labour will be restricted by a more or less confined set of needs, and . . . no boundless thirst for surplus labour will arise from the character of production itself. (345)

Furthermore, because this appropriation occurs in a society characterized by wage labor, laborers are not going to experience their surplus-value production in the same way that serfs and slaves experience surplus labor (the fetishism of market exchange hides it). Marx uses the *corvée* system in central Europe as an illustration. Here, the laborer was forced to contribute a certain number of labor days to the landowner such that the appropriation of surplus labor is totally transparent. The freeing of the serfs through the Russian edict of 1831 actually created a situation in which the *corvée* system that replaced it, organized under the *Règlement organique*, allowed certain definitions of a day's work to be made fluid and open. The landowners (the boyars) argued that a day's labor is not measured by an actual day, but by how much work *should* be accomplished. This work requirement could not possibly be done in a day, so that it took more and more actual days to do a formal day's work, until "the 12 *corvée* days of the *Règlement organique* ... amount to 365 days in the year" (348).

There is the germ of a very important idea here which we are going to encounter several times in *Capital*. The measure of time is flexible, it can be stretched out and manipulated for social purposes. In this instance, 12 labor days become 365 actual days. This social manipulation of time and temporality is a fundamental feature of capitalism also. As soon as the extraction of surplus labor-time becomes fundamental to the replication of class relations, then the question of what time is, who measures it, and how temporality is to be understood moves to the forefront of analysis. Time is not simply given; it is socially constructed and perpetually subject to reconstruction (just think, for example, how time horizons for decision making in, say, the financial sector have shifted in recent years). In the *Règlement organique* case, the stretching of time was obvious. Laborers knew full well how much surplus labor they were giving up to the lord and how time stretching by a ruling class contributed to this result. But the thrust of the Factory Acts in Britain in the nineteenth century—the centerpiece of much of this chapter—was very different: it was to "curb capital's drive towards a limitless draining away of labour-power by forcibly limiting the working day on the authority of the state, but a state ruled by capitalist and landlord" (348).

Marx's formulation poses an important question: why would a state ruled by capitalist and landlord agree to, or even contemplate, curbing the length of the working day? So far in *Capital* we have only encountered the figures of the laborer and the capitalist, so what on earth is the landlord doing here? Clearly, as Marx seeks to analyze a real historical situation, he has to look at the existing class configuration and how class alliances might work when the workers do not have direct access to state power. The British state in the first half of the nineteenth century was essentially organized through the power relation of capitalists and landlords, and it would have been impossible to analyze the politics of the period without paying attention to the role of the landed aristocracy. The power of the working-class movement was in the background. "Apart from the daily more threatening advance of the working-class movement," Marx writes,

> the limiting of factory labour was dictated by the same necessity as forced the manuring of English fields with guano. The same blind desire for profit that in the one case exhausted the soil had in the other case seized hold of the vital force of the nation at its roots. Periodical epidemics speak as clearly on this point as the diminishing military standard of height in France and Germany. (348)

If labor is a key resource, like the land, in the creation of national wealth, and if it is overexploited and degraded, then the capacity to continue production of surplus-value is undercut. But it is also in the state's interest to have laborers who can become an effective military force. The health and fitness of the working classes is therefore of political and military interest (as is remarked in the lengthy footnote [348–9]). In the Franco-Prussian War of 1870–1, for example, the rapid defeat of the French at the hands of the Germans was in part attributed to the superior health of the German peasantry relative to the impoverished French peasantry and working class. The political implication is that it is militarily dangerous to permit the degradation of the working classes. This issue became important in the US during World War II, particularly when it came to mobilizing elements from impoverished and in some instances racially distinct populations.

The British Factory Acts, which Marx focuses on, were imposed by the state and designed for both economic and political/military reasons, to limit the exploitation of living labor and prevent its excessive degradation. The law is one thing, but enforcement is another. This brings us to the important figure of the factory inspectors: who were they and where did they came from? They were certainly not radical Marxists! They came from the professional bourgeoisie. They were civil servants. But they did a pretty good job of collecting information, and they pushed hard to discipline the industrial interest according to state requirements. Marx would not have been able to write this chapter without the abundant information they supplied. So why would a state regulated by capital and landlords employ factory inspectors to do this work? This is where "the degree of civilization in a country" enters into the picture, as well as bourgeois morality and the military concerns of the state. In nineteenth-century Britain, there were strong currents of bourgeois reformism (e.g., Charles Dickens) that thought some of the labor practices then in play should not exist in any civilized society. This introduces into the discussion that same "historical and moral element" which affects the value of labor-power. So while the working-class movement was indeed growing stronger, it would not have gotten as far as it did without the assistance of bourgeois reformism, particularly that strain represented by the factory inspectors.

The factory inspectors had to confront the problem of how the working day might be defined in practice. At what times should laborers get to work? Is the start-up time inside the factory or outside the factory? And what about breaks for lunch? Marx quotes an inspectors' report:

> 'The profit to be gained by it' (over-working in violation of the Act) 'appears to be, to many, a greater temptation than they can resist' . . . These 'small thefts' of capital from the workers' meal-times and recreation times are also described by the factory inspectors as 'petty pilferings of minutes', 'snatching a few minutes' or, in the technical language of the workers, 'nibbling and cribbling at meal-times'.

Marx then quotes the key idea: "'Moments are the elements of profit'" (352). I think this a crucial formulation. Capitalists seek to capture every moment of the worker's time in the labor process. Capitalists do not simply buy a worker's labor-power for twelve hours; they have to make sure every moment of those twelve hours is used at maximum intensity. And this, of course, is what a factory disciplinary and supervisory system is all about.

If you can believe old movies, telephone operators once had time to chat with you (I am old enough to remember even flirting with them). Operators now have a strict schedule of calls to handle every hour. If they don't meet that schedule, they get fired. And the schedule is constantly tightening, so you are now privileged if you can claim more than two minutes of their time. I've read about an operator who spent half an hour on the phone with a child whose mother evidently had died; the operator was fired for failing to keep to schedule. This is characteristic of labor processes generally. The capitalist wants the time, wants those moments that are the elements of profit. This is a corollary of the fact that value is socially necessary labor-*time*. For all its abstractness, the value theory reveals something important about daily practices and experiences on the shop floor. It touches the reality of how the capitalist behaves, and it touches the reality of the worker's life.

In the third section of this chapter, Marx discusses at length "Branches of English Industry without Legal Limits to Exploitation." I am not going to go over these, because the appalling accounts of the labor practices in the match industry, wallpaper, linens and baking in particular (where night work and the adulteration of the bread were a big issues) are fairly self-evident. Marx also cites the accidents that can come from overwork, such as one on the railways where the coroner noted that the workers' lack of attention that led to the accident probably resulted from their excessively long hours. Then there is the famous case of Mary Anne Walkley, "20 years old, employed in a highly respectable dressmaking establishment"—in a situation where "girls work, on an average, 16½ hours without a break, during the season often 30 hours, and the flow of their failing 'labour-power' is maintained by occasional supplies of sherry, port or coffee"—who quite simply died from overwork (364–5). Dying from overwork is not something that is confined to the nineteenth century. The Japanese have a technical term for it, *karōshi*. People do die from overwork, and many people's lifetimes are shortened through the overwork they suffer or from the work conditions they encounter. In 2009, the United Farm Workers sued California Occupational Safety and Health Administration for not protecting farmworkers in the state from deadly heat, citing three cases of needless death from heat exhaustion.

Marx is here describing what happens when the power relationship between capital and labor becomes so lopsided that the labor force is reduced to a position of degradation and even driven to untimely deaths. This problem is exacerbated by the rise of the relay system described in the fourth section of this chapter. Unemployed capital is lost capital, and capital, recall, is not a machine or a sum of money, but value in motion. If a machine is not being used, it's dead capital, so there is pressure to use it all the time. The continuity of the production process becomes important, particularly in those industries, such as blast furnaces and heavy-metal engineering, employing large amounts of fixed-capital equipment. The need to keep the fixed capital employed mandates a twenty-four-hour workday. Since individual workers cannot work twenty-four hours, the relay system is devised and then supplemented by night work and the shift system. Remember: workers not only produce surplus-value, they reanimate constant capital. The result is night-shift work via the relay system. There is, therefore, no such thing as a "natural working day," only various constructions of it in relation to the capitalist requirement to maintain a continuity of flow at all costs.

Section 5 takes up the struggle for a normal working day. What is the length of time during which capital may consume the labor-power whose daily value it has paid for? Capital, plainly, is going to take as much as it can get. For capital,

> it is self-evident that the worker is nothing other than labour-power for the duration of his whole life, and that therefore all his disposable time is by nature and by right labour-time, to be devoted to the self-valorization of capital [i.e., the production of surplus-value]. Time for education, for intellectual development, for the fulfilment of social functions, for social intercourse, for the free play of vital forces of his body and his mind, even the rest time of Sunday . . . what foolishness! But in its blind and measureless drive, its insatiable appetite for surplus labour, capital oversteps not only the moral but even the merely physical limits of the working day. It usurps the time for growth, development and healthy maintenance of the body. It steals the time required for the consumption of fresh air and sunlight. It haggles over the meal-times, where possible incorporating them into the production process itself. (375–6)

I always remember the assembly-line scenes from Charlie Chaplin's *Modern Times* when I read these passages. Capital

> reduces the sound sleep needed for . . . restoration, renewal and refreshment . . . [It] asks no questions about the length of life of labour-power. What interests it is purely and simply the maximum of labour-power that can be set in motion in a working day. It attains this objective by shortening the life of labour-power, in the same way as a greedy farmer snatches more produce from the soil by robbing it of its fertility. (376)

The parallel between exhaustion of the soil and of the vital powers of the laborer echoes the formulation in chapter 1 where Marx cites William Petty's comment that "labour is the father of material wealth, the earth is its mother" (134). But this also implies that excessive exploitation of the resources required to produce all wealth poses a danger for capitalism itself. At some point or other, the capitalist will also think that a normal working day might not be a bad idea.

> If then the unnatural extension of the working day, which capital necessarily strives for in its unmeasured drive for self-valorization, shortens the life of the individual worker, and therefore the duration of his labour-power, the forces used up have to be replaced more rapidly, and it will be more expensive to reproduce labour-power, just as in the case of a machine, where the part of its value that has to be reproduced daily grows greater the more rapidly the machine is worn out. It would seem therefore that the interest of capital itself points in the direction of a normal working day. (377)

The problem, however, is that individual capitalists in competition with one another cannot stop pushing toward the overexploitation of their fundamental resource bases, labor and the land. The potential exists for a conflict between the class interest of capitalists in a "sustainable" labor force and the short-term individual behaviors of capitalists faced with competition. Therefore some limit has to be put on competition between them.

Slave owners, Marx points out, can, if they wish, afford to kill off their slaves through excessive work provided they have a new source of cheap slaves at hand. But this is also true for the labor market:

> for slave trade, read labour-market, for Kentucky and Virginia, Ireland and the agricultural districts of England, Scotland and Wales, for Africa, Germany. We have heard how over-work has thinned the ranks of the bakers in London. Nevertheless, the London labour-market is always over-stocked with German and other candidates for death in the bakeries. (378)

Marx here introduces another important concept: that of a surplus population. This permits capitalists to super-exploit their workers without regard for their health or well-being. Of course, the surplus population has to be accessible to capital. Marx here cites the case of the Poor Law commissioners, who were instructed to "send the 'surplus population' of the agricultural districts to the north, with the explanation 'that the manufacturers would absorb and use it up.'" (378). Agricultural districts conveniently rid themselves of their Poor Law obligations, at the same time as they provided surplus labor for the manufacturing districts.

> What experience generally shows to the capitalist is a constant excess of population, i.e. an excess in relation to capital's need for valorization at a given moment, although this throng of people is made up of generations of stunted, short-lived and rapidly replaced human beings, plucked, so to speak, before they were ripe ... Experience shows too how the degeneration of the industrial population is retarded only by the constant absorption of primitive and natural elements from the countryside, and how even the agricultural labourers, in spite of the fresh air and the 'principle of natural selection' that works so powerfully amongst them, and permits the survival of only the strongest individuals, are already beginning to die off. (380)

A surplus population affects whether the capitalist has to care about the health, well-being and life expectancy of the labor force. As individual human beings, capitalists may care. But forced to maximize profit come what may under conditions of competition, individual capitalists have no choice.

> Après moi le déluge! is the watchword of every capitalist and of every capitalist nation. Capital therefore takes no account of the health and the length of life of the worker, unless society forces it to do so. Its answer to the outcry about the physical and mental degradation, the premature death, the torture of over-work, is this: Should that pain trouble us, since it increases our pleasure (profit)? But looking at these things as a whole, it is evident that this does not depend on the will, either good or bad, of the individual capitalist. Under free competition, the immanent laws of capitalist production confront the individual capitalist as a coercive force external to him. (381)

No matter whether they are good- or bad-hearted, capitalists are forced by competition to engage in the same labor practices as their competitors. If your competitors shorten the lives of their laborers, you have to, too. That is how the coercive laws of competition work. This phrase, "the coercive laws of competition," is going to come back into the argument several times. And it's important to notice at what point these coercive laws play a decisive role, as they do here.

This brings Marx to consider the "centuries of struggle between the capitalist and the worker" that have led to "the establishment of a normal working day." He interestingly notes that "the history of this struggle displays two opposite tendencies" (382). In medieval times, it was very difficult to get people to be wage laborers. If they couldn't make a living off the land for themselves, people became vagabonds, beggars or even highway robbers (like Robin Hood). So legislation was enacted to codify the wage relation, extend the length of the working day and criminalize beggars and vagabonds. In effect, a disciplinary apparatus was created (and Marx will take this up again in part 8) to socialize the population into the role of wage laborers. Vagabonds were whipped and put into the stocks before being mandated to do a good day's labor. And a good day's labor was defined as a workday of twelve hours in the first such statutes, which date from 1349. This was how labor discipline was imposed in Britain. You will find similar issues being raised by colonial authorities during the nineteenth century and later. They would report that, say, the problem in India or Africa is that you can't get the indigenous population to work a "normal" working day, let alone a "normal" working week. They typically work for a bit and then disappear. The local notion of temporality doesn't fit with the idea of clock time and hinders the ability of capitalists to extract value as moments that are the elements of profit. The lack of time discipline of local populations was a frequent complaint among colonial administrators, and tremendous efforts were made to instill labor discipline and an appropriate sense of temporality. (I have heard contemporary university administrators make similar complaints about students and even once suffered a course from the educational geniuses of Harvard, who insisted that the first thing we had to do to teach undergraduates properly was to instill a proper sense of time discipline.)

There is now an extensive literature on the medieval and late-medieval attitude toward time, as well as on the transitions that occurred in temporality with the rise of capitalism (or, as some prefer to speak of it, of "modernity"). For instance, we all too easily forget that the hour was largely an invention of the thirteenth century, that the minute and the second became common measures only as late as the seventeenth century and that it is only in recent times that terms like "nanoseconds" have been invented. These are not natural but social determinations, and their invention was not irrelevant to the transition from feudalism to capitalism. When Foucault talks about the rise of governmentality, what he is really talking about is that moment when people started to internalize a sense of temporal discipline and to learn to live by it almost without thinking. To the degree that we all have internalized this sense, we become captive to a certain way of thinking about temporality and the practices that attach thereto. For Marx, this temporality arises in relationship to the emergence of value as socially necessary labor-time. And for him, the role of class struggle is central in ways that Foucault tends to evade or downplay. Says Marx,

> It has been seen that these highly detailed specifications, which regulate, with military uniformity, the times, the limits and the pauses of work by the stroke of the clock, were by no means a product of the fantasy of Members of Parliament. They developed gradually out of circumstances as natural laws of the modern mode of production. Their formulation, official recognition and proclamation by the state were the result of a long class struggle. (394–5)

It is no longer a matter of saying that "between equal rights, force decides," but of recognizing the class character of hegemonic forms of temporal thinking about the world. And it is not only temporality that is involved here, because the issue of spatiality also arises. To ideologists like the anonymous author of *An Essay on Trade and Commerce* of 1770, the problem is a "fatal" inclination to "ease and indolence" on the part of the working population (387). Marx quotes the essay:

> 'The cure will not be perfect, till our manufacturing poor are contented to labour six days for the same sum which they now earn in four days.' To this end, and for 'extirpating idleness, debauchery and excess,' promoting a spirit of industry [and] 'lowering the price of labour in our manufactories' . . . our 'faithful Eckart' . . . 'proposes the well-tried method of locking up workers who become dependent on public support . . . in 'an ideal workhouse'. Such an ideal workhouse must be made a 'House of Terror . . . [where] the poor shall work 14 hours in a day, allowing proper time for meals, in such a manner that there shall remain 12 hours of neat labour.' (388)

Marx then makes his reply. The equivalent of such a House of Terror for paupers, he writes,

> only dreamed of by the capitalist mind in 1770, was brought into being a few years later in the shape of a gigantic 'workhouse' for the industrial worker himself. It was called the factory. And this time the ideal was a pale shadow compared with the reality. (389)

Spatial organization is part of the disciplinary apparatus brought to bear on the worker. This almost certainly inspired Foucault's various studies of spatially organized disciplinary apparatuses (with the panopticon as his template) in books like *Madness and Civilization*, *Discipline and Punish* and *The Birth of the Clinic*. It is ironic, I think, that Foucault is so often viewed in the English-speaking world as a thinker radically at odds with Marx when he so clearly takes Marx's analysis of the working day as one of his inspirations. Foucault does a magnificent job, in my view, of generalizing Marx's argument and giving it substance. Although in some of his later works he departs from what the Marxists (and more particularly the Maoists and Communists in France at the time) were saying, his early fundamental texts about asylums, prisons and clinics should, in my view, be read as continuations of rather than departures from Marx's arguments concerning the rise of a disciplinary capitalism in which workers have to be socialized and disciplined to accept the spatiotemporal logic of the capitalist labor process.

The problem of how to create and sustain worker discipline is still with us, of course. Then there is the problem of what to do with people who don't conform and are therefore dubbed odd or even deviant. And this is Foucault's as well as Marx's point: they are called mad or antisocial and incarcerated in insane asylums or prisons; or as Marx notes, they get put in the stocks, mocked and punished. To be a "normal" person, therefore, is to accept a certain kind of spatiotemporal discipline convenient to a capitalist mode of production. What Marx demonstrates is that this isn't normal at all—it's a social construct that arose during this historical period in this particular way and for these particular reasons.

Clearly, capitalists initially had to struggle mightily to extend the working day and normalize it to, say, ten or twelve hours (as it was in Marx's time). "Working time" in precapitalist societies varied a great deal depending on circumstances, but in many instances it was not much more than four hours a day, the rest of the day given over to socializing and other activities that could not be deemed "productive" in the sense of contributing to material survival. In our form of society, a four-hour workday would be considered ludicrous, unfortunate and uncivilized, which raises some questions about the "degree of civilization" that exists in our own culture. Presumably, a socialist alternative would aim to restore the four-hour workday!

In section 6, we get the story of what happened through the 1830s and 1840s as workers sought to fight back against the excessive lengthening of the working day in industrial Britain. Marx relates a particular political dynamic, which goes something like this (and here I tell it my way to help clarify Marx's description). In the 1820s in Britain, the landed aristocracy still dominated political power. It had Parliament, it had the House of Lords, it had the monarchy and dominated the military and the judiciary. But there was also a rising bourgeoisie, partly constituted by traditional mercantile and financial interests (located in London and the port cities like Bristol and Liverpool that made a lot of their money out of the slave trade) but now supplemented by an increasingly powerful industrial interest centered on cotton manufacturers in the Manchester region. The latter became powerful advocates for a particular version of economic theory that was dominated by freedom of the market and free trade (Manchester was, recall, where Senior went to learn his economics). Although increasingly wealthy, the industrial capitalists were politically disempowered relative to the landed aristocracy. They therefore sought to reform the parliamentary system in such a way as to gain greater power within the state apparatus. In this they had to fight a serious battle against the landed aristocracy. And in fighting that battle, they looked for support from the mass of the people, particularly the professional middle classes and an articulate, self-educated, artisanal working class (distinct from the mass of uneducated laborers). The industrial bourgeoisie, in short, sought an alliance with artisanal working-class movements against the landed aristocracy. And through massive agitations toward the end of the 1820s, they forced through the Reform Act of 1832, which transformed the system of parliamentary representation in their favor and liberalized the electoral qualification so that modestly endowed property owners could vote.

But all kinds of political promises had been made to the working classes in the agitation leading up to the reform, including extending the vote to artisans, regulating the length of the working day and doing something about oppressive conditions of labor. The Reform Act was soon dubbed "the great betrayal" by the workers. The industrial bourgeoisie got most of the reforms it wanted, while the working classes got nothing very much. The first Factory Act regulating the length of the working day in 1833 was weak and ineffectual (although it did set the precedent of state legislation on the topic). The workers, angered by the betrayal, organized a political movement, called Chartism, which started to agitate against the conditions of life of the mass of the population as well as against the appalling conditions of industrial labor. During this time, the landed aristocracy became even more antagonistic toward the rising power of the industrial bourgeoisie (read a Dickens or a Disraeli novel and this tension is omnipresent). They were therefore inclined to support the workers' demands in part on the grounds of the national (military) interest but also through the typical aristocratic politics of *noblesse oblige*, depicting themselves as the good paternalistic folk who don't exploit people the way those nasty industrialists do. This was, in part, where the factory inspectors are coming from. They were being promoted by the landed aristocracy in order to curb the power of a ruthless industrial bourgeoisie. By the 1840s, the industrial bourgeoisie was being pushed hard by this coalition of landed aristocracy and a working-class movement that was "daily more threatening," as Marx puts it (348). Stronger versions of the Factory Act were mooted and passed in 1844, 1847 and 1848.

There is, however, another piece in this jigsaw puzzle of class relations and alliance formation. The Manchester School of economics was a great advocate of *laissez-faire* and free trade. This led to a struggle over the Corn Laws (N.B., in Britain at that time "corn" referred to "wheat" and not, as in America, to what the British called "maize"). High tariffs on imported wheat protected the incomes of the landed aristocracy from foreign competition. But the result was a high cost of bread, a basic foodstuff for the working classes. The industrial bourgeoisie launched a political campaign, led by Cobden and Bright in Manchester, for the abolition of the Corn Laws, pointing out to the workers that this would mean cheaper bread. Attempts were made (not very successful, since workers remembered the "great betrayal" all too well) to forge an alliance with workers. Eventually there were Corn Law reforms in the 1840s which reduced tariffs on wheat in ways that seriously impacted the wealth of the landed aristocracy. But when bread became cheaper, the industrial bourgeoisie reduced wages. In Marx's terms, since the value of labor-power is determined in part by the price of bread, cheaper imports of wheat lead to lower bread prices which lead in turn (other things being equal) to a fall in the value of labor-power. The industrialists could pay their workers less because the workers needed less money to buy their daily bread! At this point in the 1840s, the Chartist movement strengthens, and workers' demands and worker agitation escalate, but there is not a solid alliance against them because of the intense division between industrial (bourgeois) and landed (aristocratic) interests.

The industrial bourgeoisie sought to undermine the operation of the Factory Acts of the 1840s. Like the boyars, they played around with notions of temporality. Since the workers did not have timepieces, the employers altered the factory clock times to get extra labor-time. The employers organized work schedules to work in bits, "hounding him hither and thither, in scattered shreds of time" (403), so that, like an actor on the stage, they participated for ten hours of work but had to be present for fifteen. Workers had "to gulp down [their] meals in a different fragment of time" (404). The employers used the relay system to confuse the times and "denounced the factory inspector as a species of revolutionary commissioner reminiscent of the Convention, who would ruthlessly sacrifice the unfortunate factory workers to his mania for improving the world" (396–7). The earlier legislation tended to focus particularly on the employment of women and children, which sparked a debate as to the age at which children become adults. "According to the anthropology of the capitalists, the age of childhood ended at 10, or, at the outside, 11" (392). So much for the degree of civilization among the industrial bourgeoisie! And as one of the factory inspectors, Leonard Horner, vociferously complained, there was no point going to the courts, since all they ever did was to exonerate the employers. But as Marx notes, "the Tories"—the landed aristocracy—"were panting for revenge" (395) over the Corn Laws and pushed through a new Factory Act that would limit the working day to ten hours in 1848.

But in 1848, there erupted one of those periodic crises of capitalism, a major crisis of overaccumulation of capital, a huge crisis of unemployment across much of Europe that sparked intense revolutionary movements in Paris, Berlin, Vienna and elsewhere; at the same time, Chartist agitation in Britain peaked. In the face of this, the whole of the bourgeoisie got nervous about the revolutionary potential of the working class. In Paris, in June of 1848, there was a violent repression of working-class movements that had asserted power, followed by the establishment of an authoritarian regime which became the Second Empire, led by Louis Bonaparte in 1852.

In Britain, events were not so dramatic, but the fear of unrest was widespread. There,

> the fiasco of the Chartist party whose leaders had been imprisoned and whose organization dismembered, had shattered the self-confidence of the English working class. Soon after this the June insurrection in Paris and its bloody suppression united, in England as on the Continent, all fractions of the ruling classes, landowners and capitalists, stock-exchange sharks and small-time shopkeepers, Protectionists and Freetraders, government and opposition, priests and free-thinkers, young whores and old nuns [frankly, I have no idea what they had to do with it] under the common slogan of the salvation of property, religion, the family and society. (397)

It is amazing to contemplate how frequently "property, religion, the family and society" gets trotted out as an ideological mantra in the quest to protect the established bourgeois order. We don't have to look much further than the recent history of the United States, where the Republican Party in particular would not exist were it not for its vehement declaration of loyalty to these principles. In Britain in 1848 it meant that "everywhere the working class was outlawed, anathemized, placed under the '*loi des suspects*'. The manufacturers no longer needed to restrain themselves" and "broke out in open revolt" against "all the legislation since 1833 that had aimed at restricting to some extent the 'free' exploitation of labour-power." This "rebellion" was prosecuted "with a cynical recklessness and a terroristic energy which were so much the easier to achieve in that the rebel capitalist risked nothing but the skin of his workers" (397–8). All of which sounds very much like the Reagan/Thatcher neoliberal counterrevolution of the 1980s. Under the Reagan administration, much of the work that had been done on labor relations (via the National Labor Relations Board and the Occupational Safety and Health Administration) was reversed or left unenforced. In this case, too, it was the shifting character of class power and class alliances within the state apparatus that played the vital role.

In Britain, something interesting happened after 1850. The

> apparently decisive victory of capital was immediately followed by a counter-stroke. So far, the workers had offered a resistance which was passive, though inflexible and unceasing. They now protested in Lancashire and Yorkshire in threatening meetings. The so-called Ten Hours' Act, they said, was thus mere humbug, a parliamentary fraud. It had never existed! The factory inspectors urgently warned the government that class antagonisms had reached an unheard-of degree of tension. Some of the manufacturers

> themselves grumbled: 'On account of the contradictory decisions of the magistrates, a condition of things altogether abnormal and anarchical obtains. One law holds in Yorkshire, another in Lancashire; one law in one parish of Lancashire, another in its immediate neighbourhood.' (405)

What the capitalists had in effect done was to use the law to fragment decisions here, there and everywhere so that actually the law was no longer consistent. But the serious threat of unrest in 1850 forced a

> compromise between manufacturers and men, given the seal of parliamentary approval in the supplementary Factory Act of 5 August 1850. The working day for 'young persons and women' was lengthened from 10 to 10½ hours for the first five days of the week, and shortened to 7½ hours on Saturdays. (405)

Certain groups, such as the silk manufacturers, procured exemptions, and there the children "were quite simply slaughtered for the sake of their delicate fingers" (406). But by 1850,

> the principle had triumphed with its victory in those great branches of industry which form the most characteristic creation of the modern mode of production. Their wonderful development from 1853 to 1860, hand-in-hand with the physical and moral regeneration of the factory workers, was visible to the weakest eyes. The very manufacturers from whom the legal limitation and regulation of the working day had been wrung step by step in the course of a civil war lasting half a century now pointed boastfully to the contrast with the areas of exploitation which were still 'free'. The Pharisees of 'political economy' now proclaimed that their newly won insight into the necessity for a legally regulated working day was a characteristic achievement of their 'science'. It will easily be understood that after the factory magnates had resigned themselves and submitted to the inevitable, capital's power of resistance gradually weakened, while at the same time the working class's power of attack grew with the number of its allies in those social layers not directly interested in the question. (408–9)

Who were these allies? Marx does not say, but it probably comes back mainly to professional classes and the progressive wing of the reformist bourgeoisie. These were crucial elements in a situation where the working classes did not vote. "Hence the comparatively rapid progress since 1860" (409).

While Marx does not comment on it, this reformism was not confined to the conditions of factory labor, and to the degree that it became clear that they, too, could benefit, even the industrial interest increasingly participated. This was best symbolized by the Birmingham industrialist Joseph Chamberlain, who became mayor of the city and was often then referred to as "Radical Joe" because of his commitments to municipal improvements in education, infrastructure (water supply, sewage, gas lighting, etc.) and better housing for the poor. At least a segment of the industrial bourgeoisie had learned by the 1860s that it did not necessarily have to be reactionary on these topics if it was to maintain its profits.

This whole dynamic calls for some commentary. It's clear from the data that up until 1850 or so, the rate of exploitation in the British industrial system was horrendous and that the hours of work were equally horrendous, with dreadful consequences for the conditions of working and living. But this super-exploitation slackened after 1850 without any marked negative effect on profitability or output. This occurred in part because the capitalists found another way to gain surplus-value (to be taken up shortly). But they also discovered that a healthy and efficient labor force, on a shorter working day, could be more productive than an unhealthy, inefficient, falling-apart, constantly turning-over and dying-off labor force of the sort that it had utilized during the 1830s and 1840s. The capitalists could then trumpet this discovery and their benevolence and sometimes overtly support a certain level of collective regulation and state interference to limit the effects of the coercive laws of competition. If, from the standpoint of the capitalist class as a whole, curbing the length of the working day turned out to be a good idea, then what does this say about the struggle by workers and their allies to limit it? It says that workers may well be doing capital a favor. Capitalists get pushed into a reform which is not necessarily against their class interest. In other words, the dynamics of class struggle can just as easily help equilibrate the system as disrupt it. Marx in effect concedes here that capitalists, when they finally succumbed after fifty years of struggle to the idea of regulating the working day, found it worked for them just as well as it did for the workers.

In section 7, Marx examines the impact of British factory legislation on other countries, chiefly France and the United States. In so doing, he first recognizes that a mode of analysis that focuses merely on the individual worker and his or her contract is insufficient.

> The history of the regulation of the working day in certain branches of production, and the struggle still going on in others over this regulation, prove conclusively that the isolated worker, the worker as 'free' seller of his labour-power, succumbs without resistance once capitalist production has reached a certain stage of maturity. The establishment of a normal working day is therefore the product of a protracted and more or less concealed civil war between the capitalist class and the working class. (412–13)

In other countries, this struggle is affected by the nature of political traditions (the "French revolutionary method," for example, is far more heavily dependent on declarations of "universal rights") and actual conditions of labor (in the United States, under conditions of slavery, "labour in a white skin cannot emancipate itself where it is branded in a black skin") (414). But in all cases, the laborer who appears as a "free agent" in the marketplace discovers he is no free agent in the realm of production, where "the vampire will not let go 'while there remains a single muscle, sinew or drop of blood to be exploited'" (415–16) (here Marx quotes Engels). The lesson that must be learned is that

> for 'protection' against the serpent of their agonies, the workers have to put their heads together and, as a class, compel the passing of a law, an all-powerful social barrier by which they can be prevented from selling themselves and their families into slavery and death by voluntary contract with capital. In place of the pompous catalogue of the 'inalienable rights of man' there steps the modest Magna Carta of the legally limited working day, which at last makes clear 'when the time which the workers sells is ended, and when his own begins'. (416)

There are a couple issues that arise from this conclusion. Marx's dismissal of the "inalienable rights of man" is a reaffirmation that "rights talk" is not going to be able to address fundamental issues, such as the determination of the length of the working day. The courts cannot do it, either. But here, for the first time, Marx argues that workers have to "put their heads together" and work as a class, and how they do so is going to have a huge impact on the conditions of labor and the dynamics of capitalism. This struggle is central to the very definition of freedom itself. I here quote from the third volume of *Capital*:

> The realm of freedom really begins only where labour determined by necessity and external expediency ends; it lies by its very nature beyond

> the sphere of material production proper. Just as the savage must wrestle with nature to satisfy his needs, to maintain and reproduce his life, so must civilized man, and he must do so in all forms of society and under all possible modes of production. This realm of natural necessity expands with his development, because his needs do too; but the productive forces to satisfy these expand at the same time. Freedom, in this sphere, can consist only in this, that socialized man, the associated producers, govern the human metabolism with nature in a rational way, bringing it under their collective control instead of being dominated by it as a blind power; accomplishing it with the least expenditure of energy and in conditions most worthy and appropriate for their human nature. But this always remains a realm of necessity. The true realm of freedom, the development of human powers as an end in itself, begins beyond it, though it can only flourish with this realm of necessity as its basis. The reduction of the working day is the basic prerequisite.[1]

But we also see that capitalists, impelled onward by the coercive laws of competition, are likely to behave in such a way as to seriously impair the prospects for their reproduction as a class. If the laborers organize as a class, and thereby force the capitalists to modify their behavior, then the collective power of the workers helps save the capitalists from their own individual stupidity and short-sightedness, thus forcing them to recognize their class interest. The implication is that collective class struggle can be a stabilizer within the capitalist dynamic. If workers are completely powerless, then the system goes awry because *Après moi le déluge!* is no way to run a stable capitalist economy. Clearly, the coercive laws of competition that drive the capitalists down such a self-destructive path need to be contained. This is as serious a problem with respect to the super-exploitation of the land and the pillaging of natural resources as it is for the qualities and quantities of labor supply.

Now, this is a difficult conclusion to reach since Marx is purportedly a revolutionary thinker. In this chapter, he hemmed himself in by the initial assumption that both capital and labor pursue their rights in terms of the laws of exchange. In these terms, the only possible outcome for the workers is a "modest Magna Carta" of a fair day's wage for a fair day's labor. There is no overthrow of the capitalist class or abolition of class relations

1. Karl Marx, *Capital*, Vol. III, trans. David Fernbach (London: Penguin, 1981), 958–9.

here. Class struggle merely equilibrates the capital-labor relation. Class struggle can all too easily be internalized within the capitalist dynamic as a positive force that sustains the capitalist mode of production. While this does mean that class struggle is both inevitable and socially necessary, it sheds very little light on the prospects for a revolutionary overthrow of capitalism.

How are we to interpret the politics of all this? My own view is to agree with the proposition that a certain empowerment of the workers' movement is socially necessary for capitalism to function effectively, and that the sooner the capitalists recognize this and submit to it, the better off they will be. There is plenty of historical evidence to support this conclusion, even to the point where the state, as happened in the United States during the New Deal, deliberately empowered the trade-union movement in order not to overthrow capitalism but to help stabilize it. Struggles over the value of labor-power and over the length of the working day are fundamental to the achievement of a modicum of stability within capitalism for social and political as well as purely economic reasons. It is perhaps no accident that the phase of strong social-democratic governance in the 1950s and 1960s in Europe and the social compact between capital and labor in the United States were associated with strong capitalist growth and that the Scandinavian states with their strong social support systems have remained relatively successful competitors on the international stage even during the recent turn toward neoliberalism elsewhere. Marx will also insist that this finding as to the socially necessary state of class struggle has to be inserted theoretically into an otherwise silent bourgeois political economy in order to understand the dynamics of capitalism.

But there is also a point at which struggle over the length of the working day and the empowerment of a working-class movement can go beyond trade-union consciousness and morph into more revolutionary demands. It is one thing to say that the working day should be limited to ten or eight hours, but what happens when it drops to four? At that point, capitalists get a little jumpy. As happened in France, even a thirty-five-hour week and six weeks' mandated vacation time have been seen as excessive and sparked a strong movement on the part of the capitalist class and their allies for much greater "flexibility" in labor laws. The question here is, at what point does reform go too far and actually challenge the very basis of capitalism?

If there is an equilibrium point for class struggle, it is not fixed, nor is it known. But it does depend on the nature of the class forces and the degree of flexibility that capitalists have in relation to new requirements. For example, a far shorter working day permits capitalists to push toward intensification and increasing efficiency of labor in ways that compensate for the shorter hours. It is virtually impossible to maintain a high level of intensity over a twelve-hour workday. An interesting example of this occurred in the miner's strike against the Edward Heath government in Britain in the early 1970s. In the face of power shortages, Heath mandated a three-day workweek, but the subsequent evidence showed that productive activity did not diminish in the same proportion. He also mandated no television broadcasting after ten at night, which ensured he got booted out at the next election (there was also, I recall, an interesting blip upward in the birthrate some nine months later).

I cannot resist ending consideration of this chapter with a few comments on its relevance to contemporary conditions. Plainly, the dynamics of class struggle (including class-alliance formation) have continued ever since Marx's time to play a crucial role in the determination of working days, weeks, years and lifetimes as well as in the degree of regulation of working conditions and levels of wages. While in certain places and times, the more horrendous and appalling conditions that Marx dwells on at length have been very much circumscribed, the general issues he describes (such as much lower life expectancies than average in many occupations such as mining, steel and construction) have never disappeared. But over the past thirty years, with the neoliberal counterrevolution that places much greater emphasis on deregulation and the pursuit of more vulnerable workforces through globalization, there has been a recrudescence of the sorts of conditions that the factory inspectors so graphically described in Marx's time. By the mid-1990s, for example, I would give the students in my *Capital* class the following exercise. I would ask them to imagine they had had a letter from home that noted they were taking a course on *Capital* and that commented that while the book perhaps was historically relevant, the conditions it describes had long ago been superseded. I gave the students bundles of excerpts from official reports (by the World Bank, for instance) and clippings from respectable newspapers (the *New York Times*, etc.) describing working conditions in plants producing Gap clothing in Central America, Nike plants in Indonesia and Vietnam or Levi Strauss products in Southeast Asia and describing how that great lover of children Kathy Lee Gifford was shocked to find that her line of clothing for Wal-Mart was produced either in plants in Honduras employing young children at almost no wages or in sweatshops in the New York region where people had not been paid for weeks. The students wrote great essays, though they balked when I suggested they might like to send them home.

Regrettably, conditions have grown worse. In May 2008, an Immigration and Customs Enforcement raid on an Iowa meatpacking plant netted 389 suspected illegal immigrants, several of whom were underage and many of whom worked twelve-hour days six days a week. The immigrants were treated as criminals; many of the 297 convicted were jailed for five months or more prior to deportation, while the authorities only began slowly to move against the company for its appalling labor practices as the moral outrage began to build through public exposure. As the students in my class had also concluded, it is all too easy to insert any number of contemporary accounts of labor practices into Marx's chapter on the working day without noticing the difference. This is where the neoliberal counterrevolution and the loss of power on the part of the labor movement have brought us. Sad to report, Marx's analysis is all too relevant to our contemporary condition.

CHAPTER 11: RATE AND MASS OF SURPLUS-VALUE

Chapter 11 is a typical link chapter. It moves out of one set of questions in order to pose another. Marx's method returns to the somewhat dryly algebraic before taking a substantive twist. Capitalists, he suggests, are most interested in maximizing the mass of surplus-value because their individual social power depends on the total money power they command. The mass of surplus-value is given by the rate of surplus-value multiplied by the number of laborers employed. If the number of laborers employed diminishes, the same mass of surplus-value can be gained by increasing the rate of surplus-value. But there is a limit on the rate of surplus-value given not only by the twenty-four hours in a day but also by all the social and political barriers discussed earlier. Faced with this limit, capitalists can increase the number of laborers employed. But at some point, another limit is encountered, which is the total variable capital available and the total supply of the laboring population. The outer limit here would be, of course, the total population, but again there are reasons why the available workforce is far less than this. Faced with these two limits, capital has to come up with an entirely different strategy for increasing the mass of surplus-value.

As often happens in transitional chapters, Marx provides us, in capsule form, with a conceptual map as to where we have been and where we are going:

> Capital developed within the production process until it acquired command over labour, i.e. over self-activating labour-power, in other words the worker himself. The capitalist, who is capital personified, now takes care that the worker does his work regularly and with the proper degree of intensity . . . [But] capital also developed into a coercive relation, and this compels the working class to do more work than would be required by the narrow circle of its own needs. (424–5)

Capital personified, in its thirst for surplus labor and its incessant pursuit of surplus-value,

> surpasses all earlier systems of production . . . in its energy and its quality of unbounded and ruthless activity . . . [But] at first capital subordinates labour on the basis of the technical conditions within which labour has been carried on up to that point in history. It does not therefore directly change the mode of production. The production of surplus-value in the form we have so far considered, by means of simple extension of the working day, appeared therefore independently of any change in the mode of production itself. (425)

But all that is about to change, both logically and historically. When "we view the production process as a process of valorization," then the means of production are changed into "means for the absorption of the labour of others. It is no longer the worker who employs the means of production, but the means of production which employ the worker." This historical and logical reversal lies at the core of an astonishing transformation in how a capitalist mode of production has to be understood. "Instead of being consumed by him as material elements of his productive activity," the means of production "consume him as the ferment necessary to their own life-process, and the life-process of capital consists solely in its own motion as self-valorizing value" (425). This all follows from the simple fact that the only way in which the value of the means of production (the dead labor congealed in factories, spindles and machines) held by the capitalists can be preserved (let alone augmented in the form of surplus-value) is by the absorption of fresh supplies of living labor. To the "bourgeois brain" it then follows that laborers exist only to valorize capital through the application of their labor-power!

Capitalism abhors limits of any sort, precisely because the accumulation of money power is in principle limitless. Capitalism perpetually strives, therefore, to transcend all limits (environmental, social, political and geographical) and to convert them into barriers that can be bypassed or circumvented. This gives a definite and special character to the capitalist mode of production and imposes specific historical and geographical consequences on its development. We now turn to consider how the limits encountered in this chapter—of total available labor force and rate of exploitation—are converted by capital into a barrier that can be overcome.

CHAPTER SIX

Relative Surplus-Value

CHAPTER 12: THE CONCEPT OF RELATIVE SURPLUS-VALUE

Chapter 12 proposes a simple argument with a few complicated wrinkles. Yet it is a chapter that it is all too easy to get wrong. The initial argument goes like this:

The value of a commodity is determined by the socially necessary labor-time congealed in it, and this value diminishes with increasing productivity. "In general, the greater the productivity of labour, the less the labour-time required to produce an article, the less the mass of labour crystallized in that article, and the less its value" (131).

The value of labor-power as a commodity is affected by all manner of historical, cultural and social circumstances. But it is also tied to the value of the commodities that laborers need to reproduce themselves and their dependents at a given standard of living.

> The value of labour-power can be resolved into the value of a definite quantity of the means of subsistence. It therefore varies with the value of the means of subsistence, i.e. with the quantity of labour-time required to produce them. (276)

Other things remaining equal, therefore, the value of labor-power will decline with rising productivity in those industries producing the goods laborers need to reproduce themselves.

> In order to make the value of labour-power go down, the rise in the productivity of labour must seize upon those branches of industry whose products determine the value of labour-power, and consequently either belong to the category of normal means of subsistence, or are capable of replacing them. (432)

For the capitalists, this means that they can lay out less in the way of variable capital because the workers need less money to meet their needs (as fixed by a given standard of living). If capitalists have to lay out less for variable capital, then even if the length of the working day is fixed, the ratio s/v, or the rate of exploitation, rises. A greater mass of surplus-value thereby accrues to the capitalist even though the length of the working day is fixed.

This process in no way involves any infringement of the laws of exchange. To be sure, capitalists will seek to purchase whatever labor-power they can at less than its value, and that will augment the mass of surplus-value they receive. "Despite the important part which this method plays in practice, we are excluded from considering it here by our assumption that all commodities, including labour-power, are bought and sold at their full value" (431). So once again, acceptance of the market logic and the theses of classical political economy take precedence over the study of actual practices, demonstrating once more Marx's commitment to deconstructing the utopian theses of classical political economy on their own terms. One other peculiar result arises out of Marx's mode of reasoning. "An increase in the productivity of labour in those branches of industries which supply neither the necessary means of subsistence nor the means by which they are produced leaves the value of labour-power undisturbed" (432). Therefore, reducing the value of luxury goods by increasing productivity does not yield relative surplus-value. It is only the declining value of wage goods that matters.

This produces a conundrum. Why would individual capitalists raise the productivity in their own particular industry producing a wage good, when all capitalists will benefit? This is what is now called a free-rider problem. The individual capitalist who goes out, innovates, reduces the price of a wage good and so reduces the value of all labor-power gains no particular or singular benefit from so doing. The benefit accrues to the whole capitalist class. Where is the individual incentive to do that?

Could relative surplus-value arise through a class strategy? While Marx does not mention it in this chapter, he earlier related a case where this was so—the abolition of the Corn Laws (tariffs on wheat imports) as a result of the collective agitation of the Manchester industrialists. The cheaper wheat imports that resulted brought down the price of bread, and this allowed wages to be reduced. This sort of class strategy turns out to have been of great historical importance. The same reasoning exists now in the United States with respect to the supposed advantages of free trade. The Wal-Mart phenomenon and cheap imports from China are welcomed because cheap goods reduce the cost of living to the working classes. The fact that money wages have not risen much for workers over the past thirty years is made more palatable since the physical quantity of goods they can acquire has increased (provided they shop at Wal-Mart). In exactly the same way that the nineteenth-century British industrial bourgeoisie wanted to reduce the value of labor-power by allowing cheap imports, so the reluctance to block cheap imports in the United States today derives from the need to keep the value of labor-power stable. Protectionist tariffs, while they might help keep jobs in the United States, would result in price increases which would create pressures for higher wages.

It turns out historically that there have been many state-organized strategies to intervene in the value of labor-power. Why, for example, does the State of New York not charge sales taxes on food? Because that is seen as fundamental to the determination of the value of labor-power. On occasion, the industrial bourgeoisie has supported rent control, cheap (social) housing and subsidized rents and agricultural products because that, too, keeps the value of labor-power down. So we can identify many situations where there have been and still are class strategies worked out through the state apparatus to reduce the value of labor-power. To the degree that the working classes gained a modicum of access to state power, they could use it to increase their income in kind (through state provision of many goods and services) and so raise the value of labor-power (in effect claiming back a part of the potential relative surplus-value for themselves).

Marx eschews any mention of these kinds of issues in this chapter almost certainly for the same reason he dismissed the way capitalists perpetually seek to purchase labor-power at less than its value. Conscious class strategies and state interventions are not admissable in the theoretical framework Marx has established. We don't necessarily have to follow him all the way on this, particularly to the degree we are interested in actual histories. But he nevertheless accomplishes something very profound by sticking to the restrictive assumptions of free-market utopianism. He shows how and why individual capitalists might be impelled to innovate (without any class or state interventions) even though the return on their innovation goes to the whole capitalist class.

"When an individual capitalist cheapens shirts, for instance, by increasing the productivity of labour, he by no means necessarily aims to reduce the value of labour-power and shorten necessary labour-time in proportion to this." The individual capitalist does not act on the basis of a generalized class consciousness even though "he contributes towards increasing the general rate of surplus-value" through his actions. Marx then warns: "the general and necessary tendencies of capital must be distinguished from their forms of appearance." This peculiar phrasing signals that something special is going on (the odor of fetishism is in the air). So what's he getting at?

> While it is not our intention here to consider the way in which the immanent laws of capitalist production manifest themselves in the external movement of the individual capitals, assert themselves as the coercive laws of competition, and therefore enter into the consciousness of the individual capitalist as the motives which drive him forward, this much is clear: a scientific analysis of competition is possible only if we can grasp the inner nature of capital, just as the apparent motions of the heavenly bodies are intelligible to someone who is acquainted with their real motions, which are not perceptible to the senses. (433)

Now we need to think long and hard, critically and carefully, about what he is saying. I earlier suggested you remain alert for when the coercive laws of competition come into the argument, and plainly they do so here. Yet Marx seems to want to downplay their import even as he recognizes that he cannot do without them. At this point, I can only offer my own interpretation, knowing full well that many will disagree with me. I think there is a certain parallel between the way in which Marx analyzes the role of supply and demand fluctuations and the role of competition. In the case of supply and demand, Marx concedes that these conditions play a vital surface role in generating price movements for a particular commodity, but when supply and demand are in equilibrium, he argues, supply and demand fail to explain anything. Supply and demand cannot explain why shirts exchange for shoes on average in the ratio that they do. This has to be explained by something totally different, congealed socially necessary labor-time, or value. This does not mean that supply and demand are irrelevant, because without them there could be no equilibrium price. Supply and demand relations are a necessary but not sufficient aspect of a capitalist mode of production. Competition between individual capitalists within a particular line of commodity production plays a similar role. In this instance, however, it redefines the equilibrium position—the average price or value of the commodity—through changes in the general level of productivity in that line of commodity production. Competition as Marx here depicts it is a sort of epiphenomenon that occurs on the surface of society, but, like exchange itself, it has some deeper consequences that cannot be understood by reference to competition. This was the position he took in the *Grundrisse*: competition does not establish the laws of motion of capitalism

> but is rather their executor. Unlimited competition is therefore not the presupposition for the truth of the economic laws, but rather the consequence—the form of appearance in which their necessity realizes itself . . . Competition therefore does not explain these laws; rather it lets them be seen, but does not produce them.[1]

Let use see how this process works out in this instance. "For the understanding of the production of relative surplus-value, and merely on the basis of the results already achieved, we may add the following remarks" (433). The value of a commodity, recall, is fixed by the socially necessary "labour-time required to produce any use-value under the conditions of production normal for a given society and with the average degree of skill and intensity of labour prevalent in that society" (129). What happens if an individual capitalist departs from this social average and sets up a productive system which is super-efficient and instead of producing ten widgets in an hour produces twenty? If one capitalist does that but all the others still produce at the rate of ten, then this one capitalist can sell at or close to the social average of ten while producing and selling twenty. "The individual value of these articles is now below their social value; in other words, they have cost less labour time than the great bulk of the same article produced under the average social conditions" (434). The innovative capitalist gains an extra profit, extra surplus-value, by selling at or close to the social average while producing at a rate of productivity far higher than the social average. This gap is crucial and yields a form of relative surplus-value to the individual capitalist. In this case, it does not matter whether the capitalist is producing wage goods or luxuries. But how does this capitalist sell the extra ten widgets per hour at

1. Marx, *Grundrisse*, 552.

the old social-average price? Here the laws of supply and demand come into play. And the answer is, probably, that they cannot be sold at the old price. So prices begin to decline. As prices decline, the other capitalists are faced with less profit. This amounts to a redistribution of surplus-value from those with inferior technologies to those with superior technologies. Those working with an inferior technology, therefore, have an increasing competitive incentive to adopt the new technology. Once all capitalists in this line of production follow suit and adopt the new technology to produce twenty widgets an hour, so the socially necessary labor-time congealed in widgets declines.

This form of relative surplus-value, which accrues to the individual capitalist, only lasts as long as he or she has a superior technology in relationship to everybody else. It is ephemeral.

> This extra surplus-value vanishes as soon as the new method of production is generalized, for then the difference between the individual value of the cheapened commodity and its social value vanishes. The law of the determination of value by labour time makes itself felt to the individual capitalist who applies the new method of production by compelling him to sell his goods under their social value; this same law, acting as a coercive law of competition, forces his competitors to adopt the new method. (436)

So the first form of relative surplus-value considered in this chapter is a class phenomenon. It accrues to the whole capitalist class, and it is as permanent as conditions of class struggle over the value of labor-power allow. The second form is individual and ephemeral. It is this second form, the one that confers individual advantage, that individual capitalists are forced to pursue via the coercive laws of competition. The result is that all capitalists at some point or other are forced to adopt the same technology. The two forms of relative surplus-value are not unrelated, since ephemeral innovations in the wage-goods sector will also drive down the value of labor-power at a physically fixed standard of living. "Capital therefore has an immanent drive, and a constant tendency, towards increasing the productivity of labour, in order to cheapen commodities, and, by cheapening commodities, to cheapen the worker himself" (436–7).

But if you are a savvy capitalist, you will know that you can always get this second ephemeral form of relative surplus-value, provided you always have a superior technology. This generates some interesting results. Suppose the new technology is a new machine. Marx has argued that machines, since they are dead labor, can't produce value. But what happens when you get extra relative surplus-value because of your new machine? While machines are not a source of value, they can be a source of relative surplus-value to the individual capitalist! Once these machines become general, they can then appear to be a source of the relative surplus-value to the whole capitalist class because of declines in the value of labor-power. This produces a peculiar result: machines cannot be a source of value, but they can be a source of surplus-value.

From the way Marx has set up the argument, we see that there is a tremendous incentive for leapfrogging technological innovations among individual capitalists. I get ahead of the pack, I have a superior, more efficient production system than you, I get the ephemeral surplus-value for three years, and you then catch up with me or even go beyond me and get the ephemeral surplus-value for three years. Individual capitalists are all hunting ephemeral surplus-value through new technologies. Hence the technological dynamism of capitalism.

Now, most other theories of technological change treat it as some sort of *deus ex machina*, some exogenous variable outside the system, attributable to the inherent genius of entrepreneurs or simply to the immanent capacity of human beings for innovation. But Marx is typically reluctant to attribute something as crucial as this to some external power. What he does here is find a simple way to explain why capitalism is so incredibly technologically dynamic from the inside (endogenously, as we like to say). He also explains why capitalists hold the fetishistic view that machines are a source of value, and why all of us are also subject to the same fetish conception. But Marx is resolute. Machines are a source of relative surplus-value but not of value. Since capitalists are interested in the mass of surplus-value, and since they would generally prefer to gain relative surplus-value rather than confront class struggles over absolute surplus-value, then the fetish belief in a "technological fix" as an answer to their ambitions is all too understandable. We even have a hard time disabusing ourselves of it.

But there is another interesting inference to be drawn that Marx refrains from examining, though he does lightly allude to it elsewhere. Suppose workers live on bread alone, and the cost of bread is cut in half because of increases in productivity. Suppose that capitalists cut wages by a quarter. They gain the collective form of relative surplus-value, thus increasing the general rate of exploitation. But at the same time, the workers can buy more bread and raise their physical standard of living. The general question this poses is, how are gains from increasing productivity shared between the classes? One possible result, which Marx unfortunately neglects to emphasize, is that the physical standard of living of workers can rise, as measured by the material goods (use-values) they can afford, at the same time as the rate of exploitation, s/v, increases. This is an important point, because one of the criticisms frequently heard about Marx is that he believes in a rising rate of exploitation. How can that be, ask the critics? Workers (at least in the advanced capitalist countries) now have cars and all these consumer goods, so obviously the rate of exploitation cannot be increasing! Are not the workers so much better off? One part of the answer is that it is perfectly feasible, in the terms postulated in Marx's theory, for steady increases to occur in the standard of living of labor at the same time as the rate of exploitation either increases or remains constant. (The other part might be to point to the benefits that accrue to one portion of the global working class as a return on imperialist practices of exploitation of the other portion, but that cannot be appealed to here.)

I say it was unfortunate that Marx did not emphasize this point in part because it would have easily forestalled an erroneous, spurious line of theoretical and historical criticism. But it would have also made us focus more clearly on the question of how benefits from gains in productivity get shared as a crucial aspect of the history of class struggle. In the case of the United States, some share of the gains from higher productivity went to the workers from the Civil War period onward. A typical union bargaining strategy is to agree to collaborate with increasing productivity in return for higher wages. If the benefits from technological dynamism are spread around, then opposition to that technological dynamism becomes muted even as capitalists are cheerfully raising the rate of exploitation. Political opposition to capitalism in general also may become less strident, even if the rate of exploitation is increasing, because workers are at least gaining a higher physical standard of living. The odd thing about the United States is that it is only in the past thirty years or so that workers have failed to gain from rising productivity. The capitalist class has appropriated almost all the benefits. This lies at the core of what the neoliberal counterrevolution has been about and what distinguishes it from the Keynesian welfare-state period, when gains from productivity tended to be shared more evenly between capital and labor. The result has been, as is well documented, a tremendous increase in levels of social inequality in all those countries that have moved down neoliberal lines. In part this has to do with the balance of class forces and the dynamics of class struggle in different places, while in the United States, cheaper imports (and imperialist practices) have also helped workers maintain an illusion that perhaps they may be benefiting from capitalist imperialism. But all this lies way beyond what Marx's text is proposing. I find it helpful, however, to extend his key insights in these directions.

CHAPTER 13: CO-OPERATION

The three chapters that follow deal with the various ways in which capitalists can procure relative surplus-value of the individual sort. The overall focus is on whatever it is that raises the productivity of labor, and it is clear that this depends on organizational forms (cooperation and divisions of labor), as well as on machinery and automation (technology, as we usually think of it). This can create some confusion, since Marx sometimes bundles all these strategies together under the heading "productive forces," but then on occasion uses the term "technology" as if it were the same thing. He is clearly as interested in organizational form (the software, as it were) as he is in the machines (the hardware). I think it best to assume that Marx's theory of technology/productive forces is machinery plus organizational form. I find his stance on this particularly relevant since, in recent times, transformations in organizational form—subcontracting, just-in-time systems, corporate decentralization and the like—have played a major role in the quest to increase productivity. While the profitability of Wal-Mart has its basis in the exploitation of cheap Chinese labor, the efficiency of its organizational form sets it apart from many of its competitors. Similarly, the Japanese conquest of the US auto market at the expense of Detroit had as much to do with the organizational form (just-in-time and subcontracting) of the Japanese car companies as with the new hardware and automation they deployed. Indeed, ever since time-and-motion studies (and what became known as Taylorism) became fashionable around 1900, there has always been a strong link between the hardware and the software of capitalist production systems.

Marx begins by examining how two organizational forms—cooperation and divisions of labor—can be used by capital under existing technological conditions of artisanal and handicraft labor to increase productivity. Innovations in these two aspects of organizational form have been integral to the acquisition of relative surplus-value throughout the history of capitalism, and we should never forget them. As in the chapter on the labor process, however, where the potential nobility of the process is stressed in contrast to its alienated form under capitalism, Marx casts neither cooperation nor division of labor in an inherently negative light. He views them as potentially creative, beneficial and gratifying for the laborer. Cooperation and well-organized divisions of labor are wonderful human capacities that add to our collective powers. Socialism and communism would presumably have great need of them. What Marx will seek to show is how these positive potentialities are seized on by capital to its own particular advantage and thereby turned into something negative for the laborer.

"When numerous workers work together side by side in accordance with a plan, whether in the same process, or in different but connected processes, this form of labour is called co-operation." Note the word "plan" here, since it's going to become an important idea. Cooperation permits, for example, an increasing scale of production, and the resultant economies of scale can generate increases in labor efficiency and productivity. This is made much of in conventional economic theory, and Marx does not demur. "Not only do we have here an increase in the productive power of the individual, by means of co-operation, but the creation of a new productive power, which is intrinsically a collective one" (443). This collective power

> begets in most industries a rivalry and a stimulation of the 'animal spirits', which heightens the efficiency of each individual worker. This is why a dozen people working together will produce far more, in their collective working day of 144 hours than twelve isolated men each working for 12 hours. (443–4)

Furthermore, "co-operation allows work to be carried on over a large area" while rendering

> possible a relative contraction of its arena. This simultaneous restriction of space and extension of effectiveness, which allows a large number of incidental expenses . . . to be spared, results from the massing together of

> workers and of various labour processes, and from the concentration of the means of production. (446)

There is an interesting tension here between geographical expansion (work conducted over a large area) and geographical concentration (bringing workers together for purposes of cooperation in a particular space). The latter, as Marx points out, can have political consequences as workers get together and organize.

He insists, however, that "the special productive power of the combined working day is, under all circumstances, the social productive power of labour, or the productive power of social labour. This power arises from co-operation itself." Furthermore, "when the worker co-operates in a planned way with others, he strips off the fetters of his individuality, and develops the capabilities of his species" (447). This is one of those instances where Marx reverts to some notion of universal species being, which was an important theme in the *Economic and Philosophical Manuscripts* of 1844. At this point, it is hard to view this discussion of cooperation in a negative light. We strip off the fetters of our individuality and develop the capability of the species. To the degree that this capability has not been realized, we have yet to realize the potentiality of our species being.

But what happens when we return to the world of "our would-be capitalist"? First off, the capitalist needs an initial mass of capital in order to organize cooperation. How much, and where does it come from? There are what we now usually refer to as barriers to entry into any production process. In some instances, the start-up costs can be considerable. But there are ways to ameliorate this problem. Marx here introduces an important distinction. "At first, the subjection of labour to capital was only a formal result of the fact that the worker, instead of working for himself, works for, and consequently under, the capitalist." But as time goes on, "through the co-operation of numerous wage-labourers, the command of capital develops into a requirement for carrying on the labour process itself, into a real condition of production" (448). The distinction here is between the "formal" subsumption of labor under capital versus its "real" subsumption.

What does this difference mean? Under what was called the putting-out system, merchant capitalists would take materials to laborers in their cottages and return to collect the worked-up product at a later date. The laborers would not be supervised, and the labor process would be left up to the cottagers (it often entailed family labor and was dovetailed with subsistence agricultural practices). But the cottagers depended on the merchant capitalists for their monetary incomes and did not own the product they worked up. This is what Marx means by formal subsumption. When laborers are brought into the factory for a wage, then both they and the labor process are under the direct supervision of the capitalist. This is real subsumption. So the formal is out there, dependent, while the real is inside the factory under the supervision of the capitalist. The latter entails more start-up costs, more initial capital; in the early stages of capitalism, when capital was scarce, the formal system of exploitation could well be more advantageous. Marx believed that over time, the formal would give way to the real. But he was not necessarily correct in this. The revival of contract work, home working and the like in our times indicates that some reversion to formal kinds of subjection and subsumption is entirely possible.

When laborers are brought into a collective structure of cooperation in a factory, they come under the directing authority of the capitalist. Any cooperative endeavor requires some directing authority, much as a conductor directs an orchestra. The problem is that "the work of directing, superintending and adjusting becomes one of the functions of capital, from the moment that the labour under capital's control becomes co-operative." Furthermore, "as a specific function of capital, the directing function acquires its own special characteristics." This function is to recognize that moments are the elements of profit and to squeeze as much labor-time out of the laborer as possible. On the other hand, "as the number of co-operating workers increases, so too does their resistance to the domination of capital, and, necessarily, the pressure put on by capital to overcome this resistance" (449).

The struggle between capital and labor, which we earlier encountered in the labor market, gets internalized on the shop floor. This happens because cooperation is organized through the power of capital. What was once a power of labor now appears as a power of capital.

> The interconnection between their various labours confronts [the laborers], in the realm of ideas, as a plan drawn up by the capitalist, and, in practice, as his authority, as the powerful will of a being outside them, who subjects their activity to his purpose. (450)

The capitalist's purpose is to secure "on the one hand a social labour process for the creation of a product, and on the other hand capital's process of valorization," i.e., the production of surplus-value. This entails the development of a specific kind of labor process in which the "work of direct and constant supervision of the individual workers and groups of workers" results in "a special kind of wage-labourer. An industrial army of workers under the command of a capitalist requires, like a real army, officers (managers) and N.C.O.s (foremen, overseers)." A certain structure of supervision of the workers emerges which is both authoritarian and "purely despotic." In this, the capitalist acquires a distinctive role as orchestrator of the labor process in all its aspects. "It is not because he is a leader of industry that a man is a capitalist; on the contrary, he is a leader of industry because he is a capitalist. The leadership of industry is an attribute of capital" (450–1). Only by way of command over the labor process can capital be both produced and reproduced. Laborers, on the other hand,

> enter into relations with the capitalist, but not with each other. Their co-operation only begins with the labour process, but by then they have ceased to belong to themselves. On entering the labour process they are incorporated into capital. As co-operators, as members of a working organism, they merely form a particular mode of existence of capital.

Workers lose their personhood and become mere variable capital. This is what Marx means by the real subsumption of the laborer under capital.

> The socially productive power of labour develops as a free gift to capital whenever the workers are placed under certain conditions, and it is capital which places them under these conditions. Because this power costs capital nothing, while on the other hand it is not developed by the worker until his labour itself belongs to capital, it appears as a power which capital possesses by its nature—a productive power inherent in capital. (451)

An inherent power of labor, the social power of cooperation, is appropriated by capital and made to appear as a power of capital over the workers. Historical examples of enforced cooperation abound—the Middle Ages, slavery, colonies, slave labor—but under capitalism the connection of organized cooperation to wage labor is manifest in special ways. This had a key role in the rise of capitalism.

> The simultaneous employment of a large number of wage-labourers in the same labour process . . . forms the starting-point of capitalist production. This starting-point coincides with the birth of capital itself. If then, on the one hand, the capitalist mode of production is a historically necessary condition for the transformation of the labour process into a social process, so, on the other hand, this social form of the labour process is a method employed by capital for the more profitable exploitation of labour, by increasing its productive power. (453)

This originary status of a certain form of cooperation is perpetuated throughout the whole history of capitalism.

> Simple co-operation has always been, and continues to be, the predominant form in those branches of production in which capital operates on a large scale, but the division of labour and machinery play only an insignificant part . . . Co-operation remains the fundamental form of the capitalist mode of production, although in its simple shape it continues to appear as one particular form alongside the more developed ones. (454)

It is impossible to imagine the capitalist mode of production without cooperation, albeit cooperation under the despotism of capitalists who organize and direct a supervisory authority and fragment the working class into distinctive hierarchical groupings. It is, therefore, no longer adequate to think merely about *the* wage laborer, because the working class is stratified according to both the status and the differential financial reward attached to the different functions required to constitute the despotism of a cooperative apparatus dedicated solely to the production of surplus-value.

CHAPTER 14: THE DIVISION OF LABOUR AND MANUFACTURE

Chapter 14 examines divisions of labor. Marx concentrates here on the reorganization of existing handicrafts, existing skills, existing tool technologies and the like into a new system that he calls "manufacturing." The reorganization can be done in two ways. The first is to bring together in the same workshop, "under the control of a single capitalist . . . workers belonging to various independent handicrafts" (455). The example he uses is carriage making, where wheels, upholstery, frame, etc. all have to be made separately and then assembled. This contrasts with making nails or needles. In this case, the process starts with raw materials and passes through a continuous process until it comes out as a nail or a needle. But in both cases, "whatever may have been its particular starting-point, its final form is always the same—a productive mechanism whose organs are human beings." That is, human beings are brought together into a certain kind of relationship to one another inside the cooperative regime of the production space.

Such reorganizations do not, however, leave the original skills untouched. "The analysis of a process of production into its particular phases here coincides completely with the decomposition of a handicraft into its different partial operations" (457). When the production process is seen as a whole, opportunities arise to split it up into smaller fragments and get specialized workers to engage on each fragment, either in terms of the continuous sequence or in terms of the heterogeneity of many different handicrafts. Nevertheless, "handicraft remains the basis, a technically narrow basis which excludes a really scientific division of the production process into its component parts." This plainly constitutes a barrier to the progress of capitalist production, and as I have already argued, capital doesn't like barriers and perpetually seeks to overcome them. The difficulty in this case is that

> every partial process undergone by the product must be capable of being done by hand, and of forming a separate handicraft. It is precisely because the skill of the craftsman thus continues to be the foundation of the production process that every worker becomes exclusively assigned to a partial function and that his labour-power becomes transformed into the life-long organ of this partial function.

The result is that workers, instead of having the freedom to move from one activity to another, are increasingly locked into a particular skill, a particular handicraft, the use of a particular set of specialized tools. "A worker who performs the same simple operation for the whole of his life converts his body into the automatic, one-sided implement of that operation" (458). Is the worker in control of the tool or is the tool in control of the worker? Marx suggests that the social imprisonment of workers in a particular specialization within the division of labor puts them in a position of being so connected to their specialized tools that they lose their freedom. This has not always been so.

> A craftsman who performs the various partial operations . . . must at one time change his place, at another time his tools. The transition from one operation to another interrupts the flow of his labour and creates gaps in his working day, so to speak.

But capital doesn't like such gaps in the working day, since moments are the elements of profit. These gaps "close up when he is tied to the same operation the whole day long." On the other hand, this can be counterproductive since "constant labour of one uniform kind disturbs the intensity and flow of a man's vital forces, which find recreation and delight in the change of activity itself" (460).

This is a partial concession to Fourier's view of the importance of variety and stimulus in the labor process as opposed to the dull imprisonment of one person, with one tool, in the division of labor, for a lifetime. The positive and negative aspects of how the division of labor is organized under capitalist control start to enter into the argument. This argument has not gone away, even within capitalism. The attempt to raise efficiency and productivity in the labor process by introducing "quality circles" and variety of tasking to counteract the monotony of labor has been the focus of many experiments by capitalist firms in certain lines of production.

In section 3, Marx sets up a more systematic contrast between two fundamental forms of manufacture—heterogeneous (bringing together many skills, as in carriage and locomotive making) and organic (continuous, like nail making). But he here takes the opportunity to introduce the concept of the "collective worker," who, he says, is

> formed from the combination of the many specialized workers, draws the wire with one set of tooled-up hands, straightens the wire with another set, armed with different tools, cuts it with another set, points it with another set, and so on. The different stages of the process, previously successive in time, have become simultaneous and contiguous in space. (464)

Productivity and efficiency depend not on the individual worker but on the proper organization of collective work.

This means careful attention must be paid to the space-time organization of production and the efficiencies that can be gained through spatiotemporal reconstruction of the labor process as a whole. Marx points out that by *not* losing any time, you gain in productivity.

By rationalizing the way in which space is organized, you can save on movement costs. So the whole space-time structure becomes an organizational question for how capitalism works. This was the big innovation that the Japanese introduced into the labor process in the 1970s with just-in-time production, the tight scheduling of flows of goods in space and time such that you had almost no inventory anywhere in the system. This was *the* innovation which gave the Japanese car industry its competitive advantage over all others during the 1980s, and the Japanese raked in the ephemeral form of relative surplus-value until everyone else caught up. The downside of this system is that it is vulnerable to disruption. If one link in the spatiotemporal chain is stopped by, for example, a strike, then everything has to close down because there is no inventory.

Marx here clearly recognizes that a major organizational aspect of a capitalistic system is how space and time get set up and understood. The capitalist has to come up with a plan for an efficient spatiotemporal production system. But this in turn implies an important distinction between what happens in the marketplace and what happens within the firm. "The rule that the labour-time expended on a commodity should not exceed the amount socially necessary to produce it is one that appears, in the production of commodities in general, to be enforced from outside by the action of competition" (note the importance of competition once more). But "in manufacture, on the contrary, the provision of a given quantity of the product in a given period of labour is a technical law of the process of production itself" (465). This distinction (contradiction) between what market logic enforces and what can be done by internal planning is vital for the argument that follows. But the full flowering of this contradiction is hindered by the existence of a barrier due to the fact that we are still dealing with handicrafts and artisanal labor. This prompts a general comment of some importance:

> The Roman Empire handed down the elementary form of all machinery in the shape of the water-wheel. The handicraft period bequeathed to us the great inventions of the compass, gunpowder, type-printing and the automatic clock. But on the whole, machinery played that subordinate part which Adam Smith assigns to it in comparison with division of labour. (468)

That is, up until the end of the eighteenth century, capitalists were not really homing in on new machinery as a primary way to improve their productive efficiency. They were generally content to use existing methods of production and reorganize them. Of course there were innovations, like compass and gunpowder and all the rest of it, but capitalism had not yet internalized the dynamic of perpetual technological innovation in the heart of the labor process itself. That happened later on, with the rise of machinery and modern industry (the subject of chapter 15).

The capitalist reorganization of labor processes has serious impacts on the worker. "The habit of doing only one thing converts him into an organ which operates with the certainty of a force of nature, while his connection with the whole mechanism compels him to work with the regularity of a machine." Workers "are divided, classified and grouped according to their predominant qualities," and the result is "a hierarchy of labour-powers, to which there corresponds a scale of wages" (468–9). The distinction between skilled and unskilled laborers becomes particularly marked.

> Alongside the gradations of the hierarchy, there appears the simple separation of the workers into skilled and unskilled. For the latter, the cost of apprenticeship vanishes; for the former, it diminishes, compared with that required of the craftsman . . . In both cases the value of labour-power falls.

Capitalist reorganizations and reconfigurations of tasks tend to produce deskilling, as tasks that were once complicated become simplified into component parts. This also has the effect of reducing the value of labor-power employed.

> The relative devaluation of labour-power caused by the disappearance or reduction of the expenses of apprenticeship directly implies a higher degree of valorization of capital; for everything that shortens the necessary labour-time required for the reproduction of labour-power, extends the domain of surplus labour.

But "an exception to this law occurs whenever the decomposition of the labour process gives rise to new and comprehensive functions, which either did not appear at all in handicrafts or not to the same extent"

(470). In any reorganization of the labor process there can be a double movement, it must be conceded, of mass deskilling alongside usually a much smaller group that's reskilled (e.g., assembly-line engineers). The latter segments of the working class are usually empowered and privileged relative to other segments of labor.

Section 4, titled "The Division of Labour in Manufacture, and the Division of Labour in Society," is significant and has some potentially fraught implications. Marx here returns to the distinction between the detailed division of labor in the workshop, which occurs under the planned design and direct supervision of the capitalist, and the division of labor achieved through competition in the market. These two forms originate from "diametrically opposed" starting points but relate to each other. Marx provides a brief and, I have to say, not at all satisfactory discussion of the historical movement. "Within a family and, after further development, within a tribe, there springs up naturally a division of labour caused by differences of sex and age, and therefore based on a purely physiological foundation." This is an oversimplification based, as is the case with some of his other historical commentaries, on very little evidence. "Exchange," he hypothesizes,

> springs up at the points where different families, tribes or communities come into contact; for at the dawn of civilization it is not private individuals but families, tribes, etc. that meet on an independent footing. Different communities find different means of production and different means of subsistence in their natural environment. Hence their modes of production and living, as well as their products, are different.

Exchange relations arise between different communities with different assets, different resources, different products. "The foundation of every division of labour which has attained a certain degree of development, and has been brought about by the exchange of commodities, is the separation of town from country." The dialectic of town-country relations is, he suggests (correctly, in my view), important historically, but he does not elaborate on how and where. Furthermore, an adequate "number and density of the population" is relevant to the rise of capitalism (471–2). This is, he says, "a pre-condition for the division of labour within society."

> [But] this density is more or less relative. A relatively thinly populated country, with well-developed means of communication, has a denser population than a more numerously populated country with badly developed means of communication. In this sense, the northern states of the U.S.A. for instance, are more thickly populated than India.

Marx's appeal here to a relative theory of space-time relations is quite innovative. The geographical terrain on which capitalism developed was not fixed but varied, depending not only on density of populations but also on transport and communication technologies. His central point is that the division of labor in manufacture assumes that society has already "attained a certain degree of development. Inversely, the division of labour in manufacture reacts back upon that . . . society, developing and multiplying it further" (473). He argues for what is called increasing roundaboutness in and complexity of production. The movement is from a simple situation where somebody makes one thing to a situation where several people make parts of that thing and trade those parts in the market until all the parts get assembled by someone else at the end. This increasing roundaboutness generates increasing possibility for territorial specialization.

> The territorial division of labour, which confines special branches of production to special districts of a country, acquires fresh stimulus from the system of manufacture, which exploits all natural peculiarities. The colonial system and the extension of the world market, both of which form part of the general conditions for the existence of the manufacturing period [an important point that we should note well], furnish us with rich materials for displaying the division of labour in society.

But while there are "analogies and links" between the division of labor in society and within the workshop, they "differ not only in degree, but also in kind" (something that Adam Smith, as Marx rightly acknowledges, was concerned with) (474).

> The division of labour within society is mediated through the purchase and sale of the products of different branches of industry, while the connection between the various partial operations in a workshop is mediated through the sale of the labour-power of several workers to one capitalist, who applies it as combined labour-power. The division of

> labour within manufacture presupposes a concentration of the means of production in the hands of one capitalist; the division of labour within society presupposes a dispersal of those means among many independent producers of commodities. While, within the workshop, the iron law of proportionality subjects definite numbers of workers to definite function, in the society outside the workshop, the play of chance and caprice results in a motley pattern of distribution of the producers and their means of production among the various branches of social labour.

In the latter case, he argues, "the different spheres of production constantly tend towards equilibrium," but they do so only through market mechanisms. And he then explains why, going back over the laws of exchange of commodities. This means that the "constant tendency on the part of the various spheres of production towards equilibrium comes into play only as a reaction against the constant upsetting of this equilibrium" (475–6). That is, when demand and supply get out of kilter (and here, note, we cannot do without supply and demand mechanisms), market-price fluctuations force the necessary adjustment toward the underlying value relations as producers change what they are producing and how much. The result is a marked contrast between "the planned and regulated *a priori* system on which the division of labour is implemented within the workshop" and, on the other hand, "the division of labour within society," ruled by

> an a posteriori necessity imposed by nature, controlling the unregulated caprice of the producers, and perceptible in the fluctuations of the barometer of market prices. Division of labour within the workshop implies the undisputed authority of the capitalist over men, who are merely the members of a total mechanism which belongs to him. The division of labour within society brings into contact independent producers of commodities, who acknowledge no authority other than that of competition, of the coercion exerted by the pressure of their reciprocal interests, just as in the animal kingdom, the 'war of all against all' more or less preserves the conditions of existence of every species. (476–7)

In these passages, note the dependence on both supply and demand mechanisms and the coercive laws of competition as necessary to the achievement of some sort of equilibrium in which value relations prevail.

Capitalism, Marx concludes, lives always in the midst of contradiction between "anarchy in the social division of labour and despotism in the manufacturing division of labour." These two aspects of the division of labor, furthermore, "mutually condition each other." Marx attaches, however, some controversial and fraught political commentary to this conclusion:

> The same bourgeois consciousness which celebrates the division of labour in the workshop, the lifelong annexation of the worker to a partial operation, and his complete subjection to capital, as an organization of labour that increases its productive power, denounces with equal vigour every conscious attempt to control and regulate the process of production socially, as an inroad upon such sacred things as the rights of property, freedom and the self-determining 'genius' of the individual capitalist. It is very characteristic that the enthusiastic apologists of the factory system have nothing more damning to urge against a general organization of labour in society than that it would turn the whole of society into a factory. (477)

These statements require some careful parsing. Capitalists love the planned organization of production within their factory but abhor the idea of any kind of social planning of production in society. The ideological complaint that planning is a bad thing, and in particular for capitalists to attack it on the grounds that it would remake the world in the image of their own awful factories, is revealing. The condemnation of planning does not mesh with what goes on inside Toyota or Wal-Mart. Successful corporations deploy sophisticated planning techniques of total quality management, input-output analysis and optimal scheduling and design, and plan everything down to the finest detail. But it is one thing for Marx to point out the hypocritical approach of the capitalists to planning in the social realm, quite another to suggest that their undoubtedly sophisticated techniques, deployed in the quest for relative surplus-value, might be adequate for the planning of a socialist society seeking to augment the material well-being of everyone. Would it, in short, be reasonable to turn the world into a centrally planned economy, in effect into one large factory, in the quest for socialism? Obviously, there would be problems in doing so given Marx's account of the appalling conditions of factory labor. But if the problem is not the techniques but the fact that they are used to gain relative surplus-value for the capitalist rather than to produce enough output to satisfy the material needs of all, then Lenin's advocacy for Fordist productionism as a goal for Soviet industry becomes more understandable. We will return to this question later.

Certainly, the argument that centralized planning is impossible because of the level of complexity or because it infringes on private property relations does not wash, given the complexity involved in any large corporation, producing, say, electronics, and the dispossession of the laborer's right to the fruits of his or her own labors. The incredible inefficiencies of the market system (particularly with respect to the environment) and the periodic brutality of the coercive laws of competition, along with the increasing despotism this coercion typically produces in the workplace, are hardly great advertisements for the superiority of market coordinations. And the idea that innovation is only possible given individual property rights and the coercive laws of competition is surely far-fetched both logically and historically. For what I think impresses Marx most here is the appropriation of the productive powers of labor by capital. Again and again, he insists to the working class that all these powers of cooperation and of divisions of labor are *their* productive powers and that capital is appropriating them.

> The productive power which results from the combination of various kinds of labour appears as the productive power of capital. Manufacture proper not only subjects the previously independent worker to the discipline and command of capital, but creates in addition a hierarchical structure amongst the workers themselves.

The implications for the workers are far-reaching.

> It converts the worker into a crippled monstrosity by furthering his particular skill as in a forcing-house, through the suppression of a whole world of productive drives and inclinations, just as in the states of La Plata they butcher a whole beast for the sake of his hide or his tallow. Not only is the specialized work distributed among the different individuals, but the individual himself is divided up, and transformed into the automatic motor of a detail operation, thus realizing the absurd fable of Menenius Agrippa, which presents man as a mere fragment of his own body. (481–2)

So the body politics of this is that workers are reduced to being fragments of themselves. "Unfitted by nature"—and Marx is being ironic here—"to make anything independently, the manufacturing worker develops his productive activity only as an appendage of [the capitalist's] workshop." Sadly,

> the possibility of an intelligent direction of production expands in one direction, because it vanishes in many others. What is lost by the specialized workers is concentrated in the capital which confronts them. It is the result of the division of labour in manufacture that the worker is brought face to face with the intellectual potentialities . . . of the material process of production as the property of another and as a power which rules over him.

Intellectual labor becomes a specialized function, separating mental from manual labor, with the former brought increasingly under the control of capital.

> This process of separation starts in simple co-operation . . . It is developed in manufacture, which mutilates the worker, turning him into a fragment of himself. It is completed in large-scale industry, which makes science a potentiality for production which is distinct from labour and presses it into the service of capital. (482)

The result of this is an "impoverishment of the worker" and a serious loss of "individual productive power." Political and intellectual subjectivities do not remain immune. And here Marx cites Adam Smith, not necessarily approvingly but as voicing what increasingly becomes a matter of fact:

> 'The understandings of the greater part of men,' says Adam Smith, 'are necessarily formed by their ordinary employments. The man whose whole life is spent in performing a few simple operations . . . has no occasion to exert his understanding . . . He generally becomes as stupid and ignorant as it is possible for a human creature to become.' After describing the stupidity of the specialized worker, he goes on: 'The uniformity of his stationary life naturally corrupts the courage of his mind . . . It corrupts even the activity of his body and renders him incapable of exerting his strength with vigour and perseverance in any other employments than that to which he has been bred. His dexterity at his own particular trade seems in this manner to be acquired at the expense of his intellectual, social, and martial virtues. But in every improved and civilized society, this is the state into which the labouring poor, that is, the great body of the people, must necessarily fall.' (483)

Marx seems partially inclined here to accept to some degree Smith's characterization of the situation, and I, too, think it important to ask the general question: to what degree do our ordinary employments corrupt the courage of our minds? I think the problem is widespread, not confined to workers at all. Journalists, media personalities, university professors—we all have this problem (I have plenty of personal experience of it). The widespread reluctance to protest the militarism, the social injustices, the repressions, that surround us at every turn have as much to do (and in a more insidious way) with the mentalities and political subjectivities that derive from our ordinary employments as they do with the sophisticated organization of bourgeois repression. "Some crippling of body and mind is inseparable even from the division of labour in society as a whole," Marx concedes, and results in what he calls "industrial pathology" (484). Again, we are treading on dangerous ground here. Surely it would not be right to pathologize the whole of the working class? Yet it would be utopian to suppose that all of this has no impact on people's abilities to react, to think. For those of you who have ever organized with those working two jobs (eighty hours a week), you will know the problem all too well. Workers in that condition have little or no time to think about (let alone read about) most of the things that we think they should think about, given their working-class position. They are so busy trying to make ends meet, get enough food on the table for their kids and do other domestic chores that they don't have time for anything else outside work. Smith took the argument to an extreme, drawing the unfortunate conclusion that therefore it was both the job and the duty of a small elite to do all the thinking and organizing, but there is something to Marx's description that we deny at our political peril.

The reorganization of the division of labor, both within the labor process and in society at large, is the hallmark of what Marx dubs the "manufacturing period" in capitalism's history. But this manufacturing system has limits. "Manufacture was unable either to seize upon the production of society to its full extent, or to revolutionize that production to its very core. It towered up"—and Marx is really admiring of it—

> as an artificial economic construction, on the broad foundation of the town handicrafts and the domestic industries of the countryside. At a certain stage of its development, the narrow technical basis on which manufacture rested came into contradiction with requirements of production which it had itself created. (490)

The pressure was on to go beyond these barriers. It is, of course, "machines that abolish the role of the handicraftsman as the regulating principle of social production" (491). This takes us into the next chapter, in which machines and the organizational form of the modern factory move to center stage.

CHAPTER SEVEN

What Technology Reveals

CHAPTER 15: MACHINERY AND LARGE-SCALE INDUSTRY

In the introduction, I noted that Marx rarely comments on his methodology. It has therefore to be reconstructed by way of careful perusal of occasional side comments, supplemented by a study of his practices. Chapter 15, "Machinery and Large-Scale Industry," provides an opportunity to grapple with this question at the same time as it advances the general arguments as to the character of a capitalist mode of production. The chapter is long, but the sections are logically ordered. It repays to go over this logical ordering both before and after studying this chapter.

An Important Footnote

I begin, however, with the chapter's fourth footnote, where Marx, in the cryptic fashion he often deploys in describing methodological considerations, links together a slew of concepts in a configuration that actually provides a general framework for dialectical and historical materialism. The footnote unfolds in three phases. The first focuses on Marx's relation with Darwin. Marx had read *On the Origin of Species* and was impressed with the historical method of evolutionary reconstruction that Darwin had outlined. Marx clearly envisaged his work as some sort of continuation of Darwin's, with the emphasis on human as well as (rather than opposed to) natural history. His aim, he stated in the preface to the first edition, is to view "the development of the economic formation of society" from "the standpoint" of "natural history." From this standpoint, the individual cannot be held "responsible for relations whose creature he remains, socially speaking, however much he may subjectively raise himself above them" (92).

In the footnote, Marx first focuses on "a critical history of technology." This

> would show how little any of the inventions of the eighteenth century are the work of a single individual. As yet such a book does not exist.

> Darwin has directed attention to the history of natural technology, i.e. the formation of the organs of plants and animals, which serve as the instruments of production for sustaining their life. Does not the history of the productive organs of man in society, of organs that are the material basis of every particular organization of society, deserve equal attention? And would not such a history be easier to compile, since, as Vico says, human history differs from natural history in that we have made the former, but not the latter? (493)

Vico's argument was that natural history was God's domain and that since God moved in mysterious ways, it was beyond human understanding, but we could certainly understand our own history since we had made it. Marx earlier broached the historical approach to technological change and noted some vital transitions associated with transformations in the mode of production. Having followed Benjamin Franklin in defining man "as a tool-making animal" in chapter 7, he went on to observe that the

> relics of bygone instruments of labour possess the same importance for the investigation of extinct economic formations as do fossil bones for the determination of extinct species of animals. It is not what is made but how, and by what instruments of labour, that distinguishes different economic epochs. Instruments of labour not only supply a standard of the degree of development which human labour has attained, but they also indicate the social relations within which men work.

Then, in a footnote: "the writers of history have so far paid very little attention to the development of material production, which is the basis of all social life, and therefore of all real history" (286). In chapter 14 he argued that

> the Roman Empire handed down the elementary form of all machinery in the shape of the water wheel. The handicraft period bequeathed to us the great inventions of the compass, gunpowder, type-printing and the automatic clock. But on the whole, machinery played that subordinate part which Adam Smith assigns to it in comparison with division of labour. (468)

This idea that there has been a human evolutionary process in which we can discern radical shifts not only in technologies but in whole modes of social life is clearly very important to Marx.

Marx did not read Darwin uncritically. "It is remarkable," he wrote to Engels, "how Darwin recognizes among beasts and plants his English society with its division of labour, competition, opening up of new markets, 'inventions' and the Malthusian struggle for existence."[1] The problem, as Marx sees it, is Darwin's ahistorical approach to a purely natural evolution without reference to the role of human action in changing the face of the earth. The reference to Malthus is also telling because in his introduction to *On the Origin of Species*, Darwin attributed some of his key ideas to Malthus. And since Marx couldn't abide Malthus, it must have been hard for Marx to swallow the thought that Malthus had so inspired Darwin. Interestingly, the Russian evolutionists who were not exposed to ruthless British industrialism (Darwin was married to a daughter of Josiah Wedgwood, the famous pottery industrialist, and so was familiar at first hand with competition and the division of labor and of function) put much greater emphasis on cooperation and mutual aid, ideas which were translated by the Russian geographer Kropotkin into the fundamentals of social anarchism.

But what Marx appreciated was Darwin's approach to evolution as a process open to historical reconstruction and theoretical investigation. Marx is committed to understanding the human evolutionary process in like fashion. This is where Marx's emphasis on processes rather than things comes in. The chapter on machinery and large-scale industry should be read as an essay on the history of technology in this spirit. It is about how the industrial form of capitalism emerged out of the world of handicraft and manufacturing. Up until this point, nobody had really thought of writing such a history, so this chapter constitutes a pioneering effort that later spawned a whole field of academic study called the history of science and technology. Read in this way, the chapter's argument makes a lot more sense. But like Darwin's theory, there is far more here than just history. There is a theoretical engagement with processes of social transformation, and as such, there is a good deal to debate and discuss.

The second part of the footnote proffers a short, but in my view extremely important, statement that requires elaboration:

> Technology reveals the active relation of man to nature, the direct process of the production of his life, and thereby it also lays bare the process of the

---

1. Marx to Engels, June 18, 1862, in *Selected Correspondence*, ed. S. W. Ryazanskaya, trans. I. Lasker (Moscow: Progress, 1965), 128.

production of the social relations of his life, and of the mental conceptions that flow from those relations. (493)

Marx here links in one sentence six identifiable conceptual elements. There is, first of all, technology. There is the relation to nature. There is the actual process of production and then, in rather shadowy form, the production and reproduction of daily life. There are social relations and mental conceptions. These elements are plainly not static but in motion, linked through "processes of production" that guide human evolution. The only element he doesn't explicitly describe in production terms is the relation to nature. Obviously, the relation to nature has been evolving over time. The idea that nature is also something continuously in the course of being produced in part through human action has also been long-standing; in its Marxist version (outlined in chapter 7), it is best represented in my colleague Neil Smith's book *Uneven Development*,[2] where capitalist processes of production of nature and of space are explicitly theorized.

How, then, are we to construe the relationships between these six conceptual elements? Though his language is suggestive, Marx leaves the question open, which is unfortunate since it leaves lots of space for all manner of interpretations. Marx is often depicted, by both friends and foes alike, as a technological determinist, who thinks changes in the productive forces dictate the course of human history, including the evolution of social relations, mental conceptions, the relation to nature and the like. The neoliberal journalist Thomas Friedman, for example, in his book *The World Is Flat*,[3] happily admits to the charge of being a technological determinist; when someone pointed out to him (erroneously) that this was Marx's position, he expressed his admiration for Marx and approvingly cited a lengthy passage from the *Communist Manifesto* to prove his point. In a review of Friedman's book, the conservative political philosopher John Gray confirmed Marx's technological determinism and argued that Friedman was indeed merely following in Marx's footsteps.[4] These observations by those generally unsympathetic to Marx

---

2. Neil Smith, *Uneven Development: Nature, Capital, and the Production of Space*, 3rd edn. (Athens, GA: University of Georgia Press, 2008 [1984]).

3. Thomas Friedman, *The World Is Flat: A Brief History of the Twenty-first Century* (New York: Farrar, Straus and Giroux, 2005), 201-4.

4. John Gray, "The World Is Round," *The New York Review of Books* 52, No. 13 (August 11, 2005).

are paralleled within the Marxist tradition. The strongest version of the thesis that the productive forces are the leading agent in history comes from G. A. Cohen in his book *Karl Marx's Theory of History: A Defence*.[5] Cohen, having inspected all Marx's texts from the standpoint of analytic philosophy, defends this interpretation of Marx's theory.

I do not share this interpretation. I find it inconsistent with Marx's dialectical method (dismissed by analytic philosophers such as Cohen as rubbish). Marx generally eschews causal language (I defy you to find much of it in *Capital*). In this footnote, he does not say technology "causes" or "determines," but that technology "reveals" or, in another translation, "discloses" the relation to nature. To be sure, Marx pays a lot of attention to the study of technologies (including organizational forms), but this does not warrant treating them as leading agents in human evolution. What Marx is saying (and plenty of people will disagree with me on this) is that technologies and organizational forms *internalize* a certain relation to nature as well as to mental conceptions and social relations, daily life and labor processes. By virtue of this internalization, the study of technologies and organizational forms is bound to "reveal" or "disclose" a great deal about all the other elements. Conversely, all these other elements internalize something of what technology is about. A detailed study of daily life under capitalism will, for example, "reveal" a great deal about our relation to nature, technologies, social relations, mental conceptions and the labor processes of production. Similarly, the study of our contemporary relation to nature cannot go very far without examining the nature of our social relations, our production systems, our mental conceptions of the world, the technologies deployed and how daily life is conducted. All these elements constitute a totality, and we have to understand how the mutual interactions between them work.

I find this a helpful way to think about the world. For instance, I was on a jury to select ideas for the design of a new city in South Korea. We, the members of the jury, had all the designs in front of us. The jury was made up mainly of engineers and planners, with a few distinguished architects and landscape designers. The latter dominated the initial discussion on the criteria we should deploy in reaching our decisions, and it mainly

5. G. A. Cohen, *Karl Marx's Theory of History: A Defence*, expanded edn. (Princeton, NJ: Princeton University Press, 2000 [1978]).

devolved into a discussion of the relative symbolic strengths and practical implications of circles and cubes in built forms. In other words, decisions were to be made largely on the basis of geometric and symbolic criteria. At some point, I intervened to ask: if you are building a new city, what are the things you would want to know? I would want to know, what kind of relation to nature is going to be created here (the ecological footprint, etc.)? What kinds of technologies are going to be embodied in this city, and why? What kinds of social relations are envisaged? What systems of production and reproduction are going to be incorporated? What is daily life going to be like, and is that the kind of daily life we would want? And what mental conceptions, symbolic and all the rest of it, are going to be engaged here? Is this going to be built as a nationalist monument or as a cosmopolitan place?

The other jurors seemed to find this formulation both innovative and interesting. We discussed it for a while until it got a bit too complicated relative to the time at our disposal. One of the architects then suggested that out of the six criteria, only mental conceptions really mattered, which came down to the symbolism of forms, which brought us neatly back to the question of the relative strengths of circles and cubes! But afterward I was asked where they could find out more about such an interesting way of thinking. I made the mistake of saying it's in footnote 4 of chapter 15 of Marx's *Capital*. I should have known better, because there are two typical reactions to saying this kind of thing. One is nervous and even fearful, for to concede that Marx might have said something so powerfully obvious and interesting is tantamount to admitting Marxist sympathies, and that would be horrible for one's professional and even personal prospects. The other is to regard me as an idiot, so lacking in ideas that I can only parrot Marx and, even worse in this instance, fall so low as to cite a mere footnote! So the conversation stopped. But this is, I think, an interesting way to evaluate urban design and to critique the qualities of urban life.

This framework helps ground the theory of historical materialism in a fundamental way, and there is strong evidence, as I hope to show, that it grounds much of Marx's tangible approach to understanding the evolution of capitalism. Let me expand on this for a moment. Imagine a framework of thought in which these six elements hang together in a single space but in intense interrelation (see figure opposite). Each of the elements is internally dynamic such that we consider each constituting a "moment" in the process of human evolution. We can study this evolution from the perspective of one of the moments or examine interactions among them, such as transformations in technologies and organizational forms in relationship to social relations and mental conceptions. How are our mental conceptions altered by the technologies available to us? Do we not see the world differently once we have microscopes, telescopes and satellites, X-rays and CAT scans? We understand and think about the world in a very, very different way now, because of the technologies we have. But by the same token, somebody somewhere must have had the mental conception that making a telescope was an interesting thing to do (recall Marx's take on the labor process and the worst of architects). And when that person had that idea, he had to be able to find lens grinders and glassmakers and all the elements necessary in order to make the idea a reality through the production of the telescope. Technologies and organizational forms do not descend from the sky. They get produced out of mental conceptions. They also arise out of our social relations and concretely arise in response to the practical needs of daily life or of labor processes.

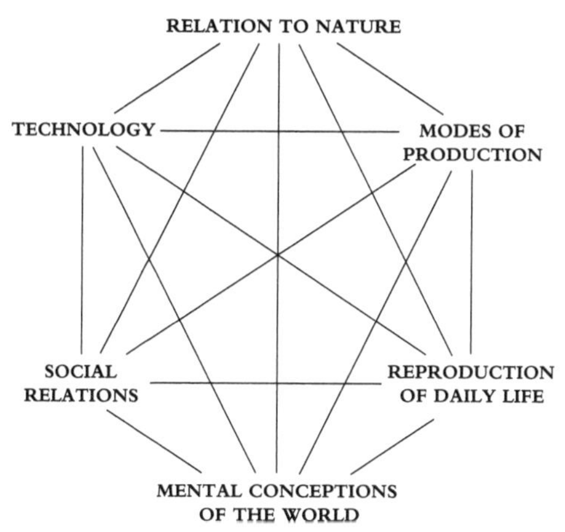

I like the way Marx sets this up, provided it is viewed dialectically, not causally. This way of thinking permeates *Capital*, and the book should be read with this framework in mind. It also provides a standard of critique, because we can analyze Marx's own performance by how well he links these different elements together. How exactly does Marx bring together mental conceptions, social relations and technologies, and does he do it adequately? Are there aspects, such as the politics of daily life, that are left in the shadows? In other words, the dialectic between this formulation and Marx's practices needs to be scrutinized.

So let me summarize. The six elements constitute distinctive moments in the overall process of human evolution understood as a totality. No one moment prevails over the others, even as there exists within each moment the possibility for autonomous development (nature independently mutates and evolves, as do ideas, social relations, forms of daily life, etc.). All these elements coevolve and are subject to perpetual renewal and transformation as dynamic moments within the totality. But it is not a Hegelian totality in which each moment tightly internalizes all the others. It is more like an ecological totality, what Lefebvre refers to as an "ensemble" or Deleuze as an "assemblage," of moments coevolving in an open, dialectical manner. Uneven development between and among the elements produces contingency in human evolution (in much the same way that unpredictable mutations produce contingency in Darwinian theory).

The danger for social theory is to see one of the elements as determinant of all the others. Technological determinism is as wrongheaded as environmental determinism (nature dictates), class-struggle determinism, idealism (mental conceptions are in the vanguard), labor-process determinism or determinism arising out of (cultural) shifts in everyday life (this is the political position taken by Paul Hawken in his influential text *Blessed Unrest*[6]). Major transformations, such as the movement from feudalism (or some other precapitalist configuration) to capitalism, occur through a dialectic of transformations across all the moments. This coevolution developed unevenly in space and time to produce all manner of local contingencies, albeit contingencies limited by the interplay within the assemblage of elements implicated in the evolutionary process and the growing spatial (and sometimes competitive) integration of economic-development processes in the world market. Perhaps one of the biggest failures of the conscious attempt to build socialism and communism on the basis of capitalism was the failure to recognize the need to engage politically across all these moments in a way that was sensitive to geographical specificities. The temptation for revolutionary

6. Paul Hawken, *Blessed Unrest: How the Largest Movement in the World Came into Being and Why No One Saw It Coming* (New York: Viking, 2007).

communism was to reduce the dialectic to a simple causal model in which one or another moment was placed in the vanguard of change, and that was supposed to be that. This approach inevitably failed.

On the surface, the third phase of the footnote appears to contradict my interpretation of the second:

> Even a history of religion that is written in abstraction from this material basis is uncritical. It is, in reality, much easier to discover by analysis the earthly kernel of the misty creations of religion than to do the opposite, i.e. to develop from the actual, given relations of life the forms in which these have been apotheosized. The latter method is the only materialist, and therefore the only scientific one. (493–4)

Marx considered himself a scientist, and he is here asserting that this means a commitment to materialism. But his materialism is different from that of the natural scientists. It is historical. "The weaknesses of the abstract materialism of natural science, a materialism which excludes the historical process, are immediately evident from the abstract and ideological conceptions expressed by its spokesmen whenever they venture beyond the bounds of their own speciality" (494). Darwin's findings on evolution were flawed because he ignored the impact of the historical context on his theorizing (the power of the metaphors that he drew from British capitalism) and failed to carry over his argument onto and integrate his findings with human evolution. Marx was writing before Social Darwinism became popular, of course, but he prefigures a critical response to the way in which the Social Darwinists legitimized capitalism as "natural" by appealing to Darwin's theory of evolution. Since Darwin's theory drew its guiding metaphors from capitalism and was inspired by the social theory of Malthus, it was hardly surprising to see capitalism confirmed as wholly consistent with supposedly natural processes of competition, struggle for survival and, of course, survival of the fittest (without paying attention to Kropotkin's mutual aid).

Marx's general point is that natural scientists, because they failed to understand their historical moment and were barred by their methodological commitments from integrating human history into their models of the world, frequently ended up with at best partial and at worst serious misinterpretations of that world. At worst, they concealed their historical and political assumptions under a supposedly neutral and objective science. This critical perspective, which Marx pioneered, is now standard practice within the field of science studies, where it has repeatedly been shown that the importation into science of social metaphors about gender, sexuality or social hierarchies leads to all kinds of misreadings of what the natural world is actually about, even as it is understood that without metaphors scientific inquiry would go nowhere.

But there is a much deeper issue here that needs to be addressed. In the first lecture, I talked about Marx's way of moving by descent: you start with the surface appearance, then dive deep down beneath the fetishisms to uncover a theoretical conceptual apparatus that can capture the underlying motion of social processes. That theoretical apparatus is then brought step by step back to the surface to interpret the dynamics of daily life in new ways. This is, Marx confirms in the footnote, "the only materialist and therefore the only scientific (method)." We have already seen a specific example of this method at work in the chapter on the working day. Value as socially necessary labor-time internalizes a specific capitalist temporality, and a vast field of social struggles on the surface of society ensues, concerning the appropriation of the time of others. The fact that "moments are the elements of profit" leads capitalists to be obsessed with time discipline and time control (and will shortly also explain why they are obsessed with speed-up).

But how are we to think about the relation between, say, the deep-value theory and the unpredictable ferment of surface struggles over the length of the working day? Back on page 175, Marx approvingly cites (in yet another footnote!) a famous passage from an earlier work, *A Contribution to the Critique of Political Economy*:

> My view is that each particular mode of production, and the relations of production corresponding to it at each given moment, in short 'the economic structure of society', is 'the real foundation, on which arises a legal and political superstructure and to which correspond definite forms of social consciousness' [mental conceptions, if you like], and that 'the mode of production of material life conditions the general process of social, political, and intellectual life.

He leaves out the following sentence from the *Critique*, which explains that it is in the superstructure that we become conscious of political issues and fight them out.

This is what is usually referred to as the base-superstructure model. The supposition is that there is an economic base on which there arise frameworks of thought as well as a political and legal superstructure that collectively define how we become conscious of problems and fight them out. This formulation is sometimes read deterministically: the economic base *determines* the political and legal infrastructure, determines the forms of struggle that are found there and, to the degree that there are transformations occurring in the economic base, actually determines the outcomes of political struggles. But I can't see how the argument can be viewed as deterministic or even causal. This is not how the chapter on the working day unfolds at all. There are class alliances, conjunctural possibilities, discursive shifts in sentiments, and the outcome is never certain. But there is always such a deep concern over the appropriation of the time of others that the issue never goes away. It is a perpetual point of contestation "between equal rights" within capitalism that can never arrive at some ultimate solution. Struggles over time are fundamental to the capitalist mode of production. This is what the deep theory tells us, and no matter what happens in the superstructure, that imperative cannot be overcome without overthrowing capitalism.

In any case, productive forces and social relations cannot exist without expression and representation in the political and legal superstructure. We have seen this with money, which is a representation of value surrounded by all manner of institutional and legal arrangements, and certainly an object of struggle and political manipulation (as is also the case with legal frameworks of private property rights). But Marx has also shown that without money (or a legal framework of private property rights), value could not exist as a foundational economic relation. Things get worked out in the monetary sphere in very particular ways depending on the dynamics of class struggle, and this has implications for how the value theory works. Is money in the political superstructure or down in the economic base? The answer, surely, has to be both.

Similarly, one would not say, from the chapter on the working day, that the outcome of the working-day struggle was determined by movements in the economic base. Furthermore, the political restriction on the length of the working day in part led capitalists to look for another way to gain surplus-value, i.e., relative surplus-value. Marx clearly does not intend this base-superstructure model to operate mechanically or causally, but he does use it dialectically.

Yet it is also true that the "working out" that goes on in the realm of struggle over the length of the working day is a working out of the fundamental fact that moments are the elements of profit, which derives from the definition of value as socially necessary labor-time. There was not a concerted struggle over the length of the working day in precapitalist societies or even in ancient Rome. Only within the rules of a capitalist mode of production does this sort of struggle make sense. Formal issues such as the length of the working day (week, year, lifetime) get thrown up precisely because of the deep structure of what capitalism has become. How these struggles get resolved depends on you and me and everybody else. And indeed, the struggle could potentially be resolved in such a way as to entail the abolition of the capitalist mode of production. A society would be constructed in which moments are *not* the elements of profit. Can you imagine what that would look like? Sounds rather nice, no?

My main point here is that the ways in which these things get worked out—through political and legal means, the balance of class forces, hegemonic mental conceptions and the like—are not ineffectual in relation to the deep concept of the circulation of value as capital. The real scientific method is to identify those deep elements which explain to you why certain things go on in our society the way they do. We saw that in the struggle over the length of the working day. We also see it in the struggle over relative surplus-value, which explains why capitalism has to be so technologically dynamic. We seem not to have choices over whether or not to grow or to invent because that's what the deep structure of capitalism mandates. The only interesting question is, therefore, how is growth going to occur, and with what kinds of technological change? This forces us to consider the implications for mental conceptions, the relation to nature and all the other moments. If we don't like these implications then we have no recourse except to engage in struggle with respect not only to one or another of the moments but to all of them simultaneously, until we ultimately come to terms with having to transform the very rule of value itself.

The circulation of capital is, however, the driver of the dynamics under capitalism. But what is socially necessary for this process to be sustained? Consider, for example, the necessary mental conceptions. If you go down to Wall Street with a big banner saying, "Growth Is Bad, Stop It Now," would that be considered an anticapitalist sentiment? You bet it would. You would be dismissed, however, not necessarily for being anticapitalist but for being antigrowth, because growth is considered both inevitable and good. Zero growth signals serious problems. Japan hasn't grown much at all in recent times, poor folk. But the growth in China has been spectacular, so the Chinese are the grand success story. How can we emulate them? We all happily sit around and say growth is good, technological change is good and so capitalism, which requires both, must also be good. This is the sort of common belief system that Gramsci often referred to as "hegemony." The same sorts of issues arise concerning institutional arrangements. Capitalism requires adequate legal arrangements to function effectively. The more the Chinese moved down a capitalistic path, the less plausible it was for them to maintain a legal system that didn't acknowledge some sorts of private property rights. But there is a great deal of latitude and contingency in the institutional arrangements that might work.

Sections 1–3: Machine Development, Value Transfers and Effects on Workers

So, finally, let us take up the materials assembled in this long chapter. I suggest you pay careful attention to the sequence of the section headings. These define a logical line of argument that structures Marx's inquiry into the rise of the factory system and the use of machinery. He begins, however, with John Stuart Mill's surprise at the fact that mechanical inventions, supposedly designed to lighten the load of labor, had done nothing of the kind. In fact, they had generally made matters worse. Marx himself is in no way surprised, since machines are used to produce surplus-value, not to lighten the load of labor. But this means, notice, that "the machine is a means for producing surplus-value" (492). This sounds odd, since Marx has argued that machines are dead labor (constant capital) and cannot produce value. Yet they can, however, be a source of surplus-value. The reduction in the value of labor-power through rising productivity in the wage-goods sector yields relative surplus-value to the capitalist class, while the capitalist with the best machinery will acquire the temporary form of relative surplus-value that accrues to the producer with higher productivity. No wonder capitalists hold to the fetish belief that machines produce value!

Marx then considers the difference between tools and machines. To "call a tool a simple machine and a machine a complex tool" and "see no essential difference between them" misses something essential, most notably "the historical element" (that element that he, incidentally, makes so much noise about in the footnote) (492–3). Marx was one of the first people ever to use the phrase "industrial revolution" and to make it central to his historical reconstruction. So what constitutes the heart of this industrial revolution? Was it simply a change of technology, the fact that tools become machines? Is the difference between machines and tools that machines have an external source of power? Does it entail a radical shift in social relations to parallel the transformations in productive forces? The answer is all of the above.

> The machine, which is the starting-point of the industrial revolution, replaces the worker, who handles a single tool, by a mechanism operating with a number of similar tools and set in motion by a single motive power, whatever the form of that power. Here we have the machine, but in its first role as a simple element in production by machinery. (497)

This is predicated, however, on a transformation in the positionality (social relation) of the worker. This is just as important as the machine itself. While workers can continue to provide the motive power, at some point or other the need arose to supplement that power from an external source. Water power had long been pressed into service, but its application was limited and restricted by location.

> Not till the invention of Watt's second and so-called double-acting steam-engine was a prime mover found which drew its own motive power from the consumption of coal and water, was entirely under man's control, was mobile and a means of locomotion, was urban and not—like the water-wheel—rural, permitted production to be concentrated in towns instead of—like the water-wheels—being scattered over the countryside and, finally, was of universal technical application, and little affected in its choice of residence by local circumstances. (499)

The steam engine liberated capital from dependence on localized sources of power, because coal was a commodity that could, in principle, be shipped anywhere. But be careful not to read too much into this invention, because "the steam-engine itself . . . did not give rise to any industrial revolution. It was, on the contrary, the invention of machines that made a revolution in the form of steam-engines necessary" (496–7).

And while Marx doesn't mention it, coal also eliminated the acute rivalry, which had limited industrial development before this time, between the use of land for food production and the use of land's biomass as an energy source. All the time wood and charcoal were primary fuel sources, the competition for land between food and biofuels raised the cost of both. With coal it became possible to mine the stored energy of the Carboniferous period; then, with oil, that of the Cretaceous period. This liberated the land for food and other forms of raw-material production and liberated industry to proliferate using cheap fuels, with all kinds of implications both for urbanization and, of course, for the way we live our lives right now. Interestingly, a response to fuel scarcities in recent times has been to go back to the land for fuel (ethanol, in particular), and this has had the predictable consequence of rapidly increasing food and other raw-material prices (with all manner of social consequences, such as food riots and increasing hunger; even my bagel has gone up in price by thirty cents). We are currently re-creating the barriers to capital accumulation that the shift to fossil fuels in the late eighteenth century so successfully circumvented by revolutionizing the relation to nature.

But the hallmark of the industrial revolution was more than just a shift in energy production. The "co-operation by division of labour which is peculiar to manufacture" now appears "as a combination of machines with specific functions." There is a significant evolution in social relations.

> In manufacture, it is the workers who, either singly or in groups, must carry on each particular process with their manual implements. The worker has been appropriated by the process; but the process had previously to be adapted to the worker. This subjective principle of the division of labour no longer exists in production by machinery. Here the total process is examined objectively, viewed in and for itself, and analysed into its constitutive phases. The problem of how to execute each particular process, and to bind the different partial processes together into a whole, is solved by the aid of machines, chemistry, etc.

The result is the evolution of "an articulated system composed of various kinds of single machine, and of groups of single machines," and this "becomes all the more perfect the more the process as a whole becomes a continuous one" (501–2).

There are a number of points to make about this statement. First is the importance of continuity in the production process, which is crucial because the continuity of the circulation of capital requires it, and machinery helps achieve this. Second, note that social relations are being transformed alongside the technical relations. Third, the analysis of the production process into its constitutive phases entails a mental transformation which brings a science (such as chemistry) to bear on technology. In other words, there is an evolution in mental conceptions. At least three of the elements examined in the footnote come into play here, while the relation to nature and to locational requirements also shifts as coal resources replace waterfalls and biomass as primary sources of energy. We see in paragraphs of this sort how Marx's formulation in the footnote is working. The different elements flow easily together to constitute a compelling narrative of coevolution rather than causation. The outcome is an "organized system of machines to which motion is communicated by the transmitting mechanism from an automatic centre," and this, he says, "is the most developed form of production by machinery. Here we have, in place of the isolated machine, a mechanical monster"—Marx loves images of this sort, as we have already seen—"whose body fills whole factories, and whose demonic power, at first hidden by the slow and measured motions of its gigantic members, finally bursts forth in the fast and feverish whirl of its countless working organs." But, Marx reminds us, "the inventions of Vaucanson, Arkwright, Watt and others could be put into practice only because each inventor found a considerable number of skilled mechanical workers available, placed at their disposal by the period of manufacture." That is, the new technologies could not have come on line if the necessary social relations and labor skills had not already been in place. In some cases, these workers "were independent handicraftsmen of various trades," while others were already "grouped together" (503).

But the evolutionary process had its own momentum. "As inventions increased in number, and the demand for the newly discovered machines grew larger, the machine-making industry increasingly split up into numerous independent branches, and the division of labour within these manufactures developed accordingly." Social relations were in full flood of transformation. "Here, therefore in manufacture, we see the immediate technical foundation of large-scale industry. Manufacture produced the machinery with which large-scale industry abolished the handicraft and manufacturing systems in the spheres of production it first seized hold of." After the system had "undergone further development in its old form," it finally created "for itself a new basis appropriate to its own mode of production" (503–4). Capitalism, in short, discovered a technological basis more consistent with its rules of circulation.

This is, in my view, an evolutionary, not a determinist, argument. The contradictions of capitalism as they arose in the manufacturing and handicraft period could not be resolved given the nature of the technologies which existed. Therefore, there was considerable pressure to come up with a new technological mix. Marx is telling the story of how capitalism came to "create for itself a new basis appropriate to its own mode of production." But this whole process was

> dependent on the growth of a class of workers who, owing to the semi-artistic nature of their employment, could increase their numbers only gradually, and not by leaps and bounds. But, besides this, at a certain stage of its development large-scale industry also came into conflict with the technical basis provided for it by handicrafts and manufacture. (504)

The expansionary force of capital encountered limits. The capitalist system had arrived at the point where it needed skilled workers to make the machines that would facilitate its development at the same time as its own technological basis acted as a drag on the capacity of built machines.

But the evolutionary process was hard to stop. "The transformation of the mode of production in one sphere of industry necessitates a similar transformation in other spheres." Note here, by the way, Marx's use of the term "mode of production." He sometimes uses this term, as he does in the opening paragraph of *Capital*, to contrast, say, the capitalist and feudal modes of production. But here it means something much more specific: the mode of production in a particular industry. These two meanings interrelate: the mode of production in a particular industry creates new machine forms which actually are consistent with the capitalist mode of production understood in the broader sense. Here, however, we are talking about specific transformations in modes of production in particular spheres of industry and the dynamic interactions between them.

> This happens at first in branches of industry which are connected together by being separate phases of a process, and yet isolated by the social division of labour . . . Thus machine spinning made machine weaving necessary, and both together made a mechanical and chemical revolution compulsory in bleaching, printing and dyeing.

Spill-over effects between different segments of a production process create mutually reinforcing changes. Furthermore, "the revolution in the modes of production of industry and agriculture made necessary a revolution in the general conditions of the social process of production, i.e. in the means of communication and transport" (505–6). This introduces one of the other themes that I find extremely interesting in Marx: that is the importance of what he calls in the *Grundrisse* the "annihilation of space by time."[7] The evolutionary dynamic of capitalism is not neutral in terms of its geographical form. We've already seen hints of this in his discussion of urbanization, the concentration that could arise through the steam engine, and the locational freedoms conferred by steam power. Connectivity in the world market also changed.

> Hence, quite apart from the immense transformation which took place in shipbuilding, the means of communication and transport gradually adapted themselves to the mode of production of large-scale industry by means of a system of river steamers, railways, ocean steamers and telegraphs. But the huge masses of iron that had now to be forged, welded, cut, bored and shaped required for their part machines of Cyclopean dimensions, which the machine-building trades of the period of manufacture were incapable of constructing.

And here comes the final link in the argument:

> Large-scale industry therefore had to take over the machine itself, its own characteristic instrument of production, and to produce machines by means of machines. It was not till it did this that it could create for itself an adequate technical foundation, and stand on its own feet. (506)

The capacity to produce machines with the aid of machines is, in short, *the* technical foundation of a fully fledged, dynamic capitalist mode of production. In other words, the growth of engineering and the machine-tool industry is the ultimate phase of a revolution that created the "adequate technical foundation" for the capitalist mode of production in general. "As machinery, the instrument of labour assumes a material mode of existence which necessitates the replacement of human force by natural forces, and the replacement of the rule of thumb by the conscious

7. Marx, *Grundrisse*, 524.

application of natural science." This entails a revolution not only in mental conceptions but also of their application.

> In manufacture the organization of the social labour process is purely subjective: it is a combination of specialized workers. Large-scale industry, on the other hand, possesses in the machine system an entirely objective organization of production, which confronts the worker as a pre-existing material condition of production. (508)

The nature of cooperation is fundamentally changed, for example.

I have gone over this section at length, in order to show how the synergistic spread of revolutions in technology both rests on and provokes transformations in social relations, mental conceptions and modes of production (in the concrete and particular sense), as well as in spatial and natural relations. The rise of this new technological system which is suited to a capitalist mode of production (in the grand sense) is an evolutionary story in which all the elements in the footnote coevolve.

In the chapter's second section, Marx asks the following question: how is value transferred from the machine to the product? The other two modes of acquiring relative surplus-value—through cooperation and division of labor—cost capital nothing, apart from some incidental expenses. But a machine is a commodity that has to be bought in the market. This is very different from, say, merely reconfiguring the division of labor in a workplace. Machines have a value, and that value has to be paid for. Somehow the value congealed in the machine must be transferred into "the product it serves to beget," even though no physical transfer of matter is involved (509). Initially, Marx appeals to the idea of straight-line depreciation. If the machine lasts ten years, one-tenth of the value of the machine ends up in the product each year over that time. But then he goes on to derive an important limit to the deployment of machinery:

> The use of machinery for the exclusive purpose of cheapening the product is limited by the requirement that less labour must be expended in producing the machinery than is displaced by the employment of that machinery. For the capitalist, however, there is a further limit on its use. Instead of paying for the labour, he pays only the value of the labour-power employed; the limit to his using a machine is therefore fixed by the difference between the value of the machine and the value of the labour-power replaced by it. (515)

This assumes (as most economists tend to) that capitalists are rational in their decisions. If the machine is expensive and you save very little labor by it, then why buy it? The cheaper the machine and the more expensive the labor, the greater the incentive to employ machinery. The calculation that the capitalist has to make, therefore, is between the value expended to buy the machine and the value saved on labor (variable capital) employed. This limit on the deployment of machinery is typically enforced by the coercive laws of competition. Capitalists who buy costly machines but save little labor by them are going to be driven out of business.

How much variable capital gets saved depends, however, on the value of labor-power. "Hence the invention nowadays in England of machines that are employed only in North America" (516). In North America, the relative scarcity of labor meant high labor costs, so employing machines made sense, but in Britain the existence of surplus labor meant cheap labor and less incentive to use machines. This calculation on the limiting conditions to the employment of machinery is significant, both theoretically and practically. There are contemporary examples in China where, with the abundance of cheap labor, something which is made with a sophisticated and expensive machine in the United States has been broken down into smaller labor processes that can be done by hand. Instead of employing one very expensive machine with twenty laborers in the United States, you employ two thousand laborers in China using hand tools. This example counters the idea that capitalism inevitably marches onward toward ever-greater mechanization and technological sophistication. Given the importance of the limiting conditions and the value relations, then all manner of oscillations can occur in the deployment of machine technologies.

In the third section, Marx considers three consequences of machine deployment for the worker. Machinery facilitated the "Appropriation of Supplementary Labour-Power by Capital. The Employment of Women and Children." Machine technologies effectively destroyed the skill basis that existed in the handicraft period. It then became much easier to employ unskilled women and children. A number of consequences followed. It became possible to substitute the family wage for the individual wage. The latter could be reduced, but the family wage could remain constant as women and children entered the workforce. This has been an interesting and persistent theme in capitalist history. In the United States since the 1970s, individual wages have either declined or remained fairly constant in real terms, but family wages have tended to rise as more women have gone to work. What the capitalists class gets is two laborers for close to the price of one. The Brazilian economic miracle of the 1960s was likewise dominated by a catastrophic diminution of individual wages under the military dictatorship, but family wages managed to stabilize because not only women but kids went to work (child labor in the iron mines surged). This led to the famous comment by the Brazilian president Emílio Garrastazu Médici that "the economy" (he should have said the capitalist class) "is doing very well but the people are doing very badly." There are many historical circumstances where capitalists have pursued this solution to gaining surplus-value.

This also raises the question of the relationship between the individual and the family wage. The latter is necessary for the reproduction of the working class. But who bears the cost of this reproduction? Marx is not very sensitive, as many have pointed out, to questions of gender, but he does in a footnote acknowledge the importance of the relation between household work and the buying and selling of labor-power in the market. If women enter the labor force, then

> domestic work, such as sewing and mending, must be replaced by the purchase of ready-made articles. Hence the diminished expenditure of labour in the house is accompanied by an increased expenditure of money outside. The cost of production of the working-class family therefore increases, and balances its greater income. In addition to this, economy and judgement in the consumption and preparation of the means of subsistence become impossible. (518)

Consideration of the family wage raises other issues. It was very common in Marx's time for the male, particularly in the countries Marx was familiar with, to be deliverer of the whole family labor. The result was the creation of a "gang system" for labor supply. One male figure would be held responsible for delivering the labor-power of several kids, maybe the labor-power of a wife and a sister, as well as the labor-power of nephews and kin. In France, the labor market was frequently constituted as a gang system whereby a patriarchal figure would command the labor of everybody around him and deliver that labor to his employers, leaving the question of the remuneration of that labor and distribution of the benefits to the patriarchal figure. Systems of this sort are not at all uncommon in

Asia and are frequently found in the organization of immigrant groups in Europe and North America. Some of the worst aspects of this, then as now, as Marx points out in a footnote, arose (and arise) through trafficking in children and the equivalent of slave dealing. Relying very much on the reports of the factory inspectors (suffused with Victorian morality that Marx does not criticize) and Engels's account in *The Condition of the Working Class in England*, Marx focuses on the "moral degradation which arises out of the exploitation by capitalism of the labour of women and children," and the weak attempts by the bourgeoisie to counter this moral degradation through education (522). As in the case of the Factory Acts, a contradiction emerges between what individual capitalists are compelled to do by the coercive laws of competition and what the state tries to do in the way of educating children. Marx does therefore raise, albeit in a not very adequate way, issues concerning the reproduction of life (again an important but somewhat neglected element in footnote 4).

The second subsection deals with "The Prolongation of the Working Day". Machinery in fact creates new conditions not only permitting capital to lengthen the working day but also creating "new incentives" to do so.

> Because it is capital, the automatic mechanism is endowed, in the person of the capitalist, with consciousness and a will. As capital, therefore, it is animated by the drive to reduce to a minimum the resistance offered by man, that obstinate yet elastic natural barrier.

The machine is in part designed to overcome worker resistance, which is in any case "lessened by the apparently undemanding nature of work at a machine, and the more pliant and docile character of the women and children employed by preference" (526–7). This is, of course, a typical Victorian prejudice. In fact the women were by no means docile, any more than the children were.

But the heart of the problem here is the temporality and continuity of production. The machine wears out faster the more it is used, and there are strong incentives to use up the machine as fast as possible. To begin with, "the physical deterioration of the machine is of two kinds. The one arises from use," and the other from non-use, i.e., it just rusts away. "But in addition to the material wear and tear, a machine also undergoes what we might call a moral depreciation." I always find this term strange. What

Marx really means is economic obsolescence. If I bought a machine for two million dollars last year, and this year all my competitors can buy it for one million (or, what amounts to the same thing, buy a machine for two million dollars which is twice as efficient as mine), then the value of commodities produced will fall, and I will lose half the value of my machine. "However young and full of life the machine may be, its value is no longer determined by the necessary labour-time actually objectified in it, but by the labour-time necessary to reproduce either it or the better machine." The threat is that the machine will be "devalued to a greater or lesser extent" (528). To protect against this threat, capitalists are impelled to use their machinery up as fast as possible (keeping it employed twenty-four hours a day if possible). This means lengthening the working day (or, as we will see, resorting to shift work and relay systems). Machines supposed to get around lengthening the working day actually stimulate a need to further lengthen it.

Capitalists fall in love with machines because they are a source of surplus and relative surplus-value. The fetish of a "technological fix" becomes ingrained in their belief system. Yet machines are also the source of "an immanent contradiction" because "of the two factors of the surplus-value created by a given amount of capital, one, the rate of surplus-value, cannot be increased except by diminishing the other, the number of workers" (531). And since the mass of surplus-value, so crucial to the capitalist, depends on the rate of surplus-value and the number of workers, labor-saving innovations may leave the capitalist no better off. Throwing workers out of work through technological innovations from this standpoint does not seem a good idea, because the real value producers are lost from production. This contradiction will be made much of in the third volume of *Capital*, where the dynamics of technological innovation are seen as destabilizing and a source of serious crisis tendencies.

But the incentive for capitalists to keep on innovating is all-powerful. The competitive search for the ephemeral form of relative surplus-value becomes overwhelming in spite of the contradictions. Individual capitalists, responding to the coercive laws of competition, behave in a way that is not necessarily in the interests of the capitalist class. But the social consequences for labor can also be catastrophic.

> Partly by placing at the capitalists' disposal new strata of the working class previously inaccessible to him, partly by setting free the workers

> it supplants, machinery produces a surplus working population, which is compelled to submit to the dictates of capital. Hence that remarkable phenomenon in the history of modern industry, that machinery sweeps away every moral and natural restriction on the length of the working day. Hence too the economic paradox that the most powerful instrument for reducing labour-time suffers a dialectical inversion and becomes the most unfailing means for turning the whole lifetime of the worker and his family into labour-time at capital's disposal for its own valorization. (531–2)

Now we see why John Stuart Mill was so right.

The third subsection explicitly takes up the question of intensification. Earlier usually mentioned in passing (as, for example, in the definition of socially necessary labor-time), intensity is here confronted head-on. Capitalists can use machine technology to change and regulate the intensity and pace of the labor process. Reducing what is called the porosity of the working day (moments when work is not being done) is a key objective. How many seconds in a working day can a worker goof off? If they are in charge of their own tools, then they can lay them down and pick them up again. Laborers can work at their own pace. With machine technology, the speed and the continuity are determined internally to the machine system, and workers have to conform to the movement of, say, the assembly line (as in Chaplin's *Modern Times*). There is an inversion in social relations, such that workers now become appendages of the machine. One of the great advances that occurred after 1850, once the industrial bourgeoisie got over the fact that they were going to have to deal with the Factory Acts and the regulation of the length of the working day, was that capitalists discovered that a shorter working day was compatible with increasing intensity. This repositioning of the laborer as an appendage to the labor process is of utmost importance in what follows.

CHAPTER EIGHT

Machinery and Large-Scale Industry

In the last chapter, I invited you to look at this long chapter on machinery through the lens of Marx's footnote 4, paying particular attention to the way "technology reveals the active relation of man to nature, the direct process of the production of his life, and thereby it also lays bare the process of the production of the social relations of his life, and of the mental conceptions that flow from those relations." When reading this chapter, it is interesting to note how Marx knits together interrelations between these different "moments" in order not only to understand the evolution of capitalist technologies but also to show what it is that the study of this evolutionary process reveals about the capitalist mode of production viewed as a totality (as an ensemble or assemblage of interactive elements). If you read this chapter this way, you will see in it a rather richer set of determinations than just a simple story about technological change.

In reading this gargantuan chapter (where it is all too easy to get lost), I also suggested it would be helpful to pay attention to the section headings in order to maintain a sense of the dynamism of the whole argument. Consider the story so far. In the first sections, he explained how capitalism evolved a unique technological basis by transforming the technologies associated with handicraft and manufacturing industries. This basis is eventually achieved by the production of machines by machines, and by the organization of many machines into a factory system. But machines are commodities that have to be paid for. Their value, therefore, has to circulate as constant capital during the machine's lifetime. If that lifetime is ten years, then one-tenth of the value of the machine ends up in the product every year. But this imposes a limit—the depreciating value of the machine should be less than the value of the labor replaced by it. This creates the possibility for uneven geographical development. If labor costs are high in the United States relative to Britain, then the incentive to employ machinery in the United States is greater. Trade-union power in West Germany from the mid-1970s on sustained high wage rates, which produced a strong incentive for technological innovation. The West German economy then gained relative surplus-value vis-à-vis the rest of the world through technological advantage, but the labor-saving innovations produced structural unemployment.

In the third section, Marx examined the implications for the laborer (the relationship between technologies and social relations). The transformation from skilled crafts to machine minding permits the employment of women and children in ways that might not have been possible earlier on. This allows the substitution of family labor (the family wage) for individual labor (the individual wage), with savings for the capitalist and widespread ramifications for family structures, gender relations and shifts in the role and form of domestic economies. But the introduction of machinery also creates an incentive to prolong the working day to confront the problem of "moral depreciation" (economic obsolescence) and the danger of the devaluation of old machinery by the introduction of new and better machines. Capitalists therefore strive to recuperate the value congealed in the machine as fast as they can, which means keeping the machine employed twenty-four hours a day if possible. Machinery can also be used to intensify the labor process. Capitalists can take control of both the continuity and the speed of the labor process and thereby reduce the porosity of the working day. Intensification emerges as an important capitalist strategy for squeezing more surplus-value out of the laborer. This is the story so far.

Sections 4–10: *Workers, Factories, Industry*

The seven remaining sections of the chapter on machinery both deepen and broaden our perspectives on what can be "revealed" about capitalism through an examination of technological evolution. In section 4, Marx examines the factory per se. This is the centerpiece of his concern, not simply as a technical thing but as a social order. But here I need to insert some critical caveats. Marx relies heavily on two sources for his understanding of the factory system. Engels's firsthand experience of Manchester-style industrialism was critical and was supplemented by the writings of Babbage and Ure, who were the day's leading pro-capitalist ideologists and promoters of principles of efficient industrial management. Marx tends to universalize what is going on in Manchester as if this is the ultimate form of capitalist industrialism, and he is, in my judgment, a bit too accepting of Babbage and Ure's ideas. If Engels had been in Birmingham, Marx's presentation might have been quite different. The industrial structure there was small-scale but assembled in such a way as to realize economies of agglomeration. It was more craft-oriented, with workshops producing guns, jewelry and various metallurgical products, and it seems to have been highly efficient and characterized by very different labor relations from those found in the huge cotton factories of the Manchester region. Marx evidently knew very little about what we might call the Birmingham model of capitalist industrialism and therefore failed to address a distinction that has been long-lasting in the history of capitalist development. South Korean industrialism since the 1960s has been Manchester-like, but Hong Kong's has been more Birmingham-like. Bavaria, what is called the Third Italy and other similarly organized industrial districts (Silicon Valley being a special case) have been critically important in recent phases of industrialism, and this is very different from the Manchester-like industrial forms in the Pearl River Delta of China. The point, however, is that all the industrial world was not and is not like the factories of Manchester. Marx's account of the factory, while compelling, is one-sided.

Marx begins by noting that

> along with the tool, the skill of the worker in handling it passes over to the machine. The capabilities of the tool are emancipated from the restraints inseparable from human labour-power. This destroys the technical foundation on which the division of labour in manufacture was based. Hence, in place of the hierarchy of specialized workers that characterizes manufacture, there appears, in the automatic factory, a tendency to equalize and reduce to an identical level every kind of work that has to be done by the minders of the machines; in place of the artificially produced distinctions between the specialized workers, it is natural differences of age and sex that predominate . . . In so far as the division of labour reappears in the factory, it takes the form primarily of a distribution of workers among the specialized machines. (545)

Workers can move from one machine to another. They become, in effect, machine minders.

Marx is here describing the deskilling that accompanies the rise of the factory system, such that all labor is rendered increasingly homogeneous. If you can mind this machine, you can mind that machine. The continued significance of deskilling throughout the history of capitalism has been the subject of considerable debate in more recent times (beginning with Harry Braverman's *Labor and Monopoly Capital*,[1] which provoked a lot of commentary and study from the 1970s onward). Furthermore, "the motion of the whole factory proceeds not from the worker but from the machinery," and for that reason "the working personnel can continually be replaced without any interruption in the labour process" (546). The result is that workers are reduced to the lifelong task of serving particular machines. Plainly, the worker and social relations are being transformed along with the worker's work, such that workers become mere appendages of machines.

> In handicrafts and manufacture, the worker makes use of a tool; in the factory, the machine makes use of him. There the movements of the instrument of labour proceed from him, here it is the movements of the machine that he must follow. In manufacture the workers are the parts of a living mechanism. In the factory we have a lifeless mechanism which is independent of the workers, who are incorporated into it as its living appendages ... Even the lightening of the labour becomes an instrument of torture, since the machine does not free the worker from the work, but rather deprives the work itself of all content ... [The] conditions of work employ the worker. However, it is only with the coming of machinery that this inversion first acquires a technical and palpable reality. Owing to its conversion into an automaton, the instrument of labour confronts the worker during the labour process in the shape of capital, dead labour, which dominates and soaks up living labour-power. The separation of the intellectual faculties of the production process from manual labour, and the transformation of those faculties into powers exercised by capital over labour, is, as we have already shown, finally completed by large-scale industry erected on the foundation of machinery. (548–9)

In other words, mental conceptions are now divided from physical labor. The mental conceptions lie with the capitalists—they are the ones who are designing things. Laborers are not supposed to think; they are just simply supposed to mind machines. This may not be true in fact, of course, but the point is that this is the structure for which the capitalist class struggles day and night, and as a consequence the whole structure

1. Harry Braverman, *Labor and Monopoly Capital: The Degradation of Work in the Twentieth Century* (New York: Monthly Review Press, 1974).

of mental conceptions, social relations, reproduction of life, relation to nature and so on is being transformed along class lines.

> The special skill of each individual machine-operator, who has now been deprived of all significance, vanishes as an infinitesimal quantity in the face of the science [read mental conceptions], the gigantic natural forces [read the relation to nature], and the mass of social labour embodied in the system of machinery, which, together with those three forces, constitutes the power of the 'master'.

But this transformation is predicated on that capacity to so degrade the positionality of workers that they are no more than appendages of machines, unable to use any of their mental powers and subjected to the capitalists' "autocratic power" (549) and despotic rules. Skill now resides only with those who design the machines, the engineers and so on, who become a small group of highly specialized workers. But as Marx earlier remarked, as a counterpoint there emerges "a superior class of workers, in part scientifically educated, in part trained in a handicraft; they stand outside the realm of the factory workers, and are added to them only to make up an aggregate" (545–6).

Transformations of this sort were bound to provoke resistance, particularly from skilled workers. This is the focus of section 5, dealing with "The Struggle Between Worker and Machine." The so-called Luddite movement (named after a fictional character called Ned Ludd) was a machine-breaking movement in which workers would protest their deskilling and loss of jobs by smashing the machines. They saw the machines as their competitors, as the destroyer of their skills and the creator of their job insecurity. But Marx notes an evolution in the politics of this revolt:

> The large-scale destruction of machinery which occurred in the English manufacturing districts during the first fifteen years of the nineteenth century, largely as a result of the employment of the power-loom, and known as the Luddite movement, gave the anti-Jacobin government, composed of such people as Sidmouth and Castlereagh, a pretext for the most violent and reactionary measures. It took both time and experience before the workers learnt to distinguish between machinery and its employment by capital, and therefore to transfer their attacks from the material instruments of production to the form of society which utilizes those instruments. (554–5)

This statement calls for careful evaluation. Marx seems to suggest here that the problem is not machines (the technology), but capitalism (the social relations). It may be inferred (wrongly in my view) that machines are in themselves neutral, that they can therefore be used in the transition to socialism. It seems to have been historically true that the workers themselves gave up on indiscriminate machine breaking in favor of targeting those capitalists who were using machine technology in the most brutal manner. But this seems to violate the spirit of Marx's general line of argument, particularly given my reading of the fourth footnote, in which technologies and social relations are integral to each other. Under this reading, there is bound to be a problem with machines, too, since they have been designed and set up in such a way as to internalize certain social relations, mental conceptions and ways of producing and living. That workers are being turned into appendages of machines is not, surely, a good thing. Nor is the deprivation of mental capacities associated with capitalist machine technologies. So when Lenin praised Fordist techniques of production, set up factory systems for production similar to those being created by US corporations and made the argument that the transformation of social relations wrought by the revolution was what fundamentally mattered, he was treading on dangerous ground. Marx himself appears ambiguous in these passages. Elsewhere, he is more critical of the nature of the technologies through which capitalism has found its own basis. The technologies discussed in this chapter are those suited to a capitalistic mode of production. This should lead us automatically to pose the problem of discovering those distinctive technologies appropriate to a socialist or communist mode of production. If you take the technologies of a capitalist mode of production and try to construct socialism with them, what are you going to get? You are likely to get another version of capitalism, which is what tended to happen in the Soviet Union with the spread of Fordist techniques. In the same way that Marx critiqued Proudhon for merely instantiating bourgeois notions of justice, so Marx is in danger here of endorsing the instantiation of capitalist technologies.

One way to defend Marx is to go back to how he depicts the rise of capitalism. In the manufacturing period, capitalist development rested on late feudal handicraft and manufacturing technologies (while changing their organizational form), and this was necessarily so given the conjunctural conditions. It was only later that capitalism came to define its specific technological basis. In exactly the same way, socialism was bound to make use of capitalist technologies in its early revolutionary stages, and given the exigencies of the moment (war and mass disruption), Lenin was therefore correct to turn to the most advanced capitalist technological forms in order to revive production and so protect the revolution. But a socialist revolutionary project in the long term cannot, given my reading of the footnote, avoid the question of the definition of an alternative technological basis as well as alternative relations to nature, social relations, production systems, reproduction through daily life and mental conceptions of the world. And this, it seems to me, has been one of the acute failures in the history of actually existing communisms. This issue is, of course, broader than communism, since the question of appropriate technologies to realize certain social and political aims, be they feminist, anarchist, environmentalist or whatever, is a general matter deserving of close consideration. Technologies, we have to conclude, are not neutral with respect to the other moments in the social totality.

The problematic class character of capitalist technologies is actually confirmed in Marx's text. "Machinery," he writes,

> does not just act as a superior competitor to the worker, always on the point of making him superfluous. It is a power inimical to him, and capital proclaims this fact loudly and deliberately, as well as making use of it. It is the most powerful weapon for suppressing strikes, those periodic revolts of the working class against the autocracy of capital. According to Gaskell, the steam-engine was from the very first an antagonist of 'human power', an antagonist that enabled the capitalists to tread underfoot the growing demands of the workers . . . It would be possible to write a whole history of the inventions made since 1830 for the sole purpose of providing capital with weapons against working-class revolt. (562–3)

So capitalists consciously construct new technologies as instruments of class struggle. These technologies not only serve to discipline the laborer within the labor process but also help to create a labor surplus which will depress wages and worker aspirations.

Marx here introduces the idea of technologically induced unemployment for the first time. Labor-saving innovations put people out of work. Indeed, over the past thirty years, strong technological changes and incredible increases in productivity have generated unemployment and job insecurity and made it much easier to discipline labor politically.

The tendency has been to blame outsourcing and competition from low-wage labor in Mexico and China for the ills of the US working class, but studies show that about two-thirds of the job losses there are due to technological change. When I arrived in Baltimore in 1969, Bethlehem Steel was employing more than twenty-five thousand workers, but twenty years later it was employing fewer than five thousand workers, producing about the same amount of steel. "The instrument of labour strikes down the worker" (559).

The claim that technologies are used as weapons of class struggle is not hard to substantiate. I recall reading a memoir of an industrialist, a machine-tool innovator, working in Second Empire Paris. He gave three motivations for innovation: first, to lower the price of the commodity and improve competitive position; second, to improve efficiency and eliminate waste; third, to put labor in its place. From the Luddites onward, the class struggle over technological forms has been an endless feature within capitalism.

Section 6, "The Compensation Theory," focuses on the aggregate relationship between capital and labor as a consequence of technological changes. If capitalists save variable capital by employing fewer laborers, then what do they do with the capital they save? If they expand their activities, then some of the labor rendered redundant is reabsorbed. On this basis, bourgeois economists of the time invented a compensation theory to prove that machines in aggregate did not cause unemployment. Marx does not deny that there can be some compensation, but how much is problematic. You can pick up 10 percent of the laborers you just made redundant, or 20 percent. There is no automatic reason why all will be reabsorbed. "Machinery necessarily throws men out of work in those industries into which it is introduced," but it may, "despite this, bring about an increase in employment in other industries. This effect of machinery, however, has nothing in common with the so-called theory of compensation" (570). Even if most workers eventually get re-employed, there is still a serious transitional problem. "As soon as machinery has set free a part of the workers employed in a given branch of industry, the reserve men"—that is, the reserve army which is always out there—"are also diverted into new channels of employment, and become absorbed in other branches; meanwhile, the original victims"—those thrown out of work—"during the period of transition, for the most part starve and perish" (568). There are also adaptation problems: steelworkers cannot become computer programmers overnight.

> Therefore, since machinery in itself shortens the hours of labour, but when employed by capital it lengthens them; since in itself it lightens labour, but when employed by capital it heightens its intensity; since in itself it is a victory of man over the forces of nature but in the hands of capital it makes man the slave of those forces; since in itself it increases the wealth of the producers, but in the hands of capital it makes them into paupers, the bourgeois economist simply states that the contemplation of machinery in itself demonstrates with exactitude that all these evident contradictions are a mere semblance, present in everyday reality, but not existing in themselves, and therefore having no theoretical existence either. (568–9)

The machine always has to be seen in relation, therefore, to the capitalist use of it. And there is no question but that capitalist uses are often ruthlessly and needlessly oppressive. But if the machine is viewed "in itself" as a "victory of man over the forces of nature," as well as "in itself" endowed with potentially virtuous possibilities (such as lightening the load of labor and increasing material well-being), then we are back to the dubious proposition that capitalist technology "in itself" can lay the basis for alternative forms of social organization without any major adjustment, let alone revolutionary transformation. The question is posed once more of the positionality of organizational forms, of technologies and machines in the transition from feudalism to capitalism and from capitalism to socialism or communism. This is one of the big questions raised in this chapter, one that deserves long and hard thought.

Compensation also arises because the introduction of machines increases employment in the machine-tool industry. But recall, "the increase in the labour required to produce the instruments of labour themselves, the machinery, coal, etc. must be less than the reduction in labour achieved by the employment of machinery" (570). Then there is the possibility of increasing employment in raw-material extraction. But in the case of cotton, this unfortunately meant the intensification and expansion of slave labor in the US South rather than the expansion of wage employment. But if all these possibilities for compensation are blocked, then the original problem of what the capitalists should do with their excess capital remains. They acquire this excess, either individually or as a class, as the value of labor-power declines and as the number of laborers they employ tends to decrease.

What is posed here, albeit in somewhat shadowy form, is the problem of what the bourgeoisie should do with all its surplus capital. This is a huge and fundamental problem. I call it the capital-surplus-absorption problem. Capitalists necessarily end up with more of something, a surplus, at the end of the day, and then they've got the problem of what do they do with that surplus the next day. If they can't find anything to do with it, they are in trouble. This is the central problem that gets taken up in later volumes of *Capital*. Marx does not attempt to analyze this in all its fullness here, but he does throw out some suggestions. "The immediate result of machinery is to augment surplus-value and the mass of products in which surplus-value is embodied. It also increases the quantity of substances for the capitalists and their dependants to consume" (572). So "the production of luxuries increases" while the market for surplus product may also be increased through the expansion of foreign trade.

> The increase in means of production and subsistence, accompanied by a relative diminution in the number of workers, provides the impulse for an extension of work that can only bear fruit in the distant future, such as the construction of canals, docks, tunnels, bridges and so on. (573)

Investments in long-term physical infrastructures which don't bear fruit for many years can become vehicles for surplus absorption. Remarks of this sort eventually led me to theorize, in *The Limits to Capital*, the crucial role of geographical expansions and long-term investments (particularly in built environments) in the stabilization of capitalism.

In addition,

> the extraordinary increase in the productivity of large-scale industry, accompanied as it is by both a more intensive and a more extensive exploitation of labour-power in all other spheres of production, permits a larger and larger part of the working class to be employed unproductively. Hence it is possible to reproduce the ancient domestic slaves, on a constantly extending scale, under the name of a servant class, including men-servants, women-servants, lackeys, etc.

This class of unproductive people includes

> all who are too old or too young for work, all 'unproductive' women, young persons and children; . . . the 'ideological groups', such as members of the

> government, priests, lawyers, soldiers, etc.; . . . all the people exclusively occupied in consuming the labour of others in the form of ground rent, interest, etc. (574)

All this large population has to be supported out of the surplus. With reference to England and Wales, Marx cites the 1861 census figures, which show that "all the persons . . . employed in textile factories and metal industries, taken together, number 1,039,605," while those in mining accounted for 565,835, compared with the 1,208,648 persons in the servant class (or "modern domestic slaves") (574). We tend to think that the radical shift from manufacturing to services occurred in the past half century, but what these figures illustrate is that this is not a new sector at all. The big difference is that Marx's servant class was not for the most part organized along capitalist lines (a lot of servants lived in). There were no stores whose signs said "Nails," "Cleaners," "Hair Salon" or whatever. But the population numbers involved in this form of employment were always large and too often neglected in economic analyses (including that of Marx), even though they outnumbered the working class in the classic sense of factory workers, miners and the like.

Section 7, on the "Repulsion and Attraction of Workers through the Development of Machine Production," examines the temporal rhythms of employment corresponding to the ebb and flow of business cycles. Profits, Marx argues, "not only form a source of accelerated accumulation, they also attract into the favoured sphere of production a large part of the additional social capital that is constantly being created, and is always seeking out new areas of investment" (578). But as surplus capital flows into these newly favored areas, it encounters certain barriers such as "those presented by the availability of raw materials and the extent of sales outlets" (579). Where are you going to get the new raw materials from, and whom are you going to sell your surplus product to? These, as we shall see, are key questions, and we will come back to them in the final section, "Reflections and Prognoses."

The immediate answer that Marx proffers here is India! You go wreck the domestic industries of India and turn that vast population into your market, at the same time as you also turn India into a raw-material producer for your own market. That is, you engage in imperialist and colonialist practices and geographical expansions. The problem is solved by what I call a spatial fix. As a result,

> a new and international division of labour springs up, one suited to the requirements of the main industrial countries, and it converts one part of the globe into a chiefly agricultural field of production for supplying the other part, which remains a pre-eminently industrial field. (579–80)

Now all this lies, as yet, outside the grasp of Marx's theoretical apparatus. But what we clearly see from this section is the social necessity within a capitalist mode of production to solve its capital-surplus disposal problem through geographical and temporal displacements.

Ebbs and flows in the industrial cycle are characteristic of capitalism.

> The factory system's tremendous capacity for expanding with sudden immense leaps, and its dependence on the world market, necessarily give rise to the following cycle: feverish production, a consequent glut on the market, then a contraction of the market, which causes production to be crippled. The life of industry becomes a series of periods of moderate activity, prosperity, over-production, crisis and stagnation. The uncertainty and instability to which machinery subjects the employment, and consequently the living conditions, of the workers becomes a normal state of affairs, owing to these periodic turns of the industrial cycle. Except in the periods of prosperity, a most furious combat rages between the capitalists for their individual share in the market. This share is directly proportional to the cheapness of the product. Apart from the rivalry this struggle gives rise to in the use of improved machinery for replacing labour-power, and the introduction of new methods of production, there also comes a time in every industrial cycle when a forcible reduction of wages beneath the value of labour-power is attempted so as to cheapen commodities. (580–2)

This broad-brush description of cyclical movements in the economy lacks any theoretical underpinning, and the exact mechanisms that produce such movements remain unexplored. Marx moves, as it were, from the terrain of theory to a schematic description of the cycles of boom and bust characteristic of the British economy in his time. What follows is a history of the boom and bust cycles in the British cotton industry, the main purpose of which appears to be to simply illustrate his historical point. He summarizes the story:

> We find, then, in the first forty-five years of the English cotton industry, from 1770 to 1815, only five years of crisis and stagnation; but this was

> the period of monopoly. The second period from 1815 to 1863 counts, during its forty-eight years, only twenty years of revival and prosperity against twenty-eight of depression and stagnation. Between 1815 and 1830 competition with the continent of Europe and with the United States sets in. After 1833, the extension of the Asiatic markets is enforced by 'destruction of the human race'. (587)

A footnote makes clear that the "human destruction" he is referring to was that wrought by the British as they forcibly used the opium grown in India to sell in China in return for Chinese silver that could be used to buy British goods.

In Section 8, "The Revolutionary Impact of Large-Scale Industry on Manufacture, Handicrafts and Domestic Industry," Marx examines what happens as different labor systems are brought into competition with one another. This section raises some intriguing questions. In Marx's time, there were domestic labor systems, handicraft systems, manufacturing systems and factory systems all coexisting, sometimes in the same region. When brought into competition with one another, these systems underwent adaptations, sometimes producing new hybrid forms, but with the general result that conditions of work became absolutely appalling if not totally intolerable in all sectors. Handicraft workers had to work five times as hard to compete with the products of power looms, for example. But Marx seems to believe that, ultimately, the factory system was going to prevail. I say "seems" because he does not explicitly say so. But there are many hints here of some sort of teleological progression, such that capitalism necessarily and increasingly moves toward a factory-based system. The older and hybrid labor systems, hanging on by organizing totally inhumane systems of exploitation (which Marx, with the help of the factory inspectors, will describe in graphic detail), could not possibly last. If this is what he is saying, then there are grounds for disagreement.

I prefer to read him in another way, possibly against the grain of his own thinking. Capitalists, I would argue, like to preserve a choice of labor system. If they can't make sufficient profit by the factory system, they want the option to go back to a domestic system. If they can't make it that way, they'll go off to a kind of quasi-manufacturing system. That is, instead of taking the conditions Marx describes in this chapter as temporary and transitional, I prefer to read them as permanent features (options) of a capitalist mode of production in which competition between different labor systems becomes a weapon to be used by capital against labor in the struggle to procure surplus-value. Using Marx's account of the devastating consequences of competition between labor systems this way provides a better understanding of exactly what's going on in the world right now. The revival of sweatshop and family labor systems, putting-out systems, subcontracting systems and the like has been a marked feature of global neoliberal capitalism over the past forty years. The factory system has not always worked to capital's advantage, and Marx does have some good insights as to why. Workers, brought together in a large factory, can become all too aware of their common interests and become a potentially powerful collective political force. Industrialization in South Korea after 1960 or so produced a large-scale factory labor system, and one result was a strong trade-union movement that became a politically potent force until disciplined in the crisis of 1997–8. The labor system in Hong Kong rested on sweatshop family labor and subcontracting structures, and there is little in the way of a trade-union movement there. There are, of course, all sorts of other factors that come into play, but the point is that the availability of a choice of labor system is important to capital in the dynamics of class struggle.

I therefore find it most valuable to read these sections of *Capital* as a cautionary tale of how capitalists, endowed with a choice of labor process and labor system, use that choice as a weapon in class struggle over surplus generation. The factory workers are disciplined by competition with the sweatshops, and vice versa. The heightening of competition between labor systems has made matters much worse for labor in recent times compared with, say, the 1960s or 1970s, when in many parts of the capitalist world there were largish factory systems and strong labor organizations that supported social movements with some degree of political influence and political power. Back then, it was tempting to think that the factory system was indeed going to drive out all else and that the politics that flowed from this would lead on to socialism. Many people who read *Capital* during the 1960s favored such a teleological interpretation.

Consider, then, Marx's account in greater detail. First we get the subsection "Overthrow of Co-operation Based on Handicrafts and on the Division of Labour," which describes a distinctive displacement of one labor system by another. Second, the impact on manufacture and domestic industries is examined. In this instance, the theme is adaptation and not overthrow.

> The principle of machine production, namely the division of the production process into its constituent phases, and the solution of the problems arising from this by the application of mechanics, chemistry and the whole range of the natural sciences, now plays the determining role everywhere. (590)

In other words, the mental conceptions associated with machine technologies penetrated into the reorganization of the older systems. Science and technology only began to coalesce with industry in the nineteenth century, which indeed entailed breaking down labor processes scientifically into component phases, routinizing and mechanizing them. But this implied a mental revolution in the way we understood the world, such that it became possible to apply scientific method to all labor systems (including artisanal ones). To be sure, this did not happen automatically in manufacture and the domestic industries, where older forms of thinking had long prevailed. But the consequences for those industries that were reorganized according to scientific and technical principles were horrific, if Marx's account of lace production (596–9) is anything to go by.

The form domestic industry now took had, in fact, "nothing but the name in common with the old-fashioned domestic industry." It had "been converted into an external department of the factory, the manufacturing workshop, or the warehouse." In this way, capital "sets another army" of workers in motion holding them together "by means of invisible threads." He cites the example of a shirt factory employing 1,000 workers along with "9,000 outworkers spread over the country districts." This form of labor organization remains common to this day, particularly in Asia where the Japanese automobile industry, to take just one example, rests on the basis of a vast network of domestic subcontractors producing auto parts. "Shameless exploitation" is characteristic of these "modern" forms of domestic industry in part because "the workers' power of resistance declines with their dispersal" and because "a whole series of plundering parasites insinuate themselves between the actual employer and the worker he employs" (591).

The widespread transformations in all labor systems were complicated in their specifics. "The revolution in the social mode of production which is the necessary product of the revolution in the means of production is accomplished through a variegated medley of transitional forms" (602). But, and this is the closest Marx gets to endorsing a teleological perspective, "the variety of these transitional forms does not, however, conceal the tendency operating to transform them into the factory system proper" (603). This is, however, a tendency and not a law, and when Marx uses the word "tendency," it is important to note, he nearly always has in mind counteracting tendencies that make actual outcomes uncertain. But in this instance he does not examine potential countertendencies.

Marx does describe how "this industrial revolution, which advances naturally and spontaneously, is also helped on artificially by the extension of the Factory Acts to all industries in which women, young persons and children are employed" (604). Only the largest businesses, he notes, had the resources to comply with the regulations.

> Though the Factory Acts thus artificially ripen the material elements necessary for the conversion of the manufacturing system into the factory system, yet at the same time, because they make it necessary to lay out a greater amount of capital, they hasten the decline of the small masters, and the concentration of capital. (607)

Big capital consequently often supports the rigorous enforcement of all kinds of regulatory regimes on, for example, occupational safety and health, particularly if small businesses can't afford them, leaving the whole field to the large corporations. What is called "regulatory capture" has long been a feature in the history of capitalism. Corporations capture the regulatory apparatus and use it to eliminate competition. When Mini Coopers first came out in Britain in the early 1960s, the regulatory regime in the United States excluded them by insisting that headlights had to be this much off the ground, whereas for the Mini Cooper, they were only that much. So much for the real practices of free trade!

The seasonality that characterizes some lines of production poses another set of problems to which capital has to adapt. One of the reasons I find *Capital* such a prescient book is that Marx often identifies tendencies at work in the capitalism of his time which are all too easy to identify in ours. There has, for example, been a tendency within capitalism to construct what came to be known in the 1980s, as a result of Japanese innovation, as "just-in-time" systems. Marx noted in his day how fluctuations in demand and supply, both seasonal and annual, called for flexible modes of response. He cites a contemporary commentator:

> 'The extension of the railway system throughout the country has tended very much to encourage giving short notice. Purchasers now come up from Glasgow, Manchester, and Edinburgh once every fortnight or so to the wholesale city warehouses which we supply, and give small orders requiring immediate execution, instead of buying from stock as they used to do. Years ago we were always able to work in the slack times so as to meet the demand of the next season, but now no one can say beforehand what will be in demand then.'

For this flexibility to be achieved, however, the creation of an adequate infrastructure of transport and communications was necessary. "The habit of giving such orders becomes more frequent with the extension of railways and telegraphs" (608).

Section 9, on "The Health and Education Clauses of the Factory Acts," poses another set of interesting contradictions. "Factory legislation," Marx begins by noting,

> that first conscious and methodical reaction of society against the spontaneously developed form of its production process, is, as we have seen, just as much the necessary product of large-scale industry as cotton yarn, self-actors and the electric telegraph. (610)

The Acts not only sought to regulate the hours of work but also had something to say about health and education, topics which most industrialists resisted vociferously. Nevertheless,

> as Robert Owen has shown us in detail, the germ of the education of the future is present in the factory system; this education will, in the case of every child over a given age, combine productive labour with instruction and gymnastics, not only as one of the methods of adding to the efficiency of production, but as the only method of producing fully developed human beings.

Why are we suddenly talking about "fully developed human beings" in a chapter rife with stories of the destruction of the dignity and the appropriation of all the capacities of the laborer by capital? Could it be that individual capitalist resistance to health and education provisions is irrational from a capitalist class perspective? "As we have seen, large-scale industry sweeps away by technical means the division of labour characteristic of manufacture" and reproduces "this same division of labour in a still more monstrous shape . . . by converting the worker into a living appendage of the machine" (614). The effects on children are particularly devastating. But there are some positive signs in the midst of all this.

> Right down to the eighteenth century, the different trades were called 'mysteries' (*mystères*), into whose secrets none but those initiated by their profession and their practical experience could penetrate. Large-scale industry tore aside the veil that concealed from men their own social process of production and turned the various spontaneously divided branches of production into riddles, not only to outsiders but even to the initiated. (616)

The modern science of technology entailed a veritable revolution in our mental conceptions of the world. "The varied, apparently unconnected and petrified forms of the social production process were now dissolved into conscious and planned applications of natural science, divided up systematically in accordance with the particular useful effect aimed at in each case." (616–17)

The result was an industrial revolution in every sense of the term.

> Modern industry never views or treats the existing form of a production process as the definitive one. Its technical basis is therefore revolutionary, whereas all earlier modes of production were essentially conservative. By means of machinery, chemical processes and other methods, it is continually transforming not only the technical basis of production but also the functions of the worker and the social combinations of the labour process. At the same time, it thereby also revolutionizes the division of labour within society, and incessantly throws masses of capital and of workers from one branch of production to another. Thus large-scale industry, by its very nature, necessitates variation of labour, fluidity of functions, and mobility of the worker in all directions. (617)

This necessity generates a major contradiction. On the negative side, large-scale industry "reproduces the old division of labour with its ossified particularities" and "does away with all repose, all fixity and all security as far as the worker's life-situation is concerned; . . . it constantly threatens, by taking away the instruments of labour, to snatch from his hands the means." This results "in the reckless squandering of labour-powers, and in the devastating effects of social anarchy" (617–18). But then there is the positive side.

> Large-scale industry, through its very catastrophes, makes the recognition of variation of labour and hence of the fitness of the worker for the maximum number of different kinds of labour into a question of life and death. This possibility of varying labour must become a general law of social production, and the existing relations must be adapted to permit its realization in practice. That monstrosity, the disposable working population held in reserve, in misery, for the changing requirements of capitalist exploitation, must be replaced by the individual man who is absolutely available for the different kinds of labour required of him; the partially developed individual, who is merely the bearer of one specialized social function, must be replaced by the totally developed individual, for whom the different social functions are different modes of activity he takes up in turn. (618)

Capitalism requires fluidity and adaptability of labor, an educated and well-rounded labor force, capable of doing multiple tasks and able to respond flexibly to changing conditions. Herein lies a deep contradiction: on the one hand, capital wants degraded labor, unintelligent labor, the equivalent of a trained gorilla to do capital's bidding without question, at the same time as it needs this other kind of flexible, adaptable and educated labor, too. How can this contradiction be addressed without giving rise to "revolutionary ferments" (619), particularly when it would be difficult for individual capitalists, intensely pursuing their own self-interest and impelled by the coercive laws of competition, to act on it?

One collective class answer lay in the educational clauses inserted into the Factory Acts. Such clauses were not necessarily enforced, Marx notes, particularly in the face of individual capitalist resistance. Nevertheless, the fact that the clauses were deemed necessary in a state which, as we earlier noted, was governed by capitalists and landlords is significant. It suggested that "technological education" for the working class, "both theoretical and practical, will take its proper place in the schools of the workers." Again:

> There is also no doubt that those revolutionary ferments whose goal is the abolition of the old division of labour stand in diametrical contradiction

> with the capitalist form of production, and the economic situation of the workers which corresponds to that form.

So mark well: the development of these sorts of "contradictions of a given historical form of production is the only historical way in which it can be dissolved and reconstructed on a new basis" (619).

The development of this fundamental contradiction is crucial to understanding transformations in the reproduction of the labor force. Large-scale industry plays an important role in "overturning the economic foundation of the old family system, and the family labour corresponding to it." It has "also dissolved . . . old family relationships," revolutionized relationships between parents and children and curbed the misuse of parental power that arises through the gang system. The capitalist mode of exploitation, by sweeping away the economic foundation which corresponded to parental power, made the use of parental power into its misuse" (620). But,

> however terrible and disgusting the dissolution of the old family ties within the capitalist system may appear, large-scale industry, by assigning an important part in socially organized processes of production, outside the sphere of the domestic economy, to women, young persons and children of both sexes, does nevertheless create a new economic foundation for a higher form of the family and of relations between the sexes. (620–1)

It is obvious, Marx concludes,

> that the fact that the collective working group is composed of individuals of both sexes and all ages must under the appropriate conditions turn into a source of humane development, although in its spontaneously developed, brutal, capitalist form, the system works in the opposite direction. (621)

The quest for fluidity, flexibility and adaptability of labor revolutionizes the family as well as relations between the sexes! Pressures of this sort continue to be with us, at the same time that the negative side of the contradiction Marx here identifies continues to be omnipresent. This is, we should conclude, a permanent rather than transitory contradiction within the heart of capitalism.

So what we suddenly encounter at the end of this long chapter, full of negative imagery, are some positive and revolutionary potentialities for the education of the working classes and a radical reconfiguration (with the aid of state power) in its conditions of reproduction. Capital needs fluidity of labor and therefore has to educate the laborers while breaking down old paternalistic, patriarchal rigidities. These ideas aren't really well worked out in Marx's text. But it's interesting that he would find it important to insert them into this account. And in the same way that the politics of the working day was derived to save capital from its self-destructive tendencies, here, too, that politics contains the kernel of a working-class politics to overthrow the whole capitalist system.

This brings Marx, after a lengthy and detailed review of the Factory Acts, to his conclusion, in which once again he flirts with a teleological formulation:

> If the general extension of factory legislation to all trades for the purpose of protecting the working class both in mind and body has become inevitable, on the other hand, as we have already pointed out, that extension hastens on the general conversion of numerous isolated small industries into a few combined industries carried on upon a large scale; it therefore accelerates the concentration of capital and the exclusive predominance of the factory system. It destroys both the ancient and the transitional forms behind which the dominion of capital is still partially hidden, and replaces them with a dominion which is direct and unconcealed. But by doing this it also generalizes the direct struggle against its rule. While in each individual workshop it enforces uniformity, regularity, order and economy, the result of the immense impetus given to technical improvement by the limitation and regulation of the working day is to increase the anarchy and the proneness to catastrophe of capitalist production as a whole, the intensity of labour, and the competition of machinery with the worker. By the destruction of small-scale and domestic industries it destroys the last resorts of the 'redundant population', thereby removing what was previously a safety-valve for the whole social mechanism. By maturing the material conditions and the social combination of the process of production, it matures the contradictions and antagonisms of the capitalist form of that process, and thereby ripens both the elements for forming a new society and the forces tending towards the overthrow of the old one. (635)

Section 10, "Large-Scale Industry and Agriculture," brings "the relation of man to nature" back into the picture, making, as it were, a brief but important cameo appearance in the overall argument. "In the sphere of agriculture," Marx claims, "large-scale industry has a more revolutionary effect than elsewhere," in part because "it annihilates the bulwark of the old society, the 'peasant', and substitutes for him the wage labourer," which in turn generates class conflict in the countryside. The extension of rational scientific principles to agriculture simultaneously revolutionizes relations between agriculture and manufacturing and "creates the material conditions for a new and higher synthesis" between agriculture and industry. But this potentially positive outcome occurs at the expense of disturbing

> the metabolic interaction between man and the earth, i.e. it prevents the return to the soil of its constituent elements consumed by man in the form of food and clothing; hence it hinders the operation of the eternal natural condition for the lasting fertility of the soil. (637)

This problem is exacerbated by increasing urbanization. "All progress in capitalist agriculture," Marx concludes,

> is a progress in the art, not only of robbing the worker, but of robbing the soil; all progress in increasing the fertility of the soil for a given time is a progress towards ruining the more long-lasting sources of that fertility. The more a country proceeds from large-scale industry as the background of its development, as in the case of the United States, the more rapid is this process of destruction. Capitalist production, therefore, only develops the techniques and the degree of combination of the social process of production by simultaneously undermining the original sources of all wealth—the soil and the worker. (638)

The relationships between technology, nature, the production and reproduction of life take a negative turn even as revolutions in mental conceptions and social relations open up positive possibilities. Marx does not advocate going back to a society where production processes were "*mystères*." He plainly believes that the application of science and technology can have progressive implications. But the big problem in this chapter is to figure out where, exactly, these progressive possibilities might lie and how they can be mobilized in the quest to create a socialist mode of production. Marx, while he does not solve this problem, poses it and forces us to reflect on it. Technological and organizational changes are not a *deus ex machina*, but deeply embedded in the coevolution of our relation to nature, processes of production, social relations, mental conceptions of the world and the reproduction of daily life. All these "moments" get combined in this chapter, some far more prominently than others. This chapter can and should be read as an essay on thinking through these relations. But the sense of method that then arises permits an interrogation of Marx's argument on Marx's own terms.

CHAPTER NINE

From Absolute and Relative Surplus-Value to the Accumulation of Capital

Considerable attention has been paid in the preceding chapters to the various ways in which relative and absolute surplus-value can be procured. When Marx sets up a conceptual bifurcation of this kind, he invariably brings the duality back into a state of unity: finally, there is only one surplus-value, and its two forms are conditional on each other. It would be impossible to gain absolute surplus-value without an adequate technological and organizational basis. Conversely, relative surplus-value would have no meaning without a length of working day that allowed the appropriation of absolute surplus-value. The difference is only one of capitalist strategy that "makes itself felt whenever there is a question of raising the rate of surplus-value" (646). As usually happens when Marx moves to a point of synthesis, he both highlights materials already presented and takes them to a different vantage point whence it is possible to see the terrain of capitalism in a novel way. The new perspectives in chapter 16 have been more than a little controversial, and they therefore call for careful scrutiny.

Consider, first, the concept of the collective laborer, already appealed to several times in earlier chapters. Surplus-value is no longer seen as an individual relationship of exploitation but as part of a larger whole in which laborers, in cooperation and spread across the detail division of labor, collectively produce the surplus-value that the capitalists appropriate. The difficulty with this concept is to define where the collective laborer begins and ends. The simplest way would be to take, say, the factory as a whole and designate everyone in it, including the cleaners, janitors, warehouse managers and even trainees, as part of the collective laborer, even though many workers of this sort play no direct part in the actual production of commodities.

> In order to work productively, it is no longer necessary for the individual himself to put his hand to the object; it is sufficient for him to be an organ

> of the collective labourer, and to perform any one of its subordinate functions. (643–4)

But a lot of labor does not take place in factories, and the tendency in recent times has been to resort to outsourcing and subcontracting behind which lie even other subcontractors. And what do we say about advertising, marketing and design functions as well as business services that are essential to the selling of commodities but are usually but not always separated from immediate production activities? Or do we confine ourselves solely to activities within the factory? The exact definition is hard to come by, and there seems to be no exact solution—hence the controversy. But without the help of such a concept, it would be difficult to make the move toward a more macro-theoretic approach to the dynamics of capitalism. So Marx plows ahead, asserting that the analysis so far "remains correct for the collective labourer, considered as a whole," even as "it no longer holds good for each member taken individually."

The second move is to contrast this broadening of the definition of productive labor with a narrowing of its compass such that "the only worker who is productive is one who produces surplus-value for the capitalist." To depict everyone else as "unproductive" risks an emotive reaction because it sounds like a slur on all those who work extremely hard to make ends meet. But, as Marx hastens to point out, under capitalism, "to be a productive worker is therefore not a piece of luck, but a misfortune" (644). Marx's notion of "productive" is not normative or universal, but a definition historically specific to capitalism. As far as capital is concerned, those who do not contribute to the production of surplus-value are considered nonproductive. The task for socialism would therefore be to redefine "productive" in a more socially responsible and beneficial manner.

But even within the context of capitalism, there are legitimate challenges on the issue of how "productive" might be defined. Feminists have long argued, for example, that unpaid domestic labor reduces the market value of labor-power and is therefore productive of surplus-value for the capitalist. Marx does not address this issue, but he does take up the question of the supposedly "natural basis" of productivity, and his analysis provides some clues as to how he might have approached some of these other questions. Productivity, he concedes, can be "fettered by natural conditions" or advantaged because "the greater the natural fertility of the soil and the kindness of the climate, the smaller the amount of labour-time necessary for the maintenance and reproduction of the producer." All other things being equal, "the quantity of surplus labour will vary according to the natural conditions within which labour is carried on, in particular the fertility of the soil" (647–8). There is no reason not to say, therefore, that surplus labor will equally vary according to the social conditions (e.g., the productivity of family labor). We leave aside some odd passages that echo nineteenth-century thinking on environmental determinism and the domination of nature ("where nature is too prodigal with her gifts, she 'keeps him in hand like a child in leading strings'"); Marx then concludes that "favourable natural" (to which we might now add social) "conditions can provide in themselves only the possibility, never the reality of surplus labour, nor . . . the reality of surplus-value and a surplus product" (649–50). That is, the dynamic relation to nature (or to daily life conditions and household labor) forms a necessary but not sufficient backdrop to the social processes and class relations whereby surplus-value is created and appropriated.

Marx urges us to recognize that the "capital-relation arises out of an economic soil that is the product of a long process of development," such that the productivity of labor "is a gift, not of nature, but of a history embracing thousand of centuries" (647). Furthermore, he reminds us, "before [the laborer] spends [leisure time] in surplus labour for others, compulsion is necessary." And the ultimate irony is that "both the historically developed productive forces . . . and its naturally conditioned productive forces, appear as productive forces of the capital into which that labour is incorporated" (651). The crux of the matter for Marx, rightly or wrongly, always lies in the specific configuration of surplus-value appropriation by capital from labor in the matrix of elements that define the totality of an ever-evolving capitalist mode of production. Had he addressed the issue, almost certainly Marx would have taken up the travails of domestic labor in the same way as he treats of the relation to nature (hinted at in his footnote on page 518).

The two moves, of both broadening and narrowing the definition of productive labor, are not independent of each other. Taken together, they help Marx move from an individual micro-perspective, in which the dominant image is of the individual worker being exploited by a particular capitalist employer, to a macro-analysis of class relations in which it is the exploitation of one class by another class that takes center stage. This class perspective is going to dominate in the remaining chapters.

Interestingly, all forms of economic theory encounter problems of some sort in moving from a micro- to a macro-theoretical terrain. Bourgeois political economy had no way to make the move since it had (and still has) no theory of the origins of surplus-value. Ricardo ignored the problem entirely and while John Stuart Mill at least recognized that it had something to do with labor he could not identify exactly what because he could not see the difference between what labor gets and what labor makes. Alas poor Mill: "on a level plain," scoffs Marx, "simple mounds look like hills, and the insipid flatness of our present bourgeoisie is to be measured by the altitude of its 'great intellects'" (654). While Marx's theory of surplus-value does facilitate the move, the way he does it, as we have seen, is not above criticism. But we, too, have to plow on in order to harvest the fruits of his thinking.

The following two chapters do not pose any substantial issues. In chapter 17, all that Marx does is to recognize that surplus-value will vary according to three variables: the length of the working day, the intensity of labor and the productivity of labor, so that capitalists have, in effect, three strategies they can deploy. The diminution of possibilities on one dimension can be compensated for by resort to another. The underlying point is to emphasize, as Marx so often does, the flexibility of capitalist strategies in the search for surplus-value: if they cannot get it this way (by increasing intensity) then they will get it that way (by increasing the hours of labor). I emphasize this point because Marx is so often depicted as a rigid thinker operating with rigid concepts. Chapter 18 merely goes over (once again!) various formulae for interpreting the rate of surplus-value. There is a lot of repetition of this sort in *Capital*. It sometimes reads as if Marx is nervous that we have not quite got the point, so he feels constrained to repeat it just to make sure.

CHAPTERS 19–22: WAGES

The short chapters on wages, chapters 19–22, are relatively self-explanatory. Consequences flow, as might be expected, from the fact that it is the *representation* in money-form—wages—rather than the value of labor-power that provides the field of social action. This immediately poses the problem of the fetish mask that hides social relations beneath the ferment of representational politics. Marx begins, however, by reminding us that there is a huge difference between "the value of labor" (the term that classical political economists used) and "the value of labor-power."

> It is not labour which directly confronts the possessor of money on the commodity-market, but rather the worker. What the worker is selling is his labour-power. As soon as his labour actually begins, it has already ceased to belong to him; it can therefore no longer be sold by him. Labour is the substance, and the immanent measure of value, but it has no value itself.

To think otherwise is to engage in a tautology, in effect to speak of the value of value.

> In the expression 'value of labour', the concept of value is not only completely extinguished, but inverted, so that it becomes its contrary. It is an expression as imaginary as the value of the earth. These imaginary expressions arise, nevertheless, from the relations of production themselves. They are categories for the forms of appearance of essential relations. That in their appearance things are often presented in an inverted way is something fairly familiar in every science, apart from political economy. (677)

In other words, the value of labor is a fetish concept that disguises the idea of the value of labor-power and thereby conveniently evades the crucial question as to how labor-power became a commodity.

The only way in which classical political economy could resolve the problem of what it was that fixed what it incorrectly called the value of labor was to appeal to the doctrine of supply and demand. This doctrine has reappeared several times in *Capital*, but Marx is at his most explicit here in rejecting its explanatory value. Even classical political economy

> soon recognized that changes in the relation between demand and supply explained nothing, with regard to the price of labour or any other commodity, except those changes themselves, i.e. the oscillations of the market price above or below a certain mean. If demand and supply balance, the oscillation of prices ceases, all other circumstances remaining the same. But then demand and supply also cease to explain anything. The price of labour, at the moment when demand and supply are in equilibrium, is its natural price, determined independently of the relation of demand and supply. (678)

This independent determination Marx has already defined in his analysis of the buying and selling of labor-power. It is fixed by the value of the commodities needed to reproduce the worker at a given standard of living in a given society at a given time. Continuing to talk about the value of labor instead of the value of labor-power leads into all kinds of confusions. So Marx then tries to clarify matters by offering (once more!) a useful brief résumé of the theory of surplus-value on page 679.

But the laborer can be remunerated in different ways—by the hour, the day, the week or the piece. Chapter 20 is about time wages and how the time-wage system works. There is nothing very problematic here, except we must remind ourselves that the way in which this is being worked out in the market disguises the underlying social relation. Chapter 21 is about piece wages, the advantage of which for the capitalist is that workers can be forced to compete with one another in terms of individual productivity. Excessive competition between workers drives productivity up and wages down, quite possibly below the value of labor-power. On the other hand, competition between capitalists is likely to drive wages upward. So we end up once more with the idea that there is some equilibrium point where competition between capitalists and competition between workers is producing an actual wage in the market which adequately represents the value of labor-power.

The section on wages culminates in chapter 22, with an examination of national differences in wages. Marx here briefly departs from his tendency to analyze capitalism as if it were a closed system. There is an opening here to examine uneven geographical development in a globalizing system. But the treatment is too brief to go far. If the value of labor-power is fixed by the value of the basket of commodities needed to support the laborer at a given standard of living, and if that standard varies according to natural conditions, the state of class struggle and the degree of civilization in a country, then plainly the value of labor-power stands to vary geographically (from country to country, in this case) in significant ways. The history of class struggle in Germany is different from that in Britain or Spain, for example, and so there are national differences in wages (actually, there are often significant regional differences, too, but Marx does not consider that here). Similarly, variations in productivity in those industries that are producing wage goods in different parts of the world produce differentiations in the value of labor-power and wage rates. A low nominal wage in a highly productive country translates into a higher real wage, and vice versa, because workers command more goods with the wages they receive (this is what is now referred to as purchasing-power parity). So what happens to trade between countries under these conditions, and how will competition between the different countries work? Marx does not probe deeply into the question, since he mainly seems interested in how real wages and nominal wages differ primarily because of variations in productivity in the wage-goods industries in the different countries. The result will be contrasting dynamics between countries (for these were Marx's units of comparison) in how capitalism develops and how surplus-value is being pursued strategically and extracted. Almost certainly this would lead, if Marx had taken the matter further, to a serious questioning of Ricardo's doctrine of comparative advantage in foreign trade, but for some reason Marx chose not to pursue that line of argument further here. I have to say I find it hard to get excited about these chapters on wages, since the ideas are fairly obvious and the writing rather pedestrian.

PART VII: THE PROCESS OF ACCUMULATION OF CAPITAL

Part 7, however, is immensely interesting and insightful, for it is here that Marx takes up "The Process of Accumulation of Capital" as a whole. He here constructs what might best be called a "macro-analysis" of the dynamics of a capitalist mode of production. This is, unquestionably, the culminating argument of Volume I of *Capital*. A whole battery of earlier insights are brought together to create what we would now call a series of "models" of capitalist dynamics. It is vital, however, in reading part 7 to bear in mind the nature of the assumptions. Marx's conclusions are not universal statements but contingent findings, based on and limited by his assumptions. We forget this at our peril. There are far too many commentaries on Marx's work, both favorable and unfavorable, that pass over into serious misinterpretation because they neglect the impact of his assumptions. One of the most famous theses advanced here, for example, is that of the tendency toward the increasing immiseration of the proletariat and the production of ever greater class inequality. This thesis is contingent on Marx's assumptions, and when those assumptions are relaxed or replaced, the thesis does not necessarily hold. I get extremely irritated with attempts to prove or disprove Marx's findings in these chapters as if he were setting out his conclusions as universal truths rather than as contingent propositions.

Marx specifies the assumptions in the preface to part 7. He states that

> the first condition of accumulation is that the capitalist must have contrived to sell his commodities, and to reconvert into capital the greater part of the money received from their sale. In the following pages, we shall assume that capital passes through its process of circulation in the normal way. The detailed analysis of the process will be found in Volume 2. (709)

The implication of "the normal way" is that capitalists have no problem selling their goods at their value in the market or recirculating the surplus-value they gain back into production. All commodities therefore trade at their value. There is no overproduction or underproduction; everything is traded in equilibrium. In particular, there is no problem in finding a market. There is never any lack of effective demand. Is this a reasonable assumption? The answer is, not at all, for we rule out one of the major aspects of crisis formation that, for example, dominated in the Great Depression of the 1930s and became central in Keynesian theories, i.e., the lack of effective demand. Marx abandoned these assumptions in later volumes, but in the next three chapters, he holds rigorously to them. Holding effective demand to one side permits Marx to identify aspects of the capitalist dynamic that might otherwise remain opaque.

The second assumption is that the division of the surplus-value into profit of enterprise (the rate of return on industrial capital), profit on merchant capital, interest, rent and taxes (Marx does not include the latter here) has no effect. In practice, capitalist producers have to share part of the surplus-value created and appropriated with capitalists who fulfill other functions. "Surplus-value is therefore split up into various parts. Its fragments fall to various categories of person, and take on various mutually independent forms, such as profit, interest, gains made through trade"—that's merchant's profit—"ground rent," taxes, etc. "We shall be able to deal with these modified forms of surplus-value only in Volume 3" (709). Marx assumes, in effect, that there is a homogeneous capitalist class comprised of industrial capitalists alone. In Volume III of *Capital*, it becomes clear that the role of interest-bearing capital, finance capital, merchant capital and landed capital are all of considerable significance to understanding the overall dynamics of capitalism. But here all consideration of these features is laid aside. What we are left with is a highly simplified model of how capital accumulation works, and like any such model, it is only as good as its assumptions allow.

There is another tacit assumption which actually becomes explicit a bit later in a footnote.

> Here we take no account of the export trade, by means of which a nation can change articles of luxury either into means of production or means of subsistence, and vice versa. In order to examine the object of our investigation in its integrity, free from all disturbing subsidiary circumstances, we must treat the whole world of trade as one nation, and assume that capitalist production is established everywhere and has taken possession of every branch of industry. (727)

Marx assumes a closed system within which capital circulates in a "normal" way. This is an important and obviously restrictive assumption. What we are left with is a stripped-down model of the dynamics of capital accumulation derived from the theory of absolute and relative surplus-value operating in a closed system. The model turns out, as we shall see, to be very revealing of certain aspects of capitalism.

Just to set the following chapters in their full context, it is useful to contrast them with what happens in the other volumes of *Capital*. Volume II confronts that which is held constant in Volume I: the difficulties that arise in finding markets and bringing them into a state of equilibrium such that the "normal" process of capital circulation can proceed. But Volume II tends to hold constant that which is treated as dynamic in Volume I, i.e., the extraction of absolute and relative surplus-value, rapid shifts in technologies and productivities, shifting determinations of the value of labor-power. Volume II imagines a world of constant technology and stable labor relations! It then poses the questions, how is capital going to circulate smoothly (given different turnover times, including problems that derive from the circulation of fixed capital of different lifetimes), and how can it always find a market for the surplus-value being produced? Since capital accumulation is always about expansion, how can capitalists find a market when the working class is being increasingly immiserated and the capitalists are reinvesting? There is, in fact, no mention of immiseration at the end of Volume II. The problem is to ensure "rational consumption" on the part of the working classes in order to help absorb the capital surpluses being produced. The model here would be Ford's famous turn to a five-dollar eight-hour day for the workers, backed by an army of social workers to ensure that the workers consumed their wages "rationally" from the standpoint of capital. We in the US now live in a world where about 70 percent of the driving force in the economy depends on debt-fueled consumerism, which is perfectly understandable given the analysis of Volume II but not given that of Volume I.

There is, it turns out, a major contradiction between the equilibrium conditions defined in Volume I and those defined in Volume II. If things are going right according to the Volume I analysis, then they are likely to be going very badly from the standpoint of Volume II, and vice versa. The two distinctive models of the dynamics of capital accumulation do not, and cannot, concur. This prefaces the discussion of the inevitability of crises in Volume III, but my insertion of the phrase "debt-fueled" before "consumerism" signals that the terms of distribution (finance, credit and interest) may actually play a central rather than merely ancillary role in the dynamics of capitalism. Consumer power augmented by everybody (including governments) using their credit cards and going into debt up to the hilt has been central to the stabilization (such as it is) of global capitalism over the past half century. None of this will be encountered in the chapters to follow. But the highly simplified model of capital accumulation that Marx does construct and analyze is incredibly revealing, as well as deeply relevant to understanding the recent history of neoliberalism, which has been characterized by deindustrialization, chronic structural unemployment, spiraling job insecurities and surging social inequalities. We have, in short, been very much in the world of Volume I over the past thirty years. The problems of effective demand revealed in the Volume II analysis have been temporarily resolved through the excesses of the credit system, with predictably disastrous consequences.

CHAPTER 23: SIMPLE REPRODUCTION

The first chapter of part 7 models the qualities of a fictional capitalism characterized by simple reproduction. How does capital accumulation through the extraction of surplus-value get reproduced and perpetuated over time? To answer that question, we need to view capital accumulation as a "connected whole, and in the constant flux of its incessant renewal," such that "every social process of production is at the same time a process of reproduction." Furthermore, "if production has a capitalist form, so too will reproduction" (711).

Part of what the capitalist captures in terms of new wealth has to be put to reproducing the system. But this means that surplus-value has to recirculate back into simple reproduction. "This mere repetition, or continuity, imposes on the process certain new characteristics, or rather, causes the disappearance of some apparent characteristics possessed by the process in isolation" (712). The analysis so far has been concerned solely with the production of surplus-value as a one-shot event. But things look rather different when examined as a continuous process going on over time.

> What flows back to the worker in the shape of wages is a portion of the product he himself continuously reproduces. The capitalist, it is true, pays him the value of the commodity [that is, the value of labor-power] in money, but this money is merely the transmuted form of the product of his labour. While he is converting a portion of the means of production into products, a portion of his former product is being turned into money. It is his labour of last week, or of last year, that pays for his labour-power this week or this year. The illusion created by the money-form vanishes immediately if, instead of taking a single capitalist and a single worker, we take the whole capitalist class and the whole working class. (712–13)

Class relations rather than individual contracts now move center stage in Marx's thinking.

> The capitalist class is constantly giving to the working class drafts, in the form of money, on a portion of the product produced by the latter and appropriated by the former. The workers give these drafts back just as constantly to the capitalists, and thereby withdraw from the latter their allotted share of their own product. The transaction is veiled by the commodity-form of the product and the money-form of the commodity. (713)

The image this conveys is that the working class as a whole is in a "company store" relation to the capitalist class. Workers receive money for the labor-power they sell to the capitalists and then spend that money to buy back a portion of the commodities they collectively produced. This company-store relation is veiled by the wages system and is not readily discernible when the analysis focuses only on the individual worker. The meaning of "variable capital" takes another twist. In effect, the body of the worker, from the standpoint of capital, is a mere transmission device for the circulation of a portion of capital. The worker is in a continuous version of the C-M-C process. But instead of seeing this as a simple linear relation, we now have to think of it as continuous and circular. A portion of the capital flows along as workers congeal value in commodities, receive their money wages, spend the money on commodities, reproduce themselves and come back to work to congeal more value in commodities the next day. Workers stay alive by circulating variable capital in this way.

This gives rise to some interesting observations. To begin with, variable capital "loses its character of a value advanced out of the capitalist's funds . . . when we view the process of capitalist production in the flow of its constant renewal." Capitalists pay their workers only after the work is done. In effect, therefore, workers advance the equivalent of the value of their labor-power to the capitalist. There is no guarantee that the worker will be paid (if, for example, capitalists declare bankruptcy in the meantime). In China in recent years, the nonpayment of wages owed has been very common, particularly in areas such as construction. But Marx is interested in reshaping our interpretation of capital accumulation in even more radical ways. He points out that the "process must have had a beginning of some kind. From our present standpoint it therefore seems likely that the capitalist, once upon a time, became possessed of money by some form of primitive accumulation" (714). This concept will anchor the discussion of the origins of capitalism in part 8. Here he simply asserts that there must have been some original moment when capitalists somehow or other got hold of enough assets (monetary and otherwise) to start on this process of capital accumulation. The question he poses here is, how and by whom is that original capital reproduced?

Marx gives an example: if a capitalist starts off with one thousand pounds and invests it in variable capital and constant capital to produce a surplus-value of two hundred pounds, then the capitalist appropriates the two hundred pounds as his or her own in addition to gaining back the original thousand pounds. But the original capital has been preserved by the workers' productive consumption, and the surplus-value has been produced out of the workers' surplus labor-time. Suppose the next year, the capitalist once again lays out one thousand pounds (having consumed the surplus away) to produce another two hundred pounds of surplus-value. After five years of this, the workers have produced one thousand pounds of surplus-value, which is equivalent to the capitalist's original capital. Marx here makes the political argument that even if the capitalist had a right to that thousand pounds at the beginning, however he or she came by it, after five years of producing two hundred pounds of surplus-value every year, the capitalist has surely forfeited the right to the original capital. He or she has, according to Marx's accounting method, consumed the original capital away. The thousand pounds now belongs by right to the workers, given the Lockean principle (not cited here, but clearly Marx has this in mind) that property rights accrue to those who create value by mixing their labor with the land. The workers are the ones who produced the surplus-value, and by rights it should belong to them.

The politics of this argument are important but go radically against the grain of deeply entrenched ways of thinking. We would all be surprised to be told that the original money we placed in a savings account at, say, 5 percent compound interest no longer belonged to us after a number of years. Capitalism appears to be capable of laying its own golden nest eggs, as far as we are concerned. But where that 5 percent comes from is a legitimate question, and it can only be, if Marx is right, through the mobilization and appropriation of surplus-value from someone, somewhere. It is discomforting to think that perhaps the 5 percent comes from the vicious exploitation of living labor in Guangdong province in China. Our legal superstructure is insistent on preserving original property rights and preserving also the right to use those rights to gain a profit. But those property rights in turn derive from the class power of capital to extract and maintain command over the surpluses, because labor-power has, by specific historical processes, become a commodity bought and sold in the labor market. The implication of what Marx is saying here is that in order to challenge capitalism, it is necessary to challenge not only the whole notion of rights, how people think about rights and how people think about property, but also the material processes whereby surpluses are both created and appropriated by capital. Then, indeed, after five years

> not a single atom of the value of his old capital continues to exist . . . Therefore, entirely leaving aside all accumulation, the mere continuity of the production process, in other words simple reproduction, sooner or later, and necessarily, converts all capital into accumulated capital, or capitalized surplus-value. Even if that capital was, on its entry into the

> process of production, the personal property of the man who employs it, and was originally acquired by his own labour, it sooner or later becomes value appropriated without an equivalent, the unpaid labour of others. (715)

There happens to be an interesting example of a practical plan that reflects Marx's way of thinking (whether it derived from Marx, I do not know). A Swedish labor economist called Rudolf Meidner, who played a major role in the construction of the highly successful Swedish welfare state in the 1960s and early 1970s, came up with what became known as the Meidner Plan. Confronting inflation, the powerful trade unions were urged to exercise collective wage restraint. In return, the extra profits (surplus-value) that would accrue to capital because of that restraint would be taxed away and placed in a worker-controlled social-investment fund that would purchase shares in capitalist corporations. The shares purchased were deemed untradeable, and over time (more than the five years of Marx's example) control over the corporation would pass over to the social-investment fund. In other words, the capitalist class would quite literally be bought out (peacefully) over time and replaced by total worker control over investment decisions. The plan was greeted with horror by the capitalist class (who promptly awarded the so-called Nobel Prize in economics—it actually has nothing whatsoever to do with Nobel—to neoliberals like Friedrich Hayek and Milton Friedman and set up anti-union think tanks and mobilized fierce opposition in the media). The social-democratic government of the time got cold feet and never attempted to implement the plan. But when you think about it, the idea (much more complicated in its details, of course) is broadly consistent with Marx's argument, at the same time as it offers a peaceful way to buy out capitalist class power. So why not think more about it?

When put together with the company-store relation of labor to capital, Marx's argument leads to even deeper insights at the same time as it raises crucial (and in this instance, unfortunately, unanswered) questions. "Since, before [the laborer] enters the process, his own labour has already been alienated . . . from him"—that is, he has given over the use-value of labor-power to the capitalist—"appropriated by the capitalist, and incorporated with capital, it now, in the course of the process, constantly objectifies itself so that it becomes a product alien to him." Neither the product nor the labor congealed in it belong to him.

> Therefore, the worker himself constantly produces objective wealth, in the form of capital, an alien power that dominates and exploits him; and the capitalist just as constantly produces labour-power, in the form of a subjective source of wealth which is abstract, exists merely in the physical body of the worker, and is separated from its own means of objectification and realization; in short, the capitalist produces the worker as a wage-labourer. This incessant reproduction, this perpetuation of the worker, is the absolutely necessary condition for capitalist production. (716)

I find this an interesting and troubling formulation, worthy of serious reflection. "The worker himself constantly produces *objective* wealth, in the form of capital," and that objective wealth becomes an alien power that now dominates the worker. The worker produces the instrument of his or her own domination! This is a theme that echoes and reverberates throughout *Capital*. It poses a general historical question of the penchant of human beings to produce all manner of instruments of their own domination. But in this case, the capitalist produces the *subjective* source of wealth, which is abstract, through the "physical body of the worker" which is "separated from its own means of objectification and realization." The capitalist produces and reproduces the worker as the active but alienated subject capable of producing value. And this, please note, is the fundamental socially necessary condition for the survival and maintenance of a capitalist mode of production.

The worker engages in productive consumption and individual consumption (a distinction encountered earlier). Workers not only produce the equivalent of the value of variable capital, i.e., their own living, but they also transfer and thereby reproduce the value of constant capital. Through their labor, workers reproduce both capital and the laborer. The chapters on division of labor and machinery showed how the worker was necessarily transformed into an appendage of capital inside the labor process. But now we also come to see the worker as an "appendage of capital" in the marketplace and in the home. That is what the circulation of variable capital really means: capital circulates through the body of the worker and reproduces the worker as an active subject who reproduces capital. But the worker not only has to be reproduced as an individual person. "The maintenance and reproduction of the working class remains a necessary condition for the reproduction of capital" (719).

This raises a host of questions that Marx glosses over. The politics of class reproduction were, Marx holds, in his time brutal and simple. "The capitalist may safely leave" the daily grind of actual class reproduction to "the worker's drives for self-preservation and propagation. All the capitalist cares for is to reduce the worker's individual consumption to the necessary minimum" (718). But Marx is sliding over something important here that cries out for deeper analysis. The huge and fundamental question of the reproduction of the working class involves questions of propagation, self-preservation, social relations within the class and a host of other issues that Marx conveniently leaves to the workers themselves to sort out because that is what capital supposedly does. Actually, even in a state controlled by capitalists and landlords, matters of social reproduction are never left solely to the workers themselves, and certainly the conditions of class struggle and "the degree of civilization" in a country enter in here with at least the same force as they do with respect to questions of the working day, if not with even greater force. The earlier discussion of the educational clauses of the Factory Acts provided an example of state intervention in the politics of working-class reproduction, and the state has always been active in the fields of public health (given that cholera had the awkward habit of transcending class boundaries) and reproductive rights, population policies and the like. Issues of this sort need far more detailed consideration than Marx provides. But Marx's general point is well taken. Simple reproduction is *not* a technical question. The crucial question is the reproduction of the class relation.

> Capitalist production therefore reproduces in the course of its own process the separation between labour-power and the conditions of labour. It thereby reproduces and perpetuates the conditions under which the worker is exploited. It incessantly forces him to sell his labour-power in order to live, and enables the capitalist to purchase labour-power in order that he may enrich himself. It is no longer a mere accident that capitalist and worker confront each other in the market as buyer and seller. It is the alternating rhythm of the process itself which throws the worker back onto the market again and again as a seller of his labour-power and continually transforms his own product into a means by which another man can purchase him. In reality, the worker belongs to capital before he has sold himself to the capitalist. (723)

As a result, Marx concludes,

> the capitalist process of production, therefore, seen as a total, connected process, i.e. a process of reproduction, produces not only commodities, not only surplus-value, but it also produces and reproduces the capital-relation itself; on the one hand the capitalist, on the other the wage-labourer. (724)

CHAPTER 24: THE TRANSFORMATION OF SURPLUS-VALUE INTO CAPITAL

For a variety of reasons, as we will shortly see, the idea of a capitalist mode of production in a stable, nongrowth state is improbable if not downright impossible. Chapter 24 examines how and why the surplus-value gained yesterday is converted into tomorrow's new money capital. The resultant "production of capital on a progressively increasing scale" involves combining "additional labour-power, annually supplied by the working class in the shape of labour-powers of all ages, with the additional means of production." For this to happen requires that capital must first produce the conditions for its own expansion.

> Accumulation requires the transformation of a portion of the surplus product into capital, But we cannot, except by a miracle, transform into capital anything but such articles as can be employed in the labour process (i.e. means of production), and such further articles as are suitable for the sustenance of the worker (i.e. means of subsistence). Consequently, a part of the annual surplus labour must have been applied to the production of additional means of production and subsistence . . . In a word, surplus value can be transformed into capital only because the surplus product, whose value it is, already comprises the material components of a new quantity of capital. (726-7)

The production of luxuries or other useless products (such as military hardware and religious or state monuments) does not work no matter how profitable such production may be. The new means of subsistence and of production have to be produced and organized in advance. Then and only then "the cycle of simple reproduction alters its form and . . . changes into a spiral" (727). Another way of looking at it (given the analysis of the preceding chapter) is that "the working class creates by the surplus labour of one year the capital destined to employ additional labour in the following year. And this is what is called," writes Marx with heavy irony, "creating capital out of capital."

The laborer is, however, the active subject in this process. Marx continues, however, to assume that market processes "conform to the laws of commodity exchange, with the capitalist always buying labour-power and the worker always selling it at what we shall assume is its real value." Again, I emphasize the importance of such assumptions in Marx's analysis. "It is quite evident from this that the laws of appropriation or of private property, laws based on the production and circulation of commodities, become changed into their direct opposite through their own internal and inexorable dialectic." The inversion of Locke's principle of mixing labor with the land to create value as grounding the right to private property is clear.

> The exchange of equivalents, the original operation with which we started, is now turned round in such a way that there is only an apparent exchange, since, firstly, the capital which is exchanged for labour-power is itself merely a portion of the product of the labour of others which has been appropriated without an equivalent. (729)

As a consequence, "the relation of exchange between capitalist and worker becomes a mere semblance belonging only to the process of circulation, it becomes a mere form, which is alien to the content of the transaction itself, and merely mystifies it" (729–30). Amplifying, Marx continues:

> the constant sale and purchase of labour-power is the form; the content is the constant appropriation by the capitalist, without equivalent, of a portion of the labour of others which has already been objectified, and his repeated exchange of this labour for a greater quantity of the living labour of others. Originally the rights of property seemed to us to be grounded in a man's own labour. Some such assumption was at least necessary, since only commodity-owners with equal rights confronted each other, and the sole means of appropriating the commodities of others was the alienation of a man's own commodities, commodities which, however, could only be produced by labour. Now, however, property turns out to be the right, on the part of the capitalist, to appropriate the unpaid labour of others or its product, and the impossibility, on the part of the worker, of appropriating his own product. The separation of property from labour thus becomes the necessary consequence of a law that apparently originated in their identity. (730)

Marx has here returned (once more!) to the question of how equivalent exchange can produce a non-equivalent, i.e., surplus-value, and how the original notion of property rights gets inverted into being a right of appropriation of the labor of others. What then follows is a reprise, for what seems like the umpteenth time, of the theory of surplus-value (so if you are still unsure what it's all about then read it carefully—pages 730–1). But Marx does go on to note that what can be derived from the standpoint of the individual doesn't work out to be the same thing from the standpoint of class relations.

> The matter looks quite different if we consider capitalist production in the uninterrupted flow of its renewal, and if, in place of the individual capitalist and the individual worker, we view them in their totality, as the capitalist class and the working class confronting each other. But in doing so we should be applying standards entirely foreign to commodity production. (732)

This is so because freedom, equality, property and Bentham prevail in the marketplace, rendering invisible the production of surplus-value in the labor process.

> The same rights remain in force both at the outset, when the product belongs to its producer, who, exchanging equivalent for equivalent, can enrich himself only by his own labour, and in the period of capitalism, when social wealth becomes to an ever-increasing degree the property of those who are in a position to appropriate the unpaid labour of others over and over again . . . This result becomes inevitable from the moment there is a free sale, by the worker himself, of labour-power as a commodity. (733)

Bourgeois freedoms and rights mask exploitation and alienation. "To the extent that commodity production, in accordance with its own immanent laws, undergoes a further development into capitalist production, the property laws of commodity production must undergo a dialectical inversion so that they become laws of capitalist appropriation" (733–4). There is, to revert to the language of the preface to *A Contribution to the Critique of Political Economy*, a superstructural adjustment to legitimate and legalize the appropriation of surplus-value by appeal to concepts of the rights of private property. Hence Marx's fundamental objection to any and all attempts to universalize bourgeois conceptions of right and justice. It merely provides the socially necessary legal, ideological and institutional cover for the production of capital on a progressively increasing scale.

Classical political economy, saddled with bourgeois conceptions of rights, produced all manner of "erroneous conceptions of reproduction on an increasing scale" (as the name of section 2 has it). To begin with, the relationship between capital accumulation and hoarding (saving) was left in a state of utter confusion. The classical political economists were, however, "quite right to maintain that the consumption of the surplus product by productive, instead of unproductive, workers is a characteristic feature of the process of accumulation" (736). But given Marx's definition of "productive," this means that yesterday's surplus product has to be put to creating more surplus product and surplus-value today. The actual dynamics of this are tricky. Classical political economy focused exclusively on the extra labor and therefore extra variable capital (increase in wage outlays) that were called for. But as in the case of Senior's last hour, which Marx so effectively mocked earlier, classical political economy tended to forget entirely about the necessity to procure new means of production (constant capital) with each round of accumulation (which entailed transformations in the relation to nature through raw-material extractions). This was the second "erroneous conception" that Marx had to rectify.

This brings us to the central question: when capitalists have surplus-value at their command, why don't they just have a good time and consume it away? Some of the surplus-value is indeed consumed by the capitalists as revenue. The capitalist class consumes away a portion of the surplus in pursuing its pleasures. But part of it is reinvested as capital. Another question then arises: what governs the relationship between the capitalist consumption of revenues and the reinvestment of surplus-value as capital? Marx's answer is worth quoting at length.

> Except as capital personified, the capitalist has no historical value, and no right to that historical existence which, to use Lichnowsky's amusing expression, 'ain't got no date'. It is only to this extent that the necessity of the capitalist's own transitory existence is implied in the transitory necessity of the capitalist mode of production. But, in so far as he is capital personified, his motivating force is not the acquisition and enjoyment of use-values, but the acquisition and augmentation of exchange-values.

Capitalists, Marx avers, are necessarily interested in and therefore motivated by the accumulation of social power in money-form.

> He is fanatically intent on the valorization of value; consequently he ruthlessly forces the human race to produce for production's sake. In this way he spurs on the development of society's productive forces, and the creation of those material conditions of production which alone can form the real basis of a higher form of society, a society in which the full and free development of every individual forms the ruling principle. Only as a personification of capital is the capitalist respectable. As such, he shares with the miser an absolute drive towards self-enrichment. But what appears in the miser as the mania of an individual is in the capitalist the effect of a social mechanism in which he is merely a cog. Moreover, the development of capitalist production makes it necessary constantly to increase the amount of capital laid out in a given industrial undertaking, and competition subordinates every individual capitalist to the immanent laws of capitalist production, as external and coercive laws. It compels him to keep extending his capital, so as to preserve it, and he can only extend it by means of progressive accumulation. (739)

The capitalist, according to Marx, has no real freedom, either. Poor capitalists are mere cogs in a mechanism, who have to reinvest because the coercive laws of competition force them into it. As capital personified, their psychology is so focused on the augmentation of exchange-value, on the accumulation of social power in limitless money-form, that money accumulation becomes the fetish focus of their deepest desires. Herein lies the similarity between the miser and the capitalist. They both want social power, but the social power of capitalists comes from constantly augmenting their wealth by releasing it into circulation, whereas the miser tries to hold on to it by not using it. And if capitalists individually show any sign of drifting away from their central mission, then the pesky coercive laws of competition (once more slid into the argument in a central role of policing the system) bring them back into line.

Faced with this reality, the bourgeois apologists create a noble fiction. The capitalists, they say, are creating capital and engaging their noble mission to create that "higher form of society" that even Marx concedes can be a product of their endeavours, through abstinence! I have to say, living in New York, I have never noticed the capitalist class abstaining too much. But Marx does suggest that capitalists face a Faustian dilemma. He even quotes *Faust*: "Two souls, alas, do dwell within his breast; The one is ever parting from the other" (741). They are forced by the coercive laws of competition to accumulate and reinvest on the one hand and are plagued by the desire to consume on the other. Coerced restraint with respect to the latter is then converted into an ideology of voluntary bourgeois virtue. Profit can even be interpreted as a return on virtue! Reinvestment, the story goes, is a virtue (it creates jobs, for example), and therefore deserves to be admired and rewarded. All those tax cuts for the ultrarich that George W. Bush set up during his presidency were construed as a reward for virtuous investors whose abstinence supposedly played a crucial role in job creation and economic growth. The fact that the rich soon acquired the habit of throwing ten-million-dollar parties for their kids' graduations or their trophy wives' birthdays hardly squared with this theory. Marx, however, once again heavily influenced by the story of Manchester capitalism, suggests that the struggle between the "two souls" dwelling in the capitalist's breast underwent a gradual evolution. In the initial stages, capitalists indeed were forced to exercise restraint on consumption (hence the significance of Quaker ideology among some early capitalists in England). But as the spiral of accumulation on a progressively increasing scale got under way, so the restraints on consumption slackened. In Manchester, during "the last thirty years of the eighteenth century . . . 'expense and luxury have made great progress,'" Marx reports, quoting an account from 1795 (742). Under such conditions, "production and reproduction on an increasing scale go on their way without any intervention from that peculiar saint, that knight of the woeful countenance, the 'abstaining' capitalist" (746).

Driven by the coercive laws of competition and the desire to augment their social power in limitless money-form, capitalists reinvest because this is, in the end, the only way they can stay in business and maintain their class position. This leads Marx to a central conclusion concerning the essence of a capitalist mode of production.

> Accumulate, accumulate! That is Moses and the prophets! 'Industry furnishes the material which saving accumulates.' Therefore save, save, i.e. reconvert the greatest possible portion of surplus-value or surplus product into capital! Accumulation for the sake of accumulation, production for the sake of production: this was the formula in which classical economics expressed the historical mission of the bourgeoisie in the period of its

> domination. Not for one instant did it deceive itself over the nature of wealth's birth-pangs. But what use is it to lament a historical necessity? If, in the eyes of classical economics, the proletarian is merely a machine for the production of surplus-value, the capitalist too is merely a machine for the transformation of this surplus-value into surplus capital. (742)

What this means quite simply is this: capitalism is always about growth. There can be no such thing as a capitalist social order that is not about growth and accumulation on a progressively increasing scale. "Accumulation for the sake of accumulation, production for the sake of production." Just read the press reports on the state of the economy every day, and what are people talking about all the time? Growth! Where's the growth? How are we going to grow? Slow growth defines a recession, and negative growth a depression. One or 2 percent growth (compounded) is not enough, we need at least 3, and only when we reach 4 percent is the economy deemed to be "healthy." And look at China with its sustained 10 percent growth rates over many years: that is the real success story of our times compared with Japan, which after decades of stellar growth fell into the sick bay of global capitalism, with close to zero growth throughout the 1990s.

To this imperative attaches a fetish belief, a whole ideology, centered on the virtues of growth. Growth is inevitable, growth is good. Not to grow is to be in crisis. But endless growth means production for production's sake, which also means consumption for consumption's sake. Anything that gets in the way of growth is bad. Barriers and limits to growth have to be dissolved. Environmental problems? Too bad! The relation to nature must be transformed. Social and political problems? Too bad! Repress critics and send recalcitrants to jail. Geopolitical barriers? Break them down with violence if necessary. Everything has to dance to the tune of "accumulation for the sake of accumulation, production for the sake of production."

This is, for Marx, one of the defining characteristics of capitalism. To be sure, he arrives at this conclusion on the basis of his assumptions. But these assumptions are consistent with the inherent vision internalized within classical political economy as to the "historical mission" of the bourgeoisie. And it defines a very important and powerful regulative principle. Has the history of capitalism been about compounding growth rates? Yes. Have capitalist crises come to be defined as lack of growth? Yes. Are policy makers throughout the capitalist world obsessed with stimulating and sustaining growth? Yes. And do you see anybody really questioning the growth principle, let alone doing anything about it? No. To question growth is irresponsible and unthinkable. Only cranks, misfits and weird utopians think that endless growth, no matter what the environmental, economic, social and political consequences, might be bad. To be sure, problems deriving from growth, such as global warming and environmental degradation, need to be addressed, but rarely is it said that the answer to the problem is to stop growth altogether (even though there is evidence that recessions relieve pressures on the environment). No, we have to find new technologies, new mental conceptions, new ways of living and producing, such that growth, endless compounding capital accumulation, can continue.

This has not been a regulative principle of other modes of production. To be sure, empires grew and social orders episodically expanded, but then they also just as often stabilized and in some instances stagnated and even faded away. One of the big criticisms of actually existing communisms in, for example, the former Soviet Union and Cuba, has been that they didn't grow enough and so could not compete with the incredible consumerism and growth performance of the West, centered on the US. I do not say this in praise of the USSR but merely to point up how automatic our responses tend to be to nongrowth—stagnation is unforgivable. So now we have enough SUVs, Coca-Cola and bottled water around to satisfy accumulation for accumulation's sake with all manner of disastrous environmental and health consequences (such as the epidemic of diabetes, which incidentally, continues to be rare in Cuba compared with the US). It bears thinking about that the endless three percent compound rate of growth that has characterized capitalism since the mid-eighteenth century might be singularly hard to maintain. When capitalism was constituted by an economic zone of about forty square miles around Manchester and a few other smaller locations, a three percent compound rate of growth was one thing, but now it covers Europe, North and South America and above all East Asia, with strengthening implantations in India, Indonesia, Russia and South Africa. Starting from this base, the consequences of a three percent compound rate of growth over the next fifty years are unimaginable. At the same time, it makes Marx's suggestion in the *Grundrisse* that it is time for capital to be gone, and to make way for some more sensible mode of production, more imaginable if not absolutely imperative.

There are, it turns out, a variety of ways to gain surplus-value without producing anything. Reducing the value of labor-power by reducing the standard of living opens up one path. Indeed, Marx writes, quoting John Stuart Mill, "if labour could be had without purchase, wages might be dispensed with." But then

> if the workers could live on air, it would not be possible to buy them at any price. This zero cost of labour is therefore a limit in a mathematical sense, always beyond reach, although we can always approximate more and more nearly to it. The constant tendency of capital is to force the cost of labour back towards this absolute zero. (748)

And Marx notes some ways to do this, such as providing recipes to workers so they can feed themselves more cheaply. Later this sort of thing became part of the practice of, for example, the Russell Sage Foundation and of the practices of social workers as they sought to educate other workers to proper modes of consumption. But plainly, taking this path creates problems of effective demand, which Marx does not consider here since he has ruled it out by assuming that all commodities trade at their values. Saving on constant capital (including cutting down on waste) can also be helpful while capitalists are constantly on the lookout for "something provided by nature free of charge" (751). "It is once again the direct action of man on nature which becomes an immediate source of greater accumulation, without the intervention of any new capital" (752). Changing the productivity of social labor through other means (motivation and organization) is also free of charge, and using old machines beyond their lifetime helps, as does the mobilization of past assets (e.g., built environments) for new purposes. Finally, "science and technology give capital a power of expansion which is independent of the given magnitude of the capital actually functioning" (754). Accumulation can be expanded by all these different means without resort to the capitalization of surplus-value.

"It has been shown in the course of this inquiry," Marx concludes at the beginning of section 5,

> that capital is not a fixed magnitude, but a part of social wealth which is elastic, and constantly fluctuates with the division of surplus-value into revenue and additional capital. It has been seen further that, even

> with a given magnitude of functioning capital, the labour-power, science and land (which means, economically speaking, all the objects of labour furnished by nature without human intervention) incorporated in it form elastic powers of capital, allowing it, within certain limits, a field of action independent of its own magnitude. In this inquiry we have ignored all relations arising from the process of circulation [he is here reminding us of the initial assumptions about the market], which may produce very different degrees of efficiency in the same mass of capital . . . [and] we disregarded any more rational combination which could be effected directly and in a planned way with the means of production and the labour-power at present available.

Once again, Marx insists on the incredible flexibility and maneuverability of capital. "Classical political economy," in contrast, "has always liked to conceive social capital as a fixed magnitude of a fixed degree of efficiency." That poor man Jeremy Bentham, a "soberly pedantic and heavy-footed oracle of the 'common sense' of the nineteenth-century bourgeoisie," had a particularly fixed vision of how capitalism constructed a labour fund (758).

Capital is not a fixed magnitude!! Always remember this, and appreciate that there is a great deal of flexibility and fluidity in the system. The left opposition to capitalism has too often underestimated this. If capitalists cannot accumulate this way, then they will do it another way. If they cannot use science and technology to their own advantage, they will raid nature or give recipes to the working class. There are innumerable strategies open to them, and they have a record of sophistication in their use. Capitalism may be monstrous, but it is not a rigid monster. Oppositional movements ignore its capacity for adaptation, flexibility and fluidity at their peril. Capital is not a thing, but a process. It is continually in motion, even as it itself internalizes the regulative principle of "accumulation for the sake of accumulation, production for the sake of production."

CHAPTER TEN

Capitalist Accumulation

CHAPTER 25: THE GENERAL LAW OF CAPITALIST ACCUMULATION

In chapter 25, Marx operationalizes a synoptic model of capitalist dynamics under the assumptions laid out at the beginning of part 7: accumulation is occurring in its normal way (there is never any problem in the market and everything trades at its value, with the exception in this chapter of labor-power); the system is closed (no trade with an outside); surplus-value is being produced through the exploitation of living labor in production; and the division of the surplus-value between interest, profit of merchant's capital, rent and taxes has no impact. In this stripped-down model of the accumulation process, everything is contingent on these assumptions. When these assumptions are dropped, as they are in Volume II, the results look different.

A Commentary on the Value Composition of Capital

In this chapter, Marx focuses on one particular substantive issue. He wants to examine the implications of the accumulation of capital for the fate of the working class. This is why he allows the remuneration of labor-power to fluctuate above and below its value. To aid him in this task, he sets up a conceptual apparatus concerning what he calls "the composition of capital" (762). He uses three terms: technical composition, organic composition and value composition. These terms were, it seems, introduced fairly late into the argument, in part to reflect some of the work he was doing in Volume III on contradictions and crises. So the terms don't do that much work in this chapter, and it is possible to understand his argument without them.

If you find this part of the discussion esoteric and perplexing (which it is), then pass straight on to the next section. But since these terms play a key role in Volume III and have been the subject of much argument and controversy in Marxian theory more generally, I think it important to examine them here.

The term "technical composition" simply describes the physical ability of a worker to transform a certain quantity of use-values into a commodity in a given period of time. It is the measure of physical productivity. It refers to the number of socks, tons of steel, loaves of bread, gallons of orange juice or bottles of beer produced by a worker per hour. New technologies transform these physical ratios, so that, for example, the number of socks produced per hour per worker increases from ten to twenty. The concept of technical composition is clear and unambiguous. Problems arise in differentiating between the organic and value compositions, both of which are value ratios. The value composition is the ratio of the value of the means of production consumed in production to the value of the variable capital advanced. Conventionally, we represent this as c/v, the amount of constant capital divided by the variable capital. The organic composition, which is also measured as a value ratio of c/v, is defined as changes in the value composition that arise because of physical changes in productivity.

Why the difference? The implication is that changes in value composition can occur other than those related to physical changes in productivity. Since changes of this nontechnological sort were listed at the end of the preceding chapter, this interpretation is more than merely plausible. But note that these changes, such as gifts of nature, economizing on waste, or depressing the physical standard of living of workers, can affect the value of both the constant and the variable capital laid out, such that the c/v ratio can either increase or decrease as a result. There is another possible interpretation that Marx does not to my knowledge explicitly develop, but we could infer it. This interpretation depends on where the changes in physical productivity are occurring. If I change the physical productivity of sock making by employing new machinery, then the ratio c/v (let's call this the organic composition of capital) typically increases within my firm because of my actions. But this ratio will also likely change without my doing anything because the value of the constant and variable capital I purchase (at its value, given Marx's assumptions) is fixed by the changing physical productivity in the industries producing the wage goods that fix the value of labor-power and the other industries producing the means of production that I purchase (constant-capital inputs). In this instance, the ratio c/v (let's call this the value composition of capital) will rise or fall depending on the relative pace of changes in physical productivity in these two different sectors of the economy (even though physical productivity within my firm has not changed). This interpretation focuses on the difference between what is possible for the individual capitalist to do about the c/v ratio and what happens to the c/v ratio in the market outside individual capitalist control. It is hard to sustain this interpretation here, given that Marx in this chapter is working at the aggregate level of relations between the capitalist and working classes. But yet it is also plausible given the theory of relative surplus-value, which emphasizes that it is the individual capitalist's search, operating under the coercive laws of competition, for the ephemeral form of relative surplus-value that truly drives the technological dynamism that produces relative surplus-value of the aggregate sort.

The reason all this is so important is that in Volume III of *Capital*, Marx takes up the question of why there might be a tendency for the rate of profit to fall. Ricardo had explained this in Malthusian terms, that in the end diminishing returns on the land would so increase the price of natural resources that profits were bound to decline to zero. In other words, the problem resides in the relation to nature (when faced with a falling rate of profit problem, Marx elsewhere quipped, Ricardo "flees from economics to seek refuge in organic chemistry"[1]). Marx dismisses this claim and argues instead that it is the internal dynamics of technological change within capitalism, the search for relative surplus-value, that increases the organic (value?) composition of capital, c/v, which in the long run will lead to a falling rate of profit (s/[c + v]) under the assumption of a limit on the rate of exploitation (s/v). Put differently, labor-saving innovations remove the active value producer from the labor process and so make it more difficult (other things being equal) to produce surplus-value. The argument is ingenious and has the undoubted virtue of (correctly in my view) internalizing the dynamics of crisis formation within the framework of capitalist social relations and the development of its productive forces. Unfortunately, the argument is incomplete and problematic because, given the second line of argument advanced above, there is no definite reason why the ratio c/v should increase in the way Marx suggests it would.

In this chapter, Marx argues forthrightly in favor of a law of rising value composition of capital. He begins by pointing out that from the standpoint of the whole capitalist class, the changing value composition of capital has both direct and indirect aspects in relation to production.

---

1. *Grundrisse*, 753–4.

We are talking about not only machines and factories but also railways, roads and all manner of physical infrastructures (built environments) that provide the necessary preconditions for capitalist production and realization to proceed. If these preconditions are to be fulfilled, there has to be an astonishing increase in the ratio of the total stock of constant (and increasingly fixed) capital in relationship to the number of laborers employed. (Marx fails to register here a point he makes elsewhere: that if past investments in, say, the built environment have already been amortized, then they operate as a "free good"—much like gifts of nature—for capitalist production to proceed. That is, unless a pesky landlord class gets in the way and starts extracting rent from them.) The movement from relatively simple handicraft production to more complex and integrated processes of production in itself entails a historical tendency for the ratio of c/v to increase with time. This leads Marx to assert that the

> law of the progressive growth of the constant part of capital in comparison with the variable part is confirmed at every step . . . by the comparative analysis of the prices of commodities, whether we compare different economic epochs or different nations in the same epoch. The relative magnitude of the part of the price which represents the value of the means of production, or the constant part of the capital, is in direct proportion to the progress of accumulation, whereas the relative magnitude of the other part of the price, which represents the variable part of the capital, or the payment made for labour, is in inverse proportion to the progress of accumulation. (773–4)

There is, he clearly proposes here, a "law" of rising value composition of capital over time, and it is this law that plays such a crucial role in the theory of the falling rate of profit in Volume III. But Marx does recognize that there can be a decrease in the value (as opposed to the physical presence) of constant capital because of technological change. Indeed, he suggests that the reason the c/v ratio has not increased more than it has "is simple: with the increasing productivity of labour, the mass of the means of production consumed by labour increases, but their value in comparison with their mass diminishes." As a result of rising productivity in the production of means of production,

> their value therefore rises absolutely, but not in proportion to the increase in their mass. The increase of the difference between constant and variable

> capital is therefore much less than that of the difference between the mass of the means of production into which the constant capital, and the mass of the labour-power into which the variable capital, is converted. (774)

The supposed "law" of a rising value composition of capital is subject to modification, but not in a way that controverts its fundamental direction. The accumulation of capital and the search for relative surplus-value "give to each other, that change in the technical composition of capital by which the variable component becomes smaller and smaller as compared with the constant component" (776).

But what Marx needs to do to consolidate his argument is to disaggregate the economy into sectors producing wage goods and means of production, respectively, and then examine relative rates of change in physical productivity in both sectors. He does this at the end of Volume II (written after the drafts of Volume III that have come down to us), but his main concern there is to examine the problem of how the market can keep the two sectors in equilibrium (if at all). He therefore assumes away the technological dynamism that lies at the heart of the Volume I analysis and is so vital to the Volume III analysis of falling profits. The concept of value composition is not mentioned. He does open up the probability of crises of disproportionality (too many wage goods in relation to means of production, or vice versa) and even the possibility of generalized crises of underconsumption (lack of effective demand) but does nothing to illuminate the issue of falling profit rates due to technological changes. What subsequent theoretical work has shown, however, is that there is a pattern of technological change between the two sectors (wage goods and means of production) that can keep the c/v ratio steady in perpetuity, but that no mechanisms exist to ensure such an outcome. Hence the likelihood of frequent crises of disproportionality and occasional generalized crises deriving from the instabilities generated out of technological changes is considerable.

Plainly, we cannot resolve all these issues here. My own view (which many will disagree with) is that Marx's intuition that patterns of technological change are destabilizing to the point of producing crises is correct but that his explication of rising value compositions and falling profits is not. However, the main line of argument that unfolds in this chapter is readily understandable without deploying the value-composition concept.

The First Model of Capital Accumulation

If capitalists take part of the surplus-value they appropriated yesterday and invest it in more production today, then this requires more labor-power, assuming for the moment that there is no technological change. So the first obvious effect of the accumulation of capital under these conditions is increased demand for labor-power. "Accumulation of capital is therefore multiplication of the proletariat" (764). Where are the extra laborers going to come from, and what are the implications of increasing the demand? At some point, increasing demand will lead to an increase in wages. The "spiral" of accumulation therefore entails more capital being generated, more laborers being employed and at some point higher wages, such that labor-power is either sold above its value (an exception to the assumption that all commodities trade at their value) or that the value of labor-power rises as laborers gain a higher standard of living. But this only means "that the length and weight of the golden chain the wage-labourer has already forged for himself [is] loosened somewhat" (769).

> At the best of times an increase in wages means only a quantitative reduction in the amount of unpaid labour the worker has to supply. This reduction can never go so far as to threaten the system itself. Apart from violent conflicts over the rate of wages . . . a rise in the price of labour resulting from accumulation of capital implies the following alternatives: . . . Either the price of labour keeps on rising, because its rise does not interfere with the progress of accumulation. (769–70)

That is, capitalists can afford some increase in the price of labor, because the mass of capital they can appropriate continues to increase as they employ more laborers. Remember, capitalists are primarily interested in the mass of profit, and the mass depends, as we saw in chapter 17, on the number of laborers employed, the rate of exploitation and the intensity. In the face of a diminishing rate of exploitation, increasing the number of laborers employed can increase the mass of capital gained by the capitalist by a substantial amount. In this scenario, there is, therefore, no conflict between rising wages and capital accumulation. "The other alternative" is that

> accumulation slackens as a result of the rise in the price of labour, because the stimulus of gain is blunted. The rate of accumulation lessens; but

> this means that the primary cause of that lessening itself vanishes, i.e. the disproportion between capital and exploitable labour-power. The mechanism of the capitalist production process removes the very obstacles it temporarily creates. (770)

Marx's model here is quite simple. Accumulation of capital, assuming constant productivity, increases demand for labor. Whether or not this leads to a rise in wages depends on the available population. But as more and more of the available population are brought into employment, wages will go up, which diminishes the rate of exploitation. But the mass of surplus-value can continue to rise because more laborers are employed. If at some point, for whatever reason, the mass of surplus-value begins to diminish, then the demand for labor tails off, the pressure on wages slackens and the rate of exploitation recovers. Over time, therefore, we would likely see countervailing oscillations in wage and profit rates. Wages rise, accumulation slackens, wages fall back, profits and accumulation revive. Marx here describes an automatic adjustment system between the demand and supply of labor and the dynamics of accumulation.

There is, Marx suggests, historical evidence for processes of this sort. In eighteenth-century England there was a tendency, made much of by a contemporary commentator called Eden, for wages to rise because of the rapid expansion of capital accumulation. The working classes were becoming better off alongside a capitalist class that was plainly doing very well. The temptation, to which Eden succumbed, was to declare therefore that capital accumulation was good for the workers as well. But all it does, says Marx, is to lengthen "the golden chain" that ties labor to capital. Besides, this idea had earlier been vigorously contradicted in the famous tract of Mandeville, *The Fable of the Bees*. Mandeville had produced a scurrilous polemic against the "drones" that exist in English society and in so doing established that such a society had a desperate need for poor people, the poorer the better, because they would then demand less in the way of goods and services, leaving more for the rich. If we didn't have the poor, then the rich could not be rich. This pillorying of the conditions in England in the eighteenth century upset Adam Smith and the humanists, who could not accept the proposition that the poor shall always be with us and that the poor serve such a vital function for the rich. Smith's response was to attempt to show that everybody, including the poorest, stood in the end to be better off if the market mechanism was mobilized effectively to increase national wealth. The significance of Mandeville for Marx is the idea that the accumulation of capital requires the prior existence of not only an available population but an available population that is sufficiently impoverished, is sufficiently ignorant, is sufficiently oppressed and desperate, that it can be recruited as low-wage labor into the capitalist system at the drop of the proverbial hat.

The Second Model of Capital Accumulation

The second model of accumulation analyzes what happens when the increasing productivity of social labor becomes "the most powerful lever of accumulation" (772). The impacts of technological and organizational changes on productivity need to be placed in a central position in relation to the dynamics of accumulation. This leads Marx to elaborate at some length on the "law" of increasing value composition of capital in the manner already outlined. But while "the progress of accumulation lessens the relative magnitude of the variable part of capital . . . this by no means thereby excludes the possibility of a rise in its absolute magnitude," because, as we have seen in the first model, more laborers can be employed to counteract the falling rate of surplus-value (774).

The deployment of cooperation, new divisions of labor and the application of machinery, science and technology as ways to increase labor productivity depends, in the first instance, on there having been sufficient initial or "primitive" accumulation of money wealth to set the whole process in motion. Marx has introduced this term, "primitive accumulation," before, but again prefers to delay any detailed consideration of it until part 8. "How it itself originates we need not investigate as yet" (775). But once accumulation gets under way, the progress of increasing productivity also depends on processes of concentration and centralization of capital. Only in this way can all possible economies of scale be realized. Wealth increasingly concentrates in a few hands, he says, because at each round of accumulation the capitalist acquires an increasing mass of capital in the form of money power. Growth occurs at a compound rate, and the concentration of wealth and power accelerates, though in a way that is limited by the rate of surplus-value and the number of laborers employed. This process of concentration may also be partially offset, however, by the opening up of new small businesses in new lines of production.

> Therefore not only are accumulation and the concentration accompanying it scattered over many points, but the increase of each functioning capital is thwarted by the formation of new capitals and the subdivision of old. Accumulation, therefore, presents itself on the one hand as increasing concentration of the means of production, and of the command over labour; and on the other hand as repulsion of many individual capitals from one another. (776–7)

The "fragmentation of the total social capital into many individual capitals, or the repulsion of its fractions from each other," must also be taken into account. This is typical Marx: there are countervailing tendencies at work: concentration on the one hand, subdivision and fragmentation on the other. Where is the balance between them? Who knows! The balance between concentration and decentralization is almost certainly subject to perpetual flux (countering any teleological interpretation of the evolution of machinery and large-scale industry).

Centralization, on the other hand, arrives at concentration of capital by a different path—takeovers, mergers, the ruthless destruction of competitors. There may be, Marx suggests, laws of the centralization of capital. But he admits he is not in a position to develop these laws here, though he evidently suspects that they may yet be uncovered (which would be consistent with the teleological view!). There is, however, a definite tendency toward centralization, undoubtedly fueled by a "new force [that] comes into existence with the development of capitalist production: the credit system" (777). While he is not yet in a position to introduce the credit system here (it would violate his initial assumption that the division of surplus-value between interest, rent, profit on merchant capital does not matter), he cannot resist some preparatory remarks:

> In its first stages, this (credit) system furtively creeps in as the humble assistant of accumulation, drawing into the hands of individual or associated capitalists by invisible threads the money resources, which lie scattered in larger or smaller amounts over the surface of society; but it soon becomes a new and terrible weapon in the battle of competition and is finally transformed into an enormous social mechanism for the centralization of capitals. (777-8)

The picture is compelling and in Marx's time drew much from the theories of Saint Simon on the power of associated capitals and the practices of Second Empire bankers such as the Péreire brothers in France. It also resonates in our contemporary world. Set up micro-credit and micro-finance institutions to capture what is called "the wealth at the bottom of the pyramid" and then suck out all that wealth to support ailing international financial institutions (all with the help of the World Bank and the IMF) and use that wealth on Wall Street to pay the asset and merger game . . . "Commensurately with the development of capitalist production and accumulation," Marx acutely observes, "there also takes place a development of the two most powerful levers of centralization—competition and credit" (778–9). Rapid centralization overtakes the slower processes of concentration through compound growth as the main vehicle for achieving the enormous financial scale required to implement entirely new rounds of productivity increase. Centralization can radically improve and increase the scale of production. We wouldn't be able to undertake many of the mega-projects of physical infrastructures (e.g., railways and ports) and urbanization (fixed and constant capital) without centralization (or, as he discusses elsewhere, without involving the state).

Adequate instruments of centralization are, therefore, absolutely critical to the dynamics of accumulation. But this poses the threat of monopoly power and contradicts the vision, so dear to classical political economy as well as to contemporary neoliberal theorists, of a decentralized market economy characterized by highly dispersed and individualistic decision making such that no one can corner or dominate the market. What Marx suggests here is that even if the market economy begins with small-scale, highly competitive firms, it is almost certainly going to be rapidly transformed through centralization of capital and end up in a state of oligopoly or monopoly. The result of competition, he says elsewhere, is always monopoly. Processes therefore exist internal to the capitalist dynamic that are inherently disruptive to the theory of how perfect markets work. The problem is that markets and the struggle for relative surplus-value cannot coexist for long without centralization kicking in and disrupting decentralized decision making in freely functioning markets. While Marx does not explicitly make this point here, it is, surely, one of the implications of his argument. But if the analysis of concentration is anything to go by, increasing centralization cannot entirely be a one-way process lacking any countervailing influences and forces. Unfortunately, Marx does not make this point here, but elsewhere he will talk about the way in which centralization can sometimes be countered by decentralization. Therefore, what we have to look at is the relationship between concentration, deconcentration, centralization and decentralization. But what he's introducing in here is the idea of a market dynamic of the accumulation process in which these forces have to be integrated into the argument and not set aside as some kind of accident of history. This, though, takes him beyond his remit in this chapter, which is about the condition of the working class.

A rising productivity of labor (a rising value composition of capital) has implications for the demand for labor.

> Since the demand for labour is determined not by the extent of the total capital but by its variable constituent alone, that demand falls progressively with the growth of the total capital, instead of rising in proportion to it, as was previously assumed. It falls relatively to the magnitude of the total capital, and at an accelerated rate, as this magnitude increases. With the growth of the total capital, its variable constituent, the labour incorporated in it, does admittedly increase, but in a constantly diminishing proportion. (781–2)

This implies that capitalist accumulation "constantly produces, and produces indeed in direct relation with its own energy and extent, a relatively redundant working population, i.e. a population which is superfluous to capital's average requirements for its own valorization, and is therefore a surplus population" (782). It does this by that processes we now call downsizing.

> The working population therefore produces both the accumulation of capital and the means by which it is itself made relatively superfluous; and it does this to an extent which is always increasing. This is a law of population peculiar to the capitalist mode of production. (783–4)

Once again, the theme of the production of the conditions of our own domination emerges as a supreme irony.

Mention of a "law of population" puts Marx on a collision course with Malthus, who, judging by earlier footnotes, is far from being Marx's favorite theorist and whose universal theory of population and overpopulation called for refutation. "Every particular historical mode of production," Marx writes, "has its own special laws of population, which are historically valid within that particular sphere. An abstract law of population exists only for plants and animals, and even then only in the absence of any historical intervention by man" (784). Marx's objection to Malthus is that he naturalizes unemployment and the creation of poverty by turning them into the simple relationship between population increase and pressure on resources. Marx does not hold that population growth is irrelevant or even neutral with respect to capital accumulation; indeed, there are many passages elsewhere in which he depicts strong population growth as a necessary precondition for sustained accumulation. His fundamental objection is to the thesis that poverty is produced by a working class that reproduces itself too numerously (thereby blaming the victim). Marx's concern is to show how capitalism produces poverty no matter what the state or rate of population growth. He proves Mandeville was right, that the poor are and always will be with us under a capitalist mode of production but, *contra* Mandeville, Marx shows how and why this is so.

Capitalism produces poverty by creating a relative surplus of laborers through the use of technologies that throw laborers out of work. A permanent pool of unemployed laborers is socially necessary for accumulation to continue to expand.

> But if a surplus population of workers is a necessary product of accumulation or of the development of wealth on a capitalist basis, this surplus population also becomes, conversely, the lever of capitalist accumulation, indeed it becomes a condition for the existence of the capitalist mode of production. It forms a disposable industrial reserve army, which belongs to capital just as absolutely as if the latter had bred it at its own cost.

It is not, therefore, the technology itself that is the main lever of accumulation, but the pool of surplus laborers to which it gives rise. "Independently of the limits of the actual increase of population, it creates a mass of human material always ready for exploitation by capital in the interests of capital's own changing valorization requirements" (784).

Typically, the reserve army is drawn into production and then thrown out in alternating bursts, creating a cyclical motion in the labor market. "The varying phases of the industrial cycle recruit the surplus population, and become one of the most energetic agencies for its reproduction" (785). Marx describes

> the simple process that constantly 'sets free' a part of the working class; by methods which lessen the number of workers employed in proportion to the increased production. Modern industry's whole form of motion therefore depends on the constant transformation of a part of the working population into unemployed or semi-employed 'hands'.

"Even political economy sees that the production of a relative surplus population—i.e. a population surplus in relation to capital's average requirements for valorization—is a necessary condition for modern industry." (786) Malthus, for example, "recognizes that a surplus population is a necessity of modern industry" but he fails to see that "capitalist production can by no means content itself with the quantity of disposable labour-power which the natural increase of population yields. It requires for its unrestricted activity an industrial reserve army which is independent of these natural limits" (787–8).

The ramifications of this process spread far and wide to influence the deskilling of large segments of the labor force and processes of deindustrialization through technological change that have become all too familiar to us over the past thirty years or so. The existence of this relative surplus population typically results in the overwork of those who are employed since they can be threatened with layoffs unless they work overtime and agree to increase the intensity of their labor. Since capital in our time doesn't like to bear the indirect costs of full-time employees (healthcare benefits and pensions), the preference to push the employed to work overtime, whether they want it or not, increases even as the pool of unemployed labor also increases. Agreeing to overtime sometimes becomes a condition of employment. This has become a serious problem in Europe in recent years. The result is overwork and excessive exploitation of those who are employed.

> The over-work of the employed part of the working class swells the ranks of its reserve, while conversely the greater pressure that the reserve by its competition exerts on the employed workers forces them to submit to over work and subjects them to the dictates of capital.

This becomes a remarkable "means of enriching the individual capitalists" (789). The impact on wages is also significant. "Taking them as a whole, the general movements of wages are exclusively regulated by the expansion and contraction of the industrial reserve army." Wage movements are driven by capital accumulation. This contradicts the standard view that the pace of accumulation of capital is regulated by fluctuations in wage rates driven either by population growth or, in contemporary rhetoric, by excessively greedy trade unions. The "dogma of the economists" was that "higher wages stimulate the working population to more rapid multiplication, and this goes on until the labour-market becomes over-supplied, and hence capital becomes insufficient in relation to the supply of labour" (790).

Marx's model suggests that whenever capital accumulation runs into problems of labor supply, it throws people out of work by resorting to technological or organizational innovations, the effect of which is either to bring wages down below value or to increase the length of working day and the intensity of labor for those who remain employed.

> The industrial reserve army, during the periods of stagnation and average prosperity, weighs down the active army of workers; during the periods of over-production and feverish activity, it puts a curb on their pretensions. The relative surplus population is therefore the background against which the law of the demand and supply of labour does its work. It confines the field of action of this law to the limits absolutely convenient to capital's drive to exploit and dominate the workers. (792)

Hence it is that "the mechanism of capitalist production takes care that the absolute increase of capital is not accompanied by a corresponding rise in the general demand for labour" (793). This provokes "great exploits of economic apologetics" on behalf of the bourgeoisie to justify such practices when they so clearly work to the detriment of the working classes (792). The only thing the apologists can do is to view "the misery, the sufferings, the possible death of the displaced workers during the transitional period when they are banished into the industrial reserve army," as a necessary short-term sacrifice for the greater long-term good of all that can come from progressive capital accumulation. But the reality is far more sinister.

> The demand for labour is not identical with increase of capital, nor is supply of labour identical with increase of the working class. It is not a case of two independent forces working on each other. Les dés sont pipés. Capital acts on both sides at once. (793)

That is, capital creates the demand for labor when it reinvests, but it can also manage the supply of labor through reinvestments in labor-saving technologies that produce unemployment. This ability to operate on both sides of the demand and supply equation totally contradicts the way in which markets are supposed to work.

As happened in the case of machinery, workers soon

> learn the secret of why it happens that the more they work, the more alien wealth they produce, and that the more the productivity of their labour increases, the more does their very function as a means for the valorization of capital become precarious; as soon as they discover that the degree of intensity of the competition amongst themselves depends wholly on the pressure of the relative surplus population; as soon as, by setting up trade unions [this is, surprisingly, the only time you'll see this term mentioned in *Capital*], etc., they try to organize planned co-operation between the employed and the unemployed in order to obviate or to weaken the ruinous effects of this natural law of capitalist production on their class, so soon does capital and its sycophant, political economy, cry out at the infringement of the 'eternal' and so to speak 'sacred' law of supply and demand. (793)

In a situation where the rules of market exchange are subverted by capital's ability to regulate both the supply and demand for labor-power, attempts by workers to organize on their side to protect their collective interests are fiercely condemned for infringing on the rules of the market!

Marx has constructed two models of accumulation, with and without technological change. Capitalists have a choice: accumulate with an existing technology and enter the world of model 1 (difficult to do in the face of the coercive laws of competition) or invest in technological change and enter the world of model 2. The question in the second model is, what regulates the pace of technological change? The theory of relative surplus-value showed that the pace of that change is impelled onward by the coercive laws of competition as capitalists compete for the ephemeral form of relative surplus-value that accrues to those working at higher productivity. The limit is therefore partially set by the intensity of competition (a point which Marx does not emphasize). But there is also an outer limit. Marx had earlier established that the rationale for adopting new machine technologies entailed a trade-off between the value laid out for the machine and the value of the labor-power saved by using it. Though Marx does not make the point explicitly, this means that technological innovation would continue up until the point where wage rates fall low enough (as they did in England in the nineteenth century relative to the US) to make buying the machine no longer worthwhile. This point would likely be when the working class is reduced to a condition of utter misery.

The Relative Surplus Population

In section 4 of this chapter, Marx examines the condition of the relative surplus population. He identifies three distinct strata: floating, latent, stagnant (794). By "floating" he means people who are already proletarianized, who are already full-time wage workers, who are temporarily thrown out of work for some reason, who survive somehow through a period of unemployment, before being reabsorbed back into employment as conditions for accumulation improve. In contemporary terms, the floating are roughly equivalent to the pool of unemployed, as recorded in the unemployment statistics, plus those classified as underemployed or as "discouraged workers." The latent are people who have not yet been proletarianized. In Marx's time, this particularly referred to peasant populations not yet absorbed into the wage-labor system. The destruction of peasant or indigenous subsistence agricultural systems and the proletarianization of the rural world have pushed massive numbers into the wage-labor force. This continues to be the case up until our own times (witness China, Mexico and India in recent decades). The mobilization of women and children into the wage-labor force through the disruption of domestic systems has likewise long played a role up until today (turning women into the backbone of wage labor in many parts of the developing world). The latent category can also include petty-bourgeois independent producers and artisans who get displaced by large-scale capital and were thus forced to enter the labor market. The cannibalization of family farms in the United States over the past fifty years has released their labor-power from its former confinements. You could say the same of independent producers and people who once ran the corner stores now displaced by the supermarkets. The latent is, therefore, a huge and diverse category of people comprising petty-bourgeois producers of various kinds, women and children, peasants and the like. In our time, it also encompasses groups who had escaped proletarianization only to be brought back into the fold. Medical doctors used to think they were not part of the proletariat, but an insidious process of proletarianization of the medical workforce is not too hard to identify. The proletarianization of higher education has likewise proceeded apace as the corporatist and neoliberal model of the university has become more entrenched. What Marx draws our attention to here are possible shifts in the dynamics of proletarianization and the various ways in which a latent reserve of labor-power can be mobilized. This will obviously vary a great deal from one situation to another. Furthermore, whereas the floating population is roughly confined to the areas of capitalist organization, the latent reserve has a very different geographical spread. It is potentially available everywhere, and the geopolitics of access to it through imperialist and colonial practices can play a very significant role.

The third stratum is the stagnant. This refers to that part of the population that is very irregularly employed and particularly hard to mobilize. The lowest sediment of the stagnant Marx describes as being "in the sphere of pauperism," including "vagabonds, criminals, prostitutes, in short the actual lumpenproletariat," for whom he has very little affection. Also among them there are "those [paupers] able to work," as well as "orphans and pauper children. These are candidates for the industrial reserve army, and in times of great prosperity . . . they are enrolled in the army of active workers both speedily and in large numbers." But then there are "the demoralized, the ragged, and those unable to work, chiefly people who succumb to their incapacity for adaptation." These populate what Marx calls "the hospital of the active labour-army," and they are almost impossible to mobilize into the wage-labor force (797). This is what William Julius Wilson refers to as an "underclass" (a term I don't really like).

The final and lengthy section 5 of this chapter describes in gruesome detail the situation as it then existed for those embedded in the industrial reserve army (both floating and latent). While Marx focuses on Britain (and the condition of its rural labor reserve in particular), he pays close attention to the role of urbanization and, with respect to the Irish immigrants into England, identifies something important about how these mobilizations of latent workforces so often utilize differences of ethnicity and religion (in this case), which by extension can encompass all manner of racial, gender, cultural, religious and other differences in the divide-and-rule politics deployed by the capitalist class. We could easily supply parallel materials for our own times. The long history of Puerto

Rican labor in the United States neatly parallels that of the Irish in Britain in the nineteenth century. We could also easily write out descriptions of conditions in Mexico, Guatemala, China, Bangladesh, Indonesia and South Africa that would be every bit as distressing as the conditions that Marx describes in section 5.

Marx's second model of accumulation depends primarily on the floating reserves created through technologically induced unemployment. The systemic way in which this floating population is managed (how unemployed workers stay alive and in good enough health to come back into the labor force, for example) is obviously a matter of considerable interest. But there is also a strategic question as to whether it is more advantageous for capitalism to work with floating or with latent reserves (the stagnant might be very hard to mobilize and even harder to work with). The free manipulation of floating reserves poses a number of difficulties. Strong labor organization that procures a modicum of job security can check unemployment. New technologies and new production systems may be challenged by the workers themselves before they become widespread. And the political consequences that result from the production of unemployment when it does occur can be serious under certain circumstances. In the 1950s and 1960s, for example, there was a general reluctance on the part of the bourgeois corporate class throughout much of the capitalist world to create unemployment, in part for fear of social unrest. The preference was to find latent reserves. There were two ways you could do that. You could take capital abroad or import workers. In Sweden in the 1960s and 1970s, unemployment was low, and there was almost no floating reserve at all. In the face of strong union power, lots of social legislation and a powerfully entrenched social-democratic political apparatus, the import of labor from Portugal, Yugoslavia and Central Europe became crucial to the generation of surplus-value. Shortages of labor in the French automobile industries led to state-supported in-migration of Maghrebians, while the labor surplus in Turkey fueled German industry during these years. The changes in immigration laws in the US in the 1960s were also significant in helping to mobilize latent labor-power reserves. The labor surplus in Mexico is crucial to the functioning of firms in the United States, making the current furore over migration, both legal and illegal, a difficult issue (lack of a labor surplus has led to the loss of crops at harvest time in the US West, for example).

We've got a situation today where there is considerable unemployment and a lot of latent labor. It is interesting to think about these categories in relation to the specific political history of labor control within capitalism. The floating population also raises the question of how the reserve is to be maintained in a healthy enough state to compete with the employed. The creation of social-welfare structures has been one answer, but this is less significant now given the trend toward neoliberalization. The right-wing argument is that unemployment arises when laborers put too high a reserve price on their labor. Laborers create unemployment by refusing to work below a certain minimum wage! This typically happens when welfare is too generous. Ergo, the best way to get rid of unemployment is to reduce welfare to zero. But that makes it hard for the floating population to remain a labor reserve. The same problem bedevils immigration policy. Every attempt to regulate immigration in the United States runs up against the corporate need for adequate access to surplus-labor supplies. Industries varying from agribusiness to Microsoft agitate against restrictive immigration policies.

The management of the labor supply becomes crucial. The capitalist class interest is to manage the labor supply in such a way as to create and perpetuate a reserve army (some combination of floating and latent) to keep wages down, threaten the employed laborers with being laid off, disrupt labor organization and increase the intensity of labor for those employed. Since the 1970s, this strategy seems to have succeeded reasonably well in the United States, since real wages have remained essentially flat (with a brief uptick in the 1990s) while profit rates have generally risen. This is the first era in US history in which workers have not benefited from significant increases in productivity. All the benefits from the pursuit of relative surplus-value have accrued to the capitalist class to produce immense concentrations of wealth and surging inequality.

The Liberal Utopian Dream Deconstructed

We saw in Part IV, when analysing the production of relative surplus-value, that within the capitalist system all methods for raising the social productivity of labour are put into effect at the cost of the individual worker; that all means for the development of production undergo a dialectical inversion so that they become means of domination and exploitation of the producers; they distort the worker into a fragment of a man, they degrade him to the level of an appendage of a machine,

> they destroy the actual content of his labour by turning it into a torment; they alienate . . . from him the intellectual potentialities of the labour process in the same proportion as science is incorporated in it as an independent power; they deform the conditions under which he works, subject him during the labour process to a despotism the more hateful for its meanness; they transform his life-time into working-time, and drag his wife and child beneath the wheels of the juggernaut of capital. But all methods for the production of surplus-value are at the same time methods of accumulation, and every extension of accumulation becomes, conversely, a means for the development of those methods. It follows therefore that in proportion as capital accumulates, the situation of the worker, be his payment high or low, must grow worse. Finally, the law which always holds the relative surplus population or industrial reserve army in equilibrium with the extent and energy of accumulation rivets the worker to capital more firmly than the wedges of Hephaestus held Prometheus to the rock. It makes an accumulation of misery a necessary condition, corresponding to the accumulation of wealth. Accumulation of wealth at one pole is, therefore, at the same time accumulation of misery, the torment of labour, slavery, ignorance, brutalization and moral degradation at the opposite pole, i.e. on the side of the class that produces its own product as capital. (798–9)

This is the famous concluding thesis about the increasing immiseration of the proletariat as a socially necessary consequence and condition of capitalist accumulation. A typical response to this thesis is to say that it is simply wrong, that many workers of the world are far better off today than they were one hundred years ago and that while it may be true that there are still some terrible work conditions in the factories of China and the sweatshops of Hong Kong, these are typical transitional problems en route to the creation of better material living standards that even in those countries are beginning to be evidenced. So this is one of those statements that is taken, sometimes by Marxists as well as by critics, to be one of Marx's firm predictions that can simply be tested by appeal to the historical record. And insofar as the historical record does not support it wholeheartedly, this is then taken to mean that Marx's analysis is surely wrong.

So I here need to forcefully remind you of the assumptions that govern these chapters and emphasize once again that conclusions of this sort are not absolute but contingent, broadly dependent on the limiting assumptions laid out at the beginning. This is the conclusion to Volume I of *Capital*, in which the focus is exclusively on the dynamics of production. The analysis proceeds purely from that perspective. What we will find at the end of Volume II, written from the standpoint of the realization of capital in the market, is something entirely different. There Marx will concentrate on the problems of effective demand (who has the money power to buy the expanding volume of products?). Part of the solution to this problem has to lie in what he there depicts as "rational consumption" on the part of the working class. He means two things by this. First, the working class must have sufficient purchasing power available to itself to be able to consume; second, the working class will have acquired consumption habits congenial to the absorption of the surplus product that capitalism perpetually generates. So at the end of Volume II, Marx cites the ways in which bourgeois philanthropy concentrates on teaching the working classes "proper" consumption habits (much as what happened when Ford mobilized an army of social workers to make sure those who were benefiting from the five-dollar eight-hour day he instituted in his factories spent their money wisely and not on drink, drugs and women). So what we get at the end of Volume II is a completely different story. Plainly, the working class cannot perform its socially necessary role as a consumer-demand center for capitalist products if the Volume I story is all there is.

So what, then, is the purpose and point of the Volume I story? It says that if the world were to operate in this way, then the outcome would be increasing immiseration of the workers. If we ask whether we see elements of truth in this conclusion, then the answer is surely "yes" if we go to the factories of Indonesia, Bangladesh, Vietnam and Guatemala. In these places, latent reserves of labor are being mobilized under conditions of the utmost brutality. Indeed, you will see all the "agony of toil" that Marx describes. You do not have to look far to find detailed reports of the appalling conditions of labor in many of the world's production centers (NGO and UN reports are full of it, and even the mainstream press has published some searing accounts). Furthermore, it is one of the signal facts of the past thirty years or so of neoliberal practices and policies that income inequalities have soared and billionaires have erupted all over the place (India, Mexico, China, Russia), making the picture of an accumulation of wealth at one pole and of misery at the other a very compelling metaphor for describing the conditions of contemporary global capitalism.

So it is hard to read the Volume I story without recognizing that it depicts a certain, albeit partial, truth, particularly when compared with the situation in the advanced capitalist countries of the 1950s and 1960s, when labor organization was relatively strong, social-democratic tendencies were dominant and state interventions, both in production and with respect to the distribution of wealth, were more widely accepted. In those times, the issues of rational consumption were more salient: how do we ensure that the working class purchases automobiles? Well, we build cities and suburbs in such a way that the automobile becomes a necessity rather than a luxury, which means that workers have to be paid enough to be able to afford automobiles and suburban housing and all that goes with this lifestyle. During these times, the Volume II analysis made a lot of sense, and the Volume I conclusions seemed a bit far-fetched.

Much of this has been reversed by the neoliberal turn that set in during the 1970s. There has been a massive expansion of the proletariat worldwide as some two billion people have been dispossessed of their earlier economic base and brought into the proletariat either through the destruction of rural ways of life and peasant economies (as in Latin America and South Asia) or through direct government action (as in China and East Asia more generally). The predictable result of this influx has been that the working classes in the core traditional centers of capital accumulation have not improved their lot. Astonishing increases in wealth have flowed to the top 1 percent (and even more, proportionately, to the top 0.1 percent) of the population. The pursuit of the neoliberal project has led us back into a world in which the Volume I analysis is more and more relevant.

This was a conscious project on the part of the ruling classes. The "Volcker shock," which raised United States interest rates dramatically beginning in 1979, produced surging unemployment; this, when coupled with President Reagan's attack on organized labor (beginning with taking on the air-traffic controllers' union in the strike of 1981), was clearly intended to discipline labor. The British economist Alan Budd, reflecting on his experience of being Margaret Thatcher's chief economic adviser, later confessed as to how ashamed he felt around his neighbors, because "the 1980s policies of attacking inflation by squeezing the economy and public spending were a cover to bash the workers. Raising unemployment was a very desirable way of reducing the strength of the working class. What was engineered—in Marxist terms—was a crisis of capitalism, which re-created a reserve army of labor, and has allowed the capitalists to make high profits ever since."[2] Like Reagan, Thatcher attacked union power politically in a violent suppression of the miner's strike in the 1980s. Again, the aim was to discipline labor to secure profits and endless accumulation. The terrifying thing about Marx's analysis is that such an outcome is entirely predictable and that it could be so easily articulated in Marxist terms.

What Marx has done in Volume I of *Capital* is to take the words and theories of the classical political economists seriously and ask what kind of world would emerge if they got to implement their utopian liberal vision of perfectly functioning markets, personal liberty, private property rights and free trade. Step by step, he explores what would happen in a world constructed in this image. Adam Smith had purported to show that national wealth would grow and that everyone would or could be better off in a world of decentralized and freely functioning markets (though Smith himself did not absolve the state from responsibilities when it came to the distribution of that wealth along more equitable lines). What Marx shows is that a world constructed along pure *laissez-faire* lines would in itself produce an increasing accumulation of wealth at one pole and a burgeoning accumulation of misery at the other. So who would want to construct the world according to the rules of this utopian vision? And the answer is stunningly obvious: the wealthy members of the capitalist class! So who preaches to us the virtues of this utopian free-market vision, and who has put us on our contemporary neoliberal path? Surprise, surprise! It was the wealthy who used their money power to persuade all of us that the market is always right and that Marxian theory is nonsense.

The neoliberal project (as I show in *A Brief History of Neoliberalism*[3]) has been directed toward the increasing accumulation of wealth and the increasing appropriation of surplus-value on the part of the upper echelons of the capitalist class. And in pursuing that objective, the capitalist class has taken the typical path as outlined in the models of capital accumulation set out in Volume I. Bring wages down and create unemployment by technological changes that displace workers, centralize capitalist power, attack workers' organizations as interfering

---

2. See *The Observer*, June 21, 1992.

3. David Harvey, *A Brief History of Neoliberalism* (New York: Oxford University Press, 2005).

with the market coordination of supply and demand (when, as we have seen, capital works on both sides of the market), outsource and offshore, mobilize latent populations around the world and depress welfare levels as far as possible. This is what neoliberal "globalization" has really been about. The socially necessary conditions have been created, very much in accord with the Volume I analysis, for the immense accumulation of wealth at one pole at the expense of everyone else. The problem, of course, is that this kind of neoliberal capitalism can survive only "by simultaneously undermining the original sources of all wealth—the soil and the worker" (638).

But this is not the only outcome consistent with Marx's analysis. Marx points in this chapter to the inevitability of the increasing concentration and centralization of capital under conditions of free-market utopianism. Interestingly, this has also been a marked feature of the past thirty years of neoliberalization (look at energy, pharmaceuticals, the media and above all at the increasing centralization of financial power). Excessive freedoms of the market always produce a trend toward more oligopoly and even monopoly (a fact that is recognized in antitrust legislation and some state monitoring—these days largely ineffective—of mergers and monopolies). Not only does wealth accumulate, it centralizes in the hands of an increasingly powerful capitalist class! But this also poses a problem. What happens when the conditions for harmony defined in the Volume II analysis turn so contradictory—precisely because of the polarization of wealth—as to generate a shuddering crisis of the sort that broke out in 2008? Perhaps it is no accident that the only period in US history when wealth distribution was as lopsided as it is today was the 1920s and that we are now seeing a rerun of the 1929 collapse in 2008.

It is, I think, immense testimony to the strength of Marx's analysis and the power of his method that he can get us to see clearly aspects of the historical dynamic that so often remain hidden, while he simultaneously confronts the simmering contradictions and powerful ideological constructions that produce and legitimate the kinds of results he predicts. How many Nassau Seniors are there in our economics departments! Thus it is appropriate to defend his conditional statements, recognizing that while they are not the whole story, they are still a vital and all too easily recognizable aspect of what's unfolding within capitalism today. He has indeed spelled out "*the absolute general law of capitalist accumulation*" in no uncertain terms, even as he also recognizes that "like all other laws, it is modified in its working by many circumstances, the analysis of which does not concern us here" (798). The general law is a brilliant exposition of where free-market and liberal utopianism will take us if implemented, and to the degree that the neoliberal ideological turn has taken these shibboleths, dressed them up in new guises and indeed sought to implement them, it has actually taken us in the direction that Marx predicts, replete with contradictions. We can, I think, take insight though absolutely no comfort, and acquire significant diagnostic power, from a careful reading of Marx's text and a deep appreciation of his method.

CHAPTER ELEVEN

The Secret of Primitive Accumulation

There is a marked shift in tone, content and method in part 8 of *Capital*. To begin with, it goes against the central presumption of the rest of the book, established back in chapter 2, where Marx accepts Adam Smith's theoretical world of atomistic market exchange in which freedom, equality, property and Bentham rule in such a way that all commodity exchanges occur in a noncoercive environment of properly functioning liberal institutions. Smith knew perfectly well that this is not how the world actually is, but he accepted it as a convenient and compelling fiction on which to build a normative political economic theory. Marx, as we have seen, takes this all on board in order to deconstruct its utopianism.

By this strategem, Marx was able to show, as we saw in the last chapter, that the closer we get to a regime of liberal market action, the more we will find ourselves confronting two significant consequences. The minor consequence is that the decentralized, fragmented and atomistic structure that would prevent any single power cornering and manipulating the market gives way to increasingly centralized capitalist power. Competition always tends to produce monopoly, and the fiercer the competition, the faster the tendency toward centralization. The major consequence is the production of immense concentrations of wealth at one pole (particularly on the part of the centralizing capitalists) and increasing misery, toil and degradation for the working class at the other pole.

The neoliberal project of the past thirty years, grounded in liberal utopianism, has successfully conformed to both of Marx's predicted trends. Of course, there is a good deal of divergence, geographical as well as sectoral, in the details, but the degree of centralization of capital that has occurred in various spheres has been striking, and there is general acknowledgement that the immense concentrations of wealth occurring at the very top of the wealth and income scale have never been as great as they are now, while conditions among the working classes of the world have either stagnated or deteriorated. In the United States, for example, the proportion of the national income and wealth held by the top 1 percent of the population has doubled over the past twenty years, and for the top 0.1 percent it has tripled. The ratio of income between CEOs and their median salaried workers, which stood at 30:1 back in 1970, has soared to more than 350:1 on average these past few years. Wherever neoliberalization has been rampant (as in Mexico and India since 1990 or so), billionaires have suddenly emerged on the *Forbes* list of the wealthiest individuals in the world. Carlos Slim of Mexico is now ranked as one of the wealthiest people in the world, and he rose to that position on the back of the wave of neoliberalization that occurred in Mexico in the early nineties.

Marx arrived at these counterintuitive conclusions through deconstructing the classical political economists' propositions on their own terms. But he also used their powerful abstractions critically, to probe creatively into the actual dynamics of capitalism and so reveal the origins of struggles over the length of the working day, the struggles surrounding the conditions of life of the industrial reserve army and the like. The analysis of Volume I can be read as a sophisticated and damning account of why "there is nothing more unequal than the equal treatment of unequals." The ideology of freedom of exchange and liberty of contract gulls us all. This grounds the moral superiority and hegemony of bourgeois political theory and underpins its legitimacy and supposed humanism. But when people enter this free and egalitarian world of market exchange with different resource endowments and different assets, then even minor inequalities, let alone the major divide of class position, get magnified and compounded over time into huge inequalities of influence, wealth and power. When coupled with increasing centralization, this makes for Marx's devastating reversal of the Smithian vision of "the benefit of all" that derives from the hidden hand of market exchange. This enlightens us mightily as to the class content of what, for example, the past thirty years of market-based neoliberal globalization have really been about. The upshot for Marx is a fierce critique of the theses of individual liberty and freedom that ground liberal and neoliberal theory. These ideals are, in Marx's view, as misleading, fictional and fraudulent as they are seductive and beguiling. Laborers, he early on observed, are free only in the double sense of being able to sell their labor-power to whomsoever they chose at the same time as they have to sell that labor-power in order to live because they have been freed and liberated from any and all control over the means of production!

What part 8 of *Capital* does is to take up the question of how this second kind of "freedom" was secured. Here we are forced to confront the thievery, predation, violence and abusive use of power that lay at the historical origins of capitalism as it freed up labor-power as a commodity and displaced an earlier mode of production. The assumptions that have dominated the argument in the first seven parts of *Capital* are cast aside with brutal consequences.

Capitalism depends fundamentally, as we have seen, on a commodity capable of producing more value than it itself has, and that commodity is labor-power. "Why this free worker," Marx observed early on in *Capital*,

> confronts him in the sphere of circulation is a question which does not interest the owner of money, for he finds the labour-market in existence as a particular branch of the commodity-market. And for the present it interests us just as little. We confine ourselves to the fact theoretically, as he does practically. One thing, however, is clear: nature does not produce on the one hand owners of money or commodities, and on the other hand men possessing nothing but their own labour-power. This relation has no basis in natural history, nor does it have a social basis common to all periods of human history. It is clearly the result of a past historical development, the product of many economic revolutions, of the extinction of a whole series of older formations of social production. (273)

Primitive accumulation is about the historical origins of this wage labor, as well as about the accumulation of the necessary assets in the hands of the capitalist class to employ them.

Part 8 therefore addresses the central question of how labor-power became a commodity (or, more generally, how the working class was formed). The standard bourgeois story devised by Locke and Smith was that

> long, long ago there were two sorts of people; one, the diligent, intelligent and above all frugal élite; the other, lazy rascals, spending their substance, and more, in riotous living . . . the former sort accumulated wealth, and the latter sort finally had nothing to sell except their own skins. And from this original sin dates the poverty of the great majority who, despite all their labour, have up to now nothing to sell but themselves, and the wealth of the few that increases constantly, although they have long ceased to work. (873)

This standard story depicts the transition from feudalism to capitalism as gradual and peaceful. But "in actual history," Marx argues, it was anything but:

> It is a notorious fact that conquest, enslavement, robbery, murder, in short, force, play the greatest part. In the tender annals of political economy, the idyllic reigns from time immemorial. Right and 'labour' were from the beginning of time the sole means of enrichment, 'this year' of course always excepted. (874)

This is so, because the process

> which creates the capital-relation can be nothing other than the process which divorces the worker from the ownership of the conditions of his own labour; it is a process which operates two transformations, whereby the social means of subsistence and production are turned into capital, and the immediate producers are turned into wage-labourers. So-called primitive accumulation, therefore, is nothing else than the historical process of divorcing the producer from the means of production. It appears as 'primitive' because it forms the pre-history of capital, and of the mode of production corresponding to capital. (874–5)

As a matter of historical fact, the history of primitive accumulation "is anything but idyllic" (874). It "is written in the annals of mankind in letters of blood and fire" (875).

Marx's account, radically at odds with that of Smith and Locke, poses some interesting questions. First, are merchant's capital and finance capital and usury simply antediluvian forms, or do they still have a very active role, independent of production capital, industrial capital and the like? Marx had also earlier observed that "we shall find that both merchants' capital and interest-bearing capital are derivative forms," at the same time as "it will become clear why, historically, these two forms appear before the modern primary form of capital" (267). The implication is that the transition from feudalism to capitalism occurred in stages such that merchants' capital and usury pioneered the way for the rise of production/industrial capital. The role these earlier forms of capital played in the dissolution of the feudal order is therefore open to investigation.

Second, does this mean that once capitalism has gone through primitive accumulation, once the prehistory is over and a mature capitalist society has emerged, that the violent processes he here describes become insignificant and no longer necessary to how capitalism works? This is a question to which I will return. But bear it in mind as we go forward.

In Marx's version of primitive accumulation, all the rules of market exchange earlier laid out (in chapter 2) are abandoned. There is no reciprocity, no equality. Yes, the accumulation of money is there, markets of a sort are there, but the real process is something else. It is about the violent dispossession of a whole class of people from control over the means of production, at first through illegal acts, but ultimately, as in the enclosure legislation in Britain, through actions of the state. Adam Smith, of course, did not want the state to be construed as an active agent in the victimization of a population, so he certainly could not tell a story of primitive accumulation in which state violence played a crucial role. If the origins of capital accumulation lie with the state apparatus and state power, then why now advocate *laissez-faire* policies as a primary means to augment national and individual well-being? Consequently, Smith, along with most other classical political economists, preferred to ignore the role of the state in primitive accumulation. There were exceptions. James Steuart, Marx notes, certainly understood that state violence was absolutely central to proletarianization but took the position that it was a necessary evil. Michael Perelman's book *The Invention of Capitalism*[1] provides an excellent account of how original or primitive accumulation was handled within classical political economy.

Marx's primary concern in part 8 is to unravel the history of primitive accumulation from the sixteenth century onward and to investigate how these processes were set in motion. He readily admits, of course, that

> the history of this expropriation assumes different aspects in different countries, and runs through its various phases in different orders of succession, and at different historical epochs. Only in England, which we therefore take as our example, has it the classic form. (876)

Does "classic" mean that it was a template for the transition to capitalism that everybody around the world had to follow? Marx later on denied this interpretation and stated that he viewed Britain as but one, albeit

1. Michael Perelman, *The Invention of Capitalism: Classical Political Economy and the Secret History of Primitive Accumulation* (Durham, NC: Duke University Press, 2000).

special and pioneering, example. Again, these are controversial issues to which we will have to return. How we think them through has relevance to another important but largely occluded question: is it necessary to go through primitive accumulation and the long history of capitalism in order to arrive at socialism?

CHAPTERS 27–33: PRIMITIVE ACCUMULATION

The chapters of part 8 are relatively short and arranged in a sequence that has clear implications. I shall consider them briefly, pointing out some significant elements. Chapter 27 deals with the expropriation of the agricultural population, as well as the equally important process of the dissolution of the bands of feudal retainers. The appropriation of the land was the primary means to dispossess the peasantry, but release of the retainers owed as much to the way in which money power began to be exercised within and over the feudal order (e.g., by merchant capital and usury). "The new nobility was the child of its time, for which money was the power of all powers" (879). In the *Grundrisse*, Marx is rather more explicit. He there writes of how money dissolves the traditional community, and in dissolving the traditional community, money becomes the community. So we move from a world in which "community" is defined in terms of structures of interpersonal social relations to a world where the community of money prevails. Money used as social power leads to the creation of large landed estates, large sheep-farming enterprises and the like, at the same time as commodity exchange proliferates (an idea made much of in the early chapters on money and exchange in general). The traditional community does not yield without a struggle, and in the initial stages, at least, state power attempts to preserve what E. P. Thompson later called "the moral economy" of the peasantry against raw money power.

But state power gradually yields for two reasons. First, the state depends on and thereby becomes vulnerable to money power. Secondly, money power can be created and mobilized in ways that state legislation has difficulty stopping. Under Henry VII, acts were passed trying to hold back the process of monetization and proletarianization. But the rising power of incipient capitalism demanded "the reverse of this: a degraded and almost servile condition of the mass of the people, their transformation into mercenaries, and the transformation of their means of labour into capital." The "forcible expropriation of the people received a new and terrible impulse in the sixteenth century," and after that, the resistance of the traditional social order starts to crumble (883). Instead of the illegalities of money power taking a subversive lead, the state allies with money power and starts to actively support processes of proletarianization. This trend consolidates, Marx suggests, with the Glorious Revolution of 1688, which

> brought into power, along with William of Orange, the landed and capitalist profit-grubbers. They inaugurated the new era by practising on a colossal scale the thefts of state lands which had hitherto been managed more modestly. These estates were given away, sold at ridiculous prices, or even annexed to private estates by direct seizure . . . The Crown lands thus fraudulently appropriated, together with the stolen Church estates, . . . form the basis of the present princely domains of the English oligarchy. (884)

On this basis, new and more powerful class alliances form. "The new landed aristocracy was the natural ally of the new bankocracy, of newly hatched high finance, and of the large manufacturers, at that time dependent on protective duties." In other words, there is a formation of a bourgeoisie made up of landed capitalists, merchant capitalists, finance capitalists and manufacturing capitalists in broad alliance. They bend the state apparatus to their collective will. As a result, "the law itself now becomes the instrument by which the people's land is stolen, although the big farmers made use of their little independent methods as well."

So there is a systematic theft of communal property which goes on during this period, spearheaded by a grand movement of enclosure of the commons. The "forcible usurpation, generally accompanied by the turning of arable into pasture land, begins at the end of the fifteenth century and extends into the sixteenth" (885). These circumstances, incidentally, spawned a significant literature of nostalgia for the loss of the old order. This was the world of Oliver Goldsmith and Gray's elegy, lamenting the destruction of a supposed "Merrie England." Marx chooses to comment on a later example, the spectacular case of the Highland clearances in Scotland, which dispossessed the crofters of their land in wave after wave until the later nineteenth century. He revels in the hypocrisy of the Duchess of Sutherland, who, while simultaneously expelling people from the land in the Highlands through a quasi-legal process, "entertained Mrs

Beecher Stowe, authoress of *Uncle Tom's Cabin*, with great magnificence in London to show her sympathy for the Negro slaves of the American republic" (892).

Summarizing, Marx writes:

> The spoliation of the Church's property, the fraudulent alienation of the state domains, the theft of the common lands, the usurpation of feudal and clan property and its transformation into modern private property under circumstances of ruthless terrorism, all these things were just so many idyllic methods of primitive accumulation. They conquered the field for capitalist agriculture, incorporated the soil into capital [a very interesting phrase], and created for the urban industries the necessary supplies of free and rightless proletarians. (895)

The question of what all these people kicked off the land are going to do is taken up in chapter 28. Often there was no employment for them, so they became, in the eyes of the state at least, vagabonds, beggars, thieves and robbers. The state apparatus responded in ways that continue to this day: it criminalized and incarcerated them, depicted them as rogues and visited the utmost violence on them. "Thus were the agricultural folk first forcibly expropriated from the soil, driven from their homes, turned into vagabonds, and then whipped, branded and tortured by grotesquely terroristic laws into accepting the discipline necessary for the system of wage-labour." The violence of the socialization of workers into the disciplinary apparatus of capital is at first transparent. But with the passing of time, "the silent compulsion of economic relations sets the seal on the domination of the capitalist over the worker." Once the proletariat is formed, Marx here seems to be saying, then the silent compulsion of economic relations does its job and the overt violence can fade into the background, because people have been socialized into their situation as wage laborers, as bearers of the commodity labor-power. But "the rising bourgeoisie" continues to need "the power of the state" to regulate wages, to prevent any kind of collective organization of the worker (anti-union legislation and what at the time were called the Combination Laws, banning workers' associations or even assemblies) (899). This was a crucial support, Marx points out, to the consolidation of the liberal regime (founded on private property rights).

> During the very first storms of the revolution, the French bourgeoisie dared to take away from the workers the right of association they had just acquired. By a decree of 14 June 1791, they declared that every combination by the workers was 'an assault on liberty and the declaration of the rights of man'. (903)

Bourgeois legality is used in this very specific way to inhibit the potential collective powers of labor.

Chapter 29 examines the genesis of the capitalist farmer. Marx here tells a very simple tale of how bailiffs became sharecroppers became tenant farmers and then came to pay ground (money) rent to landlords. This process of monetization and commodification underpinned an "agricultural revolution" on the land, which permitted capital to command the soil in certain ways. Capital circulated through the soil, through nature, in exactly the same way that it came to circulate through the body of the laborer as variable capital. The impact of this agricultural revolution, he says in chapter 30, was double-edged. Not only did it set free a lot of labor, it also set free means of subsistence formerly consumed on the land directly. It commoditized the food supply. The market for goods and commodities grew, in part because fewer people could subsist on their own. The result was an expansion of market exchange and an increase in the size of the market. Meanwhile, capital was destroying many of the subsidiary artisanal and household trades not only in India but also in Britain. This resulted in the creation of a stronger and larger domestic market. The growth of the internal market in Britain from the sixteenth century onward was, in Marx's view, an important element in the development of capitalism.

This leads us to consider, in chapter 31, the genesis of the industrial capitalist who takes over the leading role from merchant's capital, usurer's capital, the bankocracy (finance capital) and landed capital. This takeover from the very beginning was tightly integrated with colonialism, the slave trade and what happened in Africa and in the United States. Under feudalism, there were many barriers to turning the growing quantity of money capital into industrial capital. "The feudal organization of the countryside and the guild organization of the towns" inhibited industrial development based on wage labor, but "these fetters vanished with the dissolution of the feudal bands of retainers, and the expropriation and partial eviction of the rural population." But, Marx presciently notes,

> the new manufactures were established at sea-ports, or at points in the countryside which were beyond the control of the old municipalities and their guilds. Hence, in England, the bitter struggle of the corporate towns against these new seed-beds of industry. (915)

Industrial capitalism developed in Britain on what we would now call greenfield sites. The corporate towns like Norwich and Bristol were highly organized, and it was politically difficult to take them over and break the power of the guilds. On greenfield sites in the countryside, there was no regulatory apparatus to stop you—no town bourgeoisie, no guild organization. So most of the industrialization that occurred in Britain occurred on former village sites like Manchester (all the cotton towns were originally just small villages). Leeds and Birmingham, again, began as small trading villages. This is different from some patterns of industrialization that have occurred elsewhere, although it is still the case that capital likes to move to greenfield sites whenever it can. When the Japanese auto industry moved into Britain in the 1980s, it avoided highly unionized parts of the country and moved to areas open for new development, where the companies could start from scratch and build whatever they wanted (with the assistance of the Thatcher anti-union government, of course). In the United States, the same tendency exists. Finding spaces where regulation and union organization are lacking continues to be a significant aspect of the geographical and locational dynamic of capitalism.

The roles of the colonial system and the slave trade cannot be ignored, either, since it was by these means that the bourgeoisie both circumvented and overturned feudal powers. There is a strong body of opinion that regards the slave plantations of the West Indies in the early eighteenth century as a pioneering stage in the organization of large-scale labor operations of the sort that reappeared later in the factory systems of Britain. "These methods depend in part on brute force, for instance the colonial system" (915). All manner of tactics were used to extract wealth from colonized populations. "Between 1769 and 1770," for example, "the English created a famine by buying up all the rice and refusing to sell it again, except at fabulous prices" (917). But all such methods

> employ the power of the state, the concentrated and organized force of society, to hasten, as in a hothouse, the process of transformation of the

> feudal mode of production into the capitalist mode, and to shorten the transition. Force is the midwife of every old society which is pregnant with a new one. It is itself an economic power. (915–16)

But we cannot understand this crucial role of the state as an organizing force, and as promoter of the colonial system, without acknowledging the significance of both the national debt and the public credit system as means whereby money power can start to control the power of the state. The merger between money power and state power from the sixteenth century onward is signaled by the rise of a "modern system of taxation" and an international credit system (921). The "bankocrats, financiers, *rentiers*, brokers, stock-jobbers, etc." who populate this system then come to play significant power roles (920). The colonial system allowed "the treasures captured outside Europe by undisguised looting, enslavement and murder" to flow "back to the mother-country" and be "turned into capital there" while "the public debt became one of the most powerful levers of primitive accumulation" (918–19).

> Colonial system, public debts, heavy taxes, protection, commercial wars, etc., these offshoots of the period of manufacture swell to gigantic proportions during the period of infancy of large-scale industry. The birth of the latter is celebrated by a vast, Herod-like slaughter of the innocents. (922)

This "slaughter" arose out of the need to find and mobilize sufficient labor-power in areas remote from the existing towns. Marx quotes John Fielden: "The small and nimble fingers of little children being by very far the most in request, the custom instantly sprang up of procuring apprentices (!) from the different parish workhouses of London, Birmingham, and elsewhere" and shipping them north to rural Lancashire (923). Marx continues himself: "While the cotton industry introduced child-slavery into England, in the United States it gave the impulse for the transformation of the earlier, more or less patriarchal slavery into a system of commercial exploitation," thereby giving a stimulus to the slave trade, which fell under the increasing dominance of the British (925). "Liverpool grew fat on the basis of the slave trade. This was its method of primitive accumulation" (924).

It took immense effort to

> unleash the 'eternal natural laws' of the capitalist mode of production, to complete the process of separation between the workers and the conditions of their labour, to transform, at one pole, the social means of production and subsistence into capital, and at the opposite pole, the mass of the population into wage-labourers, into the free 'labouring poor', that artificial product of modern history. (925)

If money "comes into the world with a congenital blood-stain on one cheek," Marx concludes, then "capital comes dripping from head to toe, from every pore, with blood and dirt" (926).

The processes of expropriation, Marx argues in chapter 32, are as drawn out as they are brutal and painful. Feudalism did not dissolve without a struggle. "New forces and new passions spring up in the bosom of society, forces and passions which feel themselves to be fettered by that society." Feudalism

> has to be annihilated; it is annihilated. Its annihilation, the transformation of the individualized and scattered means of production into socially concentrated means of production, the transformation, therefore, of the dwarf-like property of the many into the giant property of the few, and the expropriation of the great mass of the people from the soil, from the means of subsistence and from the instruments of labour, this terrible and arduously accomplished expropriation of the mass of the people forms the pre-history of capital.

This prehistory "comprises a whole series of forcible methods" that amount to a system of "merciless barbarism" (928). But once set in motion, the processes of capitalist development assume their own distinctive logic, including that of centralization.

> One capitalist always strikes down many others. Hand in hand with this centralization, or this expropriation of many capitalists by a few, other developments take place on an ever-increasing scale, such as the growth of the co-operative form of the labour process, the conscious technical application of science, the planned exploitation of the soil.

These proceed apace as the world market forms to impart an "international character of the capitalist regime." From this there also grows the revolt of the working class:

> a class constantly increasing in numbers, and trained, united and organized by the very mechanism of the capitalist process of production. The monopoly of capital becomes a fetter upon the mode of production which has flourished alongside and under it. The centralization of the means of production and the socialization of labour reach a point at which they become incompatible with their capitalist integument. This integument is burst asunder. The knell of capitalist private property sounds. The expropriators are expropriated. (929)

There is, after all, a huge difference between "the expropriation of the great mass of the people" by a few usurpers and the expropriation of a few usurpers by the great mass of the people.

This call to the barricades of revolution is the rhetoric of the *Communist Manifesto* brought back to bear on the politics of *Capital*. It is a political and polemical statement that should, surely, provide the culminating chapter to an astonishing work of deep analysis that is animated by a revolutionary spirit.

Which brings us to the last chapter, a curious chapter that deflates the messianic rhetoric and tone of the preceding chapter by offering a series of reflections on the theory of colonization. Furthermore, it is not really about the actual colonial experience and the prospects for anticolonial revolutionary struggles (the expropriation of the colonial masters by the mass of the colonized people). It is about the theories of colonization set out by a man called Wakefield, who hardly rates among the greatest political economists of all time and who wrote his book about colonization when in Newgate Prison for attempting to abduct the daughter of a wealthy family. While in Newgate, Wakefield found himself in the company of prisoners about to be transported to Australia, and this evidently set him thinking about the role of Australia in the general scheme of things. He had little idea as to what was really going on in Australia, but he saw something that Marx considered of great import because it amounted to a devastating rebuttal of Adam Smith. Wakefield simply recognized that you can take all the capital in the world to Australia—money, instruments of labor, materials of all kinds—but if you can't find any "free" (in the double sense!) laborers to work for you, you cannot be a capitalist.

Wakefield, in short, "discovered that capital is not a thing, but a social relation between persons which is mediated through things" (932).

It would be difficult to find laborers in Australia; at the time they had easy access to the land and so could support themselves as independent producers. The only way to ensure a labor supply, and thereby preserve the prospects for capitalism, was for the state to step in and put a reserve price on the land. That reserve price had to be high enough to make sure that everybody who arrived in Australia had to work as wage laborers until they could save enough capital to gain access to land. Wakefield considered that the land system in the United States (the Homestead Act) was too open and too free, and this set the price of labor too high (which, as we earlier saw, led to the faster adoption of labor-saving innovations). The United States, Wakefield correctly predicted, would have to dive back into the brutal tactics of the prehistory of capitalism if capitalism were to survive there. The struggle between "free labor" on the frontier and the increasing control of land policy by corporate (particularly railroad) interests, as well as the retention of immigrant populations as wage laborers in the city, was a vital aspect of accumulation.

"The only thing that interests us," writes Marx,

> is the secret discovered in the New World by the political economy of the Old World, and loudly proclaimed by it: that the capitalist mode of production and accumulation, and therefore capitalist private property as well, have for their fundamental condition the annihilation of that private property which rests on the labour of the individual himself; in other words, the expropriation of the worker. (940)

> Let the government set an artificial price on the virgin soil, a price independent of the law of supply and demand, a price that compels the immigrant to work a long time for wages before he can earn enough money to buy land and turn himself into an independent farmer. (938)

This, Marx says, is the "great secret" of Wakefield's plans for colonization, but it also reveals the great secret of primitive accumulation. These plans did carry considerable influence in the British Parliament and did affect colonial land policy. "The English government for years practised this method of 'primitive accumulation' prescribed by Mr Wakefield expressly for use in the colonies" (939).

Marx uses this colonial theory to rebut Adam Smith's theory of original or primitive accumulation. But there is something else going on here that may have deep relevance to the whole argument and structure of *Capital* as a book. In the preface to the second edition, Marx takes up his relationship to Hegel, noting, "I criticized the mystificatory side of the Hegelian dialectic nearly thirty years ago" (102). Almost certainly, he is referring to his lengthy *Critique of Hegel's Philosophy of Right*. There, Marx starts his critique at paragraph 250 of Hegel's exposition. But the content of the preceding paragraphs is somewhat surprising. Without any prior warning or theorization, Hegel launches into a discussion of the internal contradictions of capitalism. He notes the "dependence and distress of the class tied" to a certain kind of work, processes that lead to generalized impoverishment and the creation of a rabble of paupers which, at the same time, "brings with it, at the other end of the social scale, conditions which greatly facilitate the concentration of disproportionate wealth in a few hands." The language is very similar to that in chapter 25 of *Capital*, where Marx talks about the accumulation of wealth at one pole and of misery, toil and degradation at the other pole, occupied by the working class. "It hence becomes apparent," Hegel observes, "that despite an excess of wealth civil society is not rich enough . . . to check excessive poverty and the creation of a penurious rabble" and

> this inner dialectic of civil society thus drives it—or at any rate drives a specific civil society—to push beyond its own limits and seek markets, and so its necessary means of subsistence, in other lands which are either deficient in the goods it has over-produced, or else generally backward in industry.

A "mature civil society" is thus driven to colonizing activity "by which it supplies to a part of its population a return to life on the family basis in a new land and so also supplies itself with a new demand and field for its industry."[2]

Why might be called an "inner dialectic" produces greater and greater levels of social inequality. Furthermore, as Hegel says in one of his paragraph addendums, "against nature man can claim no right, but once society is established, poverty immediately takes the form of a wrong done to one class by another."[3] This inner dialectic founded on class

2. G.W. F. Hegel, *Hegel's Philosophy of Right*, trans. T. M. Knox (Oxford: Clarendon Press, 1957), 149–52.

3. Ibid., 277.

struggle leads civil societies to seek relief in an "outer dialectic" of colonial and imperialist activity. Whether Hegel believes that this will resolve the inner problem is not clear. But Marx is quite clear that it cannot. The penultimate chapter of *Capital*, which contemplates the expropriation of the expropriators as the ultimate outcome of the inner dialectic, cannot be countered by colonial practices that merely re-create the social relations of capitalism on a wider scale. There can be no colonial solution to the internal class contradictions of capitalism, and by the same token no ultimate spatial fix to the internal contradictions. What we now call globalization is simply, as we are again and again reminded, a temporary fix that "solves" problems in the here-and-now by projecting them onto a larger and grander geographical terrain.

COMMENTARY

There are a variety of issues posed by Marx's account of primitive accumulation that call for commentary. To begin with, it is important to recognize and appreciate the innovative and pioneering character of Marx's account. Nobody had really done this before in such a systematic and ordered way. But as so often happens in an innovative account, it's a bit exaggerated, and it glosses over a host of issues. Historians and economic historians have since done a vast amount of research on the transition from feudalism to capitalism. The consensus would probably be that the story Marx tells is partially true in some places. There were indeed plenty of moments and incidents of extreme violence in this historical geography. And the role of the colonial system, including the evolution of colonial land, labor and taxation policies, is undeniable. But there have also been instances of primitive accumulation that were relatively peaceable. Populations were not so much forced off the land as attracted off the land by employment possibilities and the prospects of a better life offered by urbanization and industrialization. The voluntary move to cities from appalling and precarious conditions of rural life, because urban wages were fairly high, has not been uncommon (even without those processes of forcible dispossession from the land that Marx refers to and for which there is plenty of historical evidence). The story of primitive accumulation is, therefore, far more nuanced and complicated in its details than the one that Marx tells. And there were important aspects to the dynamic that Marx ignores. For example, the gender dimension is now recognized as being highly significant, since primitive accumulation frequently entailed a radical disempowerment of women, their reduction to the status of property and chattel and the reenforcement of patriarchal social relations.

But Marx did sketch the broad outlines of the industrial and agricultural revolutions, of the processes of proletarianization, commodification and monetization that were necessary for capitalism to come into being. His account set a baseline for all future discussions and for this reason alone was a creative intervention. It also dramatically reminds us of the originary violence and the fierce struggles that brought capitalism into being, an originary violence that the bourgeoisie subsequently sought to deny and forget, even as we live with its trace to this day.

Throughout *Capital*, but also in many of his other writings, Marx tends to relegate processes of primitive accumulation to the prehistory of capitalism. Once that prehistory is done with, then the "silent compulsion of economic relations" takes over. Marx's political project in *Capital* is to alert us as to how these silent compulsions operate on us, often without our noticing, hidden behind the fetishistic masks that surround us at every turn. It shows us how, as I earlier argued, there is nothing more unequal than the equal treatment of unequals; how the equality presupposed in the market exchange of things deludes us into a belief in the equality of persons; how bourgeois doctrines of rights of private property and the profit rate make it seem as if we are all endowed with human rights; how illusions of personal liberty and freedom (and how and why we act on those illusions and even fight for them politically) arise out of market freedoms and free trade.

But there is, in my view, a real problem with the idea that primitive accumulation occurred once upon a time, and that once over, it ceased to be of real significance. In recent times, several commentators, including myself, have suggested that we need to take the continuity of primitive accumulation throughout the historical geography of capitalism seriously. Rosa Luxemburg put that question firmly on the agenda nearly a century ago. She insisted that we think of capitalism as being based on two different forms of exploitation.

> One concerns the commodity market and the place where surplus value is produced—the factory, the mine, the agricultural estate. Regarded in this light, accumulation is a purely economic process, with its most important

> phase a transaction between the capitalist and wage labourer . . . Here, in form at any rate, peace, property and equality prevail, and the keen dialectics of scientific analysis [and this was, she argued, Marx's signal achievement in Capital] were required to reveal how the right of ownership changes in the course of accumulation into appropriation of other people's property, how commodity exchange turns into exploitation and equality becomes class-rule.

This is indeed what Marx so brilliantly reveals in the first seven parts of *Capital*. "The other aspect of the accumulation of capital," she writes,

> concerns the relations between capitalism and the non-capitalist modes of production which start making their appearance on the international stage. Its predominant methods are colonial policy, an international loan system—a policy of spheres of interest—and war. Force, fraud, oppression, looting are openly displayed without any attempt at concealment, and it requires an effort to discover within this tangle of political violence and contests of power the stern laws of the economic process.[4]

There is, she maintains, an "organic connection" between these two systems of exploitation and accumulation. The long history of capitalism centers on this dynamic relation between continuous primitive accumulation on the one hand and the dynamics of accumulation through the system of expanded reproduction described in *Capital* on the other. Marx was therefore wrong, she argues, to confine primitive accumulation to some antediluvian point, some prehistory of capitalism. Capitalism would long ago have ceased to exist had it not engaged in fresh rounds of primitive accumulation, chiefly through the violence of imperialism.

Intuitively, there is much to suggest that Luxemburg was right in principle, even if one does not have to follow her all the way to her specific conclusions. To begin with the specific processes of primitive accumulation that Marx describes—the dispossession of rural and peasant populations; colonial, neocolonial and imperialist politics of exploitation; the use of state powers to reallocate assets to a capitalist class; the enclosure of the commons; the privatization of state lands and assets; an international system of finance and credit; to say nothing of

---

4. Rosa Luxemburg, *The Accumulation of Capital*, trans. Agnes Schwarzschild (London: Routledge, 2003), 432.

the burgeoning national debts and even the shadowy continuation of slavery through the trafficking of people (women in particular)—all these features are still with us and in some instances seem not to have faded into the background but, as in the case of the credit system, the enclosure of the commons and privatization, to have become ever more prominent.

The continuity becomes even more emphatic when we shift our gaze from the "classic" case of Britain to the historical geography of capitalism on the world stage. Luxemburg cited the so-called Opium Wars against China as an example of the processes she had in mind. One of the largest foreign markets for British goods was India, and the Indians could partly pay for those goods by supplying raw materials to Britain (as Marx points out in *Capital*). But this was not enough. So Indian opium was increasingly marketed in China in exchange for silver that could then be used to pay for the British goods. When the Chinese sought to control foreign trade in general and the opium trade in particular, the British fleet sailed up the Yangtze and destroyed the whole of the Chinese fleet in a short encounter to force open the Treaty ports. Only by these sorts of imperialist means, Luxemburg suggested, could the long-term accumulation and realization of capital be secured. According to Luxemburg's work, the continuity of primitive accumulation took place mainly on the periphery, in areas outside regions where the capitalist mode of production dominated. Colonial and imperialist practices were crucial in all this. But as we come closer to the present, the role of the periphery changes (particularly with decolonization), and the practices of primitive accumulation not only shift and proliferate in form but also become more prominent in the core regions dominated by capital.

Consider, for example, the case of contemporary China. China had been through its own developmental process under Mao with minimal relations to the outside. But in 1978, Deng Xiaoping started to open China up to the outside and to revolutionize China's economy. Agricultural reforms not only generated the equivalent of an agricultural revolution in production but also released an enormous quantity of labor, as well as surplus product, from off the land. There is no question that something equivalent to what Marx describes as primitive accumulation has been going on in China over the past thirty years. And to the degree that the opening of China has helped stabilize global capitalism in recent times, Luxemburg would probably look at it and say that this fresh round of primitive accumulation there has been fundamental to the survival of capitalism. In this case, however, events were not powered by foreign imperialist practices but set in motion by the Chinese state and its ruling Communist Party taking a quasi-capitalist road to the augmentation of national wealth. This entailed the creation of a vast low-wage urban proletariat out of an agrarian population, the initially controlled movement in of foreign capital to selected regions and cities to employ that proletariat, and the development of a network of global trading relations to market and realize the value of the commodities, even as the internal market started to boom. It is also interesting to note the role of greenfield sites in China. Just as Manchester went from a small town to a massive industrial center in a few decades, so did Shenzhen after 1980. The developmental pattern is not too different from that described by Marx, except that the levels of originary violence were muted (some would say they were effectively disguised) and that the power of the state and party has been critical throughout. In the light of this example, and the crucial role that China has played in the continuous expansion of a capitalist system dedicated to "accumulation for the sake of accumulation, production for the sake of production," it is difficult to avoid the conclusions that (a) something akin to primitive accumulation is alive and well within the dynamics of contemporary capitalism and (b) its continued existence may well be fundamental to the survival of capitalism.

But this proposition holds pretty much everywhere. The violence of extraction of natural resources (throughout Africa in particular) continues, and the expropriation of peasant populations in Latin America and throughout South and East Asia is still with us. None of this has disappeared, and in some instances it has intensified, resulting in fierce conflicts over, for example, the expulsion of peasant populations from the land in India in order to make way for "special economic zones" on greenfield sites where industry can set up activity on a privileged terrain. The killing of peasants resisting expulsions in West Bengal at Nandigram to make way for industrial development is as "classic" an example of primitive accumulation as could ever be found in seventeenth-century Britain. Furthermore, when Marx points to the national debt and the nascent credit system as vital aspects in the history of primitive accumulation, he is talking about something that has grown inordinately since then to act as a kind of central nervous system to regulate the flows of capital. The predatory tactics of Wall Street and of financial institutions (credit-card companies) are indicators of primitive accumulation by other means. So none of the predatory practices that Marx identified have gone away, and in some instances they have even flourished to a degree unimaginable in Marx's own times.

But in our times, the techniques for enriching the ruling classes and diminishing the standard of living of labor through something akin to primitive accumulation have proliferated and multiplied. For instance, United Airlines goes bankrupt, then gets the bankruptcy court to agree that it has to rid itself of all its pension obligations in order to continue as a viable business. All United Airlines employees suddenly find themselves with no pension and dependent on a state insurance fund that pays out at a very much lower rate. Retired airline employees are forced back into the proletariat. There are interviews with former United Airlines employees who said, "Well, you know, I'm sixty-seven and I thought I was going to be living happily on my retirement income of eighty thousand dollars a year, and now I'm only getting thirty-five thousand. So I have to go back and find myself a job to survive." And the big, interesting question is, where did the equivalent of all that money go? It is perhaps no coincidence that at a time when many working people were being dispossessed of their pension, healthcare and other welfare rights across the United States, the rate of remuneration of Wall Street executives and CEOs more generally was soaring into the stratosphere.

Consider, to take another example, the wave of privatization that has swept across the capitalist world since the 1970s or so. The privatization of water, education and healthcare in many of the countries that once provided them as public goods has dramatically changed how capitalism works (creating all manner of new markets, for example). The privatization of state enterprises (almost invariably at a price that allowed the capitalists to gain immense profits in very short order) has also relinquished public control over growth and investment decisions. This is, in effect, a particular form of enclosure of the commons, in many instances orchestrated by the state (as was the earlier round). The result has been a taking away of assets and rights from the common people. And at the same time as there is a taking away, there are these immense concentrations of wealth occurring at the other end of the scale.

In both *The New Imperialism*[5] and *A Brief History of Neoliberalism*,

5. David Harvey, *The New Imperialism* (Oxford: Oxford University Press, 2003).

I argued that class power was being increasingly consolidated right now through processes of this sort. Since it seems a bit odd to call them primitive or original, I prefer to call these processes accumulation by dispossession. I argued that while some of this went on in the 1950s and 1960s, particularly through the tactics of the colonialism and imperialism and in the predatory raiding of natural resources, there wasn't that much accumulation by dispossession going on within the core regions of capitalism, particularly those with strong social-democratic state apparatuses. Neoliberalization, after the mid-1970s, has changed all that. Accumulation by dispossession has been more and more internalized within the core regions of capitalism even as it has widened and deepened throughout the global system. We should not regard primitive accumulation (of the sort that might reasonably be considered to be the case in China) or accumulation by dispossession (as it has occurred through the wave of privatization in the core regions) as simply being about the prehistory of capitalism. It is ongoing and in recent times has been revived as an increasingly significant element in the way global capitalism is working to consolidate class power. And it can encompass everything—from the taking away of rights of access to land and livelihoods to the retrenchment of rights (to pensions, education and healthcare, for example) hard-won in the past through fierce class struggles by working-class movements. Chico Mendes, the leader of the rubber tappers in Amazonia, was murdered for defending a way of life against the cattle ranchers, the soybean producers and the loggers who sought to capitalize the land. The peasants of Nandigram were killed for resisting land takeover for capitalist development. The Landless Workers' Movement in Brazil (the MST) and the Zapatistas have both fought to defend their right to autonomy and self-determination in environments rich in resources and either coveted or locked away by capital. But then think of how the newly minted private-equity funds have been taking public companies private in the United States, stripping them of assets and firing as many employees as they could, before taking the restructured companies back on the market and selling them at a vast profit (for which the CEO of the private-equity fund receives an astronomical bonus).

There are innumerable examples of struggles against all these diverse forms of accumulation by dispossession. Struggles against biopiracy and the attempt to patent genetic materials and codes, struggles against the use of eminent domain to make way for capitalist developers, against gentrification and the production of homelessness in New York and London, the predatory way in which the credit system works to force family farmers off their land to make way for agribusiness in the United States . . . the list is endless. A vast array of practices exists through which accumulation by dispossession is still occurring that, on the surface at least, have nothing directly to do with the exploitation of living labor in the workplace to produce surplus-value in the way Marx describes in *Capital*.

Yet there are commonalities as well as complementarities between the two processes, as Luxemburg correctly, in my view, suggests by pointing to the "organic relation" between them. The extraction of surplus-value is, after all, a specific form of accumulation by dispossession, since it is nothing more or less than the alienation, appropriation and dispossession of the laborer's capacity to produce value in the labor process. Furthermore, in order for this form of accumulation to continue to grow, ways have to be found to mobilize latent populations as laborers and open up more land and resources as means of production for capitalist development. As has happened in the cases of India and China, for example, the creation of "special economic zones" by expelling peasant producers from the land is a necessary precursor to the continuity of capitalist development, just as the clearance of so-called slums of urban dwellers is necessary for developer capital to expand its urban operations. This taking of lands by the state through eminent domain, or some legal equivalent, has been a widespread phenomenon in recent times. Developers and construction interests in Seoul in the 1990s were desperate for access to urban land and set out to dispossess whole populations who had migrated to the city in the 1950s and built their own housing on land to which they had no title. The construction companies hired gangs of big, heavy wrestler thugs to go into the neighborhoods and smash people's houses to smithereens with sledgehammers, including all their possessions. During the 1990s you could walk around totally devastated Seoul neighborhoods, punctuated with islands of intense popular resistance.

While Marx tends to the view that expanded reproduction is *the* mechanism whereby surplus-value is accumulated and produced, it cannot continue without first realizing the necessary conditions of dispossession, which in its own right also redistributes assets directly into the hands of the capitalist class. I hold, along with Luxemburg, that accumulation by dispossession cannot be ignored, that the taking away of pension rights, of rights to the commons, of rights to Social Security (a common property resource for the entire US population), the increasing commodification of education, to say nothing of expulsions from the land and the despoliation of the environment, are all significant to how we understand the aggregate dynamic of capitalism. Furthermore, the conversion of a common property resource like education into a commodity, the conversion of universities into neoliberal corporatist institutions (with massive consequences for what is taught and how), has significant ideological and political consequences at the same time as it is both a sign and a symbol of a capitalist dynamic that leaves no stone unturned in its struggle to expand the sphere of profit making and profit taking.

In the history of primitive accumulation that Marx describes, there were all manner of violent struggles against the forcible evictions and the dispossessions. There were widespread movements in Britain—the Levellers and the Diggers, for example—that violently resisted. In the seventeenth and eighteenth centuries it would not be an exaggeration to say that the primary forms of class struggle were those resisting dispossession rather than those resisting workplace exploitation. In many parts of the world, the same thing could be said today. This raises the question of which form of class struggle constitutes or is going to constitute the core of a revolutionary movement against capitalism in a given place and time. If global capitalism in aggregate since the 1970s has not been very successful at generating growth, then the further consolidation of class power has required a much stronger turn toward accumulation by dispossession. It is probably this that has filled the coffers of the upper classes to the point of overflowing. The resurgence of the mechanisms of accumulation by dispossession has been particularly marked in the expanding role of the credit system and financial appropriations, the latest wave of which has resulted in several million people in the United States losing their homes through foreclosures. Much of this loss of assets is concentrated in poorer neighborhoods, with particularly serious implications for women and for African-American populations in older cities like Cleveland and Baltimore. Meanwhile, the Wall Street investment bankers who grew immensely rich on this business in the halcyon years even get huge bonuses when they lose their jobs because of the financial difficulties. The redistributive impact of loss of housing assets for millions of people and the huge gains on Wall Street appear as a very stark contemporary case of predation and legalized robbery typical of accumulation by dispossession.

Political struggles against accumulation by dispossession, I argue, are just as important as more traditional proletarian movements. But these traditional movements and their associated political parties tend to pay little attention to struggles over dispossession, often regarding them as secondary and not particularly proletarian in content since they focus on consumption, environment, asset values and the like. The participants in the World Social Forum, on the other hand, are far more preoccupied with resisting accumulation by dispossession and quite often take an antagonistic stance toward class-based workers'-movement politics on the grounds that such movements do not take the concerns of World Social Forum participants seriously. In Brazil, for example, the Landless Workers' Movement (the MST), an organization primarily concerned with accumulation by dispossession, has a somewhat tense relationship with the urban-based Workers' Party (the PT), led by Lula and with a more workerist ideology. The question of closer alliances between the two is therefore worthy of consideration both practically and theoretically. If Luxemburg is right, as I believe she is, to say that there is an organic relation between these two forms of accumulation, then we ought to be prepared to envision an organic relation between the two forms of resistance. An opposition force made up of the "dispossessed," no matter whether they are dispossessed in the labor process or dispossessed of their livelihoods, their assets or their rights, would require a reenvisioning of collective politics along rather different lines. I think Marx was in error in confining these forms of struggle to the prehistory of capitalism. Gramsci certainly understood the importance of building class alliances across these two different terrains, as did Mao. The idea that that the politics of primitive accumulation and by extension accumulation by dispossession belong exclusively to the prehistory of capitalism is surely wrong. But that, of course, is something you will have to decide for yourself.

Reflections and Prognoses

Once you get to the end of *Capital*, Volume I, it is a good idea to go back to the beginning and read the first chapter again. You will almost certainly find yourself reading it in a different light. You should, by now, find it a lot easier to follow. When I went back the first time, I also found it much more interesting and even downright fun to read. With the tension out of the way as to whether I would ever manage to get to the end of this huge tome, I relaxed and really began to enjoy what Bertell Ollman calls "the dance of the dialectic" and all the nuances (including the footnotes, the asides and the literary references) that I had missed first time through. Skimming back over the whole text schematically is also useful. It helps consolidate some thematic understandings. When I used to set examination papers, I would sometimes take a basic concept and ask students to comment on how it would weave into and out of the fabric of the book. How many times, I would ask, do you encounter the concept of fetishism? Commodities and money are obvious. But why do capitalists fetishize machinery, and how come all those inherent powers of labor (cooperation, divisions of labor, mental capacities and powers) appear so often as pure powers of capital? (And does the word "appear" always signal a fetishistic moment?) There are all sorts of themes that can be followed throughout, such as alienation (on this one, try beginning at the end with primitive accumulation and working backward through the text!), process-thing relations, logic-history intersections (confusions?) and the like.

Here, however, I want to look forward to some of the arguments that Marx takes up in the other volumes and elsewhere, by extending the logical implications of the framework set up in Volume I. I think it fair to do this because, as I indicated at the outset, Marx plainly intended much of his argument in Volume I to lay a theoretical and conceptual basis that would carry him forward onto a broader terrain. The occasional invocation of the omnipresent contradictions of capitalism and the possibilities they foretell of crises provide signposts as to where he might be headed. From this it is also possible to gain some political sense as to what a capitalist class politics is likely to look like and what some of the key terrains of political struggle are going to be.

Volume I of *Capital* examines a circulation process of capital that looks like this:

$$M\text{—}C \begin{cases} LP \\ MP \end{cases} \ldots\ldots\ldots P \ldots\ldots C\text{—}M + \Delta M$$

The starting point is money, armed with which the capitalist goes into the marketplace and buys two kinds of commodities, labor-power (variable capital) and means of production (constant capital). The capitalist simultaneously selects an organizational form and a technology and proceeds to combine the labor-power and the means of production in a labor process that produces a commodity, which is then sold in the market for the original money plus a profit (surplus-value). Impelled onward by the coercive laws of competition, capitalists appear (and I use that word in Marx's sense) to be forced to use part of the surplus-value to create even more surplus-value. Accumulation for accumulation's sake and production for production's sake become the historical mission of the bourgeoisie, producing compound rates of growth forever, unless capital encounters limits or insurmountable barriers. When this happens, capital encounters a crisis of accumulation (simply defined as lack of growth). The historical geography of capitalism is littered with such crises, sometimes local and at other times system-wide (as in 1848, 1929 and 2008). The fact that capitalism has survived to this day suggests that the fluidity and flexibility of capital accumulation—features that Marx emphasizes again and again—have somehow allowed limits to be overcome and barriers to be circumvented.

Close inspection of the flow of capital allows us to identify some potential points of blockage that can be the source of serious disruptions and crises. Let us go over these one by one.

(1) WHERE DOES THE INITIAL MONEY COME FROM?

This is the question that Marx's account of primitive accumulation is primarily concerned to answer. Primitive accumulation is invoked at several points in the text at large as well as in part 8, which deals directly with origins. But as more and more of the surplus-value created yesterday is converted into fresh capital, so more and more of the money invested today comes from yesterday's surplus. This does not rule out, however, the possibility of additional increments of money from the continuation of primitive accumulation, or what I would prefer to call in its modern context "accumulation by dispossession." If it were only the accumulation from yesterday that could be capitalized into expansion today, then over time we would surely see a gradually increasing concentration of money capital in individual hands. But as Marx points out, there are also methods of centralization, mainly achieved with the help of the credit system, that permit large quantities of money power to be brought together very rapidly. In the case of joint-stock companies and other corporate organizational forms, enormous quantities of money power are amassed under the control of a few directors and managers. Acquisitions and mergers have long been big business, and activity of this kind can entail new rounds of accumulation by dispossession (asset stripping of firms laying off workers, as practiced by the private-equity movement). Furthermore, there are all sorts of tricks whereby big capital can drive out the small (state regulation is frequently used as an aid, as Marx presciently notes). The dispossession of the small operators (neighborhood stores or family farms) to make way for large enterprises (supermarket chains and agribusiness), frequently with the aid of credit mechanisms, has been a long-standing practice. So the question of the organization, configuration and mass of the money capital available for investment never goes away. It acquires an added significance because of the "barriers to entry" that exist—the scale of certain activities, like building a steel mill, building a railroad or launching an airline, requires an immense initial outlay of money capital before production can even begin. Only relatively recently, for example, has it become possible for private consortia of associated capitals rather than the state to undertake massive infrastructural projects, like the Channel Tunnel that links Britain to continental Europe. As Marx notes in the chapter on machinery, such infrastructural projects become increasingly necessary as a capitalist mode of production comes into its own. Processes of centralization and decentralization of capital define a terrain of struggle between different factions of capital as well as between capital and the state (over questions of monopoly power, for example). Massive centralization of money power has all manner of implications for the dynamics of class struggle, as well as for the trajectory of capitalist development. If nothing else, it endows many elements in the privileged capitalist class (itself consolidating with centralization) with the capacity to wait, because their sheer money power gives them control over time in ways that small producers and wage laborers are often denied. But the contradictory element lies in the fact that increasing monopoly power diminishes the power of the coercive laws of competition to regulate activity (innovation in particular), and this can lead to stagnation.

(2) WHERE DOES THE LABOR-POWER COME FROM?

Marx pays a lot of attention to this in Volume I. Primitive accumulation releases labor-power as a commodity into the marketplace, but thereafter the extra labor required to expand production with a given technology comes from either mopping up the floating reserve released by previous rounds of labor-saving technological change or by mobilizing latent and *in extremis* elements within the stagnant reserve army. Marx several times mentions the ability to mobilize agricultural laborers or peasants from the countryside, as well as previously excluded women and children, into the labor force as crucial to the perpetuation of capital accumulation. For this to happen, there has to be a continuous process of proletarianization, which means continuous primitive accumulation by one or another means throughout the historical geography of capitalism. But labor reserves can also be produced by technologically-induced unemployment. Perpetual accumulation requires, Marx shows, a perpetual surplus of labor-power. This reserve army of labor is positioned more or less like a bow wave in front of the accumulation process. There must always be sufficient and accessible labor-power available. It not only needs to be accessible, it needs to be disciplined and in possession of the requisite qualities (i.e., skilled and flexible when necessary).

If, for any reason, these conditions are not met, then capital faces a serious barrier to continuous accumulation. Either the price of labor goes up, because this does not interfere with the dynamics of accumulation, or both the appetite and capacity for continuous accumulation slacken. Severe barriers in labor supply, arising either out of conditions of absolute labor scarcity or from the rise of powerful organizations of labor (trade unions and left political parties), can create crises of capital accumulation. One obvious answer to this barrier is for capital in effect to go on strike by refusing to reinvest. This amounts to the deliberate production of a crisis of accumulation so as to produce unemployment sufficient to discipline labor-power. This solution is, however, costly for capital as well as for labor. Capitalists would obviously prefer an alternative path, which brings us to the politics of the problem. If labor is too well organized and too powerful, then the capitalist class will seek to command the state apparatus either by a coup of the sort that killed Allende and the socialist alternative in Chile in 1973 or by political means in the US and Britain, in order to do what Pinochet, Reagan and Thatcher all did, which was to smash labor organization and crush left political parties. That is one way to get around the barrier. Another path is to make capital more mobile, so it can move to where there is an available proletariat or an available population that can be easily proletarianized, as in Mexico or China over the past thirty years. Open immigration policies or even state-organized immigration strategies (as in many European countries toward the end of the 1960s) provide yet another alternative. One consequence of circumventing barriers to labor supply this way is to push organized labor (and segments of the public more generally) into the position of opposing offshoring of jobs and opposing open immigration policies, culminating in domestic anti-immigrant movements among the working classes.

The contradictory aspects of labor-supply politics arise around questions not only of the value of labor-power (set by the conditions of supply of wage goods to satisfy the reproduction of labor-power at a given standard of living, itself vulnerable to definition by the state of class struggle) but also of the health, skills and training of the labor force. Capitalist class interests (as opposed to those of individual capitalists, who typically practice the politics of *Après moi le déluge!*) can rally around both subsidizing the supply of cheaper wage goods to keep the value of labor-power down and investing in improvements of the qualities of labor supply; in this latter regard, the military interests of the state can play an important supportive role. So the politics of labor supply have all manner of ramifications. They have been a central focus of struggle throughout the historical and geographical development of capitalism.

Out of this, some Marxists have distilled a distinctive theory of crisis formation. The so-called profit-squeeze theory of crisis hinges on the perpetually fraught problem of labor relations and class struggle, both in the labor process and in the labor market. When these relations pose a barrier to further capital accumulation then a crisis ensues unless some way (or, more likely, mix of ways) can be found for capital to overcome or circumvent that barrier. Some analysts, such as Andrew Glyn (see his impressive account, written with Bob Sutcliffe, in *British Capitalism, Workers and the Profits Squeeze*[1]), would interpret what happened in the late 1960s and early 1970s (particularly in Europe and North America) as an excellent example of the profit-squeeze theory in action. Certainly, the management of labor resources and the politics of labor organization and supply dominated the politics of the period. It is also true that the survival of capitalism has been contingent on the perpetual overcoming or circumvention of this potential barrier to accumulation. But at this time (2008), there is very little sign of a profit-squeeze situation as massive labor reserves exist everywhere, and as the political attack on working-class movements has reduced serious worker resistance to modest levels almost everywhere. The crisis of 2008 is hard to interpret, except in a roundabout way (and there are some versions of the theory, such as that of Itoh, that do this), in profit-squeeze terms.

(3) ACCESS TO THE MEANS OF PRODUCTION

When capitalists go into the market, they need to find there extra means of production (extra elements of constant capital) to meet their needs for reinvestment of part of the surplus in the expansion of production. The means of production are of two sorts: the intermediate products (already shaped by human labor) that are used up in the production process (through what Marx calls "productive consumption," such as energy and cloth used up in making a coat) and the machinery and fixed capital equipment, including factory buildings and the physical infrastructures such as transport systems, canals, ports, all those sorts of things that are necessary for production to proceed. The category of means of production (constant capital) is evidently very broad and complicated. Just as plainly, the lack of availability of these material inputs and conditions constitutes a potentially serious barrier to sustained capital accumulation. The auto industry cannot expand without more steel inputs. It is for this reason that Marx notes that technological innovations in one part of what we

1. Andrew Glyn and Bob Sutcliffe, *British Capitalism, Workers and the Profits Squeeze* (Harmondsworth: Penguin, 1972).

now call a "commodity chain" render innovation elsewhere necessary if it is to facilitate the general expansion of production. Innovations in the cotton industry required innovations in cotton production (the cotton gin), transport and communications, chemical and industrial dyeing techniques and the like.

From this we can derive the possibility of what are called "crises of disproportionality" within the complicated structure of inputs and outputs within the totality of a capitalist mode of production. At the end of Volume II, Marx engaged in a detailed study of how such crises might form in an economy divided into two grand departments, those industries producing means of production and those industries producing the wage goods for the workers (he later complicated the model further by introducing luxury goods). What Marx showed (and subsequent more sophisticated mathematical research by economists like Morishima has confirmed the point) was that equilibrium was far from automatic, given the tendency of capital to flow to wherever the rate of profit was highest, and that spiraling disproportionalities could seriously disrupt the reproduction of capitalism. In our own times, we see also the obvious impact of energy shortages and rising prices on capitalist dynamics. Barriers of this sort are plainly sources of perpetual concern within a capitalist system, and the equally perpetual need to overcome and circumvent barriers of this sort is often in the forefront of political activity (state subsidies and planning—particularly of physical infrastructures—research and development activity, vertical integration through mergers, etc.).

(4) SCARCITIES IN NATURE

But behind all this, there lurks a deeper problematic that Marx also raises several times in Volume I. This concerns our metabolic relation to nature. Capitalism, like any other mode of production, relies on the beneficence of a bountiful nature, and as Marx points out, the depletion and degradation of the land makes no more sense in the long run than does the destruction of the collective powers of labor, since both lie at the root of the production of all wealth. But individual capitalists, working in their own short-term interests and impelled onward by the coercive laws of competition, are perpetually tempted to take the position of *Après moi le déluge!* with respect to both the laborer and the soil. Even without this, the track of perpetual accumulation puts enormous pressures on expanding the supply of so-called natural resources, while the inevitable increase in the quantity of waste is bound to test the capacity of ecological systems to absorb it without turning toxic. Here, too, capitalism is likely to encounter barriers which will become increasingly hard to circumvent. Capitalism, Marx notes, "acquires an elasticity, a capacity for sudden expansion by leaps and bounds, which comes up against no barriers but those presented by the availability of raw materials and the extent of sales outlets" (579).

There are, however, all sorts of ways in which such barriers in nature can be confronted, sometimes overcome and more often than not circumvented. Natural resources are, for example, technological, social and cultural appraisals, and so any shortage in nature can be mitigated by technological, social and cultural changes. The dialectical relation to nature that is set up in the footnote at the beginning of chapter 15, on "Machinery and Large-Scale Industry," indicates a range of possible transformations, including the production of nature itself. The historical geography of capitalism has been marked by an incredible fluidity and flexibility in this regard, so it would be false to argue that there are absolute limits in our metabolic relation to nature that cannot be transcended or bypassed in some way. But this does not mean that the barriers are not sometimes serious and that overcoming them can be achieved without going through some kind of environmental crisis. A lot of capitalist politics, particularly these days, is about ensuring that what Marx calls the free gifts of nature are both available to capital on an easy basis and sustained for future use. The tensions within capitalist politics over these sorts of issues can sometimes be acute. On the one hand, the desire to maintain an expanding flow of cheap oil has been central to the geopolitical stance of the United States over the past fifty or sixty years. Making sure that the world's oil supplies are open for exploitation has drawn the US into conflict in the Middle East and elsewhere, and energy politics, just to take one example of a crucial relation to nature, often emerges as a dominant issue within the state apparatus. But on the other hand, the politics of cheap oil has created problems of excessive depletion, as well as global warming and a host of other air-quality issues (ground-level ozone, smog, particulate matter in the atmosphere and the like), that pose increasing risks to human populations. Land-use degradation through energy-consuming urban sprawl has been a problem at the other end of the steady depletion of natural resources to support all aspects of growth of the automobile industry.

Some Marxists (led by Jim O'Connor, who founded the journal *Capitalism Nature Socialism*) refer to the barriers in nature as "the second contradiction of capitalism" (the first being, of course, the capital-labor relation). In our own times, it is certainly true that this second contradiction is absorbing as much political attention as the labor question, if not more, and there certainly is a wide-ranging field of concern, of political anxiety and endeavor, that focuses on the idea of a crisis in the relation to nature, as a sustainable source of raw materials and land for further capitalist (urban) development as well as a sink for waste.

In O'Connor's work, this second contradiction of capitalism comes to displace the first, after the defeats of the labor and socialist movements of the 1970s, as the cutting edge of anticapitalist agitation. I leave you to make up your own mind on how far that sort of politics should be pursued. But what is certain is that the barrier in relation to nature is not to be taken lightly or treated as minor, given the framework that Marx sets out in Volume I of *Capital*. And in our own times, it is clear that the barriers in nature are looming large and that there may be an imminent crisis in our relation to nature that will require widespread adaptations (such as the development of new environmental technologies and the expansion of industries producing these goods) if this barrier is to be successfully circumvented, at least for a time, within the framework of endless capital accumulation.

(5) THE QUESTION OF TECHNOLOGY

The relations between capital and labor, as well as those between capital and nature, are mediated by the choice of organizational forms and of technologies (hardware and software). In Volume I, Marx is, I think, at his very best in theorizing where the impulsions for organizational and technological change come from and why it is that capitalists inevitably fetishize machinery, which cannot produce value, because it is a vital source of surplus-value to them both individually and collectively. The result is perpetual organizational and technological dynamism. "Modern industry," Marx notes "never views or treats of the existing form of a production process as the definitive one. Its technical basis is therefore revolutionary, whereas all earlier modes of production were essentially conservative" (617). This is a persistent motif in Marx's works. As noted in the *Communist Manifesto*,

> The bourgeoisie cannot exist without constantly revolutionising the instruments of production, and thereby the relations of production, and with them the whole relations of society . . . Constant revolutionising of production, uninterrupted disturbance of all social conditions, everlasting uncertainty and agitation distinguish the bourgeois epoch from all other ones.

But it is at this point also that the coercive laws of competition step forward, underpinning the search for relative surplus-value. The implication, which Marx for some reason is reluctant to contemplate, is that any weakening in those coercive laws, through monopolization and the increasing centralization of capital described in chapter 25, will have an impact on the pace and form of technological revolutions. The class-struggle dimensions through broad-based oppositions (e.g., the Luddite movement) or sabotage on the shop floor also have to be taken into account. As Marx noted, a stimulus to technological change arises out of the desire on the part of capital to have weapons to deploy against labor. The more laborers become mere appendages of the machine, and the more their monopolizable skills get undermined by machine technologies, the more vulnerable they become to the arbitrary authority of capital. To the degree that the actual history of technological and organizational innovations displays a distinctively wave-like character, it seems that more has to be said about these dynamics than is given to us even in the rich analysis set out in Volume I.

These questions becomes even more important because, in setting up his arguments on the organic and value composition of capital in chapter 25, Marx is clearly anticipating the view laid out in Volume III, that an ineluctable tendency toward a rising value composition of capital presages an equally compelling law or tendency for the profit rate to fall, inevitably producing long-term crisis conditions in the accumulation process. It is most emphatically here, in Marx's view, that capital has to confront a crucial barrier internal to its own nature.

The resultant crisis of profitability is solely due to the destabilizing effects of technological dynamism arising out of the persistent search for relative surplus-value. A short-cut version of the argument states that the search for relative surplus-value pushes capitalists to labor-saving technologies, and the more labor saved, the less value produced, because labor is the source of value. To be sure, there are compensating possibilities such as raising the rate of exploitation or reabsorbing displaced workers in expanded production. But there are, as I argued in chapter 10, reasons for being skeptical of any necessary and ineluctable tendency for the value composition of capital to rise. In Volume III, Marx actually lists a variety of "counteracting influences" to a falling rate of profit, including rising rates of exploitation of labor, falling costs of constant capital, foreign trade and a massive increase in the industrial reserve army that blunts the stimulus for the employment of new technologies (as noted in Volume I). In the *Grundrisse*, he had gone even further, noting the constant devaluation of capital, the absorption of capital in the production of physical infrastructures, the opening up of new labor-intensive lines of production and monopolization. My own (probably minority) view is that the falling-rate-of-profit argument simply does not work in the way that Marx specifies it, and I have laid out more fully why I think so in *The Limits to Capital*.[2]

But I also think there is no question that organizational and technological changes do have serious destabilizing effects internal to the dynamics of capital accumulation and that Marx's brilliant exposition of the forces at work impelling perpetual revolutions in technologies and organizational forms sets the stage for a better understanding of processes of both class and popular struggle over the deployment of new technologies and crisis formation. The crisis tendencies can be manifest (as "footnote 4" indicates) in labor relations, in the relation to nature as well as in all other coevolving moments in the capitalist developmental process. There are also directly destabilizing effects such as the devaluation of prior investments (machinery, plant and equipment, built environments, communications links) before their value has been recovered (amortized); rapid shifts in labor-quality requirements (e.g., skills such as computer literacy) that outpace existing labor force capacities and the investments in social infrastructures needed to create them; the production of chronic job insecurity, spiraling crises of disproportionality due to the uneven development of technological capacities across different sectors;

2. Harvey, *The Limits to Capital*, 176–189.

dramatic shifts in spatiotemporal relations (innovations in transport and communications) that entail a total revolution in the global landscape of production and consumption; sudden accelerations and speed-up in capital circulation (computer trading on financial markets can create serious problems, as we have seen); and so on. And, yes, there may be occasions in which a rising value composition of capital can be detected with consequent effects on profits.

(6) LOSS OF CAPITALIST CONTROL OVER THE LABOR PROCESS

Marx is at great pains to emphasize that the creation of surplus value rests on the ability of the capitalist to command and control the laborer on the shop floor where value is produced. This command and control over the "form-giving fire" of the labor process is always contested. The "despotism" of labor control depends on some mix of coercion and persuasion as well as upon the successful organization of a hierarchical structure of authority in labor relations. Plainly, any breakdown in this control presages a crisis, and Marx emphasizes the implicit power of workers to disrupt, sabotage, slow down or simply to cease altogether the production of value upon which the capitalist necessarily relies. The refusal to succumb to the disciplinary apparatuses set up by capital, the power of refusal to work, is of supreme importance in the dynamics of class struggle. In itself it can force a crisis (as theorists such as Tronti and Negri emphasize in the "autonomista" Marxist tradition). This power of the worker is, of course, limited in that workers have to live and without the wage they will also suffer unless they have available to them some other means of subsistence (such as cultivation of the land). The potential limit that exists within the circulation of capital at the point of production and within the labor process itself cannot, however, be ignored. Much attention is therefore paid both by individual capitalists as well as by the whole capitalist class to ensuring labor discipline and adequate forms of labor control.

(7) THE PROBLEM OF REALIZATION AND EFFECTIVE DEMAND

The seventh potential barrier comes at the end of the sequence, when the new commodity enters the market to realize its value as money through exchange. The C-M transition is always more problematic than going from the universal of money to the particular of the commodity, for reasons noted back in chapter 2. To begin with, a sufficient number of people must need, want or desire the commodity produced as a use-value. If a thing is useless then it has no value, says Marx. Useless commodities will be devalued, and the circulation process of capital will come to a crashing halt. So the first condition for the realization of value is to pay attention to the wants, needs and desires of a population. In our time, relative to Marx's, an immense amount of effort, including the formation of a whole advertising industry, is put into manipulating the nature of wants, needs and desires in a population to ensure the market for use-values. But what is involved here is something more than just advertising. What is required is the formation of a whole structure and process of daily living (the reproduction-of-daily-life component of "footnote 4") that necessitates the absorption of a certain bundle of use-values in order to sustain it. Consider, for example, the development of the wants, needs and desires associated with the rise of a suburban lifestyle in the United States after World War II. We are talking about the need for not only cars, gasoline, highways and suburban tract houses but also lawn mowers, refrigerators, air conditioners, drapes, furniture (interior and exterior), interior entertainment equipment (the TV) and a whole mass of maintenance systems to keep this daily life going. Daily life in the suburb required the consumption of all that. The development of suburbia ensured a rising demand for these use-values. In this way, "to bring forth a new need," as Marx presciently notes, becomes a crucial precondition for the continuity of capital accumulation (201). The politics of need creation are in themselves intriguing and increasingly important over time, and now it is well understood that "consumer sentiment" is a key element in the stimulus for endless capital accumulation.

But where does the purchasing power to buy all these use-values come from? There must be, at the end of this process, an extra amount of money that somebody holds somewhere to facilitate the purchase. If not, there is a lack of effective demand, and what is called a crisis of "underconsumption" results—there is not enough demand backed by ability to pay to absorb the commodities produced (see chapter 3) The barrier posed by the "extent of sales outlets" has to be overcome. (579). In part, effective demand is expressed through workers spending their wages. But variable capital is always less than the total capital in circulation, so the purchase of wage goods (even with a suburban lifestyle) is never sufficient for the realization of the whole value stream. But, and this is a point that emerges in Volume II of *Capital*, reducing wages in the manner presupposed in the Volume I analysis plainly creates deeper stresses at the point of realization and in itself can be an important component in the creation of crises of underconsumption. It was for this reason that the politics of the New Deal, at the time of a crisis that many came to regard as primarily a crisis of underconsumption, turned to supporting unionization and other strategies (like Social Security payments) to bolster effective demand across the working classes and also why, in 2008, at a point of economic stress, the federal government released a six-hundred-dollar tax rebate to most taxpayers in the US in order to jack up consumer effective demand. Raising the real wages of labor (thus countering the tendency toward increasing immiseration of the proletariat) may be necessary to the stabilization of continuous capital accumulation, but for obvious reasons the capitalist class (let alone the individual capitalist) may not be willing to contemplate any radical implementation of such a solution.

But worker demand, though an important base, can obviously never go as far as to solve the problem of realization. Rosa Luxemburg paid great attention to this. First she took up the possibility that the extra demand could come from increasing the gold supply (or in our day by simply having the central banks print more money). While obviously this can help in the short run (injecting sufficient liquidity into the system, as during the financial crisis of 2008, becomes a crucial tool for stabilizing and sustaining the continued circulation and accumulation of capital), in the long run the effect is to create yet another kind of crisis, that of inflation. Luxemburg's solution was to presuppose the existence of some latent and mobilizable demand outside the capitalist system. This meant the continuation of primitive accumulation through imperialist impositions and practices on societies not yet absorbed into the capitalist mode of production.

In the transition to capitalism, and in the phase of primitive accumulation, the stores of accumulated wealth within the feudal order could play this role along with the robbery and plundering of wealth from the rest of the world by merchant's capital. Over time, of course, what might be called the "gold reserves" of the feudal classes were steadily depleted, and the capacity of the peasantry to generate consumer power by way of taxation to support the consumerism of a landed aristocracy was also exhausted. As industrial capitalism consolidated in Europe and North America, so the plundering of wealth from India, China and other already developed noncapitalist social formations became more and more prominent, particularly from the mid-nineteenth century onward. This was the phase of an immense transfer of wealth from East and South Asia in particular, but also to some degree from South America and Africa, toward the industrial-capitalist class located in core capitalist countries. Eventually, as capitalism grew and spread geographically, the ability to stabilize the system by such means became decreasingly plausible, even if such means had ever been entirely sufficient (which is doubtful) during the phase of late-nineteenth-century high imperialism. Certainly, since 1950 or so but even more markedly since the 1970s, the capacity of imperialist practices of this sort to perform the role of grand stabilizer through opening new fields (new markets) for the realization of capital has been seriously impaired.

The most important answer, one that Luxemburg failed to notice but which follows logically from Marx's argument (though he never articulated it directly because he ruled out the problem of potential realization crises by assumption in Volume I), is that the solution lies in capitalist consumption. This, we have seen, is of two sorts: a portion of the surplus-value is consumed as revenues (e.g., luxury goods), but the other portion is put to further expanding production through reinvestment strategies that appear (and I use this word in Marx's sense) to be impelled by the coercive laws of competition. We here encounter the necessity of what Marx calls "productive consumption" as a link in the realization process. This means that surplus-value production has to internalize its own increasing monetary demand. The demand for yesterday's surplus product depends on tomorrow's expansion of surplus-value production! Capitalist consumption today, fueled by the surplus gained yesterday, forms the market for yesterday's surplus product and surplus-value. What this does is to convert what appears as a potential underconsumption crisis because of lack of effective demand into a lack of further profitable investment opportunities. In other words, the solution to the realization problems encountered at the end of the circulation process depends upon going back to the beginning and expanding even more. The logic of perpetual compound growth takes over.

(8) THE CREDIT SYSTEM AND THE CENTRALIZATION OF CAPITAL

For the circulation of capital to complete its course, two fundamental conditions must be realized. First, capitalists must not hold the money they gained yesterday. They must immediately release it back into circulation. But as Marx argues in his critique of Say's law, there is no compelling necessity that says C-M must immediately be followed by M-C, and within that asymmetry there lies the perpetual possibility not so much for monetary and financial crises but for the emergence of a barrier to the realization of surplus-value through failure to spend. In chapter 2, we considered various circumstances in which it would make perfect sense to hold on to money rather than to release it, and it is at this point that an overlap emerges between Marx's and Keynes's thinking on the possibility of crises of underconsumption. Keynes sought to bypass this barrier by resorting to a state-led set of technical strategies of fiscal and monetary management.

The second condition is that the time gap between today and yesterday needs to be bridged for continuous circulation to be assured. This gap can be filled, as Marx also shows in chapter 3, by the rise of credit moneys and the use of money as a means of account. Put bluntly, the credit system as an organized relation between creditors and debtors steps into the circulation process to play a vital function. As other options run out, this becomes the main means to cover the effective-demand problem in a way that is internal to capital circulation. In so doing, however, the credit system claims its part of the surplus in the form of interest.

At several points even in Volume I of *Capital*, Marx tacitly recognizes the crucial role of the credit system, but in order to get to what he considers the heart of the problem of the labor-capital relation in part 7, he finds it necessary to exclude the facts of distribution (rent, interest, taxes, profit on merchant's capital) from the analysis. While this helps reveal and clarify some important aspects of capitalist dynamics, it does so at the cost of pushing to one side a crucial feature in the capital-circulation process. Unfortunately, Marx continues to push this aside throughout much of Volume II (while acknowledging its crucial presence in relation, for example, to the circulation of long-term fixed capital investments), leading Luxemburg quite correctly to state that the accumulation schemata laid out at the end of that volume failed to solve the problem of realization and effective demand. It is only relatively late in Volume III that Marx gets round to examining the role of the credit system, and frankly, these chapters, though full of suggestive insights, are a mess (I tried as hard as I could—and I don't mind confessing it nearly drove me crazy doing so—to clean them up in chapters 9 and 10 of *The Limits to Capital*). He had, however, established in the *Grundrisse* that "the entire *credit system*, and the over-trading, over-speculation etc., connected with it, rests on the necessity of expanding and leaping over the barrier to circulation and the sphere of exchange."[3]

If it is the further expansion of capitalism that creates the demand for yesterday's surplus product, then this means that the realization problem cannot be solved, particularly under today's conditions of globalized capitalist development, without the construction of a vibrant and extensive credit system to bridge the gap between yesterday's surplus product and tomorrow's absorption of that surplus product. This absorption can occur either through the further expansion of surplus-value production (reinvestment) or through the capitalist consumption of revenues. In the long run, it can easily be shown, the capitalist consumption of revenues will lead to stagnation (this is the model of "simple reproduction" Marx considers in chapter 23). Only the further expansion of surplus-value generation will work in the long run, and it is this that underpins the social necessity for compound rates of growth forever as a condition of capitalism's survival.

It is at this point that Marx would surely have said, had he got to this point, that the coercive laws of competition are merely a tool to secure this absolutely necessary condition for capitalism's survival. In other words, the survival of capitalism requires the maintenance of the coercive laws of competition in order to keep the expansion of surplus-value production tomorrow on track as a means to absorb the surpluses produced yesterday. From this it follows that any slackening of those coercive powers, through, for example, excessive monopolization, will in itself produce a crisis in capitalist reproduction. This was exactly Baran and Sweezy's point in *Monopoly Capital*[4] (written during the 1960s, when monopolies like the Big Three auto companies in Detroit were

3. Marx, *Grundrisse*, 416.

4. Paul A. Baran and Paul M. Sweezy, *Monopoly Capital* (New York: Monthly Review Press, 1966).

of increasing significance). The tendency toward monopolization and the centralization of capital necessarily produced, as Baran and Sweezy clearly predicted, the crisis of stagflation (rising unemployment coupled with accelerating inflation) that so haunted the 1970s. The answer to this crisis was the neoliberal counterrevolution that not only smashed the power of labor but also effectively liberated and unleashed the coercive laws of competition as "executor" of the laws of capitalist development by all manner of strategems (more open foreign trade, deregulation, privatizations and the like).

But this process is not without its potential complications. To begin with, the presumption is that all the other barriers (e.g., the relation to nature) to the expansion of surplus-value production tomorrow are non-operative and that there is plenty of room for more production to occur. This implies, for example, a different kind of imperialism, which is not about robbing values and stripping assets from the rest of the world, but about using the rest of the world as a site for opening up new forms of capitalist production. The export of capital rather than of commodities becomes critical. Herein lies the big difference between nineteenth-century India and China, whose wealth was plundered by capitalist domination of their markets, and the United States and to some degree Oceania and parts of Latin America, where unrestricted capitalist development producing new wealth developed rapidly and in so doing provided a field for absorbing and realizing surplus product being generated in the older centers of capitalism (for instance, Britain exported capital and machinery to the US and Argentina in the nineteenth century). In recent times, of course, China has absorbed a lot of foreign capital in the development of production and in so doing has generated a huge effective demand not only for raw materials but also for machinery and other material inputs.

There are, however, two problems inherent in this solution, both of which can reconstitute barriers to the continuity of capital accumulation in the very act of seeking to bypass them. The first derives from the simple fact that the circulation process becomes by definition speculative: it rests on the belief that tomorrow's expansion will not encounter any barriers (including that of further realization), so that today's surplus can effectively be realized. The speculative element, which is fundamental rather than exceptional or excessive, means that anticipations and expectations, as Keynes for one well understood, are fundamental to the continuity of capital circulation. Marx tacitly recognizes this in Volume III when he notes that capitalist expansion is, as he puts it, very "Protestant" because it is based on faith and credit rather than on the "Catholicism" of gold, the true monetary base. Any fall-off in speculative expectations will be self-fulfilling, therefore, and generate a crisis. In this regard, it is interesting to reread Keynes's *General Theory* and notice that the technical solutions of monetary and fiscal policy occupy only a minor part of the argument compared with the psychology of expectations and anticipations. Faith in the system is fundamental, and loss of confidence, as happened in 2008, can be fatal.

The second problem arises within the money and credit system itself. The possibility of "independent" financial and monetary crises, which Marx points out but does not develop in chapter 3, is omnipresent. The underlying problem lies in the contradictions of the money-form itself (use-value as the representation of value, the particular [concrete] as representation of the universal [abstract] and the private appropriation of social power—see chapter 2). When Marx disputes Say's law, he points to the fact that there is a permanent temptation to hold on to money, and the more people do this, the greater the check to the continuity of circulation. But why would people hold on to money? One reason is that it is a form of social power. It can buy conscience and honor! In the *Economic and Philosophical Manuscripts*, Marx tells us that if "I am ugly . . . I can buy for myself the most *beautiful* of women"[5] (or beautiful of men); if I'm stupid, I can buy the presence of intelligent people; if I'm lame, I can have people carry me around. Just think what you can do with all that social power! So there are very good reasons why people want to hang on to money, particularly in the face of uncertainty. Releasing it into circulation in order to get more social power takes an act of faith, or the creation of safe and trustworthy institutions where you can save your personal money while someone else puts it back into circulation to make more money (which is, of course, what banks are supposed to do).

But the ramifications of this problem spread far and wide into the field of representations, where loss of confidence in the symbols of money (the power of the state to guarantee their stability) or in the quality of money

5. Karl Marx, *Economic and Philosophic Manuscripts of 1844*, trans. Martin Milligan, in *The Marx-Engels Reader*, ed. Robert C. Tucker (New York: W. W. Norton, 1978), 103.

(inflation) butt up against more directly quantitative considerations such as "monetary famine" and the freezing up of the means of payment of the sort that occurred in the fall of 2008.

> The bourgeois [read Wall Street], drunk with prosperity and arrogantly certain of himself, has just declared that money is a purely imaginary creation. 'Commodities alone are money,' he said. But now the opposite cry resounds over the markets of the world; only money is a commodity. As the hart pants after fresh water, so pants his soul after money, the only wealth. In a crisis, the antithesis between commodities and their value-form, money, is raised to the level of an absolute contradiction. (236)

What better description could we have of the crisis that suddenly erupted in 2008!

At the heart of the credit system there exists a range of technical and legal aspects (many of which can fail or badly distort simply by virtue of their rules of operation) coupled with subjective expectations and anticipations. And to the degree that capitalism continues to expand, so the role of the credit system as a kind of central nervous system for directing and controlling the global dynamics of capital accumulation becomes more prominent. The implication is that the control over the means of credit becomes critical for the functioning of capitalism—a positionality that Marx and Engels had recognized in the *Communist Manifesto* by making the centralization of the means of credit in the hands of the state one of their key demands (presuming, of course, control over the state by the working class). When this is added to the key role of the state with respect to the quality of the coinage and, even more important, symbolic moneys (a role which is acknowledged in chapter 3), then some sort of fusion of state and financial powers appears inevitable. This contradictory fusion was established by the formation of state-controlled central banks with unlimited reserve powers over the disbursement of the means of credit to private appropriators.

In the same way that capital can operate on both sides of the demand and supply of labor-power (see chapter 10), so it can operate through the credit system on both sides of the production-realization relation. In recent years in the United States, for example, the increasingly liberal supply of credit to prospective homeowners coupled with an equally liberal supply of credit to property developers to fuel a massive boom in housing and urban development. In this way, it was imagined that the realization problem was done away with. The only difficulty arose because real wages did not rise in parallel (as the Volume I analysis would predict, given the dominance of neoliberal policies after 1980 which meant that gains from rising productivity were not shared, but concentrated entirely in the upper classes), so that the ability of ordinary homeowners to pay off their rising debt (which tripled for US households from 1980 to 2008) was steadily diminishing. The resultant property-market crash was utterly predictable.

But an analysis of the current crash suggests yet another key role of the credit system. In the same way that Marx noted the role of credit (and usury) in extracting wealth from the feudal lords through primitive accumulation, so the credit system is well positioned to target and extract wealth from the assets held by vulnerable populations. Predatory lending practices—a form of accumulation by dispossession—eventually resulted in foreclosures, which allowed assets to be acquired at low cost and transferred wholesale to boost the long-run wealth of capitalist class interests. The foreclosure wave that began in 2006 inflicted a huge loss of asset values on, among others, vulnerable African-American populations. This second moment of "accumulation by dispossession" via the credit system is of great consequence to the dynamics of capitalism. It facilitated an immense transfer of wealth from East and Southeast Asia to Wall Street in the crisis of 1997–8, for example, as a liquidity freeze forced all manner of viable firms into bankruptcy so that they could be bought up cheaply by foreign investors and then sold back at an immense profit when the recovery came. The credit-led attack on family farming that has occurred in waves since the 1930s in the United States has in similar fashion effectively centralized agricultural wealth in the hands of massive agribusinesses at the expense of small owners, who have been forced to give up their assets cheaply, through foreclosures. Class struggle and the accumulation of capitalist class power work their way through every possible channel within the maze of credit instruments that now exist.

Marx did not investigate the credit system in a sufficiently thorough way to confront the realization problem in all its complexity. This is one of the items of unfinished business in Marx that requires a good deal of work to complete, particularly given the complexity of financial and credit markets, which makes so much of what goes on within them opaque even to their managers and users. But what is interesting about the argument of Volume I is that Marx, in making the transition from the circulation of commodities to that of capital, finds himself forced to invoke relations between creditors and debtors and the use of state-regulated money as a means of payment. He also invokes the time structure of production processes and payments as a key problem of monetary circulation that requires credit if it is to achieve the necessary continuity of capital circulation and accumulation. "Credit-money," he pointed out, takes root "spontaneously in the function of money as a means of payment."[6] This is what I mean when I say that a careful study of the Volume I argument tells us a lot about what is to come in the rest of Marx's analysis. It also helps reveal what might be missing and what therefore needs to be more fully investigated.

THE CIRCULATION OF CAPITAL AS A WHOLE

When capital circulation is looked at as a whole, it becomes apparent that the numerous potential barriers to the free and continuing flow of capital through all its moments are neither independent of one another nor systemically integrated. They are best construed as an ensemble of distinctive moments within the totality of the circulation process of capital. There has been a tendency within the history of Marxian theorizing about crises, however, to look for one dominant and exclusive explanation of the origins of the obviously crisis-prone character of a capitalist mode of production. The three big traditional camps of thought are the profit-squeeze, the falling-rate-of-profit and the underconsumptionist traditions, and the separations are often so strongly marked as to put the theories at one another's throats. The very term "underconsumptionist" in some circles amounts to a dirty word (it seems to mean you are a Keynesian and not a "true" Marxist), while fans of Rosa Luxemburg get outraged at the mean-spirited dismissal of her ideas on the part of those who place the falling-rate-of-profit argument at the center of their theorizing. In recent years, for obvious reasons, far more attention has been paid to the environmental and the financial aspects of crisis formation, and in what are called "the noughties" these aspects of crisis formation have top billing.

6. Ibid., 224.

I find it more compelling, in the spirit of the analysis laid out in Volume I alongside the extremely interesting discussion of the relations between limits and barriers in the *Grundrisse* ("every limit appears as a barrier to be overcome"[7]), to think of all the limits and barriers discussed above as potential points of blockage, each of which can slow down or disrupt the continuity of capital flow and thereby create a crisis of devaluation. I think it also important to understand the potentiality of displacement of one barrier by another. Moves made to alleviate a crisis of labor supply by generating widespread unemployment can obviously create problems of an insufficiency of effective demand, for example. Consequent moves to resolve the effective-demand problem by extensions of the credit system among the working classes can ultimately create crises of confidence in the quality of money (as registered by inflationary crises, sudden constrictions of credit supply and financial crashes). I also think it is more in keeping with Marx's frequent invocation of the fluid and flexible character of capitalist development to recognize the rapid repositioning of one barrier at the expense of another and so recognize the multiple ways in which crises can be registered in different historical and geographical situations.

Summarizing, the potential barriers are as follows: (1) inability to mass together enough original capital to get production under way ("barriers to entry" problems); (2) scarcities of labor or recalcitrant forms of labor organization that can produce profit squeezes; (3) disproportionalities and uneven development between sectors within the division of labor; (4) environmental crises arising out of resource depletion and land and environmental degradation; (5) imbalances and premature obsolescence due to uneven or excessively rapid technological changes driven by the coercive laws of competition and resisted by labor; (6) worker recalcitrance or resistance within a labor process that operates under the command and control of capital; (7) underconsumption and insufficient effective demand; (8) monetary and financial crises (liquidity traps, inflation or deflation) that arise within a credit system that depends on sophisticated credit instruments and organized state powers alongside a climate of faith and trust. At each one of these points internal to the circulation process of capital, there exists an antinomy, a potential antagonism that can irrupt as an

7. Marx, *Grundrisse*, 408.

open contradiction (to use the language that Marx frequently deploys in *Capital*).

This is not the end of the analysis of crisis formation and resolution under capitalism, however. To begin with, the dynamics of uneven geographical development together with the whole problem of spatiotemporal unfolding of capitalist development on the world stage are stressful in the extreme, as capital seeks to create a geographical landscape (of physical and social infrastructures) appropriate to its dynamic at one time only to have to destroy it and re-create yet another geographical landscape at a later point. The changing dynamics of urbanization on the world stage dramatically illustrate this process. Geopolitical conflicts (including catastrophic wars) abound and, arising as they do out of the peculiar qualities of territorialized power (requiring an adequate theorization of the state, a set of institutions and practices that is frequently invoked in Volume I but, like the credit system, left undertheorized), have a logic that does not neatly fit into the requirements of continuous capital circulation and accumulation. The recent history of global shifts in production and deindustrialization have entailed an immense amount of creative destruction, largely worked out through sometimes local but in other instances continent-wide crises (such as that which hit East and Southeast Asia in 1997–8). Furthermore, the possibility of external shocks (including hurricanes and earthquakes) triggering crises cannot be excluded. When almost all activity stopped in the United States in general and New York in particular in the wake of 9/11, the stoppage of circulation was so threatening that within a week the powers that be were everywhere urging the population to get out their credit cards and go shopping!

The spirit of Marxian inquiry into the actual history of crises should, I believe, be open to all these possibilities. Keynes was, I suspect, basically correct to interpret the crisis of the 1930s as mainly an insufficiency of effective demand (though probably for class reasons, he did not point out the relation to income inequality—not historically replicated until recently—that exploded in the 1920s owing to wage repression). This was exacerbated by the fact that people got nervous about the capacity for sustained accumulation and so started to hold on to money. And the more people held on to money, the more the system gummed up. This is what Keynes called the liquidity trap. Ways had to be found to entice money out of hiding, and one answer was debt-financed government expenditures to reinvigorate capital circulation (the other answer was to go to war). On the other hand, I think Andew Glyn and others were basically correct to see a strong element of profit squeeze in the difficulties of the late 1960s in the advanced capitalist countries, where labor scarcities and strong labor organization were clearly putting a brake on accumulation. Excessive monopolization simultaneously helped slow productivity, and this, along with a fiscal crisis of the state (associated with the US war in Vietnam), initiated a long phase of stagflation that could only be resolved by disciplining labor and liberating the coercive laws of competition. In this case, the crisis cascaded from one barrier point to another and back again. The relation to nature also affects profitability, particularly if the rent (a category which, like interest, is not handled in Volume I) on natural resources rises dramatically.

My point here is not to attempt some potted history of crises but to suggest that the insights that come from a study of Marx's works need to be used flexibly and contingently rather than formalistically. My own view of the internal dynamics of crisis theory (as opposed to independently occurring but not unrelated geopolitical struggles) rests on an analysis of the various limits and barriers encountered within the circulation process; a study of the various strategies for overcoming or circumventing these limits and barriers politically and economically; and a careful monitoring of the ways in which barriers overcome or circumvented at one point result in new barriers appearing at other points. The continuous unfolding and partial resolution of the crisis tendencies of capitalism becomes the subject of inquiry.

Behind this lies a deeper problem. Accumulation for accumulation's sake and production for production's sake and the perpetual need to achieve a compound rate of growth were all very well when the core of industrial capitalism was constituted, as it was around 1780, by activities in the forty square miles around Manchester and a few other hot spots of capitalist dynamism. But what we are now confronting is the possibility of a compound rate of growth of, say, 3 percent per year, on the basis of everything happening in China and the rest of East and Southeast Asia, an expanding core of activity in India, Russia and Eastern Europe, surging economies in the Middle East and Latin America and intense pockets of capitalist development in Africa, as well as in the traditional heartlands of capitalism in North America, Europe and Oceania. The mass of accumulation and of physical movement required in future years to keep this compound rate of growth going will be nothing short of staggering.

I view crises as surface eruptions of deep tectonic shifts in the spatiotemporal logic of capitalism. The tectonic plates are now accelerating their motion, and the likelihood of more frequent and more violent crises increases. The manner, form, spatiality and time of the consequent eruptions are almost impossible to predict, but that they will occur with greater frequency and power is almost certain, making the events of 2008 appear normal if not trivial in comparison. Since these stresses are internal to the capitalist dynamic (which does not preclude some seemingly external disruptive event like a catastrophic pandemic), then what better argument could there be, as Marx once put it, for capitalism "to be gone and to give room to a higher state of social production"?[8]

But this is easier said than done. It entails, of course, the shaping of a political project. For this we can't wait until we know everything we need to know, or even understand everything Marx has to say. Marx holds up a mirror to our reality in Volume I in such a way as to create an imperative to act, and he makes it clear that class politics, class struggle, has to center what we do. In itself, this doesn't sound particularly revolutionary. But over the past quarter century, many of us have lived in a world where we have been told again and again that class is irrelevant, that the very idea of class struggle is so old-fashioned as to be mere fodder for academic dinosaurs. But any serious reading of *Capital* shows irrefutably that we will get nowhere unless we write "Class Struggle" on our political banners and march to its drum-beat.

We need, however, to better define exactly what this might mean for our place and times. Marx in his own day was often uncertain as to exactly what to do, what kinds of political alliances would make sense, what kinds of objectives and claims should be articulated. But what Marx also shows is that even in the midst of such uncertainties, we cannot fail to act. Cynics and critics typically object that one is trying to reduce questions of, say, nature, gender, sexuality, race, religion or whatever to class terms, and that this is unacceptable. My answer to this is: not at all. These other struggles are clearly important and have to be waged in their own right. But, I would note, it is rare for any of them not to internalize a significant class dimension, the solution to which is

8. Marx, *Grundrisse*, 750.

a necessary though never sufficient condition for, say, an adequate anti-racist or pro-environmentalist politics.

Just look, for example, at the impact of the so-called subprime-mortgage crisis on conditions in the city of Baltimore. A disproportionate number of black households and households headed by single parents (mainly women) have been dispossessed of their living rights and in some cases their assets in the course of a vicious class war of accumulation by dispossession. In such a situation, we cannot walk away from the category of class and deny its relevance. We have to stop being nervous and fearful of talking class talk and of mobilizing political strategies around notions of class war.

But there is, of course, a reason for the wishful silences. Class is the one category that the powers that be do not want anyone to take seriously. The *Wall Street Journal* scathingly mocks anything smacking of class war as being gratuitously divisive when the nation should be pulling together to confront its difficulties. The ruling elite does not ever want to openly admit, let alone discuss, the one central thing it is engaged on, its class strategy to augment its wealth and power.

The one thing that Marx again and again insists on is that the concept of class, in all its ambiguous glory, is indispensable to both theory and action. But there is much to do to make the category work. For example, one of the questions that comes out of reading *Capital* is what to say about the relations between struggles waged around primitive accumulation and accumulation by dispossession on the one hand, and the class struggles typically waged around the workplace and in the labor market on the other. It is not always easy to put these two forms of struggle together. But I find it hard to ignore the vast array of struggles going on in the world against dispossession, even though some of them are merely a hardened form of retrograde not-in-my-backyard politics. The division between these two grand forms of class struggle hurts politically. But what Marx's chapter on "The Working Day" teaches is that alliances are important and that it is hard to get anywhere without them, because the capitalist class accumulates capital by whatever means are at hand, and that means at the expense of the rest of us. Capitalists get filthy rich while everyone else stagnates or suffers. This class privilege and power, Marx says, must be battled against and destroyed to make way for another mode of production.

But what Volume I also teaches is that the displacement of one mode of production by another is a drawn-out and complicated process. Capitalism did not supplant feudalism with some neat revolutionary transformation. It had to grow within the interstices of the old society and bit by bit supplant it, sometimes through force, violence, predation and seizures of assets but at other times with guile and cunning. And it often lost battles against the old order even as it eventually won the war. As it achieved a modicum of power, however, it had to build its alternative at first on the basis of the technologies, social relations, mental conceptions, production systems, relations to nature and patterns of daily life as these had long been constituted under the preceding order. It took a coevolution and uneven development of these different moments within the social totality (see chapter 6) before it found not only its own unique technological base but also its belief systems and mental conceptions, its unstable but clearly class-ridden configuration of social relations, its curious spatiotemporal rhythms and its equally strange ways of daily life, to say nothing of its production processes; before it was truly possible to say that this was capitalism, albeit constantly changing in response to its own inevitable contradictions.

I began this book by urging you to try to read Marx on Marx's own terms. Obviously, my own view as to what those terms are has played a crucial role in the mental map I have tried to construct to guide you. My purpose in this was not to persuade you that I have the correct line, the correct reading, but first to open a way for you to construct your own meanings and interpretations. Many people will, I know, dispute my reading, as you should, too, in whole or in part. For me, the second crucial task is to open up a space of dialogue and discussion in such a way as to bring the Marxian vision of the world back onto center stage, both intellectually and politically. Marx's works have far too much to tell us regarding the perils of our times to consign them to the dustbin of history. It should by now, given the events of the last year or so, be evident that we need to think "outside the box" of received wisdoms. "Events," wrote Henri Lefebvre in his little book *The Explosion*, covering the events of 1968, "belie forecasts; to the extent that events are historic, they upset calculations. They may even overturn strategies that provided for their possible occurrence." Events "pull thinkers out of their comfortable seats and plunge them headlong into a wave of contradictions."[9] What better moment to study carefully the inner contradictions of capitalism and the works of that superb dialectician who did so much to make them so luminously transparent!

---

9. Henri Lefebvre, *The Explosion: Marxism and the French Revolution*, trans. Albert Ehrenfeld (New York: Monthly Review Press, 1969), 7–8.

While mental conceptions cannot on their own change the world, ideas are, as Marx himself observed, a material force in history. Marx wrote *Capital* to better equip us to fight that struggle. But here, too, there is no easy path, any more than there is some "royal road to science." As Bertolt Brecht once wrote:

> It takes a lot of things to change the world:
> Anger and tenacity. Science and indignation,
> The quick initiative, the long reflection,
> The cold patience and the infinite perseverance,
> The understanding of the particular case and the understanding of the ensemble:
> Only the lessons of reality can teach us to transform reality.

Index